COLLECTIBLE BOOKS

SOME NEW PATHS

Edited by Jean Peters

R. R. BOWKER COMPANY
NEW YORK & LONDON, 1979

In the chapter by Thomas L. Bonn, covers of *The Good Earth*, *Wuthering Heights*, and *Rebecca*, and the Pocket Books logo, are reprinted by permission of Pocket Books, Simon & Schuster Division of Gulf & Western Corporation; covers of *Babbit*, *Valiant Is the Word for Carrie*, and *Relentless*, and the Bantam logo, by permission of Bantam Books, Inc.; the cover of *Thunder Heights*, by permission of Ace Books; and the Penguin logo, by permission of Penguin Books. The photographs that appear in the chapter by Stuart Bennett are reprinted through the courtesy of Christie's, South Kensington, London. In the chapter by Peter Howard, the jacket design by Frank Springer appearing on the uncorrected proofs of *The Nightclerk* is reprinted by permission of Grove Press; the cover of the advance reading copy of *V* is reprinted by permission of Harper & Row Publishers, Inc.; the cover of *Philip* is reprinted by permission of Harper & Row Publishers, Inc.; and the dust jacket of *But Not for Love* is reprinted by permission of the artist and Horizon Press.

Published by R. R. Bowker Company
1180 Avenue of the Americas, New York, N.Y. 10036
Copyright © 1979 by Xerox Corporation
Printed and bound in the United States of America

Library of Congress Cataloging in Publication Data
Main entry under title:
Collectible books.
   Includes bibliographies and index.
   1. Book collecting—Addresses, essays, lectures.
I. Peters, Jean, 1935–
Z987.C58   020'.75   79-20356
ISBN 0-8352-1154-1

Contents

Preface

THIS BOOK is a direct outgrowth of *Book Collecting: A Modern Guide*, a manual on the procedures and techniques of book collecting, published by the Bowker Company in 1977. While that book was still in production, it occurred to some of us who were involved with it, that there ought to be a companion volume that would deal with book collecting by subject. Traditional subject approaches were considered and discarded. There were already more than enough books available with that approach to collecting. It seemed logical that the new book should follow the collecting philosophy set forth in *Book Collecting: A Modern Guide* and consider, not conventional rarities, but imaginative approaches to unexplored areas of collecting. At a time when the diminishing supply and soaring prices of traditionally collected books make it impossible for most collectors to build the kinds of great private collections that have been formed in the past, it seemed both sensible and worthwhile to consider collecting patterns that might be shaped from neglected categories of books. We soon agreed that the kind of book we most wanted to write would be a present-day version of *New Paths in Book Collecting*, the anthology John Carter edited in 1934.

New Paths was written in reaction to the high-spot collecting and collecting "by list" that were fashionable prior to 1930. In the introduction to *New Paths*, John Carter wrote, ". . . the man of enterprise will want to strike out some new line, or give a new twist to a familiar one." Viewing the book 35 years later, he wrote in *The Book Collector* (vol. 18, no. 1 [Spring 1969]: 59) that he and his colleagues were "determined to replace tarnished shibboleths and ritual genuflection to overworked patterns by fresh ideas, more imaginative approaches, more flexible postures." *New Paths in Book Collecting* started serious collectors thinking in a new way and has become a milestone in the literature of book collecting. In the 45 years since its publication, some of the subjects written about (each revisited by Percy Muir, a contributor to *New Paths*, in his essay in this book, "A Backward Look: The Sadleir Circle in Perspective") have become accepted collecting paths, while others have nearly disappeared as collecting fields. The time is ripe to explore new paths open to modern-day collectors.

The subjects we have chosen represent broad categories of books within which exist many opportunities to develop individual collecting interests. Although many of these subjects parallel traditional collecting areas, they have been largely overlooked as categories of collectible books. Thus, this book makes a case for the collecting of non-first editions instead of the conventional "first editions"; for publishers' trade bindings instead of fine bindings; for nineteenth-century books with photographs instead of early illustrated or color-plate books; for publishers' imprints and books in series instead of press books; for American fiction since 1960 instead of "literature"; for books about film instead of such traditionally collected subjects as natural history, philosophy, or sporting books. Emphasis is on books published in the last 150 years.

This book is not intended as a beginner's guide. The reader will find no definition of terms, no description of how a book is put together, no advice on physical care of books, no bibliography on the literature of book collecting (although a list of "Further Reading" appears at the end of each chapter). For this basic information the reader is referred to the companion volume. It is, however, intended as much for the bookseller as it is for the collector, for, as Percy Muir observed, "Courage and perspicacity in opening up new paths are needed no less in the collector than the bookseller. . . ." (*Minding My Own Business.* London: Chatto & Windus, p. 57). If it is more difficult to chart a new course than to follow a traditional one, it is often times made easier by the booksellers who support this kind of collecting, who join in the search, and who share the discoveries.

The editor is grateful to Alice Koeth for the design of this book and its jacket, and to Filomena Simora and Nancy Leff of the Bowker book editorial department, who with patience and care saw the book through to publication. Special thanks are due William Matheson and G. Thomas Tanselle, who took an interest in the planning and organization of the book from the start and offered advice whenever it was needed. And to all the contributors, who themselves have formed collections of the kind this book champions and who were willing to write about them, the editor expresses deepest gratitude.

August 1979   *Jean Peters*

Introduction

William Matheson

COLLECTIBLE BOOKS: SOME NEW PATHS presupposes that the reader has gained some knowledge of book collecting from practical experience or from reading an introduction to book collecting such as the 1977 Bowker volume *Book Collecting: A Modern Guide* and is ready to be inspired by the example of the eight experienced collectors and the one antiquarian book dealer whose personal experiences in forming their collections constitute the substance of this volume. Inevitably the book is indebted in its conception to *New Paths in Book Collecting*, a distinguished and still surprisingly useful volume published by Constable in 1934 and containing an introduction by its editor, John Carter, which I recommend to you highly. Percy Muir, the only surviving contributor to the 1934 volume, recalls the circumstances of its publication in a second introduction immediately following this one, "A Backward Look: The Sadleir Circle in Perspective."

The contributors to *New Paths* were a closely knit group heavily weighted with members of the antiquarian book trade who shared common bibliographic interests. The balance has completely shifted in the present volume. Even Peter Howard, the lone representative of the trade, tells of a collecting experience: assembling for his thirty-eighth catalogue 2,752 books representing his view of the most important fiction produced by American writers since 1960. The authors of these nine chapters are scattered across the country and it is doubtful that more than three of them ever talked together at one time. Though they are not a circle, they share assumptions that are revolutionary in their implications, as I hope to make clear in the remarks that follow.

In a 1929 Rowfant Club publication, *Among My Books*, Paul Lemperly, a well-known American collector, expressed a point of view that I take to be typical of collectors of his generation: "Though he delves into many channels in pursuit of his quarry, the books receiving the attention of the collector have at all times been comparatively limited in number." Earlier in that decade Seymour de Ricci in his Rosenbach Company publication *The Book Collector's Guide* (1921) listed the "two or three thousand British and American books which fashion has decided are the most desirable for the up-to-date collector." We get from these and many similar sources a picture of a severely limited collecting field, which by the time Desmond Flower wrote "The Future of Book Collecting" in the October 1963 issue of *The Private Library* offered a gloomy prospect for the collector, faced with competition from wealthy collectors and institutions whose resources assured they would get all the good books that came on the market. He ended by saying, "There may well be one more whole generation of private collectors before we are finally swamped by institutional buying." This many years later the collector would seem to have no choice but to settle for greatly reduced goals, to buy fewer and fewer books, and to accept gaps as inevitable.

In contrast to this dismal picture the contributors to this book reveal an almost overwhelming abundance of material to collect. Thomas Tanselle in his discussion of anthologies remarks that "no person can hope to take on the entire field. . . ." Charles Gullans refers to the "enormous volume" in his field, American publishers' trade bindings, that "cannot be exhausted by any two people or by twenty." William Todd pursues 5,393 Tauchnitz volumes in "countless" variants. In the face of the "sheer quantity" of American mass-market paperbacks Thomas Bonn suggests ways to delimit the field. Daniel Leab variously refers to the "massive increase" in film-related material, the "never-lessening flood" of film books, there being "plenty of room on this path," the "need to choose," and the "proliferation of published material." In describing his interest, book catalogues, William Barlow speaks of a "million different items" falling within his potential scope and establishes "100 feet of shelf space" as the measure at which one can begin to be taken seriously as a collector of modern catalogues. In commenting on the collecting of publishers' imprints Jean Peters refers to the danger of a collector balking at the "sheer size" such a collection might eventually assume and quotes Mr. Tanselle's 1965 observation that in this field "the labors of many men for many years to come will only make a beginning." Mr. Howard, after outlining a concept of completeness in an author collection, says "an individual can take on only one or two authors in such absolute terms." Only Stuart Bennett in his chapter on "Photography as Book Illustration, 1839–1900" sees shrinking supplies and rising prices as a problem, a phenomenon not true when he first started out in the 1950s. In those years the field offered the possibility of one's being "a latter-day [Sir Thomas] Phillipps in microcosm."

Even today Mr. Bennett can suggest certain possibilities for assembling material in substantial quantity.

In a chapter in *Book Collecting: A Modern Guide* I thought it necessary to challenge the view that the goal of the collector is to collect rare books. Clearly the writers of these chapters needed no such warning. The words "rare" and "rarity" occur infrequently in these pages and when they do they are more likely to be looked at critically than used approvingly. Mr. Tanselle observes that "rarity does not make a book valuable unless there is demand for the book." Mr. Bonn indicates that mass-market paperbacks sometimes receive attention from rare-book dealers but that given the size of the first printings rarity is a "term not usually applied to soft-cover editions." "There could hardly be a book-collecting field with a wider range of rarity and a wider range of quality" than a subspecialization of Mr. Barlow's interest, library catalogues. Ms. Peters speculates that the second edition of Virginia Woolf's *Kew Gardens* "may be even rarer than the first. . . ." Mr. Howard says that after a few years the uncorrected galley proof has a "propensity for taking on an appearance of great rarity. . . ." Among other uses of the term he speaks three times of artificial rarity and once of simulated rarity. Again Mr. Bennett's field differs from those of the other contributors in being distinguished by the "extreme rarity of examples" of allegorical photographs. He cautions the reader that a dealer's referring to an item as rare "may mean simply that he has not seen it before" and urges collectors to visit as many photographic archives as possible to develop their own sense of comparative rarity. In these collectors' eyes rare books are not the quarry, but rather the exception encountered in their collecting, most usually because a collecting interest intersects a fashionable field.

Collectible Books: Some New Paths offers comforting reassurances to anyone fearful that collecting is beyond his or her means. Mr. Tanselle's non-firsts are "generally modest" in price and in the case of Meville non-firsts "likely to be ridiculously low." In the first sentence of his chapter Mr. Gullans tells us that he began to collect American publishers' bookbindings because they were "both numerous and cheap." Mr. Todd obtained a cache of Tauchnitz's Continental issues for 25 cents a volume. In referring to the early days of his collecting adventures Mr. Leab reports that he found "bargains galore" in film-related materials. Mr. Bonn warns that the "low price and easy availability" of many paperbacks can lead to the temptation to collect everything. In Mr. Barlow's experience owners of certain dealers' catalogues are sometimes "pleased to have you haul [them] away." Ms. Peters emphasizes the "decided advantage" in price offered by publishers' imprints, many of them "low-to-moderately priced," particularly the work of authors whose books are not saved for themselves and that are "always less expensive to purchase." Innumerable paperback originals, Mr. Howard notes, "were once available . . . at 25 cents or 50 cents (not so long ago) or, more recently, $1.95." Even within Mr. Bennett's tight field certain classes of photographs were "surprisingly undervalued" in the mid-1970s.

If, contrary to the views frequently voiced, the supply of books of interest to the collector is not drying up, rare books are not the collector's quarry, and book prices are not ascending to the stratosphere, surely this book leaves the first edition in place as the "most challenging and most rewarding aspect of collecting," to quote from a recent work on collecting American first editions. You will find that they are largely ignored in most of these chapters, figuring significantly in only the first and last chapters. Mr. Tanselle acknowledges their attraction in developing his argument for collecting editions other than the first. Mr. Howard knows well that the first edition is the "sacred object," its "acquisition and preservation . . . the common goal" of collectors of modern literature but he clearly wishes that the 80 percent of collectors who collect the 10 percent of available authors would turn their attention to the less fashionable 90 percent of the field.

Recent books on book collecting have frequently stressed the investment possibilities of book collecting. Pointing out that there is evidence that non-firsts will eventually be in greater demand, Mr. Tanselle notes that "an anticipated rise in market value is hardly the point." In forming his collection Mr. Leab tells us that "the thought of any kind of financial return . . . never occurred to [him] over the years." From his vantage point in the trade Mr. Howard sees that "one must recognize 'investment' as a *real* motive for book buyers, it certainly affects the market prices. But it is surely the basest motive of all." One of the collectors he holds up as an example "never collects for investment. . . ."

In general the contributors agree on the desirability of acquiring books in fine condition but they make much less of it than one might except from reading introductory manuals. Mr. Gullans was encouraged "by the excellent condition of what [he] bought" to undertake collecting all of Margaret Armstrong's bindings. Mr. Todd tells us that the "possibility of acquiring [The Landsdowne Poets] in good condition . . . is even more remote than for the Moxon series." Mr. Leab's view of condition goes against the tenor of the time: "Whether a book had its original dust jacket, whether that dust jacket was frayed, torn, or taped mattered not a whit. In general, condition only mattered to me insofar as determining that a book was usable." In collecting auction catalogues Mr. Barlow finds that "fine condition, of course, is desirable but not a practical goal on the whole." Ms. Peters states categorically that "books should be sought in dust jacket and the jackets always preserved," justifying her statement by examples of the kinds of uses to which they can be put. Mr. Howard knows that to most collectors of modern literature "condition is paramount," but he observes that recognizing the susceptibility of certain formats to wear "will help the buyer to accept (at least temporarily) condition short of ideal. . . ." His account of the hazards facing a book in a remainder pile gives the reader a perspective on the question, "what sort of book is customarily fine?"

This is a book for the collector who is not content to follow in someone else's footsteps. The nine contributors to this volume perceive that the books in short supply are those collected in the past, and they have, to one degree or another, been pioneers in their respective fields. Their nine collecting fields (the figure is quite misleading given the number of ideas for specialization and development thrown out in each chapter) are but a tiny fraction of the collecting possibilities already being developed and yet to be recognized. A 1978 publication of Ruth E. Robinson, Books, *Buy Books Where—Sell Books Where*, lists 2,300 collecting interests from E. A. Abbey to Zoroastrianism. The 1979 membership list of the Private Libraries Association enumerates close to a thousand collecting interests among its membership of less than 2,000.

Mr. Tanselle's chapter, appropriately placed first in the book, describes not a collection but rather an approach applicable to an infinite range of collecting possibilities. Acknowledging the great attraction of firsts, he directs the reader's attention to non-firsts: "they are a part of the historical evidence and thus indispensable." He distinguishes non-firsts that have been traditionally collected (every edition of a classic work, transatlantic editions, the products of particular times and places, editions incorporating new material) from non-first printings possessing none of these characteristics, pointing out the kinds of significance these neglected books possess. Though the editor did not set up the book to develop Mr. Tanselle's point, a surprising number of the chapters following his illustrate the application of either traditional or nontraditional non-first collecting. The non-firsts Mr. Gullans and Mr. Bennett might seek for their collections would be the first with a particular binding design or the first illustrated by photographs. Though Mr. Todd seeks all the countless variants in the Tauchnitz series, Mr. Bonn is chary of suggesting such an ambitious project, concentrating instead on the delights of collecting the varying cover designs of successive printings of the same text. In her imprint collecting Ms. Peters follows Mr. Tanselle in seeking non-first impressions and offers further examples of the kind of information to be gained from an assemblage of non-firsts.

In the past collecting a series or an author whose work has been described in a bibliography has been compared to stamp collecting. In reading this book I was struck by the inappropriateness of this comparison. Mr. Tanselle shows that non-firsts are largely uncharted and that the printed record, when it does exist, is frequently contradicted by the physical object. Though Mr. Todd says that "books in series impose their own order or rationale, compelling the collector to complete obeisance," he finds his Tauchnitz horizons constantly expanding, in a manner quite unlike any stamp collection of which I am aware. Within what I would have taken to be the overworked tradition of single author collecting Mr. Howard opens up an astonishing range of possibilities.

This book undermines assumptions many of us have had about the relative rarity of certain classes of material. Mr. Tanselle demonstrates that the later editions of books published during Melville's lifetime are frequently almost impossible to obtain not only because they were carelessly treated during the many years he was a neglected author but because the later printings were only a fraction of the size of the first. Our knowledge of the tremendous size of paperback printings gives us a quite erroneous sense that they must be easily obtainable. Just as the yellowback has, on Mr. Muir's testimony, all but disappeared as a collecting field since the publication of *New Paths*, the early mass-market paperback may become a vanishing species in the years ahead. Mr. Howard tells us that a paperback original is on the stands for seven weeks and "after that time . . . is likely to have gone away forever." His example of the 1969 paperback he spent ten years looking for provides support for that observation. Even in such an apparently substantial world as the trade editions of first novels by the writers of the 1960s, things are not what they seem. As a result of poor merchandising techniques these books "were not widely available for long to buyers and readers. . . ." In all his years of searching and scouting Mr. Howard reports that he has never encountered a copy of two novels by Doris Grumbach written in the early 1960s.

A word not always associated with collecting in the past appears with striking frequency in this book: "scholarly." The term is almost invariably used in favorable contexts, often in association with the words "serious" or "significant," as in Mr. Tanselle's reference to "serious collectors—that is, collectors who understand the scholarly implications of what they are about. . . ." Among many uses of these terms he speaks of collecting as a "scholarly pursuit," the "scholarliness of collectors," the "scholarly potential" of author collections, and the "scholarly value" of non-firsts in an imprint collection. Mr. Gullans says that the "urge for scholarly completeness . . . should always be obeyed" if you mean to be serious and elsewhere refers to the "scholarly interest" and "significance" of trade bindings. Mr. Leab's collecting direction was determined in part by his "scholarly interests." In the photographic field, Mr. Bennett tells us, the collector, if he is "also a scholar" may be secure in the knowledge that "any serious research he may undertake is virtually certain to be original." According to Mr. Barlow, the collecting of catalogues as catalogues arose rather recently "among the scholar-collectors who needed to use the materials they contained." Ms. Peters points out the "scholarly use," "scholarly value," and "scholarly contribution" of an imprint collection. Mr. Howard, looking at the collecting world from his perspective as an antiquarian book dealer, speaks on at least three occasions of the use of collections by scholars without applying the term to collectors themselves. His references to the "enlightened" collector, "unusually perceptive book collecting," and to a couple "who continue to educate themselves" indicate that he might be willing to apply the term "scholarly" to at least a few collectors. In one respect I find that Mr. Howard does not give collectors their due. After summarizing the various prepublication forms in which the books of the 1960s and 1970s are sometimes found, he observes that "the charm for collectors of all these advance states lies perhaps in their transitoriness. They wish to preserve what was designed to be discarded." From my observations collectors perceive possibilities for textual study in these advance states and collect them for this scholarly potential.

This marked emphasis on the serious and the scholarly seems at first glance quite at odds with Percy Muir's account of the freewheeling Sadleir circle, encouraged in its liveliness by the excellent sherry drawn from Dennis Wheatley's "ample cellars." On closer inspection *New Paths* has its own seriousness. Early in his introduction to that volume John Carter notes that the rich nonspecialist and the poorer person who buys only what he or she enjoys form collections that "do not make any substantial contribution to knowledge." In his chapter in *New Paths*, "Ignoring the Flag," Mr. Muir reveals closer ties to the present book than might have been expected when he praises Wilmarth Lewis, whose Horace Walpole collection, a complete microcosm of the period, enables him "to make new contributions to scholarship."

In 1934 John Carter identified the "following of a development of a significant form of book structure or publishing practice . . . [as] one of the most fascinating of all branches of collecting." Clearly the contributors to this volume agree about the fascination of such collecting, variously addressing anthologies, bookbindings, series, paperbacks, a publisher's total output, the early use of photographs as book illustrations, and the various prepublication forms of a text, among the many examples of book structure and publishing practice referred to in this book. The emphasis in this book, as in *New Paths*, is on books of the last 150 years. Mr. Muir makes clear that the rise of a school of bibliography in the 1920s and early 1930s drew attention to the "collectibility of authors who had not put pen to paper . . . before 1900." In part such an emphasis is inevitable in a book emphasizing nontraditional collecting areas available to a collector of moderate means. The writers of these chapters love the thrill of pursuing their quarry in unlikely places. Most of the books they seek are not yet of sufficiently high individual value to be of much interest to the major rare-book firms and specialized antiquarian bookshops. Most of the contributors to this volume can still hope to find books in flea markets, thrift shops, general secondhand shops, country auctions, yard sales, and all the other outlets available to the enterprising collector. It would be misleading to take from this emphasis that collectors seek bargains per se or that the rare-book shops and specialized firms offer less attractive possibilities than the sources just named. One of book collecting's great attractions is the range of possibilities it offers for finding the books one seeks, from the sorriest excuse for a bookshop to the greatest of the antiquarian book firms. In my chapter in *Book Collecting: A Modern Guide* mentioned earlier, I have additional things to say about the appropriate place to seek certain kinds of books. The aspiring collector should also understand that there are exciting collecting possibilities in earlier centuries, in virtually all languages, and in countless subjects not touched on here, as my earlier references to the tremendous number of collecting areas indicate.

In his introduction to *New Paths* John Carter spoke of the "infinite" possible variations on the book-collecting theme and commented as follows on the pleasure of evolving new patterns: "By rearranging familiar books according to some constructive plan, a new significance is added to them, and, which is more, the unfamiliar, the neglected books will acquire significance by their context." Mr. Tanselle carries the concept of rearranging patterns a step further: "Collecting is an organized and disciplined pursuit that results in an assemblage of material with unity and meaning; collectors are scholars who locate and segregate the patterns to be found within the seeming chaos of the total mass of material. They make their greatest contribution, of course, when they cause previously unnoticed or neglected patterns to become visible and approachable." The implication of such an approach, as Mr. Tanselle's chapter makes clear, is that every book has relevance as part of some collecting pattern. The title of this book could be taken to indicate that some books are collectible and some are not, that the difference between this book and de Ricci's *Book Collector's Guide* is in the quantity of books today's "up-to-date collector" seeks, not the kind. The book demonstrates that collectible books are the universe of books. The methods described in these nine chapters are applicable, by extension, to this entire universe, as adapted to new patterns and to the endless possibilities that exist for rearrangement.

A Backward Look:
The Sadleir Circle in Perspective

Percy Muir

In Book Collecting: A Modern Guide, the forerunner to the present volume, reference is made more than once to an oddly recruited group of bibliophiles with bees in their bonnets, now generally known by the affectionate, if somewhat irreverent, title of "biblioboys." Not the least compliment paid to them is that one of the survivors has been invited to contribute to this erudite work some account of the origin—foundation is far too formal a term—of this small group of heretics.

My old chief, A. W. Evans, who did so much to keep modern book collecting on this side of insanity, was our ringleader, and our original rallying point was at 33 Conduit Street in London. It was A. W. Evans who began the series of "Notes for Collectors" on aspects of current book collecting as short prefaces to his catalogues. The first of these appeared in February 1930. It dealt with inserted advertisements. Later "Notes" were concerned with other pitfalls from which collectors all too often needed to be rescued.

Another even more congenial innovation of his was the sherry party. The bookshop over which he presided closed for business at six o'clock and the last daily duty of William, the general factotum, was to set up on Evans's table glasses and a supply of excellent sherry drawn from the ample cellars of Dennis Wheatley, then a wine merchant in South Audley Street and an enthusiastic book collector. Any friends or customers—not always quite the same thing—who found themselves in the neighborhood were wont to look in. No business was done, but there was plenty of good talk, almost exclusively of books and most especially of bibliographical problems.

One evening in 1932 when the company was made up exclusively of booksellers, the main topic of conversation was customers, and it was not long before it turned to the less desirable habits of some of them. Jack Abbey was not yet in the forefront of the denounceables, and there was general agreement that Thomas J. Wise was by far the most ill-mannered of the baddies. It was a deplorable example of "Eclipse first and the rest nowhere," for "Eclipse" was a rank outsider.

John Carter and Graham Pollard were present, and I have related elsewhere how closely we approached the threshold of what was to become the major bibliographical sensation of our time. (It may be as well to refer to *The Book Collector*, vol. 3, pp. 11–14 where the most accurate account of that evening occurs. At the request of John Carter some modifications were made in *Minding My Own Business*, pp. 87–92. But I am quite sure that the earlier account is more accurate.)

Nothing else of such startling nature arose from the sherry-drinking causeries, but at least one other lasting project dates back to them: from its more regular attendants was recruited the front line of the small group of nonconformists so lightheartedly christened by Richard Jennings. Richard, alas, wrote very little himself but was a most fastidious book collector. To say he wrote very little is to ignore the fact that for many years he wrote the distinguished, incongruous leading articles in the *Daily Mirror*, then the only British tabloid, and also a short series of privately printed "ribald commentaries on the old villain of Heath Drive," at whose hands Richard himself had suffered when a 'prentice collector. It was not until the early 1930s that we introduced a little more formality in our ranks.

William Roberts had for many years conducted a feature in the *Times* (London) that, under his byline, was entitled "Notes on Sales." On Fridays he compiled another feature in the *Times Literary Supplement* reporting on book auctions. (I say "compiled" rather than "wrote" because it was little more than a record of prices.) When he retired, Simon Nowell Smith, by then a member of the staff, was asked to take this over. He suggested to the editor, Bruce Richmond, that he would like to try out the idea of devoting the back page, on which Roberts's column appeared, entirely to bibliographical matters. Richmond agreed, and Simon, a fairly regular attendant at the soirées, explained the position to us. Michael Sadleir, whose pioneer work with *Excursions in Victorian Bibliography* (1922) and *Trollope: A Bibliography* (1928) had already appeared, saw at once the importance of such a platform and was determined that a plan should be organized. With A. W. Evans, Michael invited about a dozen others to dine in a Soho restaurant to discuss the matter.

We were rather a ragged regiment when we met. A couple of people had declined the invitation and those present were a bit of a mixture. Evans had been a professional journalist, and Sadleir had been a writer since his undergraduate days. I was possibly in the lowest rank of all, having written nothing but a preface to a catalogue of my own compiling. Discussion, however, was lively and lengthy; but just as we were about to break up Simon reminded us that one subject had been overlooked—the back page of the *Times Literary Supplement*. And so some of us met again to discuss this exclusively. I was given the "Notes on Sales" to deal with and, in the sequel, became for several years the most regular contributor to the back page from our group—until Stanley Morison became editor and announced that it was not his intention to "cater for the sort of lunatics who bid their heads off for books in the auction rooms." This mournful edict remained in force until Alan Pryce-Jones replaced Morison in the editorial chair, and John Carter took over the back page.

The monthly meetings continued, and, although some fell out, others replaced them, until the fairly regular attendants were Michael Sadleir, John Carter, Graham Pollard, Dudley Massey, Richard Jennings, and myself. We kept our sights lined on the back page, but we discussed almost every kind of bibliophilic interest, and, quite naturally, we took note of trends in book collecting shown by the catalogues of auctioneers and booksellers. This was just one example of Evans's having built better than he knew. The Conduit Street Regulars were ready for action. It was good that we had a publisher among our number. Sadleir took over when Evans fell out.

Strange though it may seem, the atmosphere of the period was favorable. Book collecting was in the doldrums; the recession of the 1930s made disastrous inroads into the collecting world. The injudicious optimism of the 1920s added power to the avalanche; but momentum was not entirely dispersed in what may be called the aftermath of the Kern sale.

Bibliography as we know it today originated in the last years of the nineteenth century. Contemporaries of the great writers of the seventeenth and eighteenth centuries gave no thought to compiling bibliographies of their works. Dibdin and his fellow enthusiasts appear never to have considered it.

Here the devil must be given his due. Wise's bibliography of Ruskin, issued in parts (1889–1893) was not the first bibliography in which the now familiar formulae were used. It was preceded by Herne-Shepherd's bibliography of Swinburne (1883). A fine pair of rascals. Wise was a prolific bibliographer but not a very good one. Referring to F. J. Furnivall's Browning bibliography (1882) in the Ashley Catalogue (I, 137), he claimed that "the spadework was done almost entirely by me under his direction." The effrontery of this claim is monstrous in a work that sponsors three of his own forgeries classified by Carter & Pollard's *Enquiry* as "Unknown to Furnivall." Indeed Furnivall himself referred to them as "creatures of fancy." (John Carter and Graham Pollard. *An Enquiry into the Nature of Certain Nineteenth Century Pamphlets*. London: Constable, 1934, p. 88).

In 1900 Francis Murray's *A Bibliography of Austin Dobson* was published; it was not entirely superseded by the 1925 bibliography by Dobson's son.

There are few full-length bibliographies of the authors included in the Grolier Club's four volume *Contributions to English Bibliography* (1893–1905). The various attempts to produce a Dickens bibliography —Eckel in 1913, Davis in 1928, and Hatton and Cleaver in 1933—may well have done considerably more harm than good in their classification of "prime" sets of the part issues. The odds against such a set of "Pickwick" in unsophisticated form are incalculable and surely in a tiny minority of copies extant.

In 1914 an exhaustive bibliography of Oscar Wilde appeared. Stuart Mason was the pseudonym of this compiler, who was actually Christopher Millard, a former secretary to Robert Ross. A. J. A. Symons has paid tribute to this eccentric, elusive antiquarian bookseller who first drew attention to Corvo (*The Quest for Corvo*. London: Cassell, 1934, pp. 1–3). The Wilde bibliography is possibly the most maddeningly complicated one that exists; and, lacking an effective index, it is very puzzling to consult. But the information it contains is invaluable, and a facsimile edition of it has ‚ecently appeared. The first, very limited, edition of Geoffrey Keynes's John Donne bibliography appeared in the same year. A revised edition came in 1932 and a further edition in 1958.

Looking back over the period, one recognizes that the activity of bibliographers between 1922 and 1932 is truly remarkable, the more so because their work was not confined to short pieces in the transactions of learned societies but was also in volume form. Sadleir comes first with *Excursions in Victorian Bibliography* (1922), which, among other marvels, suggested Herman Melville as a collected author. There is no British auction record under his name before May 1923, when Hodgson's catalogued "The Marquesas Islands (*Typee*) 1st English edn. 1846." It fetched £2 8s. In January 1924 they catalogued "A Residence in the Marquesas (*Typee*) 1st English edn. in 2 pts. orig. buff wrappers, 1846" for £2 12s. But auctioneers did not consult bibliographies much in those days. No Melville work got into double figures before 1930 when *The Whale* brought £170.

From this diversion, we return to the 1920s. In the same year as Sadleir's *Excursions*, the Bibliographical Society published M. B. Forman's Meredith bibliography, with a supplement in 1924; Texas published the first volume of Griffith on Pope, and the first two volumes of the Ashley Library catalogue appeared in definitive form. A bibliography of Shelley appeared in 1923 and of Johnson and "Erewhon" Butler in 1925.

The year 1927 was *annus mirabilis*. The second volume of Pope, the first volume of Kipling, and, above all, the first edition of McKerrow's *Introduction to Bibliography* were published. McKerrow went out of print almost at once and was reissued in revised form in 1928. This was really the first book to tell us how to set about a bibliographical description.

As far back as 1906 Falconer Madan had published some useful notes on "Degressive Bibliography" (*Transactions of the Bibliographical Society* 9: 53–65). In 1923, he collaborated with E. Gordon Duff and Strickland Gibson to produce "Standard Descriptions of Printed Books" with an "Additional Note on Size Notation," by R. W. Chapman, at the end of which was attached a folded sheet that made clear to the veriest novice just how a book was constructed (Oxford Bibliographical Society. *Proceedings and Papers* 1, pt. 1 [1923]: 55–64).

T. J. Wise immediately joined this illustrious bandwagon as "honorary vice-president." This may have spared him the ten shilling annual subscription that was in force for the first five years and that included the quarterly journal, in which there appeared bibliographies of Thomas Heywood, Samuel Daniel, P. A. Motteux, Richard Lower, John Mayow, Thomas Fuller, John Oldham, and the remarkable Boyle bibliography by J. F. Fulton.

Bibliographies published in 1928 include Carlyle, Barrie, Galsworthy, and Conrad, as well as one, which shall be nameless, that included the following curious collation: "The first page of the text has the numeral 1 at base on right. Page 3 has numerals 1–2 at base, right hand side. . . . These numbers continue throughout the book at odd intervals."

Continuing the march of progress, in 1929 Boswell was added to the big guns; in 1930, Henry James and William Beckford; in 1931, Carroll, Scott, and Maugham; and in 1932, Leigh Hunt.

Despite the fact that Sadleir had been a director of the publishing house of Constable since 1920, his *Excursions*, published in 1922, was not published by them but by two young antiquarian booksellers, Leslie Chaundy and Euan Cox, who had recently set up in business in a bijou bookshop at 40 Maddox Street in Mayfair. When in 1930 he announced to the "biblioboys" that he was embarking upon a series of books under the collective heading of *Bibliographia*, it was significant that they were to appear with Constable's imprint. This may have been largely due to his increased authority in the firm, but it may be doubted whether Kylman, the senior partner, would have accepted the idea had it not been for the greatly increased interest in bibliography in general.

In any case the series could hardly have been regarded as commercially attractive. Each volume cost £1 and the edition was limited to 500 copies. This may have been the reason for the flimsy binding of marbled board sides with spines made of forel, which is defined in Carter's *A.B.C. For Book-Collectors* as "inferior parchment." Ironically, the first volume in the series was Sadleir's *The Evolution of Publishers'*

Binding Styles. Five of the ten volumes were written by members of the Sadleir circle; and those of us who were booksellers hammered away, popularizing the new ethic in our catalogues.

The series went out of print quite quickly, and it may be useful to mention here some of the subjects dealt with. The general title was *Studies in Book History and Book Structure,* and the first six volumes alternated between these two outlooks. Thus the first volume, already mentioned, showed how, when, and why "publishers assumed responsibility for edition binding." This was followed by Guy Chapman's Beckford bibliography, a fine work, but with a restricted audience. Subscribers to *Bibliographical Notes and Queries,* begun in 1935 as an adjunct to a bookseller's catalogue and still going strong in *The Book Collector,* may recall that the last word about *Vathek* remained (and remains?) unsaid.

Next came another study in book structure, R. W. Chapman's *Cancels.* It is rather heavy going, and some hedging and ditching was needed to make a whole book on the subject. Moreover, McKerrow had dealt with it to some extent; and bibliographers usually give details of cancels occurring in the work of the author in question. However, Chapman's book on the subject is now a standard work on "cancellands" and "cancelans." The fourth volume returned to "book history" with Worthington's *Bibliography of the Waverley Novels.* This is one of the most complicated bibliographies every compiled, not exceeded in detail even by Charles Dickens's part publications. Indeed, it might almost be said to have given bibliophilic interest in Scott a blow from which it has hardly yet recovered.

At this point Constable issued a handout announcing the next three volumes in the series. None of them was published. Number 5 was "An Index to the 'Annuals,'" by Andrew Boyle, a man in some ways like Pollard, with a brain stuffed with bibliographical knowledge, too indolent to bring any of it to fruition. In fact the book reached proof stage, but Boyle never completed the corrections and so it did not appear. (A volume dealing with the author's contributions was published by his daughter in 1967 [Andrew Boyle Booksellers Ltd.]; a second part is promised.) Boyle's unpublished volume was replaced by John Carter's *Binding Variants in English Publishing, 1820–1900,* which neatly adapted the techniques described in Sadleir's volume, with bibliographical information derived therefrom.

The other two titles in the handout were never to appear. "Part Issues: Their Rise and Fall," by A. M. Cohn, who compiled the mammoth *Cruikshank: A Catalogue Raisonné,* was a great loss. "Henry Colburn: A Publisher of the Regency—Based on His Private Notes" was unfortunately found unsuitable by the series editor; but most, if not all, of it is in Sadleir's *XIX Century Fiction,* vol. 2.

The last five volumes in the series were all concerned with bibliographical points of one kind or another; Iolo Williams's *Points in Eighteenth*

Century Verse; I. R. Brussel's two volumes, *Anglo-American First Editions,* and my own two, *Points,* which attempted, by both precept and example, to show the difference between quackery and good medicine in the collecting of modern first editions.

At this point it may be good to pause and consider how far book collectors and auctioneers were affected by the rise of a school of bibliography drawing attention to the collectibility of authors who had not put pen to paper before 1700—some not even before 1900. Bookish people, including some auctioneers, regard novelty with suspicion; but that the new movement had arrived must have reached the ears of the veriest last-ditchers, even when the fact was discernible mainly in contemptuous reference to it. Seymour de Ricci's comments on "the modern movement" betray the condescension of a vocal champion of the old school. "Sixty years ago," he writes, "there was a great craze for Bewick's woodcuts (*sic*); thirty years later, these had been superseded by George Cruikshank's illustrations. . . ." (*English Collectors of Books & Manuscripts, 1530–1930.* Cambridge: Cambridge Univ. Press, 1930. p. 182.) However, to be fair, his praise for Thomas J. Wise is luscious.

Auction records are indispensable to collectors, and, although in the nature of things, they respond to fashion rather than lead it, they do proclaim it. If Sadleir's *Excursions* are compared with *Book Auction Records* some interesting conclusions emerge. First a word about his preface, titled "Advertisement." It still makes good reading, not only for its elegance and wit, but for its soundness. "Descending from the august to the particular . . ." he writes, "the collecting of first editions is, in its present form, a diversion of recent growth." He goes on, "It is not until one undertakes seriously the collecting of the less-known Victorian novelists that one realizes how prime the sport that their assembling offers, how destitute of guide-posts is the maze of their works." His "humble chronicle of humble writers" covers the works of Anthony Trollope, Frederick Marryat, Benjamin Disraeli, Wilkie Collins, Charles Reade, G. J. Whyte-Melville, Elizabeth Cleghorn Gaskell, and Herman Melville.

Until the recent enthusiasm for almost any novel in three volumes, Whyte-Melville may be said to have sunk without a trace. There is no auction record of a first edition of any of his books between November 1932 (*Digby-Grand,* £2) and October 1970 (*Sister Louise,* £22) roughly equivalent in real money. It is noteworthy that he does not appear in *XIX Century Fiction.* The wording of his exclusion from that volume is on pp. xii and xxvi, in an enthralling Preface.

Disraeli has so far not reached great distinction in the sale rooms. On December 9, 1924, Hodgson's sold 11 of his first editions inscribed by him to his friend Mrs. Austen. The highest price was £7 15s. for *Coningsby.* Ten days later a first edition of *Alroy,* estimated by Sadleir as

Disraeli's second rarest book, sold for £8 15s. It was inscribed by the author to "William Beckford Esq." These prices would be ridiculous today when almost any three-decker goes into double figures; but what is more relevant to the present purpose is that in April 1929 at the height of the boom in the 1920s, a signed presentation copy of *Alarcos* brought only £10 at Sotheby's.

The strange perversities of collecting fashion are exemplified by Charles Reade, for whose writings the best that Sadleir could say was that some of his books were better than others. W. T. Young is kinder to him, and considers "the age rich indeed which can afford to consider [him] a minor novelist" (*Cambridge History of English Literature* 12: 429). Both would agree that *The Cloister and the Hearth* is his best book. Reade was already a collected author in 1921 when a copy of *The Cloister*, admittedly by no means a fine copy, was sold for £5; in 1929 its record was £430. His other books had remained rather in the doldrums; for instance, in that same year, a copy of *The Course of True Love* in half calf with the original covers preserved, cost only 15s., and *Love Me Little* in original cloth cost only £2 5s. A similar eccentric history will be found with Wilkie Collins and *The Woman in White*, and again with Mrs. Gaskell and *Cranford*, first editions of these books being priced out of all proportion to their author's other books.

These are representative examples of high-spot collecting, prime examples of having the courage of somebody else's opinion, fostered by such moguls as A. E. Newton, Merle Johnson, and the Grolier Club. Even Jake Blanck catered to the plutocrats at one point with *Peter Parley to Penrod*, such is the insidious influence of Gresham's law! And, indeed, the soundest of booksellers felt bound to cater to the market. Sydney Hodgson once took very badly my description of auction rooms at that time as gambling palaces, nor was he mollified by an admission that the accommodation at Hodgson's was far from palatial. One great advantage for high-spot collectors is that, given an efficient secretary, even analphabetics can join the select circle. Of course precautions should be taken against anyone so misguided as to want to read the books. Solander cases help because they are difficult to open and look much better on the shelves than plebeian original boards or cloth.

In this respect the French, with their Cartesian approach to things in general, have continued the acceptance of publication in wrappers, leaving binding to the individual taste of the buyer. Even they insist on a hostage to fortune by preserving the wrappers, including the spine. But the craziest of deckle edge fanatics would surely prefer a Fermiers-Généraux Lafontaine in morocco with Padeloup's ticket to a copy in original wrappers.

What we were after in our small group was to recover a sense of proportion; possibly the Great Depression of the 1930s was more effectual. This is not to say that this particular lunacy perished in that holocaust. Direct evidence to the contrary is easily found. Volume 20 of *Book Auction Records* covering the period October–December 1929 records on adjacent pages [Galsworthy] *From the Four Winds* £92 and [Gaskell] *Cranford* £112, both first editions, of course. That this form of perversity still prevails may be seen from the latest volume of *American Book Prices Current* where records of the Parsons Sale include the same two books at $575 and $375 respectively.

High-spot collecting is, of course, quite different from, for example, the collection of the fifth Lord Rosebery, the catalogue of whose books showed him to be not an author collector as such, but one who bought the books that he liked; and many of his books were first editions simply because he bought them when they were first published. The four volumes of the library at Chatsworth, inadequate though they be, show a similar pattern. Many of the books there belonged to the beautiful Georgiana and bear her monogram on the morocco bindings. She is said to have played with incunabula in her cradle at Althorp.

Another idiocy that we attacked, also without complete success, was the fly-speck heresy. I see that in the early pages of *Points* (1931), I wrote: "Whatever the *basis* of collecting may be, the *method* must conform to the dictates of logic." And I emphasized the danger of "becoming a collector of misprints, errors in punctuation and freak bindings rather than a collector of books." One would have thought that common sense would suggest that, in the absence of evidence to the contrary, a broken type would occur in later stages of printing. Yet it was quite common to find this being trumpeted abroad as proof of early issue, as in the case of Joseph Conrad's *The Arrow of Gold*, first published in 1919. In the English edition the *A* in "Arrow" is defective in the headline of page 67; in other copies the letter is perfect. Fortunately it was not very long before a copy was found in which the *A* had disappeared completely.

Another canard (*canard à la presse*) that arose was concerned with inserted advertisements. It was confidently stated, for example, that the first issue of Wells's *Tono-Bungay* was distinguished by having inserted advertisements dated "1.09" until someone turned up a copy of the second edition of the book with advertisements so dated, which made it clear that the information lacked significance.

Lord Esher, in the informative preface to his catalogue writes, "I invest in the established classics; I speculate in the living writers," warning against sweeping statements (*The Modern Library . . . at Watlington Park*. 1930. p. xiii). Thus, while he had found Wells's *The Sea Lady* (1902) with first edition sheets and advertisements dated 1909, which made it a stumer, of three copies of Landor's *Imaginary Conversations* (1853) only the British Museum copyright copy, received in all probability before publication, had inserted advertisements dated 1850.

In the period of which I am writing, a tiresome feature was books that bore evidence of reprinting only on the dust wrapper. If memory serves, this first arose with some of Ernest Hemingway's books. It is difficult to believe that it was necessary to point out that the only thing provable from a dust wrapper concerns that artifact alone; no conclusions should be drawn from the particular copy of a book that it clothes at any particular time.

Words that I find no less applicable to our own time than to nearly 50 years ago when they were first written refer to the "cherished illusion that there is something magical about first editions, some secret talisman, now in the possession of a few, a touchstone which, applied to whatsoever book, will react in one way if it is a first edition, and another if it is not" (M. Escoffier, *Le Mouvement Romantique, 1788–1850*. Paris: Maison du Bibliophile, 1924, p. xvi). Some familiarity with the basic principles of bibliography is essential; and, where author collecting is concerned, failure to acquire it may prove disastrous. By 1949 Bowers and McKerrow were on hand for this purpose.

It is comforting to think that the Sadleir circle had a share in guiding 'prentice hands in both the Bibliographia series (1930–1936) and in *New Paths in Book Collecting*, published in 1934 almost coincidentally with the eighth volume of the series. I have dealt hitherto in these pages with the series, for there is a direct connection between this and *New Paths*, which arises partly from the fact that Sadleir was their publisher, but also from the close association of the members of the circle—the "biblioboys."

One subject constantly explored at our meetings was "blind spots"; fields as yet generally, or in some instances totally, unexplored by book collectors. Slowly but surely the notion of a symposium emerged. Carter took charge and himself contributed one of the two outstanding chapters—"Detective Fiction." In showing the reader how to distinguish between Wright and Wrong (W. Huntington Wright, better known as S. S. Van Dine, who contributed a historical foreword to *The Great Detective Stories*, 1926; E. M. Wrong, who edited and introduced *Crime and Detection*, vol. 301 in the World's Classics, also in 1926), he packed in an astonishing amount of solid information on authors and their detectives, giving titles, dates, and publishers with warnings on priorities, drawn from his own collection, which is now in the Lilly Library at Indiana University. The extent of influence of this chapter alone is incalculable. That it was direct and great is indisputable.

(It may be worth mentioning that in 1933 *Adventures of Sherlock Holmes* cost £1 10s. at auction, and *Memoirs*, £9. To this very day there is no auction record of the first edition in book form of *A Study in Scarlet* illustrated by Doyle's father and published by Ward, Lock in 1888. The periodical *Beeton's Annual*, in which it first appeared, now fetches nearly £1000.)

The impeccability and lucidity of C. B. Oldman's chapter, "Musical

First Editions" could not do other than clarify a subject then in its infancy. I had myself under his mentorship tested this surprisingly limited market, acquiring a number of personal favorites, among them Schubert's *Erlkönig*, op. 1 (£15)—an exceedingly rare first issue—*Winterreise* (£3), and *Schwanengesang* (£6), and Schumann's *Papillons*, op. 2 (£1), *Kreisleriana*, op. 76 (10s.), *Myrthen*, op. 25 (£1 55s.), and so on. (With the quaint perversity that haunts most official bodies Oldman, a great musicologist, was not in the music section of what was then the British Museum Library, but in the printed books department.) This chapter did much to direct the attention of many collectors to the subject of music collecting. Scribner's, New York, issued nine remarkable catalogues devoted to it, Mr. Macnutt's catalogues have passed the 100 mark, and Herr Schneider's have reached 200. This is probably not entirely a case of *post hoc ergo propter hoc*, but there can be little question that Oldman's essay greatly increased the momentum. It was later issued separately.

John T. Winterich's chapter "The Expansion of an Author Collection" was addressed, not to a novice seeking a subject to collect, but to those whose collections of Hardy, Kipling, or Emily Dickinson, for example, appeared complete, suggesting means for enlarging them.

"Yellow Backs," in the hands of Michael Sadleir, is an elegant and informative chapter, later handled by him at great length and with extended lists of titles in *XIX Century Fiction*. Some new collectors may have taken it up; but these books are now hard to find, and their generally poor condition when found makes their attraction for collectors dubious.

Tom Balston's chapter, "English Book Illustrations, 1880–1900," is a greatly extended and more useful version of his two articles in *The Book Collectors' Quarterly* nos. 11 and 14 (July 1933 and April–June 1934). The greater part of his collection was acquired *en bloc* by Gordon Ray "after they had been deemed unsuitable for disposal at auction" (*The Illustrator and the Book in England from 1760 to 1914*. New York: Pierpont Morgan Library, 1976, p. xxviii). Thus, nearly 40 years after Tom Balston had written in praise of them, these 80 or so volumes were considered to be not worth auctioning. Even now they arouse comparatively little enthusiasm, although noncollectors are usually drawn to them in my wife's collection. There is still time to follow Balston's advice.

David Randall, "American First Editions 1900–1933," devoted most of his piece to discussing the extreme difficulty, tantamount to impossibility in some instances, of completing already collected authors. In any case it was already a well-trodden path. Manley and Rickert's *Contemporary American Authors* (1929) included checklists of quite a number of them, and the 1940 edition by Fred B. Millett contained checklists of 219. With one exception all the authors mentioned by Randall are checklisted in Merle Johnson, *American First Editions* (1932), and a dozen or more are collated, not always correctly, in his *High-Spots of American Literature* (1925). As an example of the rarity of a book cited by Randall, the Parsons copy of Archibald MacLeish's *Class Poem* reached $2,500 in 1977. Hardly a "new path" author. The "wide and varied range" from which the young collector might choose were the following authors: Cabell, Hergesheimer, Dreiser, Hemingway, Wolfe, Faulkner, O'Hara, Laurence Lee, Ring Lardner, Harry Leon Wilson. Two very dark horses were Randolph Bourne and William Vaughan Moody.

Pollard begins his excellent chapter, "Serial Fiction," with these words: "The axioms and definitions which Mr. Muir has set in his book, *Points, 1874–1930*, are so clear and so logical in themselves that they provide an admirable basis for disagreement. . . ." His reasons for disagreement are based on my reluctance to admit that a periodical is a book. This is typical of the mutual logic chopping in which we frequently indulged. He once raked me over the coals for citing the great collaboration as an "enquiry" and until his dying day listed it in *Who's Who* as "inquiry."

His chapter is, despite the false premise, packed with sound and fascinating information. It should be read with its sequel, the masterly preface to Brussel's *Anglo-American First Editions, 1826–1900*, the first of the two volumes.

This leaves my own two contributions. The chapter "War Books" has largely failed in its object. One book that I recommended occasionally appears in the catalogues of booksellers and auctioneers, Frederic Manning's anonymous *The Middle Parts of Fortune* (1930).

The fact that it was not until the middle 1960s that Ford Madox Ford's novels were favored by collectors has no obvious connection with my strong recommendation of four of them in 1934. But perhaps a pat on the back is due for perspicacity. Blunden, Graves, and Sassoon were already collected authors. I regret that E. H. L. Jones's *Road to Endor* (1919)—an escape story that is so fantastic that no publisher would have given it a second look as a novel—failed to attract much attention. War or no war, C. E. Montague, Maurice Baring, and R. H. Mottram were darn good writers, and their first editions have reached no great premium.

I cannot remember which of my two chapters was a makeweight, commandeered to make a book of the called-for size. I would like to think that it was "Ignoring the Flag," which I now regard as misleading. It seems to me that dogmatism on either side is unfortunate, and I cannot feel that we are much further forward when a president of the Grolier Club unfurls Old Glory in pronouncing that "The aggregate whim of collectors is a whim of iron, cannot be governed by rules, and will always prefer *Moby-Dick* to *The Whale*." What, one may ask, is the impassioned collector to prefer over Hemingway's first two books? Anyone who sticks rigidly to the native editions should not read the early pages of the bibliography of Robert Frost—a nightmare for the poor fellow.

And what should a patriotic French collector prefer when faced with Diderot's *Le Neveu de Rameau?* First appearance in print posthumously in 1805 as a translation by Goethe from the original manuscript. First edition in French in 1821 in a highly inadequate translation back from the German. In 1823 another edition in French from a dubious French manuscript, not by the author, and found to be lacking in accuracy when the text from the original Diderot manuscript was published in 1891. For any collector who died before that date the book clearly did not exist.

In our attempt at setting collectors' feet more firmly on their chosen paths we were, I think, successful on the whole. We made no attempt to hide some of the problems that faced them and were sometimes able to suggest methods for solving such difficulties. I should like to think that we persuaded our readers that the golden rule is that there is no golden rule. Every problem should be treated on its merits.

Illustrations

1

Non-Firsts

G. Thomas Tanselle

THE MOST WIDELY known term associated with book collecting is undoubtedly "first edition." Even people who have no particular interest
in books, and who certainly have no real acquaintance with book collecting, have heard of "first editions"; the assembling of "first editions,"
it is popularly assumed, is what book collectors do. There is some
validity to this position, as conversations with collectors and the perusal
of dealers' catalogues will make clear. Collectors, of course, collect in
widely divergent fields and take many different approaches to collecting, but most of the books they collect are in fact likely to be firsts.

Actually, it is first *printings*, rather than *editions*, that traditionally
have been of interest to collectors. The distinction between an *edition*
(all copies printed from a single setting of type) and a *printing* or *impression* (all copies of an edition printed at one time—that is, during a single
run of the press) has not always been carefully maintained in the
terminology of collectors or, indeed, of publishers, but if the terms have
been fuzzy, the distinction itself has not been lost. Editions from the
nineteenth and twentieth centuries—when stereotype, photography,
and other means for the reproduction of typesetting were available—
may exist in numerous impressions; and certainly no collector of so-
called "first editions" ever settled for a copy of a second, or fifth, or
tenth printing simply because it was technically a part of the first edition
(the first typesetting). The term "first edition" became prominent

to describe a desideratum for collectors at a time when collecting interests were focused on incunabula and the later printed books of the Renaissance; in the case of such books, "first edition" and "first printing" were synonymous terms, because in that period type was not in sufficient supply to keep standing for a whole book, and a demand for more copies resulted in a second *edition* (a new typesetting). But many nineteenth- and twentieth-century books have sold well and progressed through an extended series of printings without ever being accorded a second edition; in these cases first printings of first editions are naturally what collectors have sought.[1]

Book-collecting literature is full of attempts to explain the elevated status of "first editions," many of them suggesting that an attraction to firsts is an irrational, but rather endearing, eccentricity of collectors. The real reasons for the importance of firsts, however, are far more substantial. I should like to point out a few of them, for if I am to champion the cause of non-firsts, as I intend to do presently, I would not want to be misunderstood as implying that firsts have been over-rated or are unimportant. The almost universal interest in first occurrences of all kinds—the sort of information recorded in Joseph N. Kane's *Famous First Facts* (New York: Wilson, 1933, and later editions)—does not merely represent idle curiosity or a desire to be prepared for parlor games. In attempting to understand the past or the present, there is a serious purpose to be served by knowing when a particular idea, practice, invention, or anything else first occurred or gained currency. The first printing of a work that has become a classic—or that is of historical interest for any other reason—is a cultural artifact, and we would all be poorer if there had not been those persons over the years who recognized the importance of preserving this tangible evidence of our intellectual heritage. Prices that collectors will pay for firsts are of course the result of supply and demand—which is to say that they are a measure of the force for preservation. Generally the more valuable an object is in monetary terms, the more carefully it is looked after, and the more diligently it is sought.

But there are additional scholarly reasons for the significance of firsts that are not always self-evident to everyone. The text of a first impression is likely to be closer to that of the author's manuscript than are the texts of later impressions or editions, which have had more opportunity to be altered in the processes of reprinting or resetting, and many writers have been more intimately involved in the production of the first printings of their work than of the later printings or editions (proofreading more carefully, for instance). For these reasons, even when an author introduces revisions into a later printing or edition, the scholar who wishes to establish a reliable text may find that the first-impression text (if not, indeed, the manuscript) is still the most appropriate one to serve as the basic copy-text.[2] Furthermore, although a photocopy of that text may be convenient for some purposes, it is no substitute for the original. Whereas photographs can be defective or misleading, the type, paper, and physical makeup of the original can provide evidence that may have a bearing on the establishment of the text (as well as being of interest in their own right, as indicative of book-making in a particular period). Copies of the first impression may vary from one another, too, and the more copies that are available, the more evidence scholarly editors have at their disposal. First impressions thus occupy a special place in research.

Serious collectors—that is, collectors who understand the scholarly implications of what they are about—need not be reminded of these reasons for exalting firsts. But it is well to recall them, because what I wish to say about non-firsts stems directly from this way of looking at firsts. It becomes obvious that non-firsts are also part of the total historical picture and therefore constitute important evidence as well. To say that collectors have undervalued non-firsts is not to say that firsts have been overvalued; rather, one can say that the recognition quite properly given to firsts is based—though not widely understood to be so—on a rationale that logically requires attention to be paid to later editions and impressions also. It is hard to say that non-firsts should be given equal billing; firsts, after all, by virtue of their "first-ness," will always be set apart from all that follows. At the same time, one cannot really say that non-firsts are less important; they are a part of the historical evidence and are thus indispensable. In any case, the traditions of book collecting have emphasized firsts, and that in itself provides another reason for looking more closely at non-firsts: whenever a significant body of material has been neglected, it offers attractive possibilities for collecting. I should like, therefore, to make some comments on the collecting of non-firsts, and then, because many of the same points apply to collecting anthologies as well, I shall have something to say about that neglected field also.

Defining something by what it is not is always an awkward business and seems to imply that there is nothing positive to be said about the subject. In this instance, although there are numerous positive reasons for collecting books that are not firsts, the one characteristic that unites such books is their status in relation to firsts. The collecting of firsts is so well established that to talk about collecting books for the reason that they are *not* firsts forces one to label them so as to show their relationship to the better-known category. Sometimes such books are called "later printings" or "later editions," but these terms do not make entirely clear that "later" means everything from the second onward, and the phrase "printings and editions" is a cumbersome way to refer to these books as a whole. Therefore I shall speak of them simply as "non-firsts," however peculiar the term may sound. The distinction between impressions and editions, however, remains a primary means for dividing the field. Another approach, based not on printing history but on content, is to distinguish non-firsts that contain new material from those that do not. The two kinds of division cut across one another, for obviously a new impression can be supplied, for instance, with a new preface, whereas a new edition can be set in type with no new matter whatever added to it; but understandably it is more common for new editions to coincide with the category of non-firsts containing additional material.

Less needs to be said about these latter two types of non-firsts than the other two, because the collecting both of non-first *editions* and of non-firsts (whether editions or impressions) that contain new material is already relatively well established. The idea of selecting a classic work—such as *The Compleat Angler* or *Robinson Crusoe* or the *Rubaiyat* or *Moby-Dick*—and assembling every edition in which that work appears has long been a recognized form of collecting. Prices of such non-firsts are generally modest compared to those of the firsts; yet there is a sufficient market for some of them—such as for some of the non-first editions of the four books just named—to support prices that make it worthwhile for dealers to catalogue them. The existence of bibliographies or checklists of non-firsts—like those available for these four works[3]—further encourages collecting by providing guides to what is known, so that additional attention will be directed to previously unrecorded editions as dealers and collectors discover them. A collection of editions of a single work is obviously useful in illustrating the popularity and influence of that work, the textual history of the work, and styles of bookmaking considered appropriate for such a work in different periods. Collecting all the editions of an ancient Greek or Roman author—or perhaps all the translations of that author's works into a particular language—makes a contribution to the history of Western culture and of the development of scholarship and editing, and it also allows one to have examples of books from many countries produced in every century since the beginning of European printing.

This kind of collection has considerable scope and diversity and yet is tightly organized and carefully defined. The attractions and accomplishments of such collections are certainly not unknown; yet they are not as well known as they deserve to be, and rewarding opportunities for collecting still abound in this field.

Another aspect of non-first collecting that has received a considerable amount of publicity involves transatlantic editions—that is, American editions of English books and English editions of American books. The peculiarities of the copyright relations between Britain and the United States in the nineteenth century were such that British and American works were often published across the ocean before they were published in the country of their origin.[4] This situation was first given extended treatment in I. R. Brussel's two volumes of *Anglo-American First Editions* (London: Constable, 1935–1936), and it has been investigated many times since then in connection with bibliographies or editions of particular authors. Of course, both the first English edition and the first American edition of a particular book could be regarded as firsts, and certainly both are important in the textual and publication history of the work. Some of the recent multivolume editions of American writers, such as those of Melville, Howells, and Stephen Crane, provide thorough accounts demonstrating the significance of transatlantic editions for establishing texts.[5] Yet the treatment of transatlantic editions by some collectors illustrates what first-edition collecting can become at its most superficial level. At times during the past half-century various collectors have engaged in a debate that has usually been called the "follow-the-flag controversy." The issue is whether the edition to be given pride of place by collectors is the first edition to appear in the author's own country or the first to appear anywhere. It would be hard to imagine a more pointless debate or one that does more to trivialize the act of collecting; the idea that a rule can be made declaring a certain kind of first edition the most desirable to possess implies that collecting is nothing more than a frivolous activity with arbitrary rules. Anyone who understands collecting to be a scholarly pursuit finds the whole "follow-the-flag controversy" ridiculous. A first edition is the edition published first, wherever that occurred, but the first edition published on the opposite side of the Atlantic is not thereby made undesirable or of diminished historical significance. Both editions are necessary for studying the circumstances surrounding the publication of the work, and serious collectors will recognize that they must have both. Whether the editions are called "first" and "second" or "first English" and "first American," both are important and in fact take on meaning by being brought together, for then each can be looked at in relation to the other. If the collecting of transatlantic editions of major nineteenth- and twentieth-century writers is by now fairly well established, there are still many under-valued transatlantic editions waiting to be assembled into meaningful groups by alert collectors.

Still another widely recognized category of non-first editions con-sists of those that have been found interesting as products of particular times and places. Many individuals and institutions have long collected incunabula, pre-1640 English books, or colonial American imprints, and they would not hesitate to add second or third or fourth editions to their collections if those books had been printed in the appropriate areas and periods. Nor is this kind of collecting limited to earlier cen-turies: some people collect the imprints of a given locality down to the present or collect the output of certain fine printers of the twentieth century. In many cases the content of such volumes is of little interest —they may be the tenth, or the fiftieth, editions of well-known classics. But obviously they are collected for reasons other than the firstness of their texts: they are sought after as physical artifacts or as works of graphic art. Similarly, many books are highly prized for their illustra-tions, even if the books are far from being first editions of the texts they contain. These approaches to collecting are of course well estab-lished, and I mention them only to indicate the range of non-firsts that have already become collectors' items and to suggest that the ra-tionale underlying the collecting of these non-firsts logically extends to many other books as well.

When non-firsts have been written about in the past—to the extent that they have been written about at all—it normally has been non-first *editions* that were discussed, especially those that incorporate new material. Charles Norman, in his article "On Collecting Second, Third, and Nth Editions" (*Colophon*, March 1935), devoted most of his space to examples of non-first editions, from many centuries, that contain material such as introductions, postscripts, or chapters not present in the first editions. Such non-firsts, he recognized, could be—and often had been—regarded as a species of firsts by first-edition collectors. But his point was that, even so, they were still unaccountably neglected: "We know full well, that for all the lip-service the dreadnought pays to the firstness of such [later] editions, his one hundred pounds will be laid on the counter for an incomplete *first*, while complete but sub-sequent editions will continue to be listed at a guinea, if that much, to the delight of his less affluent but more serious brethren." I would not wish to go as far as Norman in suggesting that collectors of non-firsts are necessarily more serious than collectors of firsts: those who do not really understand what collecting accomplishes exist at all levels, and the scholarliness of collectors is not to be measured by their money, or lack of it. But Norman's general observation is well taken and is still valid; for although many people understand the serious purposes to be served by assembling non-firsts that contain new material, far fewer have felt inclined to collect such books, which have therefore remained relatively undervalued in the market.

Obviously, new material can be appended to the texts of later *impressions* of a work (or even be bound up with some copies of first-impression sheets), as well as being incorporated into later *editions*, so non-firsts that have aroused attention because they contain additional matter are not always new editions but may be issues or impressions of single editions. Melville's "The Story of Toby," for instance, was bound with sheets of the English edition of *Typee* in 1846, and some volumes in series of classics like the Modern Library contain new introductions by their authors, attached to texts printed from plates of the original editions. Collectors, both private and institutional, are generally aware that author collections ought to include this kind of non-first; they often define the scope of their collections in some such phrase as "first and other significant editions," where "significant editions" refers to impressions or editions that contain something new. There is, in other words, an implication that editions or impressions not known to include new material are therefore not significant, or not significant enough to be made part of a collection. In the course of preparing with Floyd Dell a new edition of Burton's *Anatomy of Melancholy*, Paul Jordan-Smith recognized the scholarly necessity of having at hand all the editions published during Burton's lifetime and the first posthumous edition, which also contained authorial revisions. But in commenting on collecting those editions he stressed the firstness of what they contained: "To each successive edition of the *Anatomy* the author made extensive additions to the text, so that to possess a complete first edition of that book requires the purchase of at least six great volumes."[6] The importance of assembling the six editions, however, does not turn on whether it takes them all to constitute "a complete first edition"; even if there had been no textual differences among them, the volumes still would represent stages in the publication history of the work and would need to be brought together so that the scholarly editor—as Jordan-Smith realized—could discover the fact that no differences existed. The value of amassing the evidence does not depend on how dramatic the conclusions turn out to be.

I suggest, therefore, that these various kinds of non-firsts, all of which have been recognized by collectors, are most often collected as an extension of the collecting of firsts: they are found desirable not because they are non-firsts but because they can be considered firsts in some sense (the first edition to contain a preface, the first edition to be published by a particular publisher, the first edition to appear in a certain locality, the first edition to contain illustrations). As a result, those who see the intrinsic importance of non-firsts and collect them as such are in effect charting a new course; even when they collect categories of non-firsts that have already received attention, they will find much that has been neglected and much that needs accomplishing.

This line of thinking naturally leads to further scrutiny of non-first *impressions*, which have been almost totally neglected, because they only rarely have any aspect of "firstness" about them (one would generally expect their texts to be identical to the first-impression texts, being from the same typesetting; and even if they are part of a first edition by a particular publisher, they are nevertheless not the first printing of that edition). But when non-firsts are regarded for what they are, rather than for the ways in which they resemble firsts, it is clear that non-first impressions are just as significant as non-first editions. Because non-firsts of the nineteenth and twentieth centuries consist much more often of impressions than of editions, non-first impressions are clearly central to the study of the publishing history and the reputation of books and authors during those years. I should like to focus on them in some detail, for they offer many attractive possibilities for putting together impressive and useful collections at modest cost. And if I may be autobiographical for a moment, I can illustrate some of the reasons for the importance of non-first printings by describing two circumstances that led me to add this category of books to the others that I was already collecting.

The first involves my association with the Northwestern-Newberry edition of *The Writings of Herman Melville.* When the project to produce this edition was organized in 1965, one of the first tasks was to locate copies of all editions and impressions of Melville's work that had appeared during his lifetime. In order to be in possession of all the textual evidence, it was of course essential to know any variants that occurred in the texts of these editions. Whenever an edition exists in more than one printing, there is always the possibility that the text differs from one printing to another; indeed, even when there is only one printing, the text may differ from copy to copy, as the result either of stop-press alterations or of the deterioration of the type during the press run. Therefore it is always necessary, in establishing a text, to collate copies of an edition against each other. When two or more impressions are known to exist, the usual practice is to collate the first impression against the last and, if variants turn up, to locate their first appearance in any intervening impressions. In order to ensure the accuracy of the results and to take account of the possibility that variants may appear within an impression, these collations need to be performed several times, using different copies each time. Sometimes, of course, the existence of non-first impressions (or some of them) is not known at the outset, either because a given impression is not readily identifiable as such or because, even if it were identifiable when found (through title-page date or some other obvious means), no allusion to such an impression is extant and no copy of it located. In the former case, multiple collations of different copies may reveal the evidence for distinguishing the unrecognized impression; in the latter, an unrecorded impression may come to light through a diligent search of the holdings of institutional and private libraries.

The implications of this kind of editorial research for collecting policy are clear: a collection will make the greatest contribution to bibliographical and textual scholarship if it contains copies of all the successive printings of any edition collected or, better yet, multiple copies of those printings. Because this kind of collecting has been extremely uncommon, however, most scholarly editors find that they must try to assemble such a collection themselves or else locate copies in public and private collections and try to make arrangements for borrowing them. Generally a combination of these approaches must be used, though both are extremely time-consuming, and often neither is entirely successful. In the case of Melville, we began with an important nucleus in the collection of Harrison Hayford (general editor of the edition), who had for years understood the value of non-firsts and who had been amassing multiple copies of all printings of Melville's books. From there on, however, our efforts to locate further copies for our work were typical, in that they clearly revealed the effect of the traditional attention to firsts on the availability of material for research. In short, there was no problem in finding copies of first impressions: many rare-book collections in research libraries contained good runs of them, and many dealers had copies available for sale or were able to find copies fairly quickly. Curators of rare-book collections are often understandably reluctant to release books on interlibrary loan; and, although photocopies can be used for collation when absolutely necessary, the advantages for textual and bibliographical research of having a supply of the original volumes physically at one place are incalculable. Indeed, some important details that have a bearing on textual matters— such as the fact that a particular gathering consists of different paper or that a particular leaf is a cancel—may not be discovered without seeing the actual copies. Many physical points, in fact, may pass un- noticed unless copies can be laid side by side for inspection; and any physical feature of a book may prove to be significant for establishing some aspect of the printing or publishing history of the book—and thus in turn to be relevant to textual work. For this reason the research for an edition and that for a descriptive bibliography go hand in hand; they complement each other and are greatly facilitated by a collection con- taining multiple copies (so-called "duplicates," which turn out sur- prisingly often—even in the case of nineteenth- and twentieth-century books—to have some differences from one another). The Melville collection formed in conjunction with the Melville editing project was conceived from the outset as one that would emphasize the assembling of bibliographical evidence and accommodate textual and biblio- graphical research, and The Newberry Library has been generous and understanding over the years in providing for the purchase of the required books.

The collecting of the firsts, then, is largely a matter of having the money to pay for them. Melville firsts are relatively scarce, and their prices have shot up rapidly over the past decade, but most of them are still generally available on the market if one is willing to pay the price. The story is very different, however, with the non-firsts: one can be ready and willing to pay well for them, but the books still may be simply unlocatable. When one does eventually track some of them down, the prices are likely to be ridiculously low. This situation perfectly illus- trates the point that rarity does not make a book valuable unless there is demand for the book. The demand for Melville non-firsts on the part of The Newberry Library and a group of Melville enthusiasts seems small in comparison to the demand for firsts that is a product of a long- standing and well-publicized tradition of collecting. Because non-firsts have been neglected, they are now more challenging to collect. What- ever is regarded as valuable is likely to be saved, and over the years people have saved what they think may be firsts but have not hesitated to discard books labeled "fourth impression" or "eighth printing"; in this procedure they have been supported by dealers, reflecting in turn the interests of collectors. In other words, the survival rate of non- firsts has not been as high as that of firsts. And in some cases—certainly it is true of Melville—there were fewer copies of non-firsts to begin

with. Whereas the first printings of Melville's books published by the
Harpers usually amounted to 3,000 or 4,000 copies, the later printings
were almost always under 300 copies. It is not surprising, therefore,
that our search for later printings was considerably more difficult
than our search for firsts. The fact that Melville's books were not widely
read or collected during the last decades of his lifetime or for several
decades thereafter exacerbates the problem of locating the non-firsts.
Nevertheless—even if Melville is in some respects a special case because of the dramatic extremes that his reputation has undergone—
the situation in which the non-firsts are harder to find than the firsts
is a common one.[7]

When Richard Colles Johnson, during the early years of the
Melville project, surveyed the holdings of Melville editions and impressions in American, Canadian, and British libraries, he found that,
whereas many of the firsts were available in 75 or more libraries, it was
rare to find a given non-first in more than about a dozen libraries, and
some were much scarcer than that.[8] At the time of his survey, for
instance, he located (outside the Newberry collection) only three copies
of the 1865 and 1871 American printings of *Typee*, of the 1858, 1863,
and 1868 *Omoo*, and of the 1855 *Moby-Dick*, and only two copies of the
1849 English printing of *Omoo* and of the 1875 American *Redburn*. More
copies undoubtedly exist, even in libraries, but because they are not
regarded as special in any way they may be discovered, for example,
in use as ordinary reading copies in small public libraries that do not
report to the National Union Catalog. Of the institutional copies reported, I have found many to be in deplorable condition in the general
stacks of university libraries; the firsts, even when rebound, get transferred to the rare-book room, but the scarcer nineteenth-century non-
firsts, whether in tattered original cloth or in library bindings, remain
on the open shelves. The Newberry collection now contains examples
of nearly all the nineteenth-century printings but still does not have a
sufficient sampling of many of them for bibliographical purposes. And
what is there was frequently very slow in coming. For a long time we
thought that the only copy of the 1875 *Redburn* available to us was the
one we borrowed from the City College of New York, but eventually
a dealer who knew about the Melville project was able to supply us with
a copy. According to the Harper records, that printing of *Redburn* consisted of 147 copies (in contrast to the first printing of 4,508). Copies
are obviously very scarce, but to the Melville editors, they are also
highly desirable; representing the last printing from the original
American plates, they had to be collated against copies of the first print-

ing to determine whether any variants entered the text during the life of those plates. I need not elaborate further on the difficulties that the Melville editors have had with non-firsts: the lesson for collectors is clear.

I do wish, however, to point out another aspect of the Newberry collection. Although the editions and impressions (in book and periodical form) dating from Melville's lifetime occupy the central place in the collection, it does not stop with them, for editorial and bibliographical scholarship involves recourse to many related materials. The collection aims at comprehensiveness in all these areas: posthumous editions and impressions (including every printing of every paperback and classroom edition), adaptations and excerpts, translations, anthology appearances, Melville's source books, biographical and critical studies (including dissertations and articles in journals), and works inspired by Melville. As it stands, the collection is one of the most thorough author collections ever assembled, and it dramatically demonstrates how much is to be gained by placing firsts in a larger context. Merely allowing one's eye to scan the shelves of editions and impressions suggests the potential of such a collection for documenting both Melville's reputation and nineteenth- and twentieth-century printing and publishing practices. The number of editions and impressions of Melville's different works, the dates of their appearance, their places of publication, their physical treatment (cloth or paper covers, illustrations, and so on), and the nature of the texts used in them are all central pieces of information for tracing the vicissitudes of his popularity and influence over the years. Of course one also needs to utilize any printers' and publishers' records that have survived and any other relevant information, such as publishers' advertisements and comments made in letters. But the books themselves are obviously the primary evidence. Furthermore, the changes in book design from the mid-nineteenth century to the present are readily apparent in the collection. Because Melville has been so widely reprinted in the twentieth century by many kinds of publishers, the volumes ranged in order along the shelves offer a revealing panorama of shifting tastes in typographic layout, binding styles, jacket designs, and the like. The descriptive bibliography of Melville that will eventually be based on this collection will include details on all these editions and impressions. Only in that way can the bibliography serve its highest function—providing a history of the publication of the author's books, which is necessarily a segment of the larger history of printing and publishing during those years. The Newberry collection of Melville shows that in author collections of the greatest scholarly potential, the firsts constitute only one part (even if normally the most expensive part) of the whole. As more collections of this kind are formed and more bibliographies grow out of them, more comprehensive and reliable histories of the book trade will be possible.

The other circumstance, besides my work on the Melville edition, that affected my thinking about non-firsts is the imprint collecting I have been engaged in for many years.[9] I have been collecting the output of some two dozen American publishing firms that were active between 1890 and 1930—firms like Stone & Kimball and Copeland & Day in the earlier part of this period and B. W. Huebsch, Mitchell Kennerley, Boni & Liveright, and Alfred A. Knopf later, firms that played an important role in the literary history of their time through their willingness to experiment and to take more risks than many of the larger, well-established firms. Although I began by collecting only the first impressions of books from these publishers, the majority of the books involved were not ones ordinarily sought by collectors of firsts. Because I was trying to bring together all books bearing these imprints and not just those by important writers, I found myself interested in many books that were actually of very little intrinsic interest but that took on an interest by being part of the context from which the more significant books emerged. Frequently, in fact, I was more intrigued by such books than by the important ones—the latter, after all, were well known and had been well studied, whereas the others, having been bypassed, were often less readily available but were equally indispensable as a part of the total picture.

Pursuing this approach led me gradually to see that later printings, when they existed, could not be ignored: the activity of a publishing firm cannot be represented simply by firsts any more than it can by high spots alone. If one title went through 15 printings while another required only a single printing, that fact should be discoverable from an imprint collection: copies of all 15 printings must be there to reflect accurately the total output of the firm, as well as to suggest the relative popularity of the titles it published. In browsing through large used-book shops, I have often come across considerable runs of different printings of particular popular books from my publishers, and seeing them side by side has revealed in many instances that the bindings (or, more accurately, the casings) vary in color, weight or texture of cloth, lettering, or some other detail. The way in which a firm treats later printings is one of the characteristics of a firm's publishing practice that a collection focusing on the firm should document: if a firm, as sometimes happens, cheapens the casing or the paper or alters the dust jackets of later printings (or those after a certain point), the exact details of the change can be discovered readily if copies of all the successive printings are assembled in one place (and some differences might not be noticed at all if copies could not be compared directly). Furthermore, when a second publisher takes over the publication of a book, at least the first form of the book to be released by that new publisher belongs in a collection of the imprints of the original publisher. Although one can often learn in other ways (in *Publishers Weekly* or in the catalogues in *Publishers' Trade List Annual* or in the publishers' archives) that certain titles were transferred from one publisher to another, the books themselves are indispensable to document the transfer: knowing whether the new publisher produced a new impression (or edition) or instead received unsold sheets from the original publisher (and issued them with a cancel title page, or a paste-over imprint label, or a casing with the new imprint) is relevant to understanding the history of the original firm and its individual titles. The physical evidence in non-firsts is thus no less important than that in firsts for establishing the details of printing and publishing history.

Another kind of information in non-firsts is the evidence they provide of a publisher's method (or lack of it) for identifying later printings and editions. Publishers vary greatly in the way they label their non-firsts, and some do not label them at all. As a result of the emphasis that has been placed on firsts, several guides have appeared —aimed principally at collectors of twentieth-century English and American books—indicating for a large number of publishers how one can distinguish firsts from non-firsts.[10] These books are not always reliable, and in any event one cannot assume that a publisher's usual practice was necessarily followed in a particular instance. There are many examples of non-first printings that are not so labeled, and distinguishing them (when that is possible at all) may involve considerable analysis of the physical evidence, including a thorough comparison of the texts. But even when the non-first printings are designated, it is still necessary to locate copies of each of them in order to establish what the run of successive printings consists of. For instance, the fourth printing of the American edition of *The Waste Land* (published by Horace Liveright) is dated April 1930 on the verso of the title page; even if the publisher's records indicating such a printing are extant, one must still see the book itself in order to verify that an April 1930 impression did actually appear and to see exactly what it consisted of. Without seeing it, one cannot know whether it matched the previous impressions in physical appearance and whether its text differed in any respect from what had gone before. Anything that is discoverable about these matters from the publisher's records or other sources must obviously take second place to the firsthand evidence of the physical object itself (though of course one cannot necessarily accept at face value the information, such as dates, printed therein).

In studying the publishing history of a book, therefore, it is essential to have copies of each impression and not to rely on any cumulative lists of impressions that sometimes appear on copyright pages. Contrary to the usual practice of the Liveright firm (earlier called Boni & Liveright), the 1930 printing of *The Waste Land* does not record the dates of the earlier printings, so clearly in that case one must have recourse to copies of earlier impressions to learn their dates. But even when the dates of all previous impressions are listed—as they are in books from many English and American publishers from the 1890s onward (including many paperback publishers)—such a list is no substitute for copies of each of the impressions so recorded. The sixth printing of *The Emperor Jones, Diff'rent, The Straw* (Boni & Liveright, March 1923) provides a provisional record of four 1921 printings (April, June, August, November) and one 1922 printing (October), but it cannot tell one at what point the style of O'Neill's name on the backstrip was changed from "Eugene G. O'Neill" to "Eugene O'Neill" (interestingly, the plates of the title page were not altered at the same time). The run of impressions of Anita Loos's *Gentlemen Prefer Blondes* (Boni & Liveright, 1925) occupies considerable space on my shelves, but it displays some changes in casing (such as the shift from red to blue backstrips on the tenth and eleventh printings), which are part of the history of the presentation of that popular book.

Providing evidence about popularity, of course, is one of the reasons for the significance of non-firsts. It is revealing, for instance, that Robinson Jeffers's *Roan Stallion, Tamar, and Other Poems*, which Boni & Liveright published a month earlier than the Loos book, was only in its third printing at the time when Loos's book was in its fourteenth (June 1926). Obviously one does not have the whole story without knowing the number of copies in these printings; but such information is not always available, and the non-firsts themselves are crucial for whatever facts they preserve. Sometimes, indeed, they specify the number of copies in, as well as the dates of, individual impressions: thus the non-firsts of Bliss Carman and Richard Hovey's *Songs from Vagabondia* (Copeland & Day, 1894; later taken over by Small, Maynard) show that the first ten printings (through June 1909) consisted of 750 copies each, with the eleventh (March 1911) moving up to 1,000, and the fourteenth through the seventeenth, occurring at intervals of about two and a half years from March 1919 through September 1926, dropping down to 500 each. Even if non-firsts were not important for any other reason, they would be worth bringing together in order to establish this kind of record of publication.

That bibliographers who see the value of such information have not found it easy to locate—given the fact that non-firsts have not generally been collected—is illustrated by Sidney Kramer's *A History of Stone & Kimball and Herbert S. Stone & Co.* (Univ. of Chicago Press, 1940). Kramer's work is careful and normally thorough, repeatedly citing facts about non-firsts to fill in the publication history of particular Stone & Kimball and Stone books; but it is obvious that, whereas he had access to the firsts, he had not been able to see all the non-firsts, and his information about them is spotty, based simply on those he chanced to come across. For instance, his entry (no. 41) for H. C. Chatfield-Taylor's *Two Women & A Fool* (1895) says, "Issued 1897 in reduced size"; but my copy labeled "Ninth thousand" bears an 1896 title page and is in reduced leaf size. Kramer's entry (no. 107) for Richard LeGallienne's *Prose Fancies, Second Series* (1896) refers to 1897 advertisements for a second printing and 1898 advertisements for a third; but if he had seen copies of those printings, he could have pointed out that the second printing is actually dated 1896 and the third 1897. For Henry Blossom's *Checkers* (1896), Kramer mentions (in entry no. 109) the date of a seventh printing but not of the preceding ones; he also reports that the twenty-fifth thousand (1899) contains a frontispiece by John T. McCutcheon, but this frontispiece and five other new illustrations as well are present in my copy of the thirteenth printing, dated 1897. Despite Kramer's statement (no. 139) that Clyde Fitch's *The Smart Set* (1897) was "apparently not reprinted," I have a copy designated "Third Impression" and dated 1899. And when he says (no. 230) that George Riddle's *A Modern Reader and Speaker* (1900) was "reprinted in 1902," he implies that no intervening impressions appeared, but I have one dated 1901. Many other similar instances could be noted in Kramer— or in most other works citing non-firsts as evidence of a book's popularity. Charles V. Genthe's *American War Narratives, 1917–1918* (New York: David Lewis, 1969), for example, states that *A German Deserter's War Experience* (1917) "went through three printings in America" (p. 126); but my collection of Huebsch imprints includes a fifth printing (August 1917, four months after publication).[11] I mention these instances not to criticize the bibliographies but to show how scholarship is weakened by the lack of accessibility of non-firsts and the virtual absence of systematic runs of them.

Once I began adding non-firsts to my imprint collections and recognized the scholarly value of assembling them, I saw no reason to limit myself to the group of publishers I have mentioned and started collecting non-firsts (British as well as American) more widely, though still largely within the 1890–1930 period. So I now have runs of non-firsts of many prominent authors published by most of the best-known firms of the time—in some cases for books of which I do not possess the firsts. In other words, I am collecting non-firsts as such, and not simply as adjuncts to the firsts. When I once purchased a copy of the twenty-first printing of *Main Street* from a Chicago dealer (having checked my list to see that I did not own it), he remarked that I was probably the only person who would have bought it *because* it was the twenty-first printing. If he was right, his comment reflects a sad fact about the collecting of twentieth-century books. In the same way that many nineteenth-century non-firsts are now extremely scarce, twentieth-century non-firsts will in the future be very difficult to locate, as more of the writers become the subjects of scholarly editions, if we do not begin to preserve the evidence now.

My shelf of Edwin Arlington Robinson's *Tristram* (Macmillan, 1927) is fairly long (the book reached its twenty-eighth printing in November 1930), but I regard the space as well used, even though the total monetary value of that shelf is far less than that of many individual Robinson firsts (which, I must admit, I have on a different shelf). The non-firsts of another Macmillan book, Edgar Lee Masters's *Spoon River Anthology* (1915), not only exhibit changes in binding style and color but the introduction, following the eighteenth printing (September 1916), of a "New Illustrated Edition, with New Poems" (October 1916; a new typesetting) and a "New Edition, with New Poems" (November 1916; the typesetting of 1915 with the new poems added, and without the Herford illustrations)—both of which were later reprinted. Although these books contain Macmillan's familiar cumulative listing of impressions, some prominent Macmillan books do not: Vachel Lindsay's *The Chinese Nightingale and Other Poems*, for instance, bearing the words "Published September, 1917," on the copyright page, occurs with various later years on the title page. In collecting the non-firsts of Edna St. Vincent Millay, one has the Harper letter codes for month and year to contend with; in collecting the non-firsts of Susan Glaspell's early books published by Stokes, one is given an exact day of the month for each printing. Some English publishers in particular distinguish impressions and editions, as in the record printed in Jonathan Cape's 1923 edition of *Main Street* (where the notation of the third impression of the previous edition, dated 1923, is followed by a line listing a "New and cheaper Edition, reset," also in 1923) or in Heinemann's 1928 edition of Willa Cather's *A Lost Lady* (where a "New impression" of November 1927 is followed by a "New Edition" of 1928). Dust jackets, too, are as important to have on non-firsts as on firsts: not only are they an element in a book's publishing history, but also they can often be a source of additional information about non-firsts, as when a book identified on the copyright page as a third printing is wrapped in a jacket labeled "10th thousand."[12] There is clearly great variety in publishers' treatments of non-firsts, and the information provided in some instances is more helpful than in others. But these differing practices are themselves part of what such a collection exists to document.

Much of what I have been saying about non-firsts has been recognized over the years by others, without having any noticeable impact on collecting patterns. The scarcity of non-firsts, for instance, is almost proverbial, because everyone realizes that the number of books requiring either a second printing or a second edition is small compared to the total number of books that appear. David Randall, known for his imaginative catalogues, recalled in his autobiography, "I once contemplated a rare book catalogue of tenth editions only but was never able to find enough."[13] And the scarcity of the non-firsts that exist is attributable more to the attitudes of collectors than to the size of the impressions or editions. William R. Cagle is one of those bibliographers who have perceived this situation. In commenting on some non-first issues of Maugham, he says, "Remainder issues, like colonial issues, have had little appeal to collectors and so have had a lower survival rate than first issues"; the scarcity of such books, he laments, "continues to plague bibliographers."[14] The artificiality of segregating what seem to be firsts from non-firsts is underscored by the fact that non-firsts sometimes appear on the market before firsts and that what are labeled as non-firsts often are in fact a part of the first impression. Christopher Morley, explaining how copies of later printings may be stacked on top of the firsts in the publisher's warehouse, points out that while one of his own books was commanding a premium in the first-impression market, there were, at the bottom of the stockroom pile, "several hundred copies of the first printing available, (oh, how available!) at their original price."[15] And Robert Lusty recounts Walter Hutchinson's custom of "stopping the run of certain titles after every five hundred copies and inserting the phrase 'second impression before publication,' and so on progressively."[16] This practice has been by no means uncommon in either the nineteenth or the twentieth century.[17] Furthermore, non-firsts have frequently been given publicity for some particular association with the author: a prominent example is Lewis Carroll's examination of the illustrations in the sixtieth and eighty-fourth thousands of *Through the Looking-Glass*.[18] James L. W. West III has shown how the shifts in Fitzgerald's reputation are reflected in the illustrations on the paperbacks of *The Great Gatsby* and concludes that "an author's image is reflected by *all* forms in which his work is presented to the public and that even such items as cheap paperback printings are collectible because of the information they reveal about an author's reputation."[19] Yet despite all the reasons for being interested in non-firsts, collectors in general have not been drawn to them, as David Magee humorously notes in the third edition of his spoof, *A Course in Correct Cataloguing* (San Francisco, 1958); it is labeled "Third (and Best) Edition" because, as he says, "Third editions are always hard to sell."

What is hard to sell will not fetch a high price, will not be highly valued by its purchaser, and will not be looked after as carefully as it would be if it had been more costly. Market values reflect the popular view as to what is desirable and thus are a powerful aid to preservation. When important material that deserves to be preserved is undervalued, surely the collector of independent mind—who is not content simply to follow in the footsteps of others—has the ideal opportunity to be a leader in developing a new field. The attractions of non-firsts are many: in a time when the supply of traditionally collectible books is shrinking and their prices soaring, the cost of non-firsts is modest; collectors who are depressed by the prospect of building collections that will be second-rate versions of those already existing in institutions will find that assembling non-firsts affords them the opportunity of making a fresh contribution and surpassing the holdings of most institutional libraries; and non-firsts are intrinsically important, being essential for textual study, for the investigation of a book's popularity, and for the understanding of printing and publishing history. The collecting of non-firsts is logically a part of other kinds of collecting. Whether one's interest in a book is its author, its subject, its printing and design, or its publication history, one is not doing justice to that interest by stopping with the firsts. One cannot hope to be fully informed without the evidence of the non-firsts. With the growing interest in publishing history and in establishing the texts of modern authors, non-firsts are eventually going to be in greater demand. But an anticipated rise in market value is hardly the point. What is more significant is that non-firsts can offer collectors the highest kind of satisfaction: assembling systematic runs of non-firsts gives one the pleasure of creating an entity greater than the sum of its parts and in the process makes a new contribution to knowledge.

This approach to collecting can affect one's attitude toward various more specific classes of material and cause one to see opportunities for worthwhile collecting that one had not considered seriously before. Anthologies as a field for collecting provide a useful case in point. Everyone, of course, is aware of certain famous anthologies, from Tottel's miscellany (*Songs and Sonnets*, 1557) and *England's Helicon* (1600) down to *The Book of the Rhymers' Club* (1892) and *Des Imagistes* (1914), that are important in literary history and have long been considered collectible. Many author collections, too, have routinely included anthologies that were important in the authors' careers: a respectable Millay collection, for instance, would have to contain *The Lyric Year* (1912), just as an E. E. Cummings collection would have to include *Eight Harvard Poets* (1917) and a C. Day Lewis collection, *Ten Singers* (1925). Anthologies that publish original material, or material that previously appeared only in periodicals, obviously qualify as first book publications and have received due attention from collectors of individual authors. What has been much less recognized is the value of putting together collections of anthologies as such—not as parts of author collections—and including among them non-firsts as well as firsts.

Non-first collecting has two aspects in connection with anthologies: there are the non-first printings or editions of particular anthologies, and there are the anthologies that contain material previously published elsewhere (thus constituting non-first editions of the individual pieces included). The anthology as a form of original publication is a phenomenon surely deserving of study in its own right. Authors frequently receive their first public exposure—or their first exposure outside magazines—in the pages of anthologies, for a publisher takes less risk in publishing several unknown writers together in an anthology than in issuing a separate volume by each of them, and an anthology may help to identify less established writers through association with a group or literary coterie, as in the series *Georgian Poetry* (1913–1922) or *Some Imagist Poets* (1915–1917). If a collection of anthologies of a given period, then, is basic to the study of the conditions of authorship and publication in that period, allowing each anthology to be examined in the context of the practice as a whole, it follows that the non-firsts of these anthologies must also be a part of the collection.

In trying to assess the influence of a particular anthology and the exposure its contributions received, one has to take into account, as part of the evidence, the history of its reprinting. Furthermore, anthologies that contain previously published material are not irrelevant. An anthology can play an important part in establishing an author's reputation even if the pieces included have already been printed in several other places (in books as well as periodicals). This kind of anthology—containing reprinted work—has generally been ignored by collectors, but for the study of an author's reputation it may be central. Anthologies of reprinted material intended for the general public (such as Edmund C. Stedman and Ellen M. Hutchinson's *A Library of American Literature* [1888–1890] or Louis Untermeyer's many volumes) or for classroom use (the enormous number of high-school and college series that have proliferated in the past half-century) may indeed have been more influential than any other publications in solidifying the reputation of certain writers or fixing the canon of what they are best known for; conversely, such anthologies also serve to reflect current reputations and changing fashions. The texts printed in anthologies also deserve scrutiny: those that appear during their authors' lifetimes may contain authorial revisions (a situation especially likely for works that had been published previously only in periodicals); but even when authorial revision is not involved, the degree of accuracy of a text that has been widely circulated and read is an important fact in literary history. Thus what was said earlier about the role of non-firsts in editing texts and in charting writers' reputations applies equally to anthologies.

It is a well-known danger of collecting that one may be lured from an initial field into related fields, and my imprint collecting is what led me into the collecting of anthologies. Nearly every publisher I collect was responsible for an important anthology (such as *Others* or *The Freeman Book* or *The Lyric Year* or *These United States*) and for several other quite useful ones. As I began placing cards in my catalogue for each of the writers represented in these volumes, I realized that a well-indexed collection of anthologies would be of considerable value for research and could provide access to a large body of material not easy to get at in other ways. Whereas periodicals are relatively well provided with consolidated indexes, anthologies are not as well covered. There are, it is true, such guides as the *Essay and General Literature Index* and Kirby Congdon's *Contemporary Poets in American Anthologies, 1960–1977* (Metuchen, N.J.: Scarecrow Press, 1978); and some library catalogues contain—unpredictably—added entries for all the authors in certain composite volumes. But this kind of coverage is haphazard and leaves much unnoted. Author bibliographies—where one has a right to expect such information—frequently exclude anthologies except those containing the "first book publication" of individual pieces. This practice is yet another indication of how the traditional emphasis on firsts has prevented many author bibliographies from even attempting to tell the full story of the publication history of those authors. One of the great merits of Jacob Blanck's *Bibliography of American Literature* (New Haven, Conn.: Yale Univ. Press, 1955–) is that, for each author covered, it does list anthologies, whether or not they contain first book appearances. But the difficulty of locating anthologies—the almost total lack of comprehensive collections of them—has made it impossible for these sections of *BAL* to approach completeness; anyone with a moderately sizable collection of American and English nineteenth-century anthologies can without much effort locate a number of entries omitted. The fault here lies not with *BAL*—which is performing a great service in providing basic lists that can now be added to—but with the traditions of collecting and library cataloguing. A bookseller's catalogue recently provided another illustration of how anthologies, especially those for classroom use, can be overlooked: it called attention to the appearance of Steinbeck's story "The Leader of the People" in a 1941 high-school anthology, even though the standard Steinbeck bibliography cites a 1942 anthology as the first book appearance of this story outside Steinbeck's volume *The Long Valley* (1938).[20]

No one person can hope to take on the entire field of anthologies. But individuals can make a beginning by specializing in anthologies of particular kinds, indexing their contents, and publishing addenda, when appropriate, to standard bibliographies. It will be a long time before anthologies are brought under effective bibliographic control, but the activity of collectors will speed up the process, and in the interval their own catalogues, however incomplete and imperfect, will be useful tools of reference. A few categories of anthologies have already been the subjects of research: Arthur E. Case's *A Bibliography of English Poetical Miscellanies, 1521–1750* (Oxford: Bibliographical Society, 1935) is the classic example. But among the anthologies of the nineteenth and twentieth centuries—which must necessarily be the period of most anthology-collectors' activity—only the literary annuals have so far received much attention.[21] The range of anthologies to choose from is very broad, however, and I shall name here, in no particular order, a few of the types (with examples noted from my shelves) that one might profitably concentrate on. There are the collections relating to, or containing writers from, particular states or areas (such as *Poets of Portsmouth* [ed. by A. M. Payson and Albert Laighton, 1865], *South Songs* [ed. by T. C. DeLeon, 1866], or *The Chicago Anthology* [ed. by Charles G. Blanden et al., 1916]); volumes devoted to the work of students or graduates of particular colleges (*Songs of the College of the City of New York* [1866], *Yale Verse* [ed. by Charles E. Merrill, 1899], *A Williams Anthology* [ed. by Edwin P. Lehman et al., 1910], *A Book of Vassar Verse* [including poems by Millay, Crapsey, and Coatsworth, 1916]); collections for public speaking or elocution (*The National Preceptor* [ed. by J. Olney, 2nd ed., 1830], *Holiday Selections for Readings and Recitations* [ed. by Sara Sigourney Rice, 1892]); anthologies organized according to subject matter (*In the Saddle: A Collection of Poems on Horseback-Riding* [1882], *Patriotic Songs of the American People* [ed. by Howard F. Brinton, 1900]); selections of writings produced during, or relating to, war or other events (*Songs from the Trenches* [ed. by Herbert A. Gibbons, 1918])[22]; collections of poems, stories, parodies, humorous pieces, or works of other genres (*The Poets of America* [ed. by George B. Cheever, 1854], *Yankee Drolleries* [ed. by George A. Sala, 1869]); selections from the work published in particular magazines or by particular firms, often issued on the occasion of anniversaries (*Fruit among the Leaves: An Anniversary Anthology* [of Appleton-Century-Crofts, ed. by Samuel C. Chew, 1950], *One Hundred Years of "The Nation": A Centennial Anthology* [ed. by Henry M. Christman, 1965]); series of annual anthologies covering particular fields or types of writing (William Stanley Braithwaite's or Thomas Moult's series on magazine verse, Franklyn Pierre Davis's series on newspaper verse, the series of O. Henry award stories); and collections intended for a broad general audience (Alexander Woollcott's *Readers* or the series of *Oxford Books*). One could also mention encyclopedias, hymnals, *Festschriften*, memorial volumes, and collections of manuscript facsimiles (like *Autograph Leaves of Our Country's Authors* [1864] and *Fame's Tribute to Children* [1892]). The varieties are inexhaustible, and this sampling of types suggests how much overlapping of contents is bound to exist and how difficult it would be to locate anthologies relevant to a given purpose through library catalogues. Individuals should take up the task, and some of their collections will eventually find their way into special collections departments of libraries.

I have already mentioned one excellent institutional anthology collection—a part of the Melville Collection at The Newberry Library —and I should like to give an example or two of the uses to which it may be put.[23] Melville presents an unusual case, for few writers with such a solidly established reputation as he now enjoys have been so ignored during the later years of their own lifetimes and as recently as the first decade or two of this century. In order to use anthologies as one measure of this situation, one must have access to anthologies that do not include Melville as well as those that do; the Newberry collection therefore admits anthologies that do not contain Melville, if they are of the sort that would now be expected to contain him as a matter of course. Thus one gains some idea of Melville's stature in 1916 by noting that Norman Foerster's *The Chief American Prose Writers* has no Melville selections. But, as the Newberry collection also shows, there were some anthologies even after the Melville "revival" of the 1920s that still reflected the older view: Henry Garland Bennett's 1935 high-school anthology *American Literature*, containing work by some 70 writers and billed as "a perfect reference book," includes no Melville, nor does Raymond W. Short and Wilbur S. Scott's *The Main Lines of American Literature* nearly 20 years later (1954). These are exceptions, of course, for the number of anthologies that have printed selections from Melville during the past 40 or 50 years is immense, and through them one can trace changing patterns of selections and differing amounts of space allotted to Melville. In contrast to the 1935 survey that excluded Melville from a group of 70 writers are two anthologies of 1962: a one-volume selection from *Twelve American Writers* (ed. by William M. Gibson and George Arms) devoting 64 pages to him, and a two-volume selection from 28 *Major Writers of America* (ed. by Perry Miller et al.) giving him 92 pages. The early preference for *Typee*, as in the seventeenth volume (1897) of Charles Dudley Warner's *Library of the World's Best Literature*, seems to have given way to *Moby-Dick*, as in Norman Foerster's *American Poetry and Prose* (1925). But by Foerster's third edition in 1947, the selections from *Moby-Dick* had been replaced by "Benito Cereno," part of the *Mosses* review, and three poems; and in the fourth edition of 1957 the space devoted to Melville was doubled by the addition of *Billy Budd*. The significance of maintaining runs of the non-firsts of anthologies is obvious.

Even a cursory examination of the Newberry collection reveals what a wide variety of selections from Melville have appeared in anthologies. Although some pieces have been relatively standard choices, there appears to have been less of a consensus on what to include than is often the case with major writers. That situation is perhaps partly the result of the more recent evolution of Melville's reputation and partly a consequence of the nature of his output—his major achievements, aside from some poems, being book-length works or long tales and sketches. The poems have been consistently more common choices than one might have expected, going back at least as far as Burton E. Stevenson's *Poems of American History* in 1908. The patterns observable in anthologies intended for classroom use do not appear to be significantly different from those in anthologies intended for the general reading public, except perhaps that the choice of poems is somewhat less predictable in the latter. In both categories of anthology, certain of the tales and sketches—especially "Bartleby" and "The Encantadas" —seem to turn up noticeably more often after 1950 than before that year. The lengths to which one must go to locate all the anthology appearances of an author are suggested by the presence in the Newberry collection of Sylvestre C. Watkins's *The Pleasures of Smoking* (1948), with two extracts from Melville, and Alistair Sutherland and Patrick Anderson's *Eros* (1961), with six. Clearly, a more systematic study of this collection would enable one to draw more detailed conclusions, both about Melville's reputation and that of other authors.

But the importance of anthologies as a force for solidifying reputations is unquestionable: Samuel Kettell, in the preface to his *Specimens of American Poetry* (1829), described the aim of his anthology as the preservation of literature that should not be lost, and many other anthologies since then have suggested in one way or another that their function is to establish a basic canon. When schoolchildren and college students are introduced to literature with these volumes year after year, their influence is bound to be enormous. It has even been asserted that anthologies affect the quality of writing: Laura Riding and Robert Graves, in *A Pamphlet against Anthologies* (London: Cape, 1928)—which is required reading for anyone interested in this field—claim that, whereas some poets try to write poems of the "best-poem type" in order to get into anthologies, others are "anti-anthology poets" who "often overreach themselves, inflicting self-protective distortions on their work—as parents in old Central Europe often deliberately maimed their sons to save them from compulsory military service. . . . The charmlessness of some of the best poetry of our time is in part due to a militant disdain of anthology standards and criticism" (p. 159). When they add that "in the long run it is almost impossible to hold out against the anthology," they are bearing witness to the power, whether for good or ill, that anthologies wield.[24] Collectors should begin to give more recognition to anthologies, both firsts and non-firsts, for the important role they play in many authors' publication history, and in literary history generally.

I hesitate to leave the subject of anthologies without saying a word about periodicals. They, too, are composite publications made up of the contributions of a number of writers, and there is no clear-cut dividing line between them and anthologies. Some anthologies, such as Braithwaite's series, appear at regular intervals like periodicals; and some publications usually regarded as periodicals, such as *The Yellow Book, American Caravan, Gutenberg Jahrbuch,* or *Studies in Bibliography,* consist of hardcover volumes that could as well be regarded as anthologies in series. As if to demonstrate this point, the *Saturday Evening Post* in 1919 published a 382-page volume entitled *One Issue,* "designed to show how one issue of *The Saturday Evening Post* would look if published in book form." What can be said about the collecting of anthologies, therefore, can also be said about the collecting of periodicals. And although periodicals as a general rule print new material, they also contain non-first printings. In addition, many numbers of periodicals, especially from the nineteenth century, exist in multiple impressions, for individual numbers of certain journals were regularly reprinted, when the need arose, just as if they had been books. Yet very little research has been done in this area; research is hampered because virtually no collections of periodicals exist with the necessary multiple copies for comparison, and the traditional collecting emphasis on book publication has provided little incentive for the formation of such collections. As a result, bibliographies that give detailed information about the books by a given author generally provide only brief entries for that writer's contributions to periodicals. But the periodicals are printed matter, just as the books are, and are subject to the same vicissitudes in the course of being printed. They deserve investigation as a significant aspect of publication history; and they thus offer another challenge to those collectors who understand the artificiality of limiting themselves to "first book appearances."

The rationale that underlies the collecting of non-firsts can be applied in this way to all kinds of material other than anthologies and periodicals. One must naturally select a particular area, for no one can collect all non-firsts, any more than one can collect all firsts. Some people may at the outset find something amusing, or perhaps slightly ridiculous, in the thought that if firsts are collectible, as they obviously are, and now non-firsts as well, then the two together amount to the totality of all books. But the point is a serious one, and precisely the point I wish to make: there is no piece of printed matter that is not a collector's item,[25] because each one is a document of historical interest, providing evidence of its time and place and worthy of preservation.[26] To say that, however, is not to say that one becomes a collector by saving every scrap of printing that comes one's way. Collecting is an organized and disciplined pursuit that results in an assemblage of material with unity and meaning; collectors are scholars who locate and segregate the patterns to be found within the seeming chaos of the total mass of material. They make their greatest contributions, of course, when they cause previously unnoticed or neglected patterns to become visible and approachable. In doing this, they also experience their greatest personal satisfaction, because they have had the pleasure of shaping a meaningful whole, not merely following guidelines imposed from without. Collecting is not a game with arbitrary rules; it is the beginning of the process by which we find meaning in the past. The stakes are higher than those of a game, and the pleasure correspondingly greater.[27]

There has always seemed to me to be something askew in the remarks that otherwise perceptive people often make about certain of their own gatherings of books being only "working collections," as if there were a clear division between collectible books and other books or as if a library amassed for the purpose of utilitarian reference could not also be a "collection." Such a gathering might be a true collection, or it might not, but the presence in it of non-firsts or other unfashionable categories of books would not be the determining factor. I am not claiming—far from it—that scholars' working libraries are necessarily significant collections, for frequently they are not. What I do wish to be understood as saying is that an assemblage of books containing not a single item ordinarily thought of as "collectible" may be of great importance as a collection, if it has been put together with sensitivity and a thorough knowledge of the subject. A. W. Pollard, in a justly famous article on book collecting for the *Encyclopaedia Britannica* (11th ed., 1910), says that so long as a book "appears likely to be easily procurable at any moment, no one has any reason for collecting it." He is right, as far as that book considered in isolation is concerned; but the book may very well have an important role to play in a collection of books and therefore be collectible. The more a person comes to understand the degree to which the intellectual content of a book is linked to the details of its physical transmission, the more that person's working library (even the "reference" books) will become a real collection; it may be full of non-firsts, but they will have been placed there consciously as elements in a chain of evidence. John Carter, our most perceptive writer on book collecting, has pointed out that the "degree and direction of the connoisseurship applied to book-collecting . . . have developed and will continue to develop."[28] Collectors who break new ground by collecting such books as non-firsts may be rebelling against current fashions but are contributing to the larger patterns of evolution in bibliophily: they are members of a continuing community of historically minded persons who assume responsibility for preserving the written products of our culture in a way that helps to reveal their significance.

Notes

1. The distinction between editions and impressions is fully discussed in Fredson Bowers, *Principles of Bibliographical Description* (Princeton Univ. Press, 1949), especially pp. 37–39, 379–393. A convenient briefer treatment occurs at the beginning of Terry Belanger's chapter titled "Descriptive Bibliography" in Jean Peters, ed., *Book Collecting: A Modern Guide* (New York: Bowker, 1977), pp. 97–115. See also G. T. Tanselle, "The Bibliographical Concepts of *Issue* and *State*," *Papers of the Bibliographical Society of America* 69 (1975): 17–66 (especially 18–21).

2. This approach to scholarly editing has become widespread in the years since W. W. Greg, "The Rationale of Copy-Text," *Studies in Bibliography* 3 (1950–1951): 19–36—reprinted in his *Collected Papers*, ed. by J. C. Maxwell (Oxford: Clarendon Press, 1966), pp. 374–391. For a survey of the literature, see G. T. Tanselle, "Greg's Theory of Copy-Text and the Editing of American Literature," *Studies in Bibliography* 28 (1975): 167–229.

3. One convenient way of locating bibliographies of individual authors is to consult T. H. Howard-Hill, *Bibliography of British Literary Bibliographies* (Oxford: Clarendon Press, 1969), supplemented by his *Shakespearian Bibliography and Textual Criticism* (Oxford: Clarendon Press, 1971), pp. 179–322; and G. T. Tanselle, *Guide to the Study of United States Imprints* (Cambridge, Mass.: Belknap Press of Harvard Univ. Press, 1971). Of the four works mentioned here, the checklist for *Moby-Dick* appeared after the publication of these two listings: G. T. Tanselle, *A Checklist of Editions of "Moby-Dick," 1851–1976* (Evanston and Chicago: Northwestern Univ. Press and The Newberry Library, 1976).

4. This situation is effectively explored in Simon Nowell-Smith, *International Copyright Law and the Publisher in the Reign of Queen Victoria* (Oxford: Clarendon Press, 1968); and in James J. Barnes, *Authors, Publishers and Politicians: The Quest for an Anglo-American Copyright Agreement, 1815–1854* (London: Routledge & Kegan Paul, 1974).

5. A convenient list of the editions produced under the auspices of the Center for Editions of American Authors is included in *The Center for Scholarly Editions: An Introductory Statement* (New York: Modern Language Association of America, 1977), pp. 5–6 (also printed in *PMLA* 92 [1977]: 583–597).

6. *For the Love of Books: The Adventures of an Impecunious Collector* (New York: Oxford Univ. Press, 1934), p. 156.

7. For some further comments on the relations between Melville collecting

and scholarship, see G. T. Tanselle, "Bibliographical Problems in Melville," *Studies in American Fiction* 2 (1974): 57–74 (especially 57–62).

8. "An Attempt at a Union List of Editions of Melville, 1846–91," *Book Collector* 19 (1970): 333–347.

9. I have commented on this part of my collection in "Collecting Modern Imprints," *Book Collector* 19 (1970): 203–213.

10. The best known is H. S. Boutell, *First Editions of To-Day and How to Tell Them,* 4th ed., rev. by Wanda Underhill (Berkeley, Calif.: Peacock Press, 1965); two recent examples are Jack Tannen, *How to Identify and Collect American First Editions* (New York: Arco, 1976), and Edward N. Zempel and Linda A. Verkler, *A First Edition?: Statements of Selected North American, British Commonwealth, and Irish Publishers on Their Methods of Designating First Editions* (Peoria, Ill.: Spoon River Press, 1977). For a comment on the problems with such books and on the Tannen book in particular, see *Papers of the Bibliographical Society of America* 72 (1978): 270–271.

11. Another example of the way in which a standard bibliography can be supplemented with regard to non-firsts is G. T. Tanselle, "Addenda to Sheehy and Lohf's *Sherwood Anderson:* Copyright Information and Later Printings," in *Sherwood Anderson: Centennial Studies,* ed. by Hilbert H. Campbell and Charles E. Modlin (Troy, N.Y.: Whitston, 1976), pp. 145–150.

12. This point is further discussed, along with other reasons for being interested in jackets, in G. T. Tanselle, "Book-Jackets, Blurbs, and Bibliographers," *Library,* 5th series, 26 (1971): 91–134.

13. *Dukedom Large Enough* (New York: Random House, 1969), p. 41. Randall cites Charles Lamb as saying that tenth editions are scarcer than first editions.

14. "Somerset Maugham's *Orientations,*" *Book Collector* 24 (1975): 291–293.

15. *Ex Libris Carissimis* (Philadelphia: Univ. of Pennsylvania Press, 1932), pp. 10–11.

16. *Bound to Be Read* (London: Cape, 1975), p. 37.

17. See Jacob Blanck, *The Title-Page as Bibliographical Evidence* (Berkeley: School of Librarianship, Univ. of California, 1966), pp. 6–8.

18. See Selwyn H. Goodacre, "Lewis Carroll's Rejection of the 60th Thousand of *Through the Looking-Glass,*" *Book Collector* 24 (1975): 251–256.

19. "The Bantam *Gatsby,*" *Book Collector's Market* 3, no. 6 (November–December 1978): 15–18.

20. See Bradford Morrow's catalogue no. 2 (Santa Barbara, 1978), item 843: the anthology is Cynthia Ann Pugh, ed., *A Book of Short Stories,* rev. ed. (New York: Macmillan, 1941). Cf. Adrian H. Goldstone and John R. Payne, *John Steinbeck* (Austin, Tex.: Humanities Research Center, 1974), entry B23.

21. Frederick W. Faxon, *Literary Annuals and Gift Books, American and English* (Boston: Boston Book Co., 1912); Ralph Thompson, *American Literary Annuals and Gift Books, 1825–1865* (New York: Wilson, 1936); Andrew Boyle, *An Index to the Annuals* (Worcester: Boyle, 1967–).

22. A listing of 131 anthologies is included in Catherine W. Reilly, *English Poetry of the First World War: A Bibliography* (New York: St. Martin's Press, 1978).

23. Richard Colles Johnson, who is in charge of the Melville collection, has re-

corded the anthologies containing Melville that were published before Melville's death in 1891: "Melville in Anthologies," *American Book Collector* 21, no. 8 (Summer 1971): 7–8. I am indebted to him and to Richard R. Seidel for their assistance in surveying the anthology collection, as well as for reading a draft of this essay.

24. Riding and Graves divide anthologies into "true anthologies" (collections for private use and those that rescue material) and "trade anthologies" (those that treat poetry "as a commodity destined for instructional, narcotic, patriotic, religious, humorous and other household uses" [p. 26]). It is the latter category, of course, that their strictures are directed against. In the process they make many useful references to anthologies of all periods.

25. I have tried to make this point in a somewhat different way (by saying that a bibliographer "approaches all books in a library as if they were 'rare books'") in "Bibliographers and the Library," *Library Trends* 25 (1976–1977): 745–762.

26. Some *copies* of a given item may of course not be in good enough condition to be worth preserving; but acceptability of condition varies according to the relative scarcity of the item.

27. Edwin C. Bolles, in *Collectors and Collecting* (Melrose, Mass.: privately printed, 1898), was thinking along the same lines when he said, "I think that a Collector can hardly fail to become a Student, unless his collecting is the mere result of a vaccination for a fashionable craze or popular fancy, and depends more on his loose purse-strings than his personal application" (p. 17).

28. *Taste & Technique in Book-Collecting* (Cambridge Univ. Press, 1948), p. 10.

Further Reading

Non-firsts have been so little discussed that there are few references for further reading that can be provided. Of course, discussions of firsts frequently say something, at least by implication, about non-firsts (as in I. R. Brussel's *Anglo-American First Editions* [London: Constable, 1935–1936]); and there are brief comments on non-firsts in various writings devoted to other bookish topics—some of which have been cited in the notes to this essay. But Charles Norman's "On Collecting Second, Third, and Nth Editions" (*Colophon*, Part 20, March 1935) practically stands by itself as a piece entirely devoted to this subject (it is concerned with non-first *editions*, not *impressions*). For general discussion of the distinction between firsts and non-firsts, one should consult Fredson Bowers, *Principles of Bibliographical Description* (Princeton Univ. Press, 1949), and G. Thomas Tanselle, "The Bibliographical Concepts of *Issue* and *State*," *Papers of the Bibliographical Society of America* 69 (1975): 17–66, or the less detailed remarks by Terry Belanger in "Descriptive Bibliography" in *Book Collecting: A Modern Guide*, ed. by Jean

Peters (New York: Bowker, 1977), pp. 97–115, and in Philip Gaskell, *A New Introduction to Bibliography* (Oxford: Clarendon Press, 1972). On anthologies, one can do no better than to read Laura Riding and Robert Graves, *A Pamphlet against Anthologies* (London: Cape, 1928). The present notes give a few examples of reference works that cite non-firsts and anthologies. In addition, a number of author bibliographies of recent years can profitably be examined for their treatment of non-firsts and anthologies—for instance, Jacob Blanck, *Bibliography of American Literature* (New Haven, Conn.: Yale Univ. Press, 1955–), Jennifer Atkinson, *Eugene O'Neill* (Univ. of Pittsburgh Press, 1974), or James L. W. West III, *William Styron* (Boston: G. K. Hall, 1977).

2

American Trade Bindings and Their Designers, 1880–1915

Charles Gullans and John Espey

In 1966 I WAS so depressed by the prices of English books, which had been rising for over a decade, that I was consciously searching for something to collect that was both numerous and cheap. Without being sure that I had made a commitment, I began gathering books by a number of minor American authors of the turn of the century—George Washington Cable, Henry Van Dyke, Paul Leicester Ford, Thomas Nelson Page—not for the authors nor for the contents of the books, but for the decorated case bindings that adorned many of their books, all of which had one thing in common, an intersecting monogram of the letters *M* and *A*. I soon found out that the letters stood for Margaret Armstrong (she is identified in the advertising back matter of books with some frequency). Three things then happened in rapid succession, and each is important.

First, when I had only some 20 books, I made a decision to collect everything designed by Margaret Armstrong that I could find. (I was encouraged in this by the low prices and excellent condition of what I had bought.) The decision to collect the total output was crucial; it rescued me from the half-knowledge of the dilettante.

Second, since I was finding other monograms, I made the casual decision to keep a record of them and the books on which they appeared. At the beginning, recording monograms was easy and fun, but it soon became onerous. The number of them and the vastly greater number of times they appeared on books—at first hundreds and then thousands—outstripped all my expectations. I soon became irritated that the recording of monograms took time away from the pleasant search for Margarets. Yet, in retrospect I realize that the urge for scholarly completeness, though it can create difficulties, should always be obeyed; the decision to record monograms was most important to understanding not only the work of Margaret Armstrong but of the larger field of trade bindings as an aspect of publishing history as well.

The third event has its own history and importance. I showed some of the covers to my colleague, novelist John Espey. By the following day, he displayed six or seven new titles on his office shelves and so thoroughly invaded my obsession with trade bindings that he has never left it since. The spirit of emulation has thoroughly imbued the collaboration. But more importantly, at each stage of collecting, there was always someone who understood the nature of the quest. It was John Espey who introduced both system and scale to our efforts, first by reading the stacks in the College and Research Libraries at UCLA and elsewhere, and second by combing the pages of *Publishers' Trade List Annual* and *Publishers Weekly* in search of documentation and clues to titles yet unseen.

If my account seems too rational and farsighted to be true, I must admit that I made at least one fundamental mistake, which had to be pointed out to me twice before I profited from the lesson. In spring 1967, Peggy Christian, a bookseller, phoned to tell me that she had found a book *by* Margaret Armstrong. (While I teach bibliography, I had been so consumed by the notion of Margaret Armstrong as a practicing artist that I neglected so obvious a research tool as the card catalogue.) Twenty minutes later I knew that Margaret Armstrong was the author, not of one, but of eight books, that two were best sellers, and that she appeared in a number of well-known biographical guides. Subsequently John Espey discovered the *Readers' Guide* for me, and the lesson was nailed home.

By August of that year we had some 85 titles. This is more than the entire life output of any English book designer of commercial bindings of the period. So, when in the same month Hamilton Fish Armstrong, the youngest brother of Margaret Armstrong, sent us a list of titles from his library, which included 66 that were new to us, we were stunned. With this development we thought we were surely near the end of our work, but the number was to climb ever higher.

In time we came to see the enormous volume of production as generally characteristic of American work. Not only were the designs produced in quantity, but they were largely for popular books that were printed in large editions. These facts are what give hope to the new collector; the field cannot be easily exhausted by two people or even by 20. Sufficient copies survive in good condition and at prices that are generally low enough for one to hope to assemble a collection, certainly of some beauty, but also of some scholarly interest—a collection marked by the vigor and variety of much American work, but one with scope and depth, that is to say, with significance.

Historical Perspective

From the first discovery that gold could be applied to cloth (1830 in England and 1831 in America), the publishers and the diesinkers (those who routed and chased the brass plates that stamped the designs on the cloth) were fascinated by the possibilities inherent in the materials. Until 1880, the work in England was very largely, and in America exclusively, produced by diesinkers, that is to say, not by artists or designers who showed some aptitude for applying their talent to book covers, but by artisans who showed some talent for design.

In general from 1870 to the late 1880s, the designs produced can be classified quite easily into two kinds, the machine-shop style and the doodle or art-lettering style. The first is illustrated by two fairly common books, Samuel Clemens, *Tom Sawyer* (1876)[1] and Edward Bellamy, *Miss Luddington's Sister* (1883).[2] The machine-shop style is compounded of everything that can be done, however difficult, in metal worked directly, in contrast to the softness of brush lines or the fluidity and life of pen lines; we find straight lines, right angles, rectilinear crosshatching, cogwheels, and other fine-line, mechanical ornament. This shades easily into the doodle or art-lettering style, first by the introduction of natural forms, twigs, leaves, cobwebs, and then by transforming the lettering into a freehand style and by unbalancing the design so that it advances from one lower corner to the opposite upper corner. The doodle style is best illustrated by Madison Cawein, *The Triumph of Music and Other Poems* (1888).[3] The freehand lettering of the style is derived from the twig constructed lettering so common on title pages in the 1840s and 1850s; this is often joined to some pictorial, as opposed to purely decorative, element in the design. Either style may freely employ tonal modeling in the pictorial elements. Both can be extensively documented from July 1885 in the pages of the *American Bookmaker*.

The technical methods by which the covers were produced are

interesting in themselves. Because the designs were regarded as forms of advertisement, the publisher decided how much to allocate to the production of the book and set the designer his limits in the number of colors, the amount, if any, of gold leaf or Dutch metal or aluminum (for silver), and the quality of cloth. The finished design, once accepted by the publisher, went to the diesinkers, who made the color separations and transferred them to metal stamps, at first by hand with a steel point, and later by photographic means. The standard metal was brass, but zinc, because it could be cheaply photoengraved, came into use during the mid-1880s, although it wore out faster. Steel came into use about the same time, because it could be used on very long runs of textbooks without wear. Originally the spaces were cut out on the stamps with hammer and chisel, but from the early 1880s this was done with a Houchin engraving machine, "which consists of a finely adjusted, swiftly revolving spindle, in which is fastened a cutting drill, working vertically. The stamp is fixed to a table, which is propelled by screws in any direction. The drill has the advantage of being instantly made to rise or fall at the will of the operator."[4] All this was performed by highly skilled artisans who prepared one stamp for each color. Matte effects in gold were achieved by rough chasing ("shading" as it was called) the proper portion of the stamps, which were then mounted in a blocking press where each color was laid on separately under great heat and pressure. The gold leaf was cut and affixed from rolls of gold leaf mounted under full metal cowlings to prevent wind disturbance, and the casings then were sent to the blocking press. The gold leaf was sometimes laid on before and sometimes after the inks. Graded tones in ink were difficult to achieve and disliked by the workers, but were effected by a divided font and a split ink roller. The brass stamps weighed a pound and a half each and were usually scrapped after a time. I have seen very few.

Evidence in *Publishers Weekly* tends to suggest that 1908 or 1909 was the last year of extensive use of decorated cloth on novels. According to Lee Thayer of the Decorative Designers (a firm discussed later in this chapter), their business died "in a month" when the illustrated paper book jacket, nothing new to be sure, suddenly caught the fancy of the reading public. The one that probably "did it" was a jacket illustrated by Howard Chandler Christy. Because the illustration on the jacket also could be used as a paper onlay front cover for the book (although the two were not by any means always the same), the cutting of many costly blocks could be eliminated. A new and popular advertising tool, which sold as effectively as decorated cloth and at less cost, had been discovered.[5]

Early Designers

Casually and unsystematically, beginning in the 1880s, publishers were seeking well-known artists to design book covers and sometimes interior pages as well. One of the first and probably the best work of this sort in the decade was Edwin Austin Abbey, *Selections from the Hesperides and Noble Numbers of Robert Herrick* (New York: Harper, 1882). He abandoned the traditional dark and unattractive cloths and used instead a pale beige cloth, with a grained texture, and added brilliant inks and gold. The design is largely conventionalized, not tonally modeled, and respects the integrity of the book cover as a flat surface. It is a monument of intelligence and taste in solving the problems of book design and owes nothing to any prior model. A number of other books were designed by artists, illustrators, and architects in this decade, but none of the other designs was so successful as Abbey's design for *Herrick*. Among the other designs are an earlier design by Abbey for Paul du Chaillu, *The Land of the Midnight Sun* (New York: Harper, 1882 [c. 1881]), and designs by Howard Pyle for *The Merry Adventures of Robin Hood* (New York: Scribner, 1883); Elihu Vedder for *The Rubaiyat of Omar Khayyam* (New York: Houghton, 1884); George Wharton Edwards for Oliver Wendell Holmes, *The Last Leaf* (Boston: Houghton, 1886 [1885]); Stanford White for *A Book of the Tile Club* (New York: Scribner, 1887); and Louis J. Rhead for Gleeson White, *Ballades and Rondeaus* (New York: Appleton, 1888). Few of these men gave much time to book covers since they were professionals in other fields; but Edwards (1859–1950) and Rhead (1860–1926), who was brought to this country in 1883 by Appleton to design book covers, did enough work to be noticed here. Although Rhead largely abandoned books for posters in the 1890s, Edwards was to have a long career. He developed a very popular style, compounded of a line derived from Walter Crane, but much thickened and somewhat dead, and rather swollen rocaille ornament. His output was large and occasionally striking, as in Edmund Spenser, *Epithalamion* (New York: Dodd, Mead, 1894); Paul Leicester Ford, *A Checked Love Affair* (New York: Dodd, Mead, 1903); and Zona Gale, *Mothers to Men* (New York: Macmillan, 1911), a series design for her works.

The Major Designers

If Edwards remained always a little behind and out of tune with the generation of the 1890s, which would wholly revamp the aesthetics of the book cover and the book, his older contemporary, Mrs. Henry Whitman, was not.

SARAH DE ST. PRIX WYMAN WHITMAN (Baltimore, 1842–Boston, June 25, 1904) spent her early childhood in Lowell, Massachusetts. She was trained under William M. Hunt in Boston and Couture in Paris and had solid academic training. Her husband was a partner in the legal firm of Weston and Whitman. She became a member of the permanent committee of the School of the Museum of Fine Arts in Boston in 1885 and was a trustee of Radcliffe from an early date. She worked in oil, pastel, and stained glass and designed the windows for Harvard Memorial Hall and Trinity Chapel. Having been an early proponent of higher education for women and for blacks, she endowed scholarships at Howard University and at Radcliffe and left large sums of money to the Boston Museum, Radcliffe, and Tuskegee Institute.

Sarah Whitman was a forerunner who was 25 years older than the reforming generation that observed, understood, and widely imitated her example in the early 1890s. Well known as a landscape artist in oil and a portraitist in pastel, she took up book design, apparently to oblige her friends, at first mainly women, because she was at the heart of Boston's literary, artistic, and social world. She produced many exceptional and memorable designs in the 1880s, and they alone might have made her famous; but at the age of 50, she began designing in an unexpected style, as brilliant as any achieved by the young artists of the 1890s and quite without precedent.

Her earliest work was for Susan Coolidge, *Verses* (Boston: Roberts, 1880), and is much indebted to Rossetti's design for A. C. Swinburne, *Atalanta in Calydon* (London: John Hotten Camden, 1865), although in a later work by Mary Lee, *A Quaker Girl of Nantucket*, she shows her interest in the illustrators of the 1860s, especially G. J. Pinwell. What she achieved at first is simple and fairly obvious, but it is difficult to appreciate so long after the fact precisely because her work was so rapidly absorbed by others. She stripped the fussy covers of the 1870s bare and started anew with minimal detail and with ornament freshly thought out. Her design for *Verses* is not brilliant, except in its white and gold, for it is frankly borrowed, but it is revolutionary. We see three round and overlapping ornaments in Japanese style, off center and surmounted by a single line of simple lettering, all in gold on cream cloth. The effect may appear a trifle anemic today, but in the context of its time it was explosive.

For some years she lost the directness of this borrowed vision of things to come and resorted to the dark, muddy cloth generally in use; but by the mid-decade she abandoned them and was using light brown ink on light beige, rough, linen-weave cloth for John Esten Cooke, *My*

Lady Pokahontas (Boston: Houghton, 1885). Or she used cream cloth for the spine, and colored brocade patterns on the palest beige cloth over the boards of her first masterpiece, Margaret Deland, *The Old Garden* (Boston: Houghton, 1886), a book that is representative of its time and place, but wholly through its novelty and its subsequent influence. It is what we would want to remember of the time, and it made her famous. In the following year it was exactly imitated by Amy Lowell's first book, *Dream Drops* (Boston: Cupples and Hurd, 1887). In the same year, Houghton first used her name in advertisements in *Publishers Weekly*.[6] Some of her other memorable designs of the decade, all for Houghton, are Edith Thomas, *Lyrics and Sonnets* (Boston: Houghton, 1887); Rodolfo Lanciani, *Ancient Rome* (Boston: Houghton, 1889); James Russell Lowell, *Heartsease and Rue* (Boston: Houghton, 1889); Mary C. Lee, *A Quaker Girl of Nantucket* (Boston: Houghton, 1889)— one of very few pictorial designs; and F. Hopkinson Smith, *A White Umbrella in Mexico* (Boston: Houghton, 1889).

In the 1890s her rustic, sans-serif lettering with its occasional Greek letters reached its complete form and appears on almost every book that came from Houghton's Riverside Press. One of the finest is Martin Brimmer, *Egypt* (Boston: Houghton, 1892), an astonishing design of three stylized papyrus stalks in gold on white vellum with a simple stitch border in gold that imitates workaday vellum bindings of the Renaissance. The design is wholly flat, wholly conventionalized, and is one of the most striking images in American book design of any period. It is masterly in its proportions, its spacing, and its daring simplification. It is important in evaluating her to understand that she thought the problems through for herself before Beardsley, before Will Bradley, and with a single example from Rossetti to guide her through the historical wilderness of the book. The achievement was neither unconscious nor accidental. She was in no doubt as to what she wanted or what she rejected, as she made clear in a talk before the Boston Art Student's Association in February 1894: "Ten years ago you would have found book covers, hundreds of them, which represented a combination of bad French art mixed with Japanese art; scrolls and arabesques, which had to do with some debased form of book cover mixed with a bit of Japanese fan, the suggestion of a sun, a stork, or strange diagonal lines, so beautiful in pure Japanese art but so fatal and terrible on a book." She speaks elsewhere in the lecture of her great respect "for the idea of a book" and demonstrates this respect in her use of the historical shapes and forms of decorations. She makes graceful allusion to medieval clasp books on Oliver Wendell Holmes, *The Autocrat of the Breakfast Table*, illustrated by Howard Pyle (Boston: Houghton, 1885), 2 volumes; and to traditional Japanese books on Lafcadio Hearn, *Glimpses of Unfamiliar Japan* (Boston: Houghton, 1894).[7] Of a brilliance equal to *Egypt* are Richard Watson Gilder, *The Great Remembrance* (New York: Century, 1893); Celia Thaxter, *An Island Garden*, illustrated by Childe Hassam (Boston: Houghton, 1894); Margaret Graham Collier, *Stories from the Foothills* (Boston: Houghton, 1895); Sarah Orne Jewett, *The Country of the Pointed Firs* (Boston: Houghton, 1896); Louise Imogen Guiney, *The Martyrs' Idyl* (Boston: Houghton, 1899); Nathaniel Hawthorne, *The Marble Faun*, Roman Edition (Boston: Houghton, 1899), 2 volumes; and Louise Chandler Moulton, *At the Wind's Will* (Boston: Houghton, 1899). These are a few masterpieces among many, and among hundreds of lesser designs.

In collecting Margaret Armstrong, we were fortunate in finding a living contact with her generation in her youngest brother. Although she was designing in 1890, she never monogrammed a work before 1895 and not always after that. The earliest work that we had came from 1894, and our eyes were not yet sufficiently accustomed to the minute variations of her style and lettering to assign the uncertain and groping style of her earliest works to her. We would simply have dismissed them without the authority of the tradition represented by Hamilton Fish Armstrong's list. Contemporary documentation is equally important. The earliest work that we know to be by Alice C. Morse (active 1887–1921) is Harold Frederick, *Seth's Brother's Wife* (New York: Scribner, 1887), which is assigned to her in the *American Bookmaker* 10 (May 1890): 125–127. But I should not have hesitated in the early days to assign the cover to Sarah Whitman. Successful covers and designers always had their imitators, and this sort of problem recurs frequently. It can be minimized by living with a constant display of the work of artists or by a careful and even minute study of the alphabets created by the various designers such as those illustrated very richly in Frank Chouteau Brown, *Letters and Lettering* (Boston: Bates & Guild, 1902). In time one can become so familiar with the characteristics of a lettering style that it is possible to distinguish between the authentic portions of a cover design and those relettered by an alien hand—but not at first and not always.

MARGARET NEILSON ARMSTRONG (New York, September 24, 1867–New York, July 18, 1944) studied with her sister, Helen Maitland Armstrong, at the Art Students' League in New York under William Merritt Chase, Rhoda Holmes Nichols, and Irving R. Wiles. She began designing covers for McClurg in 1890 and shortly after for others, including Scribner for whom she created more than half of her output. In 1893 she was the only one of five exhibitors of book covers at the World's Columbian Exhibition to win a prize. She is notable for her invention of memorable series styles for individual authors, Myrtle Reed, Henry Van Dyke, Paul Bourget, and others. As early as 1908 she began turning down commissions, and in 1912–1914 undertook the fieldwork and the 548 drawings for her *Field Book of Western Wild Flowers* (New York: Putnam, 1915). She did not return to design except incidentally and compiled books of family letters and memoirs; and in 1938–1941 she wrote three murder mysteries and two best sellers, *Fanny Kemble: A Passionate Victorian* (New York: Macmillan, 1938) and *Trelawny: A Man's Life* (New York: Macmillan, 1940).

Because of her long career and wide range of ornamental styles Margaret Armstrong is particularly difficult to discuss in a short space. She began a series for the novels of Paul Bourget with *Outre Mer* (New York: Scribner, 1895), which would culminate in the superb design for *Antigone* (New York: Scribner, 1898). But 1896 was the miraculous year in which her powers matured in Max Beerbohm, *The Works of Max Beerbohm* (New York: Scribner, 1896) and Washington Irving, *Bracebridge Hall* (New York: Putnam, 1896), a large two-volume, illustrated holiday edition with ornamental pages. The Irving titles continued, each a distinguished achievement, with *Astoria* (New York: Putnam, 1897), *The Adventures of Captain Bonneville* (New York: Putnam, 1898), *Rip Van Winkle* (New York: Putnam, 1899), and *The Legend of Sleepy Hollow* (New York: Putnam, 1900). Each comes in at least two variant bindings with the Armstrong design. She began a series in gold on olive-green silk for the poems of Henry Van Dyke with *The Toiling of Felix* (New York: Scribner, 1900), and a series for his prose with *The Ruling Passion* (New York: Scribner, 1901), all in dark blue cloth with elaborate ornamental and botanical motifs, although some few were also issued in leather with gold and blind stamping.

She also began a series for Paul Leicester Ford with *Wanted—A Matchmaker* (New York: Dodd, Mead, 1900), but the finest achievement of that year is Robert Browning, *Pippa Passes* (New York: Dodd, Mead, 1900). These have fully decorated interiors as well as elaborate covers. In the titling on the cover of Ford's book her letter forms have much thicker stems and heavier wedge serifs than ever before, and these characteristics intensified over the next few years. In 1901 the finest book is probably Denis Arthur Bingham, *The Bastille* (New York: Pott, 1901), which comes in at least three bindings. She also began a series for the poems of Paul Laurence Dunbar with *Candle Lightin' Time* (New York: Dodd, Mead, 1901). She really had begun the lavender series for Myrtle Reed with *The Spinster Book* (New York: Putnam, 1901), but the first to achieve the special look of that series is *Lavender and Old Lace* (New York: Putnam, 1902). My own favorite of the series is probably *Old Rose and Silver* (New York: Putnam, 1909).

Of her later work the choicest seem to be Elizabeth Barrett Browning, *Sonnets from the Portuguese* (New York: Putnam, 1902); Alice Duer Miller, *Calderon's Prisoner* (New York: Scribner, 1903); Robert Browning, *The Last Ride Together* (New York: Putnam, 1906); Richard Brinsley Sheridan, *The Rivals* (New York: Crowell, 1907); the Thoreau series of four titles that began with *Cape Cod* (New York: Crowell, 1908); Florence Barclay, *The Rosary* (New York: Putnam, 1910) (see Plate 1); Mabell Smith, *Twenty Centuries of Paris* (New York: Crowell, 1913); and Edna Kingsley Wallace, *The Quest of the Dream* (New York: Putnam, 1913). From 1903 on one can see her consciously searching out new forms of ornament and new kinds of composition for her tiny five-by-eight-inch canvas. And since she drew fewer and fewer designs, the books of the later years show a high concentration of striking and compelling images, such as the final item for the Myrtle Reed series in 1913.

WILL BRADLEY (Boston, July 10, 1868–Pasadena, California, 1962) lived in upper Michigan from 1879 and moved to Chicago in 1886. Self-educated as a designer and job compositor, he worked as an illustrator for *Frank Leslie's Illustrated Newspaper* and as a designer for *The Inland Printer*. He drew a revolutionary series of monthly cover designs for *The Inland Printer* (April 1893–March 1894), the first nonpermanent covers ever used, and thereby changed the look of the American magazine forever. In March 1894, he designed the first book and poster for Stone & Kimball, a new publishing firm launched in 1893 that had already done much to alter the appearance of the American book. The poster for Tom Hall, *When Hearts Are Trumps*, published on March 15, 1893, launched Bradley to international fame and did much to start the poster craze in America. Although he continued designing for Chicago firms, he moved to Springfield, Massachusetts, in 1895 and founded his own Wayside Press. There he designed hundreds of advertising brochures that radically altered advertising layout, and he published *Bradley: His Book*. But his health failed him, and in 1898 Wayside and the University Press Cambridge merged. He stayed with the firm until shortly after 1900, when he opened his own design studio in New York. Between 1903 and 1905 he undertook a campaign of type display and

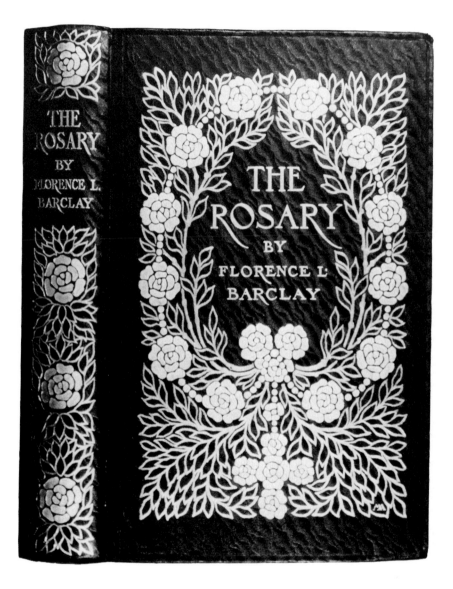

PLATE 1　Florence L. Barclay, *The Rosary*. New York: Putnam, 1910. Design by Margaret Armstrong.

publicity for American Type Founders that resulted in the twelve numbers and four broadsides of *The American Chap Book*, a source of typographic novelty for decades to follow. In 1909 he became art editor for *Collier's* and worked for Hearst in various capacities. He was art editor of all Hearst publications from 1920 to 1930, when he retired.

Will Bradley's range of achievements was enormous and a mere outline of them could fill an entire chapter, so I will restrict the discussion most stringently. His first truly original design is pictorial, for Edmund Gosse, *In Russet and Silver* (Chicago: Stone & Kimball, 1894). It depicts in radical simplification autumnal trees in maroon and silver on tan cloth; the design is of striking directness and flatness and occupies both covers and the spine. To look ahead somewhat, his only other design for Stone that is of great interest is Robert Herrick, *Love's Dilemmas* (Chicago: Stone, 1898), designed throughout by Bradley in his neocolonial style. It is one of the most important books of its decade for its typography and its brilliant double-spread cover design.

In 1895 he completely designed another very important book, R. D. Blackmore, *Fringilla* (Cleveland: Burrows, 1895). (Although it has a rather charming cover, in view of its current price, it is not a book that one is likely to collect for its cover alone.) The following year he drew his first design for John Lane, a very intricate repeat pattern for Richard Le Gallienne, *The Quest of the Golden Girl* (New York: Lane, 1896). The design was very costly to rout and chase, but Lane was aware that the covers sold books effectively, just as dust jackets do today, and he paid quite willingly.

In 1897 Bradley produced five books, all of them masterpieces of great diversity and assurance in design: Owen Meredith, *Lucille* (New York: Stokes, 1897), in several bindings; Kate M. Cleary, *Like a Gallant Woman* (Chicago: Way & Williams, 1897), a double cover design of blue on blue on blue, featuring (like *Lucille*) his beloved Caslon exaggerated to the point of impudence for display effect; George Gissing, *The Whirlpool* (New York: Stokes, 1897); John Oliver Hobbes, *The School for Saints* (New York: Stokes, 1897), the last a design for several Hobbes titles. Finally, one of his most startling and inventive designs of this or any season is the double cover, largely in display Caslon lettering in red and yellow on black cloth, for Stanley Waterloo, *The Story of Ab* (Chicago: Way & Williams, 1897). The effect is one of extraordinary elegance and immediacy of impact.

In 1898 he designed Archibald Lampman, *Lyrics of Earth* (Boston: Copeland & Day, 1898) and Richard Le Gallienne, *The Romance of Zion Chapel* (New York: Lane, 1898). The latter, with its huge areas of gold leaf on black cloth, is as dazzling as *The Story of Ab* but obviously much more expensive. According to Bradley, it broke John Lane's heart. The Le Gallienne was printed and designed at the University Press Cambridge where Bradley now presided. The output there over the next three years is of very great interest, although it is rather difficult to assign work without a monogram or signature to any particular person. We know that when Bradley went from the Wayside Press to University Press Cambridge, he took with him his two apprentices, Adrian J. Iorio (1879–1957) and Samuel L. Busha (1877–?), both of whom outstayed him at Cambridge and were designers of real merit in their own right. The University Press output from this period is worth collecting and studying; nothing that Bradley or his students touched is negligible. Two additional works definitely were done by Bradley during this period: Richard Le Gallienne, *Young Lives* (Plate 2), and *The Rubaiyat of Omar Khayyam* (New York: Lane, 1899).

The history of designs for books cannot easily be told in all its phases as a history of individual artists. Stone & Kimball were pioneers in changing the construction and appearance of the American book. Their influence, through a long series of individual artists who designed one or more books for them, was enormous and long lasting. In 1894 Frank Hazenplug joined them as house designer and established most of the series designs and individual titles for the bulk of their output. But before then and simultaneous with Hazenplug's employment, they used not only Will Bradley but Horace T. Carpenter (1874–?), who designed two works by Hamlin Garland, *Main Traveled Roads* and *Prairie Songs* (Cambridge and Chicago: Stone & Kimball, 1893); George H. Hallowell for Louise Chandler Moulton, *Arthur O'Shaughnessy* (Cambridge and Chicago: Stone & Kimball, 1894) and for Bliss Carman, *Low Tide on Grande Pré* (Cambridge and Chicago: Stone & Kimball, 1894); Pierre de Chaignon la Rose (1871–1941) for Hugh McCulloch, *The Quest of Heracles* (Cambridge and Chicago: Stone & Kimball, 1894), which I consider one of the most important pieces of book design in the decade, although its cover design is not quite so impressive. They also commissioned work by Thomas Buford Meteyard (1865–1928), Henry McCarter (1864–1942), who designed the Green Tree Library series, Bruce Rogers (1870–1957), F. R. Kimbrough (d. 1902), J. H. Twachtman (1853–1902), Blanche McManus Mansfield (1869–?), and Claude Fayette Bragdon (1866–1934).

The influence of Stone & Kimball was very great and was continued in the production of the firm of Copeland & Day in Boston.

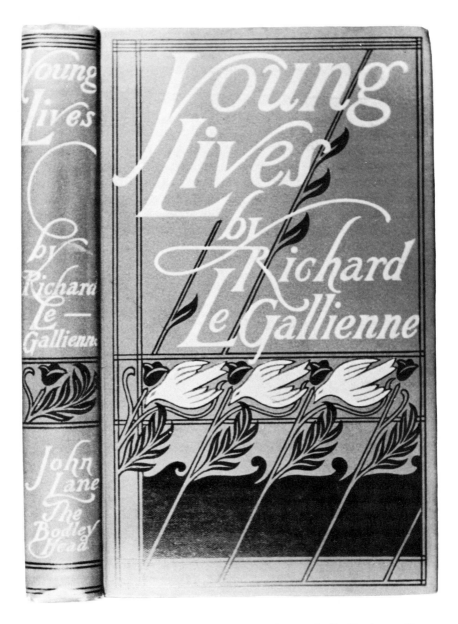

PLATE 2   Richard Le Gallienne, *Young Lives*. New York: Lane, Bodley Head, 1899. Design by Will Bradley.

They imported *The Yellow Book* and many Bodley Head publications. While a few of their books were designed by Bertram Grosvenor Goodhue, the bulk of them were designed by Frederick Holland Day himself (d. 1933); they are of real importance. But the most important figure in the United States between 1894 and 1905 was Stone & Kimball's house designer, Frank Hazenplug.[8]

FRANK HAZENPLUG (Dixon, Illinois, November 2, 1874–Santa Barbara, California, January 17, 1931) moved with his family to Chicago in 1882. He studied briefly at the Art Institute School in 1891 and again in 1895–1896. By December 1894 he was designing books for Stone & Kimball and illustrations and posters for *The Chap Book*, which made him internationally famous as early as January 1895. He designed several works for the short-lived firm of Way & Williams in 1897, including their logo and title pages, and he established the interior layout of *House Beautiful* (1897–1904). When Stone & Kimball dissolved in 1896, he stayed with Herbert S. Stone, until the latter firm dissolved in 1906. From 1903 to 1911 he was a resident and an art instructor in metalwork at Hull House. He designed extensively for Revell between 1900 and 1911 and frequently designed for McClurg, Reilly and Britton, and Rand McNally. In 1911 he moved to New York and shortened his name to Hazen, as his brother Edward had done at least as early as 1891. He began designing for George Doran, who had been a vice-president of Revell, and who had founded his own firm by importing Hodder and Stoughton sheets. Hazen designed for Doran through 1921 and for John Lane from 1913 to 1920. He gave up designing at the end of 1921 and traveled extensively in the Orient and Europe with his brother, a tea broker. In 1922 he moved to Santa Fe, seeking relief from his tuberculosis. While there he was received into the Catholic church. Late in 1930 he moved to the Cottage Hospital in Santa Barbara, where he died a few months later.

Hazenplug designed over 75 percent of the production of Stone & Kimball and created every series design for them except for the Green Tree Library; his were the Peacock Library, the English Classics, the Carnation Series, and the Blue Cloth Books. He created the typical Stone & Kimball book, one of 6¾ by 4¼ inches, with a simple rule outline on the front and back and with the title always minutely lettered on the front and spine—sometimes front, back, and spine. A typical example is David Swing, *Old Pictures of Life* (Chicago: Stone & Kimball, 1894), with gold rules on green cloth and the title lettered front, back, and spine, or R. L. Stevenson, *Vailima Letters* (Chicago: Stone & Kimball,

1895). Yet he was capable of the highest elaboration, as in the Peacock Library, with its fretted peacock feather pattern in gold on dark blue cloth, or in the large paper edition of *The Works of Edgar Allan Poe* (Chicago: Stone & Kimball, 1894 [1895]), with its intricate poppies in gold on vellum. It is in this tradition that his first real masterpiece and one of the most important designs of the decade occurs, Richard Le Gallienne, *Prose Fancies* (Chicago: Stone, 1896), although here the fine detail is subordinated to the compelling rhythmic symmetry of the stylized artichokes in gold marching across the maroon cloth. It is a design worthy of any of the great English or Continental masters of art nouveau. In general there is a curious tension in his work between an almost rococo elaboration, which is usually subdued by powerful rhythmic composition, and an expression given to almost spartan means and understatement, as in Maria Louise Pool, *In Buncombe County* (Chicago: Stone, 1896), or H. C. Chatfield-Taylor, *The Land of the Castanet* (Chicago: Stone, 1896). Sometimes both impulses join, as in Henry James, *What Maisie Knew* (Chicago: Stone, 1897), with its severe grey cloth, largely bare, but with spine ornamentation of Celtic complexity in gold. Or there is the charming, whimsical, even feminine or delicate play of design in L. H. Bickford, *Phyllis in Bohemia* (Chicago: Stone, 1897).

Of the designs that he did for McClurg, I mention only the books of Reuben Gold Thwaites, the best of which is *Down Historic Waterways* (Chicago: McClurg, 1902), with a fatted, rounded-serif Caslon, almost his favorite lettering style after 1900, and his typical broad line, derived it seems from stained glass, or perhaps from Eugène Grasset, who in turn derived it from stained glass.

For Revell he designed hundreds of books, and only a few can be pointed out. Among them are W. C. Gray, *Musings by Campfire and Wayside* (Chicago: Revell, 1902), and Nellie Lathrop Helms, *When Jesus Was Here among Men* (Chicago: Revell, 1902), two titles that could scarcely contrast more in their designer's handling of color and ornament. The first is severely restrained in black cloth and touches of gold and red; the other is on a lettuce green cloth with black outline figures decorated in blue, red, and yellow. But Fleming Revell was economical in the extreme, and Hazenplug did not often have a chance to work with either good cloth or many colors; he was compelled to invention with slim means. Two designs of utmost simplicity and frugality, but of striking poster effectiveness are Ralph Connor, *The Sky Pilot* and *Black Rock* (Chicago: Revell, 1900). With better materials he produced Lucy Rider Meyer, *Mary North* (Chicago: Revell, 1903), and a brilliant pictorial invention for Forrest Crissey, *The Country Boy*

(Chicago: Revell, 1903), in which the country boy looks through an architecturally framed window into the landscape inside the book (see Plate 3). And finally there is an understated work in one color and blind stamping, in strong contrast to the two preceding color-rich works, Robert E. Knowles, *The Attic Guest* (Chicago: Revell, 1909).

His designs for Doran also were in the hundreds, but George Doran had learned well from Fleming Revell. Aside from the covers that Hazenplug designed for the gift books imported from Hodder and Stoughton, illustrated by Dulac and Brickdale and others, the covers are run-of-the-mill in cloth and color. He designed almost every cover for Arnold Bennett, Robert W. Chambers, and Mary Roberts Rinehart, to name only Doran's most famous authors. His career, after its brilliant beginning in the heyday of decorated cloth, marked by masterpiece after masterpiece, is both sad and touching since it coincides with the slow decline of the art under the double impact of rising costs of materials and labor. And there is the final, insuperable blow, around 1908, when illustrated paper onlay covers, featuring a pretty girl drawn by Harrison Fisher or Howard Chandler Christy, caught the fancy of the reading public and replaced decorated cloth on novels, the bulk of any publisher's output. Decorated cloth persisted in special areas only, on travel books until 1929, and on illustrated books, gift books, anthologies, and special editions of the classics. What the paper onlay cover did not kill, the convenient excuse of wartime austerity brought to an abrupt end in 1917. John Lane was one of the few publishers who refused to yield to the new fashions, perhaps because he had made his fortune out of decorated books and was loath to surrender. But Hazenplug created some charming designs for him quite late in his career. Among them is a merry, cut-work design for Rena Cary Sheffield, *The Golden Hollow* (New York: Lane, 1913), although most of his work after 1910 is simple lettering in one color on a dull cloth and without the use of gold.

THE DECORATIVE DESIGNERS (1895–1931) was a unique firm in most respects, first because it was made up of several people, and second because it effected a division of labor in design work, which was novel in its day. The finished work was almost always a community effort as a result. Henry Thayer (1867–?), an architect in the firm of McKim, Mead, and White, perhaps inspired by Stanford White's book covers, decided to set up his own firm in 1895. He hired Emma Redington Lee (Troy, Pennsylvania, April 4, 1874–Coronado, California, November 18, 1973), who from 1891 had been trained in the decorative arts by Candace Wheeler at the Associated Artists (after earlier training

PLATE 3 Forrest Crissey, *The Country Boy*. Chicago: Revell, 1903. Design by Frank
Hazenplug.

at the Cooper Union from 1890 to 1892 and life classes at the Pratt Institute in 1890). At an early date, Thayer hired Rome K. Richardson and Adam Empie to handle much of the mechanical work of drawing repeats and transferring designs; later he hired Charles Buckles Falls and Jay Chambers (d. 1929), the last of whom worked for them from about 1902 to 1916. Mrs. (Lee) Thayer—as Emma Redington Lee became in 1909—was responsible for almost all of the decorative borders and designs, Jay Chambers for figures, and Henry Thayer for lettering, but each was known to render an entire design individually. While Lee Thayer enjoyed gothic lettering and excelled at it, Henry Thayer enjoyed abstract geometrical patterns and panelled designs and architectural entablatures. The output of the firm was enormous, probably in excess of 25,000 items in all branches of design.

Of Henry Thayer's work we can be certain of only a few titles, but what we know is masterly in its deployment of intricate geometrical patterns intersecting or in parallel swirls. Of these certainly the finest is William Ernest Henley, *Hawthorn and Lavender* (New York: Harper, 1901) (see Plate 4), although Ruth McEnery Stuart, *Napoleon Jackson* (New York: Century, 1902), and *George Washington Smith* (Philadelphia: Altemus, 1903) are very fine also. Jay Chambers was wholly responsible for Richard Whiteing, *The Yellow Van* (New York: Century, 1903), and Alfred Austin, *A Tale of True Love* (New York: Harper, 1902).

As impressive as these works are, it is Lee Thayer who shows inexhaustible ornamental resources: the Rackham picturesque in a number of works by Ruth McEnery Stuart, including *Solomon Crow's Christmas* (New York: Harper, 1896); an intricate repeat pattern of swirling irises, a series design for Crowell that was used on many titles, among them Lewis Morris, *The Epic of Hades* (1897); art nouveau celtic in Cyrus Townsend Brady, *Hohenzollern* (New York: Century, 1902); Jugenstil framing devices in Nathan Haskell Dole, *Famous Composers* (New York: Crowell, 1902); Japanese surimono in Charles Ross Jackson, *The Third Degree* (New York: Dillingham, 1903); and Pre-Raphaelite medievalism in Anna Robertson Brown Lindsay, *The Warriors* (New York: Crowell, 1903). There are also straightforward American inventions, indebted to no one and of an order of originality equal to Will Bradley: Gouverneur Morris, *Ellen and Mr. Man* (New York: Century, 1904); Josephine Daskam, *Poems* (New York: Scribner, 1903); Thomas Nelson Page, *On New Found River* (New York: Scribner, 1906); James Henry Breasted, *A History of Egypt*, 2nd ed. (New York: Scribner, 1909). In the latter she turns to familiar resources once again, this time to Egyptian ornament, in one of the most elaborate and costly designs in the history of deco-

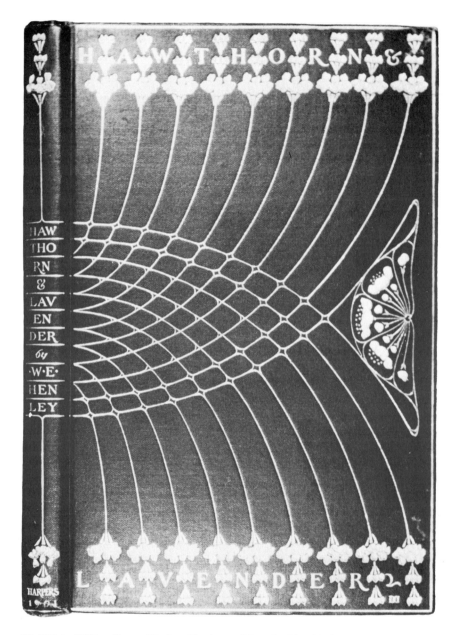

PLATE 4   William Ernest Henley, *Hawthorn and Lavender*. New York: Harper, 1901. Design by Henry Thayer.

rated cloth. The same can be said for almost all of the designs she did for the travel books of Robert Hichens—for example, *Egypt and Its Monuments* (New York: Century, 1912) and *The Near East* (New York: Century, 1913). Finally, John Luther Long, *Naughty Nan* (New York: Century, 1904), one of my favorites, is less commanding in style, less impressive in its perfection than any of those cited above, but soft and pastel in color and feminine and delicate in its effect. These are characteristics that many designers of the time quite consciously aimed to achieve, since the vast majority of the buyers of books were women who found such characteristics admirable and desirable in women and in books.

When we interviewed Lee Thayer in 1970, we learned that one of her own favorites was the design for Josephine Daskam's *Poems* (Plate 5). In the person of Lee Thayer, we were unexpectedly fortunate in finding, not merely a contact with the generation of the 1890s, but a survivor in full possession of her faculties, who was able to inform us about technical processes, assign the responsibility for design after design to the various members of the Decorative Designers firm, and reject or accept unsigned designs, which we thought likely candidates for inclusion in the canon. We were thereby given a detailed understanding that we could never have arrived at by merely looking at, and thinking about, the materials.

Other Noteworthy Designers

Such, then, are the main outlines of the subject, but it is of importance that we can document the existence of hundreds of other designers and that we have many fine bindings to which we can attach no names. Of this regiment of artists, we have picked 16 who, either by merit of some few superb designs or by the general run of their work, seem to us to deserve brief treatment. Most of them designed in sufficient quantity to be quite collectible.

ALICE C. MORSE (active 1887–1921) of Brooklyn was a considerable designer in her time. In 1890 *Publishers Weekly* commented:

> It is an interesting fact that the best designers of book covers in the United States are women. The finest work done for the leading publishers comes from them. Houghton Mifflin & Co., who give unusual attention to chaste, artistic binding, go to a woman with their most important commissions. G. P. Putnam's Sons and Harper and Brothers get many of their designs from a clever woman in Brooklyn. This lady has supplied the cover for one of Harper's Holiday Books under circumstances that bear some detail-

PLATE 5   Josephine (Dodge) Daskam, *Poems*. New York: Scribner, 1903. Design by Lee Thayer; lettering by Henry Thayer (for the Decorative Designers).

ing. Every Christmas the house illustrates something with drawings by Abbey or Alfred Parsons for a fine gift volume. Last year Parsons did the cover and the publishers were not satisfied. This year "Wordsworth's Sonnets" was the choice and Parsons did the pictures, but Miss Morse— her name slipped from the point of the pencil—was called upon to supply the quiet green and gold binding.[9]

Many of her designs seem to me only minimally interesting, and I provide a list so that the collector can become familiar with her style, but the two Irving titles are fine achievements.

Unsigned

Harold Frederic. *Seth's Brother's Wife*. New York: Scribner, 1887.
Jerome K. Jerome. *Three Men in a Boat*. New York: Holt, 1890.
R. L. Stevenson. *Ballads*. New York: Scribner, 1890.
Washington Irving. *The Alhambra*. "Darro Edition." New York: Putnam, 1891.
⸻. *The Conquest of Granada*. "Agapida Edition." New York: Putnam, 1892.
Henry Blair Fuller. *The Chatelaine of La Trinité*. New York: Century, 1892.
Owen Meredith. *Marah*. New York: Longman, 1892.
George I. Putnam. *In Blue Uniform*. New York: Scribner, 1892.

Signed

Beatrice Harraden. *Hilda Strafford*. New York: Dodd, Mead, 1896.
Paul Leicester Ford. *Tattle Tales of Cupid*. New York: Dodd, Mead, 1898.
Paul Laurence Dunbar. *Lyrics of the Hearthside*. New York: Dodd, Mead, 1899.
⸻. *Lyrics of Cabin and Field*. New York: Dodd, Mead, 1902.
Esther Singelton. *Great Paintings*. New York: Dodd, Mead, 1902.

ROME K. RICHARDSON (Tioga County, New York, April 29, 1877–?; active 1896–1917) was a pupil at the Pratt Institute and the New York School of Art, who worked for the Decorative Designers from 1896 to 1901, before launching himself on a career as a cover designer in 1902. He was perhaps encouraged in his choice of career by winning an honorable mention for book cover design at the Pan-American Exposition in Buffalo in 1901. His designs are inventive, witty, colorful, occasionally dreadful, and easy to collect. We have recorded some 65, among which are:

Owen Wister. *The Virginian*. New York: Scribner, 1902.
Frederic C. Isham. *Black Friday*. Indianapolis: Bobbs, 1905.
Meredith Nicholson. *The House of a Thousand Candles*. Indianapolis: Bobbs, 1905.

David Graham Phillips. *The Plum Tree*. Indianapolis: Bobbs, 1905.
Geraldine Bonner. *Rich Men's Children*. Indianapolis: Bobbs, 1906.
Herbert Quick. *Double Trouble*. Indianapolis: Bobbs, 1906.
Egerton Castle and Agnes Castle. *My Merry Rockhurst*. Indianapolis: Bobbs, 1907.

The UNKNOWN HARPER'S BINDER was active from 1890 to 1899 and may well have been employed directly by Harper, because most of his work is for them. The books share some common features that are distinctive and attractive, and the best are achievements of high merit. They are all bound in fine-grained cloths, they often have a standard font of letters, and they combine silver and gold (a feature not very common among the young designers but distinctly a practice in the 1880s and among the artisan designers) with sufficient frequency to suggest someone at the end, not the beginning, of a career. They are in fine condition, and their attractions are evident.

Julian Ralph. *On Canada's Frontier*. New York: Harper, 1891.
Mrs. Burton Harrison. *An Edelweiss of the Sierras, Golden Rod, and Other Tales*. New York: Harper, 1892.
W. C. Prine. *Along New England Roads*. New York: Harper, 1892.
Richard Harding Davis. *The Rulers of the Mediterranean*. New York: Harper, 1894 (1893).
_____.*The Exiles and Other Stories*. New York: Harper, 1894.
Will Carleton. *Rhymes of Our Planet*. New York: Harper, 1895.
S. R. Crockett. *The Lilac Sunbonnet*. New York: Appleton, 1896.
Sarah P. McLean Greene. *Vesty of the Basins*. New York: Harper, 1899.

BERTRAM GROSVENOR GOODHUE (1869–1924) has been extensively documented in Ingalls Kimball, *Book Decorations by Bertram Grosvenor Goodhue* (New York: Grolier, 1929), and Susan Otis Thompson, *American Book Design and William Morris* (New York: Bowker, 1977), and his career as an architect is as fully recorded as that of any American professional. Most of his work was for small Boston publishers, such as Copeland & Day and Small, Maynard; he also did some work for D. B. Updike. Although the influence of Morris was very strong, in the idiom Goodhue was a powerful and compelling designer. But it was book design (design of the whole) that he took seriously (not of the cover or of title pages alone); for this reason only a few titles are recorded here.

Anna Robertson Brown. *What Is Worth While*. New York: Crowell (c. 1893, 1897).
Richard Hovey. *Along the Trail*. Boston: Small, Maynard, 1898.
Henry W. Longfellow. *The Complete Poetical Works of Henry Wadsworth Long-*

fellow. Boston: Houghton (c. 1899). Extravagant tiger lilies in gold on green cloth (see Plate 6). The same design was used for many collected works issued by Houghton, for example, the Tennyson of the same year on blue cloth.

John Bannister Tabb. *Poems Grave and Gay.* Boston: Small, Maynard, 1899.

EDWARD STRATTON HOLLOWAY (Ashford, New York, 1859?–Philadelphia, 1939) studied at the Pennsylvania Academy of Fine Arts and specialized in marine and landscape painting, decorative designs, particularly of book covers, and decorations and bookplates. He was a specialist in American furniture and interior decoration and published several books on the subject between 1922 and 1937. He was the art adviser to J. P. Lippincott from 1891 and designed many covers for them from 1894 to 1925. His range of design techniques and sources was very wide, and his output was enormous, almost always signed, and almost always for Lippincott. Thus he is easy to find, inexpensive, and aesthetically satisfying, even if there seem to be no masterpieces.

Monogram: *H* in font.

W. R. Mackay. *The Skein of Life.* Philadelphia: Lippincott, 1897.
Sydney George Fisher. *Men, Women, and Manners in Colonial Times.* Philadelphia: Lippincott, 1898.
Charles C. Abbott. *The Freedom of the Fields.* Philadelphia: Lippincott, 1899.
Ann Hollingsworth Wharton. *Salons Colonial and Republican.* Philadelphia: Lippincott, 1900.
Philip Verril Mighels. *The Inevitable.* Philadelphia: Lippincott, 1902.
Van Zo Post. *Diana Ardway.* Philadelphia: Lippincott, 1913.

THOMAS MAITLAND CLELAND (Brooklyn, 1880–1964) was a graphic artist in all fields of design. In 1895 he studied at the Artist Artisan League in New York and began doing decorative initials, some of which appeared in the *American Bookman* in 1896, the year in which he encountered Walter Crane's *The Decorative Illustration of Books.* He first worked as a designer for Frederic Thoreau Singleton (a student of Will Bradley at the Wayside Press) at the Caslon Press owned by Singleton. Then in 1900 he was a founder of the Cornhill Press, although he completed only three books there; at the same time he did a few designs for D. B. Updike. In 1907 (or 1908) he became the art editor of McClure and designed many book covers for them from 1907 to 1913. In *The Decorative Work of T. M. Cleland*, Alfred Hamill wrote, ". . . he experimented with translating the tone effects of seventeenth- and eighteenth-century copperplate engravings into a pen and ink line technique that, when reproduced and printed on smooth paper, would compensate for [the]

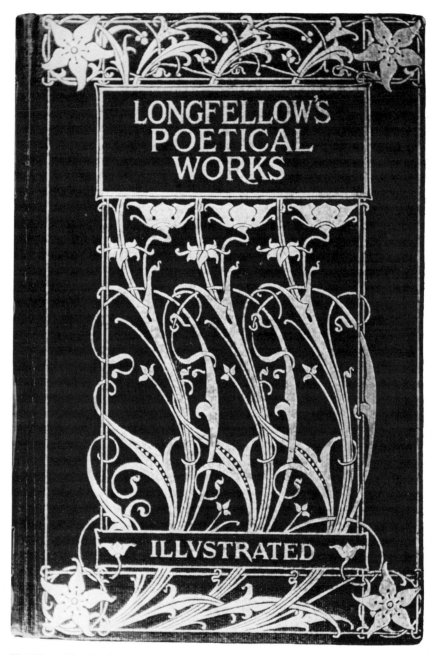

PLATE 6   *The Complete Poetical Works of Henry Wadsworth Longfellow.* Boston: Houghton, c. 1899. Design by Bertram Grosvenor Goodhue.

lack of impression and loss of 'color,' and would act as an intermedium between half-tone and the typo."[10] The style was fully developed by 1907, and its effect is of startling delicacy and sensitivity. But it was soon seized upon by many others and vulgarized in the hands of workers who did not understand what Cleland was aiming at. He worked largely on advertising campaigns in later years, for Locomobile from 1914 and Cadillac in the 1920s. His papers are in the Library of Congress.

Monogram: C in font with no serif on the terminal of the letter.

Sir Lewis Morris. *Harvest Tide*. New York: Crowell, 1901. Printed by D. B. Updike.

C. N. and A. M. Williamson. *Rosemary in Search of a Father*. New York: McClure, 1906.

———. *The Princess of Virginia*. New York: McClure, 1909.

AMY RICHARDS (active 1896–1918) is known only from her monogram and design work. She is named in the Stokes advertisements in the 1897 *PTLA* as the designer of the Besant work listed below.[11] In all we have recorded about 85 designs done by her.

Monogram: An A and R joined with a common center stroke.

Walter Besant. *The Master Craftsman*. New York: Stokes, 1896.

Henry Van Dyke. *The First Christmas Tree*. New York: Scribner, 1897.

Richard Harding Davis. *The Lion and the Unicorn*. New York: Scribner, 1899.

E. W. Hornung. *Raffles*. New York: Scribner, 1901.

William J. Locke. *A Christmas Mystery*. New York: Lane, 1910.

Edward N. Westcott. *David Harum*. New York: Scribner, 1910.

FREDERIC W. GOUDY (Bloomington, Illinois, March 8, 1865–1947) is so well documented as a type and graphic designer that he needs no new account of him here; I shall offer only a list of his book covers and note that Goudy signed himself on this early work with the monogram G. (The monogrammist of the same period who signs himself FWG, usually vertically and within a double-framed border, is in fact the Chicago banker, economist, and world authority on Japanese prints, Frederick W. Gookin.)

Monogram: G in font.

Charles Frederick Goss. *The Redemption of David Carson*. Indianapolis: Bowen (c. 1900).

Will N. Harben. *Northern Georgia Sketches*. Chicago: McClurg, 1900.

Paul Karishka. *El Reshid*. Chicago: Rand (c. 1899, 1900).

Mary Imlay Taylor. *The Cobbler of Nimes*. Chicago: McClurg, 1900. (See Plate 7.)

Katherine Tynan. *Oh, What a Plague Is Love*. Chicago: McClurg, 1900.

George Horton. *The Tempting of Father Anthony*. Chicago: McClurg, 1901.

PLATE 7   Mary Imlay Taylor, *The Cobbler of Nimes*. Chicago: McClurg, 1900. Design by Frederic W. Goudy.

Eleanor C. Reed. *The Battle Invisible.* Chicago: McClurg, 1901.
Henry Thew Stephenson. *The Fickle Wheel.* Indianapolis: Bowen (c. 1901).
Charles Frederick Goss. *The Loom of Life.* Indianapolis: Bowen (c. 1902).
Marjorie Benton Cooke. *Modern Monologues.* Chicago: Dramatic Publishing Co., 1903.

AMY M. SACKER (Boston, 1876–alive in 1940) was a prolific illustrator and poster and cover designer whose output, particularly for children's books, was probably in the thousands. The work for children is hasty and usually negligible, but Amy Sacker herself is not. Children's books were produced with a sharp eye on cost, and the material she had to work with was limited and shoddy. She began working for Joseph Knight in 1896 with Edith Robinson, *A Little Loyal Maid*, in a highly simplified "colonial" style, which remained characteristic throughout her career. Her covers are commonly found on books issued by Knight; Little, Brown; L. C. Page; and Lothrop; and from 1909 to 1917 by Houghton.

She was occasionally given design limits that were not stultifying and produced at least the two masterpieces listed below.

Monogram: *A S*, squared off and topped with a cross bar on the *A;* later, in the form of an *SAM* monogram vertically as one logo.

Theophile Gautier. *Captain Fracasse.* Boston: Page, 1901. 2 vols.
Helen Hunt Jackson. *Ramona.* Illustrated by Henry Sandham. "Monterey Edition." Boston: Houghton, 1901. 2 vols.

BERTHA STUART (active 1903–1911) is known only from her book covers. She drew some 30 for Holt from 1904 to 1913 with one isolated cover, her last, in 1916. In the years 1906–1913 she worked for Harper, Appleton, Macmillan, and several other publishers. In all we have recorded some 70 designs. Her average work has some charm, but no great distinction, as in Carroll Watson Rankin, *Dandelion Cottage* (New York: Holt, 1904), a work that, if unsigned, would have seemed a very minor product of the Decorative Designers. But she was capable of work of quite extraordinary distinction, largely silhouette designs in gold on a single rich color of grained cloth that were much indebted to Japanese prints in the firmness of their outlines and the suggestion of volume and shape achieved entirely with flat means and wholly conventionalized motifs. They are quite unexpected achievements in an otherwise rather ordinary career.

Monogram: *B S*, boldly swash.

E. V. Lucas. *The Open Road.* New York: Holt, 1906. (See Plate 8.)
Lucy H. Humphrey. *The Poetic Old World.* New York: Holt, 1909.
_____. *The Poetic New World.* New York: Holt, 1910.

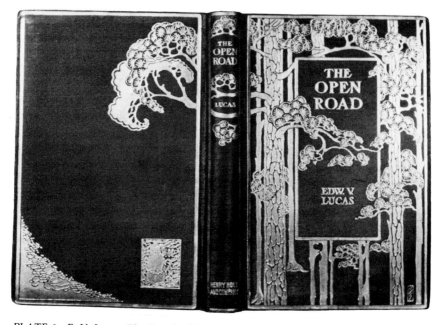

PLATE 8   E. V. Lucas, *The Open Road*. New York: Holt, 1906. Design by Bertha Stuart.

THEODORE BROWN HAPGOOD, JR. (Somerville, Massachusetts, August 28, 1871–Watertown, Massachusetts, July 2, 1938) was educated, according to W. A. Kittredge, "at the School of Drawing and Painting at the Old Art Museum in Copley Square" and "had his studio in the same building at 69 Cornhill . . . as . . . Alfred Bartlett, the well-known publisher [of the *Cornhill Booklet*], the early printing venture of T. M. Cleland, and . . . the studio of W. A. Dwiggins."[12] He designed books, bookplates, posters, book covers, and type. The Hapgood florets[13] are still in use today. He created a drawing style in imitation of early woodcuts in which the lines were generally of the same width; in that respect, they rather more markedly resemble stained glass leading than the black line of woodcut. He was a monumental letterer of distinction in many styles and was noted for his bronze work. He was prolific as a book designer, and there are works of considerable attraction. When given the materials and freed from restrictions, he produced some compelling designs in which purely ornamental motifs mingle with flowers and stems. They are works of a strange immobility, seeming to prefigure the monumental work of later years, as in the luxurious designs he did for the Lloyd, Fields, and Blanchan works listed below. The final, undated work with writhing plants and static birds is rhythmically full of motion, quite unlike the other works listed.

Monogram: *H* not in font; *TBH* in font or not; *TBH* arranged vertically with the *H* as central element, *T* within the *H* at the top, *B* within the *H* at the bottom.

> Thomas Moore. *Lalla Rookh*. New York: Crowell, n.d. (c. 1884, 1888). The design must date from about 1900.
> John Uri Lloyd. *The Right Side of the Car*. Boston: Badger, 1897. This work preceded the Robinson and was Badger's first publication.
> Ella Gale McClelland. *A Daughter of Two Nations*. Chicago: McClurg, 1897.
> George R. R. Rivers. *Captain Shay*. Boston: Little, 1897.
> Edwin Arlington Robinson. *The Children of the Night*. Boston: Badger, 1897.
> James T. Fields. *Yesterdays with Authors*. Boston: Houghton, 1901 (c. 1900).
> Theodore Cuyler. *Help and Good Cheers*. New York: Baker & Taylor, 1902.
> Neltje Blanchan. *The American Flower Garden*. New York: Dodd, Mead, 1909. Only the large paper edition limited to 1,050 copies.

FRANK BERKELEY SMITH (1869–alive 1916) was the son of the author, illustrator, and civil engineer F. Hopkinson Smith and was himself a prolific author of travel books and novels, as well as an illustrator and cover designer from 1897 to 1916. His output was huge, his line usually blunt and insensitive, but scattered among his work are some remarkable designs, largely in poster style with images drawn in outline or with pure color areas without outline. The first work listed below was one of the most famous images of the decade from the day of its publication in March 1897.[14] It is wholly characteristic of his poster style, certainly the best of his many styles.

Monogram: *S*, *BS*, *FBS*, drawn vertically or horizontally within a variety of ornamental frames.

> Anonymous. *America and the Americans*. New York: Scribner, 1897.
> F. Berkeley Smith. *The Real Latin Quarter*. New York: Funk, 1901.
> Elizabeth Wormley Latimer. *The Prince Incognito*. Chicago: McClurg, 1902.
> F. Hopkinson Smith. *The Wood Fire in No. 3*. New York: Scribner, 1905.

WILLIAM JORDAN (active 1898–1914) designed bookplates and with Jay Chambers and Wilbur Macey Stone founded the Triptych, a short-lived association for bookplate design. He was a member of the New York circle gathered around Louise Pomeroy in about 1910. He designed the beautiful Aldine colophons for McClure-Phillips in the early years of this century and many covers for them. His style is eccentrically witty and owes a great deal to Charles Rennie Mackintosh and the Glasgow school of design. Although that influence never disappears, he soon adopted somewhat slicker styles of great dash but less interest. From 1907 through 1911 he worked for other publishers, but less and less. An isolated cover of 1914 is his last known work.

Monogram: *W* over a *J*, drawn, not in font.

Samuel Johnson. *The Prayers of Samuel Johnson*, edited by W. A. Bradley. New York: McClure, 1902 (1903). Jordan designed and decorated the book throughout.

Martha McCulloch-Williams. *Next to the Ground*. New York: McClure, 1902.

Henry Somerville. *Racer of Illinois*. New York: McClure, 1902.

Booth Tarkington. *The Beautiful Lady*. New York: McClure, 1902.

Stuart Edward White. *Conjuror's House*. New York: McClure, 1903.

Henry Seton Merriman. *Barlasch of the Guards*. New York: McClure, 1904.

Willa Cather. *The Troll Garden*. New York: McClure, 1905.

Keble Howard. *The Smiths*. New York: McClure, 1907.

MARION L. PEABODY (active 1898–1910, alive in 1934) of Dorchester, Massachusetts, was the sister of the poet Josephine Preston Peabody and should be distinguished from Marian L. Peabody, née Lawrence, an artist nearly contemporary with her. She specialized in book cover decoration and designs in black and white. In 1905 she was an instructor in decorative design at the Eric Pape School of Art in Boston. Her covers are of extraordinary diversity and charm and *The Loom of Destiny* is certainly a masterpiece.

Monogram: a combined *M L P*, in which the right descender of the *M* forms the upright stroke of the *L* and *P*.

Josephine Preston Peabody. *The Wayfarers*. Boston: Copeland & Day, 1898.

Arthur Stringer. *The Loom of Destiny*. Boston: Small, Maynard, 1898. A double cover, this is found sometimes without the design on the back panel and sometimes with the design inverted with relation to the spine.

Maud Howard Peterson. *The Potter and the Clay*. Boston: Lothrop, 1901.

Dante Gabriel Rossetti. *The House of Life*. Boston: Caldwell, 1904. An embossed, double cover.

Elaine Goodale Eastwin. *Little Brother O' Dream*. Boston: Houghton, 1910.

Wilder Goodwin. *The Up Grade*. Boston: Little, 1910.

CHARLES BUCKLES FALLS (Fort Wayne, Indiana, December 10, 1874–1959) was an illustrator, letterer, and mural painter in New York, and a member of the Society of Illustrators and the Society of Mural Decorators. He became internationally famous for his Marine poster "Books wanted for our men."[15] He was the editor of *Nineteen-Ten Magazine* in 1910. He worked with the Decorative Designers for many years but also designed free-lance, largely for Dodd, Mead, from 1902 to 1913.

Monogram: *F* in font.

Sewell Ford. *Horses Nine*. New York: Scribner, 1903.

Ian Maclaren. *Our Neighbors*. New York: Dodd, Mead, 1903.

Lavinia Hart. *When a Maid Marries*. New York: Dodd, Mead, 1904.

Emily Post. *The Flight of a Moth*. New York: Dodd, Mead, 1904.
S. R. Crockett. *May Margaret*. New York: Dodd, Mead, 1905.

EARL STETSON CRAWFORD (Philadelphia, June 6, 1877; active 1909–1915; alive in 1934) was a painter of murals with academic training under Bouguereau, Ferrier, Puvis de Chavannes, and Whistler. He was a teacher at the School of Industrial Art in Philadelphia and at the Pennsylvania Academy of Fine Art. His cover designs were clearly a small part of his work, because he came to them almost as they went out of fashion, but some have real merit.

Monogram: C surmounted by a crown.

> Meredith Nicholson. *The Little Brown Jug of Kildare*. New York: Scribner; Indianapolis: Bobbs, 1908.
>
> Henry Van Dyke. *The White Bees and Other Poems*. New York: Scribner, 1909. The title page is signed by Crawford but is designed in the style that Margaret Armstrong established for this Van Dyke series and is not representative of Crawford's work.
>
> Max Beerbohm. *Zuleika Dobson*. New York: Lane, 1912.

Notes

1. Jacob Blanck, *A Bibliography of American Literature*, vol. 2 (New Haven, Conn.: Yale Univ. Press, 1957), illustration following p. 190.
2. Blanck, *A Bibliography of American Literature*, vol. 1 (New Haven, Conn.: Yale Univ. Press, 1955), illustration following p. 192.
3. Blanck, *A Bibliography of American Literature*, vol. 2, illustration following p. 118.
4. *The American Bookmaker* 1 (1885): 39, 112.
5. The complicated relationship of the designed cover to the book jacket has been dealt with by G. T. Tanselle, "Book-Jackets, Blurbs, and Bibliographers," *The Library*, 5th series, 26 (June 1971): 91–134. To his full account I can add little. Of the thousands of copies of books from the period under discussion that I have handled, I have seen only three American paper book jackets produced prior to 1900 that reproduce the full design of the front cover, although I have seen many cloth book jackets that reproduce some element of the design on the spine.
6. *Publishers Weekly*, September 24, 1887, p. 390.
7. Sarah Whitman, *Notes of an Informal Talk* (Boston: Boston Art Students Assn., 1894), [p. 3].
8. Sidney Kramer's indispensable study of the twin firms of Stone & Kimball and Herbert S. Stone, *A History of Stone & Kimball and Herbert S. Stone & Co.: With a Bibliography of Their Publications, 1893–1905* (Chicago: Norman W. Forgue, 1940), fails to give adequate mention to Frank Hazenplug, because Kramer never learned to identify his style with certainty. In turn this was

owed to the fact that Kramer studied only one firm of publishers and could not recognize Hazenplug's hand in works published by a dozen other firms as well.

9. *Publishers Weekly*, December 20, 1890, p. 990.
10. Alfred Hamill, *The Decorative Work of T. M. Cleland* (New York: Pynson Printers, 1929), unpaged.
11. *Publishers' Trade List Annual*, 1897, p. 13.
12. W. A. Kittredge, "Theodore Brown Hapgood: American Designer, 1871–1938," *Print* 3, no. 2 (Summer 1942): 2–3.
13. *Inland Printer* 21 (August 1898): 617.
14. *Book Buyer* 14 (1897): 131.
15. See *Bookman* 48 (September 1918): 45.

Further Reading

There has never been a comprehensive treatment of the field, but a number of works exist that provide convenient access. On the technical side, there is Joseph W. Rogers, "The Rise of American Edition Binding," in *Bookbinding in America*, ed. by Hellmut Lehmann-Haupt (Portland, Maine: The Southworth-Anthoensen Press, 1941), pp. 129–185; a more general treatment is provided in Brander Matthews, *Bookbindings Old and New* (New York: Macmillan, 1895), and in Matthews, "Books in Paper Covers," *Century Magazine* 50 (July 1895): 354–361. A broader and more philosophical approach is given in *Commercial Bookbinding: An Historical Sketch with Some Mention of an Exhibition of Drawings, Covers, and Books, at the Grolier Club, April 5 to April 28, 1894* (New York: The Grolier Club, 1894), a brief essay with only 20 pages of text, but a landmark in the field. Of equal importance is Victor H. Briggs and Ernest L. Briggs, *Twentieth Century Cover Design* (Plymouth, Mass.: The Briggs Brothers, 1902), which is enormously rich in illustrations and attributions of designs. Much technical information can be derived from *The American Bookmaker* 1 (1885–); *The British Bookmaker* 1 (1888–); and *The Inland Printer* 1 (1883–); and from Mary Van Kleeck, *Women in the Bookbinding Trade* (New York: Survey Associates for the Russell Sage Foundation, 1913).

Although neither is about American design or designers, still, for their approach and the kind of information they provide about the general subject, two works are invaluable: James G. Nelson, *The Early Nineties: A View from the Bodley Head* (Cambridge, Mass.: Harvard Univ. Press, 1971) and John Russell Taylor, *The Art Nouveau Book in Britain* (Cambridge, Mass.: M.I.T. Press [c. 1966]). Of similar importance is *Modern Bookbindings and Their Designers*, a special number of *The Studio* (1899–1900), which has a valuable section on American designers. But perhaps the single most helpful book for understanding the place of a designed cover in publishing practice is Sidney Kramer, *A History of Stone & Kimball and Herbert S. Stone & Co.: With a Bibliography of Their Publications, 1893–1905* (Chicago: Norman W. Forgue, 1940). And for the aesthetic milieu that produced the startling changes of the 1890s there is an invaluable book: Susan Otis Thompson, *American Book Design and William Morris* (New York: Bowker, 1977).

WHITMAN

Sarah Whitman. Boston: Merrymount, 1904. Memorial tributes to Sarah Whitman.

Giles Barber. "Rossetti, Ricketts, and Some Publishers' Bindings of the Nineties." *The Library*, 5th series, 25 (December 1970): 314–330.

ARMSTRONG

Charles Gullans and John Espey. *A Checklist of Trade Bindings Designed by Margaret Armstrong.* UCLA Library Occasional Papers, no. 16. Los Angeles: Univ. of California Library, 1968.

Hamilton Fish Armstrong. *Those Days.* New York: Harper, 1963.

BRADLEY

[Carey Bliss.] *Will Bradley: His Work—An Exhibition.* San Marino, Calif.: Huntington Library, 1951.

Will Bradley. *Will Bradley: His Chap Book.* New York: Typophiles, 1955.

Roberta Waddell Wong. *Will Bradley: Exponent of American Decorative Illustration at the End of the Nineteenth Century.* Ann Arbor, Mich.: University Microfilms, 1971.

————. *Will H. Bradley: American Artist and Craftsman (1868–1962).* New York: Metropolitan Museum of Art, 1972.

Clarence P. Hornung. *Will Bradley: His Graphic Art. . . .* With an introduction by Roberta Waddell Wong. New York: Dover, 1972.

HAZENPLUG

Sidney Kramer, *A History of Stone & Kimball,* cited above, is indispensable.

THE DECORATIVE DESIGNERS

Lee Thayer. "The Decorative Designers, A Footnote to Publishing History." *Publishers Weekly* 184 (September 5, 1953): 174–178.

Charles Gullans and John Espey. *The Decorative Designers, 1895–1932, An Essay.* Los Angeles: Univ. of California Library, 1970.

Charles Gullans. *The Decorative Designers, 1895–1932: A Guide to the Exhibition Cases. . . .* Los Angeles: Univ. of California Library, 1970.

Lee Thayer. Tapes and Transcripts of Interviews in May and June 1970, Department of Special Collections, University Research Library, UCLA.

Ernest Dressel North. "Bookbinding as a Fine Art." *Outlook* 57 (December 4, 1897): 809–817.

Other Designers

William Dana Orcutt. "Frederick Holland Day." *Publishers Weekly* 125 (January 6, 1934): 51–54.

Wilbur Macey Stone. "Jay Chambers: Artist." *Bulletin of the New York Public Library* 34 (January 1930): 9–10; and *Print Connoisseur* 10 (January 1930): 72–75.

Wilbur Macey Stone. *Book-Plates of Today.* New York: Tonnelé, 1902.

[Hannibal] Ingalls Kimball. *Book Decorations by Bertram Grosvenor Goodhue.* New York: Grolier, 1929.

Alfred Hamill. *The Decorative Work of T. M. Cleland.* New York: Pynson Printers, 1929.

Peter Beilenson. *The Story of Frederic W. Goudy.* New York: Walpole Printing Office, 1939.

Lewis Bernard. *Behind the Type: The Life Story of Frederic W. Goudy.* Pittsburgh: Department of Printing, Carnegie Institute of Technology, 1941.

Wilfred P. Truesdell. *The Bookplates of Amy M. Sacker.* Boston: Troutsdale Press, 1903.

————. *Bookplates Designed by Theodore B. Hapgood, Jr.* Boston: Troutsdale Press, 1907.

W. A. Kittredge. *Theodore B. Hapgood.* Boston: Society of Printers, 1942.

Works that Treat Several Designers

Frank Chouteau Brown. *Letters and Lettering.* Boston: Bates & Guild, 1902.

Joseph Cummings Chase. *Decorative Design: A Textbook of Practical Methods.* New York: Wiley, 1915.

J. M. Bowles. *Some Examples of the Work of American Designers.* Philadelphia: Dill & Collins (c. 1918).

3

Books in Series

William B. Todd

OF ALL THE AREAS in the great realm of book production there is none, perhaps, that at first glance is less appealing than collections of series. Unlike most other collecting pursuits, where the collector can exercise some discretion—where indeed, as the various essays in this volume generally attest, one may move freely, uninhibited by any constraints— books in series impose their own order or rationale, compelling the collector to complete obeisance. Even so, though strait and narrow is the way, that way at least is the path of rectitude and may lead on to blessings not bestowed upon less righteous bibliophiles.

Before struggling along this path collectors may first want to consult some high authority for a few directions. So forewarned, they may then look askance at several combinations of books not properly regarded as belonging to a series, hurry by others rightfully classified but possibly of little consequence, and at last dwell upon those that are worthy of complete allegiance. Amid these serried ranks I shall be escorting the reader through my own heterogeneous library but then only to books that fall into some sort of array. Surprisingly, when viewed from this new perspective, a large number of my volumes singly or in groups may justly claim adherence to some larger cause, some enterprise extending beyond the confines of a solitary book; but whether this greater purpose, however perceived, will entice the collector is a matter to be determined.

A Preliminary Assessment

Of course, for any debatable topic the immediate requisite is a useful definition. For *series* none appears to be more comprehensive than that originally provided by the *Oxford English Dictionary* (*OED*);[1] under the ninth sense of the term, three usages are given, each for our purposes more relevant than the one before:

> 1. A set of literary compositions having certain features in common, published successively or intended to be read in sequence. . . .

As the pertinent quotations indicate, ordinarily what this signifies is a series of essays within a book, or volumes of a certain order, all usually of single authorship and hence of little concern to us.

> 2. A succession of volumes or fascicules (of a periodical, the publications of a society, etc.) forming a set by itself (distinguished as *first, second*, etc., *series*).

Though no examples are provided for this definition, there can be little doubt that, for a periodical, the compilers had in mind one like *Notes & Queries* (begun in 1849 and now extending beyond its thirteenth series into a "new" one) and, for an organization, one comparable to the Royal Society (founded in 1662, with annual volumes of its transactions cumulating from 1665). As for *fascicule*, a word defined elsewhere, the *OED* itself is a splendid exemplar, having progressed through 125 separately issued sections before its conclusion on April 9, 1928.

Unquestionably these several works in senses 1 and 2, as well as others like them, are collectible, yet again they are not fully representative of what we now usually mean by *series*, since the segments remain incomplete until such time as they comprise a "set," the controlling term for each definition. So, to the third concept:

> 3. Also, in recent use, a succession of books issued by one publisher in a common form and having some similarity of subject or purpose; usually with a general title, as "the Clarendon Press Series," "the Men of Letters Series."

Here, we may agree, the emphasis has shifted in the direction we wish to take: *first* to books as separable entities within a series, *then* to the issuing agency for still other books conforming to whatever objective the series may represent.

As already intimated, on looking over our library many of us will discover that we have accidentally made the *first move:* we already possess diverse volumes, each qualifying for the purpose originally in mind but now all declaring themselves to be of various sequences. Whether we now deliberately take the *second step*, and proceed from any one to others of comparable degree, will depend upon our response to a number of crucial questions. Is the stated or implied objective of the series sufficiently intriguing to be worth the pursuit? Is it truly entrepreneurial, leading us, quite willingly, beyond our ordinary concerns? Can it sustain us, say, in the quest not for a single book but for several score, for several hundred, or, to anticipate my final, Tauchnitz example, for 5,393 volumes? Despite the "similarity of subject," is there yet sufficient diversity to enhance our interest with every new acquisition? Also, despite the "common form" the series often takes, necessarily, is there still an ever-varying appearance, provenance, or some other attribute that distinguishes each new volume? Then, too, are the books so elusive as to pose a constant challenge, yet still attainable finally? Generally, if the answer to all these queries is in the affirmative, one may confidently undertake to collect a series. If disquieting negatives begin to arise, however, the endeavor is best avoided.

While the *OED* remains close by, along with the questions definition 3 has provoked, we may conveniently consider its references to series, beginning with the two within the quotation. Since the Clarendon Press Series was intended generally for the classroom, it may be put safely aside as primarily educational or, like the Loeb Classics and countless others, to be used only for reference. Straightforward pedagogy is not one of the higher aims of a bookman. However, the English Men of Letters, to give this sequence its proper title, should be vigorously sought and all its 39 volumes carefully read. "Right from the start," as Gross remarks, "it was accorded semi-official status. . . . No comparable series has ever come so close to attaining the rank of a traditional British institution."[2] After the original Macmillan issue (1885–1894), certain of the volumes were reprinted at least nine times, and the whole series was reissued in some other guise on three separate occasions—all further indications of the enduring, stimulating value of this set. Moreover, as so often happens whenever a "best seller" appears, Macmillan was induced to publish two sequels, English Men of Action (22 in all) and Twelve English Statesmen, neither of which is now remembered.

The final account, supporting *OED*'s inclusion of sense 3 as "in recent use," is an illustrative quotation from the introduction to the 1832 magnum opus edition of Sir Walter Scott's *The Betrothed*: "The Tales of the Crusaders was determined upon as the title of the following series of these novels"—a sequence extending by the way only to one subsequent novel, *The Talisman*. Actually, the series title for these two works appeared originally in their first editions (four volumes, 1825); these in turn were preceded by three series, so designated, of Scott's *Tales of My Landlord* (1816–1819), constituting 5 novels in 12 volumes. Evidently, then, Sir Walter should receive full credit for establishing the term *series* in the sense that we now prefer—full credit also for permitting us to overlook anything that had happened before his time, before the date this "recent" usage occurred. Nonetheless, it is hard to think of Scott as having written "series," even when we contemplate the all-encompassing term "Waverley" for his historical romances. Similarly for Hardy, "Wessex" can hardly be regarded as a series title, nor for Trollope the tripartite categories "Chronicles of Barsetshire–Parliamentary Novels–Manor House Novels." Most labels of this sort are, I suspect, simply convenient designations applied sometime after the original work was done. Thus, reluctantly, I pass over the 192 volumes in my collection of Scott and all similar arrays. They have accumulated not because I am intent upon any "series" therein, real or supposed, but only because of my abiding interest in the author. Not some impersonal and external "cause," but the novelist alone, in all his/her singularity, here motivates the collector.

Early Numbered Books in Series

Coincident with Scott's early use of the word "series," in the sense now accepted, there appeared an ever-rising flood of pamphlets, none at first employing this term but many appearing eventually with serial numbers. As with periodicals, apparently it was recognized that numerical references offered some assurance that more items of the same kind had already appeared or could be expected; and as these emissions all came from sources dedicated to some high purpose there can be little doubt that all of them qualify for inclusion here. These are the tracts sponsored usually by Wesleyan organizations and directed to the unlettered masses. In all the constant message, simply phrased through parable and homily, is to lead a pious yet useful life, to do good deeds, shun all manner of sin, and be thankful for small blessings. To this end scriptural accounts are often retold but always in plain language with the moral directly expressed. So that the message could reach even the humblest household and the smallest purse, these tracts were priced not at 31s. 6d. each, as for the expansive novels of Scott's time, all "quality" fare for the literati, but at 2s. 8d. per hundred. Although they were issued in vast quantities, most of these ephemeral leaflets virtually have disappeared, and even a few specimens in one series or another are worth some passing comment.

For these the principal outlet at first was the Religious Tract Society, an organization founded in 1799 to further systematize and extend the good work earlier done by Hannah More with her "cheap repository tracts." The numbering of issues appears to have been started about 1817 as a new feature in the distribution scheme of Thomas Cordeaux, the proprietor of what was called "the Conference Office" at 14 City Road, London.[3] Of his productions I have 78, ranging from number 1 (two editions with different texts) through 193 (the last issue to bear a date—1825) and then on to 222. Many of these obviously are reprints, because certain of the earlier numbers appear over the imprint of the succeeding firm, Benjamin Bensley (later Mills, Jowett, and Mills) at 6 Bolt Court, Fleet Street.

Another, concurrent, series, done directly for the Religious Tract Society by Applegath and Cowper (later Applegath alone), though entirely undated, carries an address held by these printers only between 1820 and 1826.[4] Of these I have twenty-three in the sequence 11–179 —number 143 in two settings of the same subject and four others (21, 57, 94, 174) of a number and subject identical to those in the previously mentioned series. The British Library holds a set in the undated sequence containing only twenty-four issues, among them only four with numbers equivalent to mine.

Yet another group, bearing only the imprint of the Religious Tract Society, is of a larger quarto size, much better printed with especially designed woodcuts; each number in this group extends to 16 pages. Labeled Penny Tales for the People, the series probably appeared in the 1870s and is represented by 16 numbers within the range 75–103. Concerning this series I can find no entry in the British Library or elsewhere.[5]

Once started, there is of course no end to the numbering of books. Let me therefore simply observe that my random acquisitions from the earlier period also extend to similar series of chapbooks issued by the affiliated Glasgow Religious Tract Society (numbers 33 and 77), by several printers resident in Dublin, representing perhaps the Religious Tract and Book Society for Ireland (2, 21, 23 from John Porteous, and 20 from Thomas White), and even to a number of broadsides printed by William Fordyce in Newcastle (2, 48, 56, 143, 160, and 170). For a slightly later period (1832–1838), under the general title *Cheap Repository Tracts*, I also possess a first series representing issues 435–447 and a second series containing 449–461, collected in volumes issued by the Society for Promoting Christian Knowledge.

For all of these early tracts, and countless others, it is conceded that whatever the high resolve that actuated the purveyors and however far their influence may have extended, as collectible items these little books may now be held in rather low esteem. Even so, though oriented always toward some sectarian belief, they must be recognized as the early precursors of numerous series directed by other secular crusaders, among them in more recent times the 180 English Fabian tracts (1884–1916) and the 1,914 American Little Blue Books (1919–1951).[6] Hence the serious collector should acquire illustrative specimens throughout this long tradition of socially uplifting series, even if at the outset it seems impossible to do more.

Later Numbered Books Not in Series

Moving now to the immediate present, another tract regarded, up to 1978 at least, as highly inspirational, and revered I dare say by more people than any of the series just mentioned, is the *Quotations from Chairman Mao Tsetung*, the famous "Little Red Book." Apart from the hundreds of millions of copies first issued (1964) for internal circulation by various Chinese printing offices, from 1966 to 1972 the Foreign Languages Press of Peking circulated this "powerful ideological weapon" in 37 translations, all in the firm conviction that once Chairman Mao's "thought is grasped by the broad masses, it becomes an inexhaustible source of strength and a spiritual atom bomb of infinite power."[7] Even the Little Blue Books fall somewhat short of this stated objective, or rather this declared reality. The simple question for us, however, is whether, in the present context, the Red is really comparable to the Blue and so also properly called a series.

Superficially the *Quotations* meets every requisite so far discussed, even to the extent of provoking various sequels.[8] Nonetheless, when properly interpreted, the Chinese colophon numbers exhibit a curious circumstance: the first two translations, issued in Japanese and English respectively, are recorded as 438 and 491, and the last, in Tagalog, as 2,007. Obviously because hundreds of numbers were here employed for other works before, during, and after this sequence, the colophons must signify only the order of jobs through the press, with the *Quotations* constituting certain related issues intermittently appearing within the larger program, but not of themselves an uninterrupted series.

In view of the colophon numbers, perhaps it could be argued that the entire output of the Foreign Languages Press, like the total run of the Haldeman–Julius Little Blue Books agency, represents a complete series, one that espouses the principles of Marxism-Leninism in the Peking style. While admitting this possibility, I would yet contend that, having to my great delight acquired all variants of the *Quotations* and all known sequels, I am still not at all inclined to go any further. It suffices for me to select, rather warily, only a few specimens outside the *Quotations* sequence, among them one I cherish as an amulet against all bibliomanic tendencies, number 346 (1966), Mao's *Oppose Book Worship*.

Collectible Series

After all the provisos and exceptions so far recounted, it is time to consider the infinite variety of series, many of them once extending to great length but most of them now lost to view. Quite fortuitously, it is still possible to acquire at once a complete set of what one most desires, this usually as the benefaction of an assiduous collector earlier committed to the same purpose. Thus it happened with my Highways and Byways series (1897–1932), a sequence begun, again by Macmillan, just three years after the last of the English Men of Letters sequence and, I should say, comparable to its predecessor as "a traditional British institution"—of a citizenry always in search of nature's wonders. For some years I had fondly possessed only the first volume, . . . *in Devon and Cornwall* (by Arthur H. Norway, with illustrations by Joseph Pennell and Hugh Thomson), but that was enough for me to indulge the fantasy of meandering about that lovely part of the English countryside, so despoiled when I was later there on wartime maneuvers. More realistically, on examining other copies I also observed that this series was continuously reprinted (the original volume some ten times), testifying to its special favor among the reading public and presenting yet another credential for entry on my shelves. Now suddenly all 27 volumes are together, all invoking the greatest pleasure. Thus, on this one occasion, my submission to the publisher's intent was realized through a single order.

More often, though, the collector must be content only with stray specimens in a series, adding to them whenever possible, but dismissing all thought of completion as an impossibility. Even so, as one comes upon these interrelated books, oddly jostling with discrete or "unitary" volumes, one will find them to be somewhat more suggestive than the others; it is characteristic of series that any one generally will contain some account of all the others then available and so give the collector an idea of what presently lies beyond reach. Among my wife's miniature books I chance upon a delectable bibelot, J. G. Wood's *Croquêt* (ca. 1860), with the title page indicating that it is one of Warne's Bijou Books— one of 23 devoted to pleasant pastimes, as the list at the end relates.

To my surprise I also find on the same shelf runs of two other series, one imitating the other and both, I suspect, modeled upon my own copies of Pickering's finely produced Diamond Classics (1820– 1831, 14 volumes). The first of these, Tilt's Miniature Classical Library (1836–1837), in some 38 volumes, actually turns out to be entirely of English authors. The second, an American counterpart labeled Appleton's Classical Library (ca. 1844), presents at least 15 titles, according to its lists, a number of them identical to what Tilt had offered.

Inevitably these several reflections lead me to Moxon's Miniature Poets (admittedly a somewhat larger "miniature," 6¼ by 4¾ inches) and there initially to *A Selection from the Works of Alfred Tennyson*. An appreciative review in *The Examiner* (January 7, 1865) leaves no doubt that the series now introduced is a remarkable innovation.

> This is an exquisite little volume, in a handsome binding of blue cloth richly and tastefully adorned with gold after a design of pure ornamentation by Mr. John Leighton, who is designer also of the woodcut head and tail pieces which adorn the sightly pages of the book. The paper is thick and of the finest quality, the printing, by Messrs. Bradbury and Evans, is in a beautiful clear type, is faultless, and enclosed on each page in a square drawn with a single thin red line. . . . probably the most beautiful six-shilling gift-book ever produced in this country. . . . A series of volumes of choice poetry after this pattern as to quality, mechanical, and intellectual, will make itself a place wherever in England there is taste and education. And great credit is due to the mechanical designer of the series: for it is no mere imitation, with slight variations, of former achievements, no reproduction of the idea of the Pickering series or any other, but a perfectly new notion of the way to make a pretty book, that will supply, probably, a new point of departure to the herd of imitators.

Even beyond the aesthetic values stressed by the reviewer, these selections from contemporary poets are highly commendable, both to the scholar for the first appearance or final revision of certain verses, and to the bibliophile for the variable issues of almost every volume. Later advertisements indicate that the first book (and to some extent, all the others) was available in "Cloth bevelled, 5s.; ditto, gilt edges, 6s.; morocco gilt, 10s. 6d.; best levant morocco, 21 s.," and further, as my own collection exhibits, in a special vellum presentation binding with red and blue ruled panels on the sides. Moreover, certain of the cloth-bound volumes, including the *Tennyson*, appear in several colors (blue, green, terra-cotta, or black), on which may be displayed gilt stamp-

PLATE 9   Moxon's Miniature Poets. Illustrated is the top portion of four cover stamp-ings, each with different rules or a different border. The first three varieties may appear in any order for any of the authors published in the series. Only the fourth variety (with a name label) is demonstrably of a later issue.

PLATE 10 The Lansdowne Poets. Uniformly bound in avocado-colored cloth and stamped in black and gilt, each of these volumes has a specially designed monogram above the poet's name and a variable motif composed of the lyre, primrose, and thistle below it.

ing in any one of four styles (see Plate 9). For all of the ten poets now memorialized the avid collector may therefore need to seek out some 50 variants—five times the number I have discovered after the most persistent search.

Following Moxon's radical "point of departure" there apparently was no "herd of imitators" as the reviewer had predicted, except perhaps the series titled The Lansdowne Poets and representing some 25 earlier, noncopyright authors (Plate 10). Issued in crown octavo by Frederick Warne (ca. 1884), these too were "red line border" editions bound in "cloth extra, gilt, gilt edges, price 3s. 6d. each; or in morocco, elegant, 8s." Textually these are worthless, but the lavish gilt cover designs may be sufficiently interesting to those who desire only attractive books. However, the possibility of acquiring these in good condition is, I would say, even more remote than for the Moxon Series.

Those readers who have been noting price of issue will observe that we have been moving away from books of the Moxon order, all intended for the connoisseur, and descending once more into the mass market. Only a year or so after the Warne venture, we find available a series very cheaply priced at 3d. in paper and 6d. in cloth, well below all competition, and rapidly proceeding on the widest possible front. As announced in the London *Times* (November 30, 1885), Cassell's National Library "shall represent all periods and forms of thought, and shall include the records of history, biography, religion, philosophy, discovery, enterprise, natural science, natural history, art, and political economy, as well as plays, poems, and tales, and whatever else may be worth lasting remembrance." So proclaimed, these pleasant little books began to appear the following New Year's Day and, mass produced at an issue a week, eventually extended by 1892 to 217 volumes.[9] For each the indefatigable Henry Morley, LL.D., supplied a useful introduction, and the thoughtful publisher also provided a cloth "reading case" to protect the paper issue "from being soiled when carried in the pocket" as well as "a handsome oak or ebonized book case" to hold each yearly issue of the cloth editions. When only 150 volumes had been printed, an official of the firm declared that over 3 million copies already had been sold, "which would fill twenty-four miles of bookshelves"[10]— not so great a distance, a cynic might declare, until it is realized that with 192 pages, more or less, each volume was only about ⅜ inch thick. Today, as penciled notations read in my copies, any one of these is "very scarce."

Like other innovations the Cassell Series provoked several imitations at the same price, though these, as usual, were somewhat unsuccessful. Within several weeks, on February 10, 1886, Routledge started a World Library, with 160 pages per volume, which ran only through 50 numbers. Then on March 15, Ward, Lock began its Popular Library of World Treasures, a series aimed at 100 volumes but achieving only 22.[11] Barely surfacing to public view, these belated endeavors now seem to have sunk without trace.

Some years later, when Arnold Bennett in his *Literary Taste* (1909) came to propose an essential English library at minimal cost, apparently only two of Cassell's National Library were then in print, Mackenzie's *Man of Feeling* and Aubrey de Vere's *Legends of St. Patrick*, both still quoted at 6d. Failing to uncover any more, Bennett was therefore obliged to draw his remaining selections from 46 other series, none of them priced at less than 1s., and all of the "main" series quoted *uniformly* at that price. Included in this group are, among others, the Canterbury Poets, the Muses Library, the Scott Library (each with 15 titles selected), the Oxford World's Classics (23), the New Universal Library (33), and, far surpassing any of these, the Everyman Library (73). Though much could be said here about popular collections, and especially about the favored sequence last named,[12] I must admit that, among them all, I find nothing to sustain my interest, nothing to compel me to go on amassing one variety or another *as a series*. The very lack of variety, a certain dull monotony, all brought on by the absence of any distinctive rationale, serves to still my acquisitive propensities.

Now that our review is again taking us forward into the twentieth century I must further concede, given my backward, antiquarian bias, that with a solitary exception I can summon no great enthusiasm even for the more splendid achievements of this later time. Certainly the enormously successful Penguin Series, accompanied by its progeny of Pelicans and Puffins, deserves all the acclaim it continually receives.[13] I join in the happy chorus, though not in the attending procession. Due respect also must be accorded the Modern Library, another series of long duration that only now is coming under close bibliographic scrutiny.[14] To a much lesser extent certainly, some credit is also due to the flourishing book clubs of our time, notably the Folio Society in Great Britain and the Limited Editions Club in the United States.[15] Ordinarily the discriminating bibliophile will avoid these committee-chosen products distributed on the installment plan to apathetic subscribers.

The one exception involves a valiant effort quickly ending in dismal failure. The attempt comes from Ernest A. Baker, a principal authority on the English novel, and has its immediate antecedent in his own *Guide to the Best Fiction*, a vast index to some 4,500 novels. Apparently it occurred to Baker, while reading through all these books, that well over half were now only half remembered, if at all, and that accordingly (I conjecture here, of course) perhaps 2,250 might be worth reissuing. Thus convinced, four months after the issuance of his *Guide* Baker urged the firm of Routledge to announce, in *The Athenaeum* (July 25, 1903), a new venture titled, not surprisingly, Half-Forgotten Books, all "elegantly bound" at 2s. and offering "a series of CHEAP EDITIONS of once-famous Books which in their day enjoyed wide popularity, but which are now out of print or inaccessible in cheap and convenient forms. Each contains a careful Introduction by the Editor or another." Following this is a list of nine novels, four then "ready" (Emma Robinson, *Whitefriars;* Ann Radcliffe, *Mysteries of Udolpho;* William Godwin, *Caleb Williams;* R. Monteney-Jephson, *Tom Bulkley of Lissington*); one other available "next week" (Dickens, *Memoirs of Grimaldi*); and four more to be issued "shortly" (Judge Haliburton, *Sam Slick;* Albert Smith, *The Pottleton Legacy;* G. H. Rodwell, *Old London Bridge;* Ann Radcliffe, *Romance of the Forest*).

Baker's list is cited as final testimony of books long sought but never found. In this sequence all that I have ever discovered are six others that were published subsequently—three acquired some years ago in England and three others seized in 1977 from the cavernous basement of Dauber & Pine, New York. In a gradual cheapening of the binding decoration, these indicate a sudden termination (probably in 1905) with 22 novels as total issue, or about 1 percent of what might have been expected. Against this, the last and least fortunate of the miscellaneous series that have attracted my attention,[16] we may now compare the one that, in my view, for just over a century excelled all others.

The Tauchnitz Series

In several of the foregoing accounts the collector may be aware of certain limitations that can be very discomforting—limits in scope, in design, in the extent of the series, and in the availability of any single copy. One may also realize, rather despairingly, that the production of the more remarkable ventures is now so well documented that all one might do in this later time has been done better in times before.[17] Thus all the zest of exploration and discovery has fizzled away before one starts.

With Tauchnitz, however, we come upon something quite without precedent, a strangely foreign reference once unknown to several of my bookseller friends, yet an exploit that I dare say transcends every other. To begin with, we here contemplate an enterprise that has entirely different dimensions in many respects. Where other publishers were usually content to operate within national confines, and sometimes (as with the Moxon Series) only for a special clientele, the Leipzig-based firm of Tauchnitz could declare, in a 1937 centennial account, that its empire was spread worldwide and involved some 6,000 booksellers—a greater number, it was then affirmed, than those engaged by all the publishers of Great Britain and the United States combined.[18] Where one of the more venturesome series, Cassell's National Library, eventually "would fill twenty-four miles of bookshelves," the distance say from London to Windsor, it was said that by 1937 Tauchnitz's international issues, also averaging a book a week, could reach from London to New York.

Even though Tauchnitz was legally "prohibited" entry into Great Britain, the United States, and all their dependencies, its Collection of British (and *later* American) Authors was in fact so large and various (comprising 726 authors in some 5,393 volumes, totaling over 40 million copies)[19] that copyright restrictions actually presented no real barrier. (See Plate 11.) Most of the 1,575 volumes in my collection—all but 5 acquired these last two years—have indeed come either from England

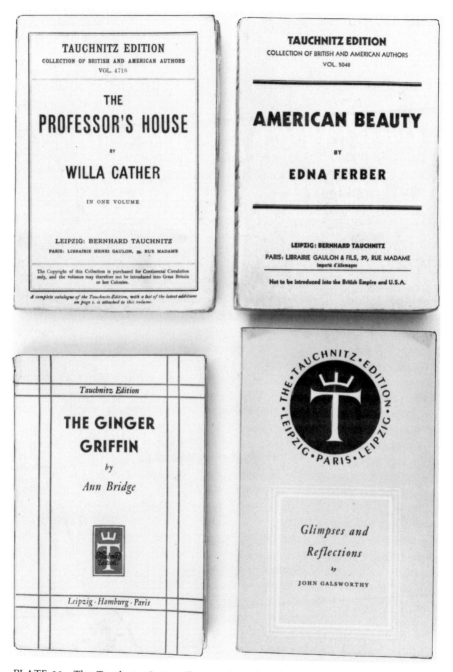

PLATE 11 The Tauchnitz Series. Illustrated are four late wrapper styles from among numerous variants; those shown enclose books dated 1926, 1932, 1935, and 1938.

or the United States and now constitute the primary base for the bibliography I am preparing.

Where my books may have been before I acquired them remains an intriguing question. Looking along my Leipzig shelves, I find here and there a Galsworthy bought in Shanghai from a German bookseller; a Lafcadio Hearn for sale on the second pier in Kobe; another impression of the same work purchased in Curaçao, D.W.I.; a Jerome K. Jerome acquired at Trondheim (where it was translated throughout by the owner into Norwegian); and the Tischendorf edition of the *New Testament*, given to someone in Madras (and since then, it appears, floated down the Ganges). These and many others document the extent of Tauchnitz's international empire.

Of those acquired as lots, all distinctively gilt bound and apparently in original impression (though of unknown origins), I am very pleased to have a 23-volume set of Bulwer-Lytton, including *Pelham*, the first number in the Tauchnitz Series (these from a dealer in Frankfurt am Main, who found them in Lund, Sweden); other extensive runs of Charles Lever (from Oxford) and Baroness Tautphoeus (New York); a 30-volume set of minor authors, choicely bound in half rose calf with black labels (Saxmundham, Suffolk); and, in bright contrast to these, 240 volumes in half green calf with red labels (London). Other large sets of a certain provenance include two groups accumulated apparently year after year by persons on vacation—one in the 1890s by Beryl Fothergill with copies inscribed and dated from Brussels, Cairo, Coblenz, Nuremberg, Paris, Rotterdam, and St. Moritz (Cambridge); the other from 1910 to 1932 by L. Gerliezy, dating from Bad Tölz, Berlin, Dresden, Eisenach, Lausanne, Munich, and Zurich (these and many others in original wrappers—at 25 cents each!—from a good friend in Washington). With Leipzig issues so easily discovered everywhere, early and late, singly or en masse, it is not surprising that "Tauchnitz" should continually occur as a kind of literary refrain or watchword in our literature, frequently cited in the novels of Henry James and intermittently on down to the latest, 1977 effusions of S. J. Perelman and William Saroyan.[20] Obviously, from 1841 to 1943 the principal series was an operation of considerable magnitude, one of some appreciable effect, and also, I must report, one of a certain complexity.

Before any intricacies obtrude, however, the curious reader may first wish to know how I became enmeshed in what admittedly is an endless and yet, I would further insist, an ever more exciting endeavor. For many years there reposed on my office shelf five lonely Leipzig editions of Mark Twain, all acquired I know not where simply as curios-

ities, mentioned once as of an order to be collated in any definitive edition of that author,[21] but then neglected as I went on with Edmund
Burke, David Hume, Adam Smith, and other concerns. Not until 1976,
when Michael Turner asked me to speak at Oxford the following year,
was I again dragged forward into the nineteenth century, and then
perforce by the announced topic for the meeting: "Publishing and the
Market for Books since 1800." About this period and subject I knew
very little, about Bernhard Tauchnitz of Leipzig nothing whatever;
but because the meeting was described as an Anglo-French Colloquium,
I thought it might be rather diverting, and truly ecumenical, for the
sole American speaker to comment on the activities of a German publisher. So resolved, and really quite bemused by my own audacity, I
proposed as much to Turner on November 5, 1976, and then hurried
over to the University of Texas Humanities Research Center where, I
vaguely remembered, Anthony Newnham's extensive collection of
Tauchnitz had been deposited many years before. There amid his 1,200
volumes, a whole new world of books, I eventually managed to assemble
enough fascinating evidence for a rough draft of my paper—one further
enhanced, some months later, by data uncovered at the British Library
and finally revised April 14, 1977, on the noonday train to Oxford. At
Blackwell's that afternoon (the day before my academic performance)
I chanced upon a Tauchnitz "1842" edition of Goldsmith's *Select Works*
and at once decided that this would be a fine exhibit for those attending,
especially since my newly acquired expertise signaled this as an impression printed not before 1859. Indeed this one book neatly exemplified a
central problem with Tauchnitz: his insistence on retaining first imprint
date on issues of far later time.

Whether I was captivated by my own talk on Friday the fifteenth,
or then incited by some searching rejoinder from Professor Robert
Escarpit of the University of Bordeaux, I do not know; yet there is no
doubt that, over the weekend, I unwittingly crossed the Rubicon. The
following Monday I was back at Blackwell's to secure, out of a large
assemblage just received, 31 additional volumes of well-known nineteenth-century authors (Bulwer-Lytton, Wilkie Collins, Disraeli, Kingsley, Kipling, Longfellow, Macaulay, Thackeray); and six months later
with many others in hand I wrote again to order whatever still remained
—by then only an odd assortment of rather obscure writers (Braddon,
Dixon, Edwards, Fontenoy, Kavanagh, Kimball, Lewes, Warburton,
Whyte-Melville). Beyond question, on this latter occasion I was no
longer interested in reputable authors per se but was entirely committed to the Tauchnitz Series, however far it might go. The "strait

and narrow" path mentioned at the beginning of this essay had veered off unexpectedly in a new direction, and what I now observed is best reported from several different perspectives.

At the outset it must be recognized that my commitment to this series, like the publisher's own original resolve, was at first not directed by any clearly enunciated principle. When at the age of 26, Tauchnitz brought out his first volume, the "1842" *Pelham,* the advertisement for this in the September 28, 1841, Leipzig *Börsenblatt für den Deutschen Buchhandel* simply remarked that the volume is in "Schiller-format" (that is, 6½ by 4¾ inches, an octavo size maintained throughout) and, as for the series now inaugurated: "Diese Taschenausgabe ist *sehr wohlfeil* und *elegant,* besonders aber empfiehlt sie sich durch *Correctheit.*" ("This pocket edition is very cheap and elegant, especially to be recommended for its correctness.") Several years thereafter, on the wrappers of a later issue (1843?–1845) of the same work, Tauchnitz's own anglophilic instincts are now more explicitly expressed:

> This collection will be particularly distinguished by its *correctness of text, elegance in exterior and cheapness of price;* it is therefore hoped that the friends of the English language and literature will be gratified with this edition. To suit the purchaser *each volume will be sold separately.*
>
> In bringing forth this edition the publisher has been solicitous to render it a popular one;—convenient in its form and valuable in its contents it will prove to be adapted not only for the public in general but for the use of schools in particular. . . .[22]

These several claims can be easily substantiated: for example, for *correctness* in the publisher's correspondence with Browning regarding a trivial misprint ("Got" for "God") overlooked by the poet;[23] for *cheapness* in the fact that Tauchnitz immediately undersold all competing firms and in later years prevailed over some eight other rival Continental publishers; for general *adaptability* in the eventual sale, already mentioned, of 40 million copies; and for *educational purposes* by Tauchnitz's early provision of companion bilingual dictionaries for every major European language. Thus by 1881, in the preface to his two-thousandth volume, the publisher could confidently predict that "the Tauchnitz Edition will still proceed in its old spirit, and continue to fulfill its mission, by spreading and strengthening the love for English literature outside England and her Colonies." Still later, in a brochure listing "Publications of 1931," it is emphasized, however, *"that the Tauchnitz Edition excludes books of an all-too superficial character."* Hence in one declaration or another there is every assurance that the books entered and thereafter sustained in the Continental Tauchnitz Series have some merit apart from, and perhaps contrary to, whatever Anglo-American critics may assert. Quite possibly, then, given this unconventional appraisal, we should begin to reassess our favorable judgment of Ainsworth, Anstey, Matthew Arnold, and James Barrie, all of whom Tauchnitz allowed to go out of print in the period 1926–1937, and arrive at some better estimate of Louisa May Alcott, Annie Alexander, and Arnold Bennett, all still maintained in stock at this later date. If at the very start our alphabetical roster subversively discloses this much, what will it divulge further on?

Usually undeclared, and also as yet beyond any ready calculation, is the kind of copy Tauchnitz produced, whether from early proofs, from original part issues, or, later, from a text especially revised in the Leipzig issue. So far at least 13 authors have been identified as occasionally complicit with this publisher in supplying something other than a direct reprint (Maurice Baring, Browning, Bulwer-Lytton, Dickens, Henry James, Charles Lever, Longfellow, George Moore, J. A. Symonds, Harriet Beecher Stowe, Thackeray, Mark Twain, and Samuel Warren); certain of these and others (for example, Wilkie Collins, G. P. R. James, Trollope, and P. G. Wodehouse) had some of their work first issued by Tauchnitz. Through 1881, as judged by signatures reproduced in the frontispiece to volume 2,000, no fewer than 173 authors were by then in direct correspondence with the publisher. Quite apart from providing a reliable foreign standard, another measure of literary excellence, with disturbing frequency the Tauchnitz Series thus appears to represent an authorized textual state varying from the one commonly accepted.

At a purely bibliographical level, as I now discover, there is also much to do, first in describing the extraordinary range of 5,393 volumes issued from 1841 to 1943, then in defining the countless variants among these, and finally in establishing exact dates of original publication. To illustrate the difficulties we need go no further than the second volume in the series, Dickens's *Pickwick Papers* ("1842"), exemplified in Karl H. Pressler's collection by *seven* different titles[24]—not to mention innumerable variables in whatever wrappers may still exist. Of the five copies of Irving's *Sketch Book* ("1843") in my own library (thirty-third volume) one has a statement on the half-title page that it was printed in 1920 and another bears wrappers dated May 1930.

The wrappers themselves, even when present (an unusual circumstance) and when dated (never before 1872 apparently), can be quite misleading, especially when they enclose catalogues of much later date or, in a few instances, of an earlier date. Thus a volume just acquired with March 1931 on the cover has quite legibly inscribed within, "Danzig 18/2/31"—two weeks earlier and 370 miles distant from the assigned time and place of issue. For every volume conclusive evidence must therefore be secured from the German trade periodicals, first from the *Börsenblatt* either for the date the book was received at that Leipzig office or sent out to the booksellers, and then from the *Allgemeine Bibliographie* or comparable journal for the date, slightly later, when it was finally issued to the public at large. The latter journal also cites a most helpful point in determining this original issue: the number of preliminary and text pages. In all respects, then, the task upon which I am engaged is very extensive, very complicated, but from book to book full of delightful surprises.

Certain other, extraneous features may well divert the collector from Tauchnitz proper, and I must say that I have succumbed to several of them. A continual enticement is the "Italian Connection," as witnessed in the work of many Tauchnitzian agents in that country, all busily covering in elaborately decorated vellum or parchment any of his paperback issues—fictional, historical, or religious—which may be of local interest. Of these bindings, each custom made and different from any other, I have about 75, some of them bearing the distinctive armorial bookplate of Edith Peruzzi de' Medici. Others (including the two illustrated in Plate 12) are further adorned with early photographs. One of these, the "1877" Thomas à Kempis *Imitation of Christ* (issued 1880–1890?, inscribed 1921), though dismissed by John Stephens as a "stunningly banal piece of kitsch,"[25] still may be regarded, by less sensitive bibliophiles, as a pleasantly garish product of the Florentine bindery of G. Giannini. The second, enclosing the two-volume issue of Hawthorne's *Transformation* ("1860") (that is, *The Marble Faun*, especially bound probably in 1879, the last year JEQ was in Rome)[26] doubtless is of Roman manufacture. It is one of twelve vellum-bound sets in my collection, containing altogether 666 early prints exhibiting the objects and scenes Hawthorne so vividly describes. A considerable number of these photographs, however, as I shall remark elsewhere, greatly misrepresent this "guide-book" so favored among American tourists—JEQ's copy, for example, illustrating in its very first print the wrong "Marble Faun."

Also to be mentioned briefly are other Tauchnitzian anomalies I hesitate to pursue, admitting at once the futility of it, and so commend to all susceptible collectors. These include:

1. Various additional "Italian Connections," especially George Eliot's

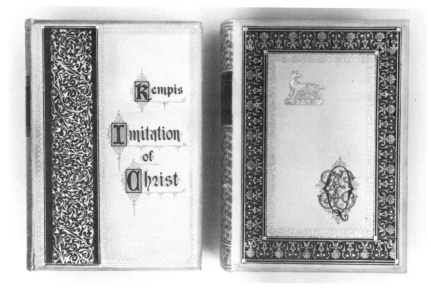

PLATE 12   Tauchnitz in Italian vellum. The Thomas à Kempis was bound in Florence, the Hawthorne probably in Rome.

Romola ("1863"), the comparable "guide-book" extra-illustrated for Florence.

2. Several "American Connections" that tend to breach the interdict against circulating these books in the United States. Among these activities are:

a. Tauchnitz's early association with the New York publishers William Appleton, Brentano's, William S. Gottsberger, Frederick Leypoldt, and Frederick A. Stokes.[27]

b. In 1885 the outright sale, by George F. Coombes, New York, of "upwards of 2,000 distinct works," in the Tauchnitz Series, these now in "special" half red morocco binding gilt-stamped with floral emblems, and all available in any quantity desired. I have yet to see a single exemplar of this American issue.[28]

c. In 1893 the dispatch to Chicago, for display in the Columbian Exposition, of a complete set of the Tauchnitz Continental editions, main series, and specimens of other publications, by then amounting altogether, I suppose, to something over 3,000 volumes. Though these too were especially bound, and it seems were afterward sold directly from the German building, I have yet to discover a solitary copy.[29]

3. Tauchnitz's *11* other series, sporadically appearing in English, French, and German over the period 1863–1943 and all of the great-

est scarcity. Among these diverse exploits, extending to several hundred volumes, I possess only ten specimens.[30]

4. The Tauchnitz volumes that were suppressed for one reason or another, none of which is represented in my collection.[31]

5. The postwar series by successor Tauchnitz firms, including the 18 "new series" volumes issued from Hamburg in 1946 and a further "new series" numbered 101–140 and published 1952–1955 in Stuttgart. Of the earlier issue I have none, of the latter only five.

Though little progress has been made along these several detours I am not at all dismayed, for at least with the main series much has already been done in a relatively short period, and in all time to come there will always be more to do. In quest of this extraordinary series, assuredly, I will remain, like Tennyson's Ulysses,

> . . . strong in will
> To strive, to seek, to find, and not to yield.

Notes

1. There are of course other definitions—notably those provided in *The Bookman's Glossary*, 5th ed., ed. by Jean Peters (New York & London: Bowker, 1975), p. 138, and in John Carter, *ABC for Book-Collectors*, 5th rev. ed. (New York: Knopf, 1978), pp. 179–180—but these do not rehearse the original distinctions given in the *OED*.

2. John Gross, *The Rise and Fall of the Man of Letters* (New York: Macmillan, 1969), p. 107. Gross is quoted in Howes Bookshop catalogue 202 (1978) where, under item 781, a complete series of the original issue is offered at £155.

3. The date is the earliest given for Cordeaux, at the City Road address, in William B. Todd, *A Directory of Printers* (London: Printing Historical Society, 1972), p. 45. Spinney's account of the earlier Hannah More tracts, the *Library* 4th series, 20 (1939): 295–340, indicates that some copies of these were numbered, but only in manuscript.

4. That is, at Duke Street, Stamford Street, Blackfriars. Todd, *A Directory of Printers*, p. 4.

5. It is possible, however, that these Penny Tales for the People may be the precursors of, or otherwise related to, Penny Stories for the People, a series that Richard D. Altick reports as having sold 18,250,000 copies. *The English Common Reader* (Chicago: Univ. of Chicago Press, 1957), p. 314.

6. Here and later I must acknowledge only by note a series avidly sought by many collectors. Because my own assemblage of Little Blue Books (a mere bucketful) came to me more by accident than by design, I would direct the reader to two useful accounts: Kansas State College of Pittsburg, *Porter Library Bulletin* 3, no. 18 (May 15, 1969), an illustrated number celebrating the fiftieth anniversary of the first book; Richard C. Johnson and G.

Thomas Tanselle, "The Haldeman-Julius 'Little Blue Books' as a Bibliographical Problem," *Papers of the Bibliographical Society of America* 64 (1970): 29–78.

7. All quotations in this sentence come from Lin Piao's "Foreword to the Second Edition," a four-page insert in later impressions of the original English edition, dated December 16, 1966. This was suppressed in subsequent issues.

8. When on October 1, 1976 ("National Day" of the People's Republic, and just three weeks after the death of Chairman Mao), the University of Texas Humanities Research Center exhibited all the exemplars I then possessed (some 32), the three sequels known to me were also displayed: *Quotations from LBJ*, 1968 (a little red book in which the section headed "Humility and Self-Criticism" is left entirely blank); *Quotations from Chairman Frank*, 1970 (wrapped in burnt orange, the university color, and celebrating the effusions of a former regent); *Quotations from Premier Chou En-lai*, 1973. Since then I have acquired two others: *Quotations from Mayor Daley*, 1969 (wrapped appropriately in Kelly green) and, doubtless the rarest of all, the *Speeches* of Enver Hoxha (Tirana, Albania), 1969. Except for the original Mao editions, the Hoxha printing is the only one to carry the Communistic caption-title "Workers of All Countries, Unite!"

9. In March 1978 a large cache (153 volumes) of this elusive series was discovered at the shop of Robin Waterfield, Oxford, and secured for the Humanities Research Center at the University of Texas.

10. Thomas Dixon Galpin, as quoted in Simon Nowell-Smith, *The House of Cassell* (London: Cassell, 1958), p. 111.

11. Nowell-Smith, *The House of Cassell*, p. 110.

12. As compared with other, routine reprint series, the Everyman Library has been described as "an institution, a benign presence, a crusade," but admittedly one that eventually became only a "featureless affair" (Gross, *The Rise and Fall of the Man of Letters*, pp. 206–207, 210). The standard account appears in Hugh R. Dent, *The House of Dent 1888–1938* (London: Dent, 1938), pp. 123–125, passim.

13. On all aspects of the emerging paperback trade, as exemplified especially in the Penguin Series, see Hans Schmoller, "The Paperback Revolution," in *Essays in the History of Publishing*, ed. by Asa Briggs (London: Longman, 1974), pp. 285–318. Of particular interest also is David J. Hall, "The Penguin Collectors' Story," *Antiquarian Book Monthly Review* 5 (September 1978): 360–367.

14. See Gordon B. Neavill, "The Modern Library Series: Format and Design, 1917–1977," *Printing History* 1, no. 1 (1979): 26–37.

15. The aims and accomplishments of the Folio Society are best summarized in F. A. Mumby and Ian Norrie, *Publishing and Bookselling*, 5th ed. (London and New York: Cape and Bowker, 1974), p. 518. The New York firm of Philip C. Duschnes has recently issued a *Complete Catalogue* 223 (1979) of the 43 series of the Limited Editions Club.

16. It is interesting to note that, while Baker is mentioned in F. A. Mumby,

The House of Routledge 1834–1934 (London: Routledge, 1934), this official account of the firm chooses to disregard his ill-fated venture into half-forgotten books: obviously all best completely forgotten.

17. I have in mind particularly Michael Sadleir's marvelous achievement, as documented in his *XIX Century Fiction: A Bibliographical Record*, vol. 2 (London: Constable, 1951; reprinted New York: Cooper Square, 1969). Yet even here, after a long and most zealous pursuit, Sadleir frequently confesses his failure to secure more than a few specimens in a number of series (for example, as noted under entries 3,466, 3,659, 3,672, 3,711). A survey of 45 nineteenth-century American publishers, some of whom produced cheap "libraries," series, and dime novels, is now being edited by Madeleine B. Stern.

18. *The Harvest: Being the Record of One Hundred Years of Publishing 1837–1937* (Leipzig: Tauchnitz, 1937), p. 25.

19. I arrive at this total, for the main series, by adding to the 5,370 numbered volumes 8 others that Tauchnitz designated "a" after a given number and 15 that he left unnumbered for one reason or another.

20. Adeline R. Tintner, "The Books in the Book: What Henry James' Characters Read and Why," *AB Bookmen's Weekly* 61 (May 15, 1978): 3470, 3488–3489. The Tauchnitz Series is also mentioned in a poem by Robert Lowell (*Life Studies* [London: Faber and Faber, 1959], p. 75) as well as in more recent work by S. J. Perelman (*Eastward Ha!* [New York: Simon & Schuster, 1977], p. 33) and William Saroyan ("Bookshop in Paris," *books and bookmen* 23 [October 1977]: 7).

21. William B. Todd, "Problems in Editing Mark Twain," *Books at Iowa* 2 (April 1965): 3–8.

22. The original wrappers bearing this advertisement, on a copy in the New York Public Library, appear to be the earliest still extant. Recently Karl H. Pressler reported as the earliest in his collection those for Lever, *Harry Lorrequer*, vol. 138, 1847. Pressler, "Die Tauchnitz Edition: Anfang und Ende einer berühmten Reihe," *Aus dem Antiquariat* 11 (November 1978): A405–415.

23. *Der Verlag Bernhard Tauchnitz 1837–1912* (Leipzig: Tauchnitz, 1912), p. 69.

24. Pressler, "Die Tauchnitz Edition," p. A409.

25. Robin Waterfield Ltd., *Catalogue 26* (Oxford, 1979), item 336.

26. The monogram JEQ on the front cover must certainly be that of the cleric identified in the *DAB* as James Edward Quigley (1854–1915), a student at the College of the Propaganda in Rome 1874–1879 and later bishop of Buffalo. His copy, carefully preserved in a custom-made case, was purchased in New York, January 27, 1979.

27. The particular connection for certain of these is specified in William B. Todd, "Firma Tauchnitz: A Further Investigation," *Publishing History* 2 (1977): 21–22, note 20.

28. The notice with accompanying illustration appears in Coombes's catalogue for October 1885, p. 258 (copy at Grolier Club Library). For this reference I am greatly indebted to G. Thomas Tanselle.

29. Copies of letters on this transaction from Bernhard Tauchnitz, Jr., to The Newberry Library's first director, William F. Poole, have kindly been provided by Diana Haskell, Curator of Modern Manuscripts. Haskell is endeavoring to discover what happened to these 3,000 volumes: no small loss from the bibliographical record! For a report of a still greater loss see Matilda Betham-Edwards's report (item H in the list of books and articles on the Tauchnitz Series in the Further Reading Section).

30. Certain of these series are recorded in *Fünfzig Jahre der Verlagshandlung Bernhard Tauchnitz 1837 bis 1887* (Leipzig: Tauchnitz, 1887), pp. 211–344; other accounts, from diverse sources, are now available in my own files.

31. Nine of these volumes are identified in the comments on items C and M in the Further Reading Section. Except for numbers 5,365–5,366, both unidentified by author or title, at least one copy has been located of each book.

Further Reading

The titles in this section are arranged in two groups. The first is an alphabetical list of commentaries on series in general; the second is a chronological list of reports on the Tauchnitz Series. For additional readings on series not considered in this section, see notes 6, 12–15, and 17 above.

General Commentaries

Altick, Richard D. *The English Common Reader*. Chicago: Univ. of Chicago Press, 1957. 430 pp. An essential work for all studies of this kind, especially of the nineteenth century.

Carter, John. "Books Issued in Parts." In Carter, *Books and Book-Collectors*, pp. 168–172. London: Rupert Hart-Davis, 1956. Important, but not especially relevant to the present account.

James, Louis. *English Popular Literature*. New York: Columbia Univ. Press, 1976. 368 pp.

Osborn, Andrew D. *Serial Publications*. 2nd ed. Chicago: American Library Association, 1973. 434 pp. On the vexing problem of library classification.

Pollard, Graham. "Serial Fiction." In *New Paths in Book Collecting*, edited by John Carter. New York: Scribner, 1934. pp. 247–277. Like the Carter essay above, this one deals with another aspect of serials.

Steinberg, S. H. "Popular Series." In Steinberg, *Five Hundred Years of Printing*, pp. 348–361. London: Penguin Books, 1961. Perhaps the best introductory essay.

The Tauchnitz Series

This is a selective list, first presenting works issued by, or on behalf of, the Tauchnitz firm and then giving other sources of commentaries. Additional Tauchnitz reports not given here may be found in item Q, pp. A414–A415, and in *Bibliographie zur Geschichte der Stadt Leipzig* (Weimar: Verlag Hermann Böhlaus, 1967), p. 124.

Tauchnitz Reports

A. *Fünfzig Jahre der Verlagshandlung Bernhard Tauchnitz 1837 bis 1887.* Leipzig: Tauchnitz, 1887, 344 pp.
    Includes record of publication to date, with main British-American series listed in two arrangements. First order is alphabetical by author, with occasional excerpts from correspondence of writers then deceased (pp. 37–164); second order is chronological, extending through volume 2,439 (pp. 165–210). Thereafter cites other series and miscellaneous publications.

B. *Der Verlag Bernhard Tauchnitz 1837–1912.* Leipzig: Tauchnitz, 1912. 126 pp.
    Edited by Curt Otto, a partner in the firm. Reprints with some additions and deletions the correspondence previously cited in item A and now includes further excerpts from writers since deceased (pp. 52–126). No listing given, but in the prefatory account (p. 15) it is noted that 4,312 volumes were now printed in the main series, 3,901 by British and 411 by American authors.

C. *Complete Catalogue of the Tauchnitz Edition of British and American Authors.* Leipzig: Tauchnitz, 1926. 333 pp.
    Only known copy at the Bodleian Library (2596. f.7). Of numerous catalogues this is perhaps the most useful bibliographical record as it appears to be the last to list essentially all volumes to date in the main series, first alphabetically by author (pp. 7–168), then chronologically through 4,730 (pp. 169–254), both records with * for volumes "out of print at present." One volume, however, is listed irregularly: 2,856, R. L. Stevenson, *Island Nights' Entertainments* (1893), replacing with the same number the 1892 volume, suppressed, of his *A Footnote to History*; two others are unnumbered: Robert Buchanan, *God and the Man* (1882), 2 vols., withdrawn for reasons given in Dennis Welland, *Mark Twain in England* (London: Chatto & Windus, 1978), p. 207; and the entries for three more silently excluded, doubtless because these books were suppressed during World War I: 4,497, Baroness von Hutten, *Maria* (1914); 4,507, 4,509, Hugo Münsterberg, *The War and America* and *The Peace and America* (1915). See item M below for further information.

D. *The Harvest: Being the Record of One Hundred Years of Publishing 1837–1937.* Leipzig: Tauchnitz, 1937, 76 pp.
    Prepared by Brandstetter & Co., successors of the firm. With six illustrations, facsimiles of letters from nine significant authors, and reproductions of letters of congratulation from the British prime minister, the archbishop of York, and twenty other notables.

E. *Tauchnitz Edition Centenary Catalogue.* Leipzig: Tauchnitz, 1937. 173 pp.
    The companion record for item D, but known only by the copy at the University of Illinois (Wells: A820/T19t). Extends to date the record given in

item C, though the "Complete" lists here are only of volumes in print. Three such lists, alphabetical (pp. 11–78), chronological through volume 5,290 (pp. 79–120), title (pp. 121–136); and two "selected" lists, special subjects (pp. 137–155) and topical (pp. 156–166).

F. *Festschrift zum 125 jährigen Bestehen der Firma Bernhard Tauchnitz Verlag 1837–1962.* Stuttgart: Tauchnitz Verlag GmbH, 1962. 16 pp.
    Text by Werner Jäckh. Appears to indicate (p. 15) the pending issue of 70 volumes and reproduces under date 1962 the title for one (Conrad, *The Secret Agent*), but none of these was issued.

Commentaries on the Tauchnitz Edition

G. Tighe Hopkins. "'The Tauchnitz' Edition: The Story of a Popular Publisher," *The Pall Mall Magazine* 25 (October 1901): 197–208.
    With eight illustrations. Summary account with quotations from various authors.

H. Matilda Betham-Edwards. "A Visit to Baron Tauchnitz." In Betham-Edwards, *Mid-Victorian Memories*, pp. 84–91. London: Murray, 1919.
    Recounts visit to Schloss Kleinschocher in 1880, where she saw in her host's private library some 3,040 volumes then published by the firm. The director of the Deutsche Bücherei, Leipzig, on April 7, 1978, advised me that an extensive investigation has failed to disclose the present whereabouts of this collection.

I. Harry Carter. "The New Tauchnitz Format." *Signature: A Quadrimestrial of Typography and Graphic Arts* 2 (March 1936): 47–50.
    On innovations brought about by John Holroyd-Reece, the founder of the rival Albatross series, who in 1934 also took over the Tauchnitz publications.

J. Percy H. Muir. "The Tauchnitz *David Copperfield*, 1849." *The Book Collector* 4 (1955): 253–254.
    Notes that two of the three volumes preceded volume publication in England.

K. Percy H. Muir. "Dickens and Tauchnitz." *The Book Collector* 4 (1955): 329.
    Further notes that six novels by Dickens and three others by Thackeray were first issued by Tauchnitz in volume form.

L. Simon Nowell-Smith. "Continental: Mainly Tauchnitz." In Nowell-Smith, *International Copyright Law and the Publisher in the Reign of Queen Victoria*, pp. 41–63. Oxford: Clarendon Press, 1968.
    Slightly revised from an article in *The Book Collector* 15 (1966): 423–436. A useful account of typographical variants, the law as it affected Tauchnitz, and his arrangements with prospective authors.

M. Ben Hutchison. "Tauchnitz Edition" and other headings. In his journal *Book Collecting & Library Monthly* (later *Book Collecting*) (November 1969–May 1978): 17–67.
    Among other features a chronological listing of all volumes in the series. Number 5,356 "Not traced" by the compiler (Vincent Sheean, *A Day of*

Battle) and numbers 5,365–5,366 "Possibly not used" (and still unidentified) all probably were suppressed by the Nazi government. For earlier suppressions see item C above.

N. William B. Todd. "Footprints in Time." [London] *Times Literary Supplement*, January 7, 1977, p. 13.
Denies a report that King George V once cast into the fire a Tauchnitz copy of *Lady Chatterley's Lover*. The firm did not publish this book.

O. William B. Todd. "Firma Tauchnitz: A Further Investigation." *Publishing History* 2 (1977): 7–26.
Further extends the range of typographical points, as first noted in item L above, and surveys the international impact of Tauchnitz publications.

P. H. Neville Davies. "The Tauchnitz Extra Christmas Numbers of *All the Year Round*." *The Library* 5th series 33 (1978): 214–222.
Tauchnitz was given advance notice and thus identifies the contributors two years before the London issue.

Q. Karl H. Pressler. "Die Tauchnitz Edition: Anfang und Ende einer berühmten Reihe." *Aus dem Antiquariat* 11 (November 1978): A405–415.
Excellent summary of all available data, with a precise illustrated account of the dates when Tauchnitz altered his typography. Pressler has in preparation a further report.

4

Film Books

Daniel J. Leab

Fɪʟᴍ ɪs the idiom of our time. More than any other medium, the cinema has both shaped and reflected our society and culture, serving as a ready provider of everything from language and belief to fashion and etiquette. Millions of women bobbed their hair to emulate the screen vamps of the 1920s; in 1934 the undershirt industry suffered a recession after Clark Gable appeared with nothing but a bare chest under his shirt in *It Happened One Night;* and in the mid-1970s *Star Wars* infused all kinds of meaning into the phrase "may the force be with you" and the letter-number combinations R2D2 and C3P0. In our advertising-dominated age, the impact of film on our society has been magnified greatly. Although it is true that "going to the movies" is no longer an end in itself, it is also true that more people than ever before are seeing both old and new movies on TV, in schools and universities, and at movie houses and noncommercial theaters. Nor has the printed word remained free from cinematic influence. As Gore Vidal pointed out in reviewing "the top ten best sellers according to the Sunday *New York Times* as of January 7, 1973," for most of the authors of these books "storytelling began with *The Birth of a Nation,*" and reading these books was like "being trapped in the 'Late, Late Show' staggering from one half-remembered movie scene to another."[1]

Recognition of the film industry's impact on the attitude and behavior of society has caused an explosion of publisher interest in film-related material and has resulted in what one English critic has described as a "never-lessening flood of books."[2] Ever since commercial distribution of motion pictures began in Europe and the United States during the 1890s, a substantial body of printed material devoted to the movies has been produced, most of the material being generated by the various national film industries to sell their product. Everyone is familiar with the fan magazines, whose gushy prose and sophisticated innuendo entertained, informed, and enthralled past generations of moviegoers. Most of the older printed material generally available, although less well known to the movie-going public, was similar in style and content, ranging from ghostwritten and thoroughly laundered memoirs to press books issued by the studios for the purpose of publicizing individual films. On the shore overlooking this stream of pap were the industry-controlled though often candid trade journals, esoteric "little magazines" devoted to a perceptive if sometimes overly intellectual or politically left-leaning criticism and analysis, and "photoplay editions" of novels that were cheap editions illustrated with stills from the movie version of the book. Rising above them in the intellectual landscape were a few serious studies dealing with historical or theoretical problems.

Until recently, then, most published material about films was occasioned by the efforts of movie companies to exploit and promote their product and was ephemeral in nature. Studio-induced material of one sort or another was the norm, and not only in the United States. Until the 1960s the worldwide literature of cinema was small, and much of what might be termed the more serious work was written by relatively few people. In France, for example, the names Henri Agel, Pierre Leprohon, Jean Mitry, Leon Moussinac, and Georges Sadoul are attached to much of the work dealing with French and world cinema published before 1965. In England, Paul Rotha published the first edition of his history of world cinema, *The Film Till Now*, in 1930 (and there were several subsequent editions and reprintings). Among his other writings in the 1930s were *Documentary Films* (1939) and *Celluloid: The Film Today* (1931).

Perhaps the most ubiquitous writer was Roger Manvell, an industry unto himself who for awhile seemed to be writing or editing all the serious material available. Manvell was the main force behind *The Penguin Film Review* (1946–1949, reprinted 1978). Among other works, he edited *The Cinema 1950* and similar volumes for 1951 and 1952 (which continued *The Penguin Film Review*); *Experiment in the Film* (1949), a collection of essays about innovative cinema developments in various countries; and *Shots in the Dark* (1951), a collection of film reviewers' opinions between 1949 and 1951. He co-authored with Rachel Low *The History of the British Film 1896–1906* (1948), the first volume in an ongoing history continued by Low. In addition, he was the author of such works as *Film* (1944, revised and enlarged 1946, 2nd rev. ed. 1950) and *A Seat at the Cinema* (1951). He remains a prolific writer, still publishing in the 1970s. Among his more recent works was *Film and the Second World War* (1974).

Despite Manvell, however, well into the 1960s most American and English publishers virtually ignored film as a subject for books. The 1960 *Publishers Weekly* Spring and Fall announcement issues together contained fewer than ten titles that could be classified as film-related works. And the *Cumulative Book Index* as late as the 1963–1964 edition listed less than a page of film books.

Given the paucity of decent monographic literature when I began collecting in the mid-1950s, and given the fact that my collecting was undertaken as a means of gathering information, much of my energy and limited resources initially went into trying to put together runs of periodicals (which in later years through considerable effort and much luck it was possible in many instances to extend backward to Vol. 1, No. 1). Although I did manage to obtain a set of *Bianco e Nero* (the uneven Italian monthly that began publication in 1937), I concentrated on English-language periodicals whose runs I then began to piece together bit by bit.

Among these periodicals were the *Monthly Film Bulletin* (a British Film Institute publication that began in 1934 as a brief series of commentaries on current educational and entertainment films and has evolved into a publication presenting idiosyncratic and comprehensive reviews of all films released in the United Kingdom); *Sight and Sound* (another British Film Institute magazine that began publication in 1932 and that for years was the only ongoing and serious—as opposed to esoteric or fan-oriented—periodical available in English); *World Film News* and its successor *Documentary News Letter* (which between 1937 and 1948 represented the point of view of the more politically oriented, mainly English, documentary filmmakers but which touched on all aspects of film); and *Close Up* (which was published from 1927 to 1933 and which represents a more esoteric approach to film—its editors were concerned with the film as an art although the periodical also contained some fascinating political commentary).

Aside from the fan magazines such as *Photoplay, Modern Screen,* and *Screen Romances,* there were few American periodicals that dealt solely with film. And most of these were short-lived, as evidenced by the four-issue run of *Film,* which was an attempt in 1939–1940 to emulate the more serious English journals, or by the publishing history of *Experimental Cinema*, an intellectually flashy effort that managed five issues over the four-year period from 1930 to 1934. I concentrated on the trade journals such as the *Motion Picture Herald* (1931–1972) and the *Moving Picture World;* laboriously acquiring copies, I managed to piece together a year here and there. The results, although better than meager, were far from satisfactory, and the almost complete run I now possess of the *Herald* and its companion the *Motion Picture Daily News* is the result of a single purchase in the early 1970s from someone who had heard that I was interested in expanding my collection of trade journals. The value of making yourself known as a collector cannot be overestimated. Finally, after years of hunting hither and yon on my part, somebody got in touch with me with an offer I could not refuse. The terms were difficult; he wanted to sell the whole run "all or nothing" and he refused to bargain over the price. Because we were meeting at John F. Kennedy Airport in New York between his flights, my decision had to be almost instantaneous. I acceded to his demands because such opportunities are rare and the building up of a run of periodicals is an arduous task, sometimes even an impossible one.

It was fortunate for me that I began collecting in the mid-1950s— during that decade and just prior to it a number of still-extant periodicals began publication, and my runs began with their first issues—or shortly thereafter when it was still easy to get back numbers. These periodicals include the Austrian *Filmkunst* (1949), a good combination of reviews and articles dealing with film past and present in Austria and elsewhere; *Cahiers du Cinema* (1951), one of the most vital and influential film magazines ever published, many of whose writers such as Jean Luc Goddard and François Truffaut became well-known filmmakers; *Jeune Cinema* (1957), a much less esoteric, French monthly; the *Continental Film Review* (1952), a British monthly self-advertised as an "illustrated magazine devoted to other than English and American films" that published sound articles but devoted much of its space to scantily clad couples or women in provocative poses; *Films and Filming* (1954), an English monthly all too often hyping the latest big-budget production but also offering cogent articles on past and present films as well as multi-issue historical surveys by such writers as Raymond Durgnat, who later proved themselves as first-rank cinema scholars; *Filmkritik* (1957), an eclectic West German monthly that at one time contained superbly informed reviews but that since the mid-1960s has undergone several permutations that have resulted in its approach becoming somewhat eccentric.

American nonfan film periodicals also proliferated in the 1950s. Among these periodicals are *Film Culture* (1955), an oddball mixture of sensitive insights and unfortunate polemicizing that gave writers such as Andrew Sarris their first chance; *Film Quarterly* (1958), an arcane but interesting American attempt at serious film criticism that began publication as successor to the *Quarterly of Film, Radio and Television,* which had suspended publication in 1952 and which itself had begun as *Hollywood Quarterly* in 1945; *Films in Review* (1950), an eccentric monthly with splendidly researched if often banal career articles as well as frequently waspish reviews; *Filmfacts* (1958), a monthly compendium of reviews of various films, with some additional information, which after sporadic interruptions in publication finally ceased in 1979.

This proliferation of film periodicals can be described as a preview of coming attractions as far as books were concerned. In the middle and late 1960s as publishers learned about this increase in film periodicals and discovered an eager nostalgia-oriented market for books on all aspects of film, they spewed forth one movie book after another—most of them undistinguished and "written without fear or research" to borrow a phrase from historian Charles Beard. This flood of film books, many of which found a deserved resting place on bookshop tables containing the cheapest-priced remainders, includes ghostwritten memoirs of cult personalities, which tended to emphasize sin rather than cinema, compilations that relied heavily on the clipping files of libraries such as the excellent performing arts research collections of the New York Public Library, dull and repetitive picture books seemingly spawned for the purpose of being endlessly discounted, and a stream of indifferent books based on ill-conceived interviews with minor figures about insignificant films. Despite the massive increase in film-related material being published, the number of worthwhile books available remained small. The well-respected film historian William Everson after surveying the film-book field in 1978 found it "incredible that there should be more than half-a-dozen books apiece on . . . John Wayne . . . and Boris Karloff, certainly two or more on . . . Liza Minelli . . . and Clint Eastwood, yet not one . . . to date on Clarence Brown, James Whale, Herbert Brenon, or William Dieterle, all of them directors of major interest and importance, whose careers spanned many years and often more than one country."[3]

This boom in film books is part of the unprecedented and still growing expansion of interest in the visual media everywhere in the world. When lecturing on film, I have found equal enthusiasm in Budapest, Cologne, and South Orange, New Jersey. The expansion of interest is splendid for the subject, but there has been an unfortunate side effect for collectors of movie material. Two decades ago the relatively few people who were interested in collecting books, periodicals, manuscripts, ephemera, or any other kind of material related to films found little private competition and almost no institutional competition. Two decades ago it was possible to browse along New York City's once fabled "Book Row," which then lined lower Fourth Avenue below Fourteenth Street, and find both new and secondhand books, periodicals, and ephemera at prices that were reasonable indeed. In those days philistine tax authorities and rapacious landlords had not yet dispersed the city's antiquarian booksellers or turned the survivors into dealers by catalogue. One could still wander easily from store to store and find all kinds of film-related material—and there were bargains galore.

Cinema was not then a trendy subject, and many times one found film books shelved with other subjects and priced accordingly. It was relatively easy to find and purchase first editions of such essential works as Terry Ramsaye's *A Million and One Nights* (a 1926 two-volume work, reprinted in 1964, which has served as a "spine" for many of the histories of the early American film industry); Benjamin Hampton's *History of the Movies* (a 1931 personal view by a one-time film industry executive, reprinted in 1970 as *History of the American Film Industry*); and Gordon Hendricks, *The Edison Motion Picture Myth* (an argumentative but thoroughly researched 1961 book—part of a trio of works, reprinted in 1971, dedicated to deemphasizing Thomas Edison's contribution to the development of movie technology).

Today such traditionally collected works are less easy to come by and, alas, much more expensive. Today one finds such institutions as Indiana University and the Wisconsin Center for Theatre Research (a cooperative venture of the University of Wisconsin and the State Historical Society of Wisconsin) building up extensive, intelligently organized research collections devoted to the cinema. Today there are dealers specializing in film, and their prices are special. When I began collecting 25 years ago, few dealers anywhere in the world specialized in movie material of any kind; today New York City alone has at least four shops whose sizable stock is devoted just to movie material and that sell both new and antiquarian film books, periodicals, and ephemera. Moreover, several shops that carry a more general antiquarian stock (and that once spurned or at best slighted film) now either have expanded or instituted film-book sections.

Although increased interest in film has meant higher prices and a market in which the unwary may well meet the unscrupulous, collecting film material remains feasible for a person of modest means. It is still a field in which knowledge and diligence will yield bargains. Excepting runs of periodicals, in a quarter-century of zealous collecting of movie material I have never paid over $100 for an individual item. And even in these expensive and inflationary times my purchases average no more than $50 a book. The most expensive book in my collection did not cost over $750. It was a limited edition of the Ramsaye with a title page filled with inscriptions by such personages as Mary Pickford, Adolph Zukor, and D. W. Griffith. This book was a birthday present from my wife, who (like me in my quest for film periodicals) took the advice of another noted film buff, John Carter: ". . . be less afraid of paying a stiff price than of letting slip some book . . . which is important to you. You cannot tell when, at what price, or even whether, you will see another."[4]

The private collector of film books and movie material is stepping along a relatively untrod path. Although institutional interest and competition has increased, there is still ample opportunity for the private collector provided that he or she carefully chooses some part of this new path in collecting and follows it both assiduously and intelligently.

Film is a very complex and in recent years much written about subject. To try nowadays to collect books and material on all aspects of this worldwide medium, especially given the recent film-book publishing boom, is trying to encompass too much of a major part of twentieth-century culture on one's own shelves. There is a need for specialization on the part of those now beginning as collectors in this field. Admittedly, as John Carter pointed out nearly a half-century ago, "specialization is an odious word, and the necessity for it in any serious collection can be qualified in many directions."[5] This specialization can take various broadly based forms. For example, a collection can deal with a subject historically, thematically, or topically. Thus it can be built around books and other material dealing with American or German cinema or parts of it (to cite just two national film industries that have been major influences on world cinema), around various directors, stars, and producers, around a specific genre such as the western or blacks in movies, or around the constantly changing technology involved in producing movies over the years. The beauty of collecting books about film is that no approach is exclusive and that any is valid provided that it has some intellectual coherence.

A springboard for an initial plunge into collecting film material could be, for example, the coming of sound to American movies in the 1920s. This fascinating and diverse subject could be very appealing, for as J. Douglas Gomery—perhaps the most thorough and perceptive recent historian of this crucial innovation—has pointed out: "the coming of sound . . . severely altered methods of film production, distribution, and exhibition, not only in the United States, but throughout the world."[6]

Any collection built around such a subject would involve contemporary material such as Fitzhugh Green's often used but rarely cited 1929 narrative, *The Film Finds Its Tongue*, and Lewis Jacobs's seminal history, *The Rise of American Film* (1939, reprinted 1968). More recent works would include the uneven and thin *The Birth of the Talkies*, a 1975 rehash by Harry Geduld, and *The Shattered Silents: How the Talkies Came to Stay*, an interesting 1978 discussion by Alexander Walker. A work perhaps overemphasizing the Warner Brothers's contribution is *Okay for Sound* (1946) by Frederick Thrasher. Interesting sidelights would be provided by the splendidly illustrated and intelligently written studies of movie theater architecture and ambiance by Ben Hall (*The Best Remaining Seats*, 1961) and Denis Sharp (*The Picture Palace*, 1969). Nor could the economic and technological aspects of the end of the silent movie be neglected, and keystone works to acquire would be Stuart Legg and F. O. Klingender, *Money behind the Screen* (1937) and Ray Fielding, *A Technological History of Motion Pictures and Television* (1967). The memoirs and biographies of personalities involved would range widely and include such otherwise dissimilar types as Joseph P. Kennedy (whose business interests in the late 1920s included the movies), John Gilbert (among the best known and perhaps the most tragic of the stars whose careers foundered with the coming of sound), and Jack Warner (one of the brothers whose studio was actively involved in the introduction of sound to the movies—it was in a Warner Brothers film, *The Jazz Singer*, in 1927 that songs burst forth from the screen and that Al Jolson spoke those few but prophetic words "You ain't heard nothing yet").

These titles will give the new collector a start, a small idea of the body of literature dealing with a turning point in the history of the American film industry. Some of these books will not be easy to find, but all should be reasonably priced. What the novice collector then decides to do will depend on his or her intelligence, diligence, point of view, and pocketbook. Different collectors will have different perspectives, but each will have ideas on how to proceed. Although the coming of sound to American film is but one aspect of collecting material about movies, it is a hop and a skip along the new path that awaits the interested collector.

Obviously there are other approaches to American film history that can be taken as well, and the reasons for use of these approaches vary. My own amble along the collecting path in this area was deter-mined in part by my scholarly interests. I assembled a collection of books and other material on the stereotyping of blacks in American movies since the 1890s as the result of writing a book on that subject.[7] The first steps in assembling the collection were easy: to accumulate as much as possible of the massive jumble of recent literature on the black mo-tion picture experience.[8] Before 1971 only one book (Peter Noble, *The Negro in Films*, c. 1947, reprinted 1971), one long pamphlet (V. J. Jerome, *The Negro in Hollywood Films*, 1950), and some articles (including a special issue of *Close Up*, August 1929) had been devoted to the subject. But in the three-year period from 1972 to 1974 alone, a variety of books were published on the subject including Donald Bogle, *Toms, Coons, Mulattoes, Mammies, and Bucks* (1973); Eileen Landry, *Black Film Stars* (1973); Edward Mapp, *Blacks in American Films: Today and Yesterday* (1972); Richard Maynard, *The Black Man on Film: Racial Stereotyping* (1974); James Murray, *To Find an Image* (1973); Gary Null, *Black Hollywood: The Negro in Motion Pictures* (1974). Most of these books were slick, superficial, and perfect examples of William Everson's charge that the proliferation of film books "resulted in a great deal of mediocrity."[9]

In addition to pulling together books by and about such stellar black performers as Harry Belafonte, Dorothy Dandridge, Lena Horne, Sidney Poitier, Paul Robeson, and Bert Williams, I also amassed works that may seem peripheral but that indicate how wide a net a collector can and should cast: Natalie Barkas, *Behind the Camera* (1934) and *30,000 Miles for the Films* (1937) are both fine examples of the "white man's burden" kind of thinking that permeated most British (and American) filmmaking about Africa; *Biograph Bulletins 1896–1908* (1971) and *Bio-graph Bulletins 1908–1912* (1973) both give an indication of the treat-ment blacks in silent films received; Ralph Ellison, *Shadow and Act* (1954) contains a splendid essay by the gifted Negro novelist about the films produced by Hollywood between 1948 and 1951 dealing with racial themes; Lillian Gish, with Anne Pinchot, *The Movies, Mr. Griffith, and Me* (1969) contains yet another apologia for D. W. Griffith, the man responsible for the blatantly racist *The Birth of a Nation*; *Playboy's Sex in Cinema* (1970–) are heavily illustrated paperbacks which highlight the rise of interracial sex in the cinema of the early 1970s; Jeffrey Richards, *Vision of Yesterday* (1973) is a wildly uneven book that, drawing on film-makers' responses to British imperialism, makes some very perceptive comments about the "imperial cinema" and its treatment of nonwhites. This list could go on and on and on. But this essay is meant to be a guide for collectors, not a bibliography for scholars.[10]

Collectors should also cast their nets widely to pull in non-book material such as articles in magazines, which in this instance are to be found in such dissimilar periodicals as *Collier's*, *Political Science Quarterly*, and the *Journal of Negro Education*. This subject also spawned article material in the early 1970s, much of it derivative and worse than useless. But for every ton of dross there was a glistening ounce of gold, an instance being the articles by historian Thomas Cripps, a careful and thoughtful scholar who later produced an excellent book, *Slow Fade to Black: The Negro in American Films 1900-1942* (1977). In addition to searching out the articles, I made some effort to obtain unpublished material such as shooting scripts of various films and copies of typescripts such as papers by various scholars on deposit at the Schomberg Collection of the New York Public Library. The research by these scholars had been incorporated into Gunnar Myrdal's *An American Dilemma* (1944), a massive and unparalleled study of the racial situation in the United States to that time. Unpublished material also included Ph.D. dissertations such as the one by William Lee Burke on "The Presentation of the American Negro in Hollywood Films, 1946–61" (1966).

Burke's analysis, like many other such dissertations that had been written earlier or were to be finished later, was a valuable work that had failed to find a publisher. Thanks to University Microfilms it has been possible for an individual to obtain "facsimile" copies of all dissertations, such as the one by Burke, deposited with the company, and most universities now participate in the deposit program. Alas, that was not always so. And there are some other drawbacks as well—the copies provided are "perfect bound" and, as the company notes in its statement of "information to users," there is always the possibility that "some pages may have indistinct print."

Still the availability of the dissertation is a great boon, even in those instances when a version of the dissertation becomes a published monograph. Given the stringent cost controls recently implemented by all publishers, it was and is unlikely that a long dissertation would be published uncut. And sometimes trimming does more than just cut fat; it also cuts sinew and bone, as in the case of James Monaco's detailed 1974 study of cinema and society in France and Germany between 1919 and 1929. Published commercially in 1976, *Cinema and Society: France and Germany during the Twenties* was about one-third of its length as a dissertation, and it suffered accordingly. Some of the documentation was cut, as was most of the detailed analysis of the films.

A significant number of dissertations (and some M.A. essays) have also become available in hardback, Smyth-sewn copies; for one happy effect of the film-book publishing boom was the establishment of an

Arno Press Series, ably edited by social historian Garth Jowett, of past and present dissertations that for a variety of reasons—lack of scholarship not being one of them—had failed to achieve publication through more traditional means. Arno's reproduction of the typescript of the dissertations made available in a more permanent fashion scholarly work that was not considered commercial, such as Timothy Lyons's first-rate 1974 history of the American Film Manufacturing Company from 1910 to 1921, or work that had been finished before the film-book boom began, such as John Rimberg's fascinating 1959 sociological analysis of movies in the Soviet Union between 1918 and 1952.

Totalitarian states such as the Soviet Union and Nazi Germany are very conscious of the impact of film, and they pay close attention to what films are produced and shown. Lenin, for example, shortly after the Bolsheviks seized power in Russia, had declared that "for us the cinema is the most important of all the arts."[11] The subject of film in a totalitarian state intrigued me at one time. A command of German resulted in my concentrating on Nazi Germany—about whose film industry a great deal has been written, both during and after the Hitler era.

A collector may find the contemporary literature fascinating; I know I did, and I was also surprised that it was not so hateful as one might expect. Perhaps the most blatant Nazi analysis is Carl Neumann, Curt Belling, and Hans Walther Betz, *Film-Kunst, "Film-Kohn," Film-Korruption* (1937), which is a strong attack on the supposed pre-Nazi domination of the German film industry by Jewish and/or Communist filmmakers. There are also strains of virulence in a number of the more serious works dealing with the film industry, for example, Fritz Hippler's *Betrachtungen zur Filmschaffen* (1942), as might be expected in any book of reflections on filmmaking authored by an important Nazi official in the film industry. More usual, however, was a quiet distortion such as is found in the Nazi-era histories of German film by Oskar Kalbus (*Vom Werden Deutscher Film Kunst*, 2 vols., 1935) or world film by Rudolf Oertel (*Filmspiegel: Ein Brevier aus der Welt des Films*, 1941). The twenty-fifth anniversary of the giant German film concern UFA (Universum Film Aktiengesellschaft) also resulted in the reshuffling of some facts in the histories by Hans Traub (1943) and Otto Kriegk (1943). When one looks at the run-of-the-mill literature about the movies published during the Nazi period it is remarkable how, apart from a cursory bow to the state's racial policies or a nod to Der Fuehrer, the literature seems ordinary—and how little it reflects the true situation in Germany. Leni Riefenstahl, *Schoenheit in Olympischen Kampf* (1937) is essentially a coffee-table book about the 1936 Olympics held in Berlin, with some mention of the film Riefenstahl made; J. Gregor, *Meister Deutscher Schauspielkunst* (1939), despite its high-flown language about masterful German actors, is a fan-oriented book; and the same holds true for H. E. Weinschenk, *Wir von Buehne und Film* (1939), which deals with both stage and screen personalities.

The books published since 1945 on the Nazi film industry tend not to be monolithic in their approach. Siegfried Kracauer's *From Caligari to Hitler: A Psychological History of the German Cinema* (1947) transcends the subject, being among the first and most controversial of the content-analysis works (and a prize for any collector of film books). Kracauer saw the cinema of Weimar Germany as leading in only one direction— that of the Nazi takeover. His book has had an enormous influence on writing about the Nazi cinema—to the extent that other works, such as Gerd Albrecht, *Nationalsozialistische Filmpolitik* (1969), found it necessary to use Kracauer as a reference point for attack or contradiction. Almost all of these works are anti-Nazi, but some, such as Curt Reiss, *Das Gab's Nur Einmal* (1956), are nostalgic for the films; some, such as David Stewart Hull, *Film in the Third Reich* (1969) and Pierre Cadar and François Courtade, *Le Cinéma Nazi* (1972), are straightforward history; some deal in depth with one aspect of the Nazi cinema as does Wolfgang Becker, *Film und Herrschaft* (1973), which analyzes the Nazi organizational structure within the film industry, or as does Jürgen Spiker, *Film und Kapital* (1974), which investigates the financing of German films between 1933 and 1945. There are also first-rate examinations of the anti-Semitic policies of the Nazis on screen (Dorothy Hollstein, *Antisemitische Filmpropaganda: Die Darstellung des Juden in Nationalsozialistischen Spielfilm*, 1971) and in the industry (Joseph Wulf, *Theater und Film in Dritten Reich: Eine Dokumentation*, 1964). All the works I have listed are but the tip of the iceberg, as any collector who wishes to explore the subject would soon find out. There is still plenty of room on this path.

The internationalization of collecting has made it easier to find such books, but when I began my scholarly work on the Nazi film industry, American research libraries contained few of these books and relatively little useful material on German filmmaking at any point in time. I therefore undertook a quest for material in Europe, a quest that resulted in a significant expansion of my collection and that illustrates a role that dealers play in assisting collectors.

While in Zurich I visited Hans Rohr Buchhandlung and chatted with Hans Peter Manz, who oversaw and built up the shop's stock of cinema materials. I told him about my difficulties in finding source material on the Nazi film industry, and he responded by telling me about a small collection of books and other material on the subject that was available for purchase. The collection had been offered to Manz, but it did not seem a good investment for the store. I got in touch with the man who had offered the collection and found that he was acting as an agent for somebody else. More importantly, in addition to the Nazi film material he himself had non-German material for sale, and he could offer me duplicates from a German library that covered all aspects of world cinema. After some involved negotiations, complete with three-language party-line conversations across the Atlantic and a trip to Germany to crawl through some sub-basements to check out the material, agreement was reached. Shortly thereafter I went one rainy night to Kennedy Airport to sign for a small container of books, magazines, and ephemera. Manz's referral is an indication of how important it is for a collector to establish good rapport with dealers. They will pass on to a favored customer otherwise unobtainable information, such as news about collections for sale, especially if they themselves cannot take advantage of the situation.

In the quest for books and other materials, no bookstore can or should be ignored. I discovered Rohr by accident some years ago while walking aimlessly in Zurich. A window display that had nothing to do with film caught my eye and I went in to look over the stock. In 1963 Manz's operation occupied but a corner of the store. Since then it has expanded to a separate shop that also has display space for antiquarian material. Luck certainly played a role in my finding of Rohr, and luck also played a role in my becoming acquainted with an English dealer who now advertises—and without too much exaggeration—"Europe's Largest Collection of New, Rare, and Out-of-Print Film Books, Magazines, Stills, Posters, Pamphlets, Programmes, Lobby Cards, and Ephemera." Yet when my wife and I literally ran into Fred Zentner while going for a walk in London in 1967, his place of business was nothing more than some rows of shelves in the basement of a seedy bookshop specializing in the occult and the mysterious. Even then Zentner ("escaping," as he put it, from "the rag trade," or garment industry) had some interesting titles for sale. As he moved above ground and as The Cinema Bookshop moved to larger if not grander locations I continued to browse his shelves and to find the effort extremely rewarding. Equally important, he often succeeded in finding good copies of the books on my want lists.

Obviously, not every visit to a bookshop leads to an ongoing relationship with a dealer, but it does pay to browse wherever and whenever one can, and not just in bookshops specializing in cinema. Any bookshop anywhere may yield happy surprises. During the early 1960s while on a visit to Copenhagen I visited a shop whose name I have now forgotten. But I still remember with glee my purchase of a complete run of the rare *World Film News*, and no matter where my tourist or scholarly activities have taken me, and the points are as disparate as Dallas and Moscow, I have never missed a chance to stop in a bookshop and browse. If there is one rule that should guide any collector, it is this: never pass a bookstore without looking in to see what is on the shelves. Browsing is serendipitous, rewarding, and wonderful. Because the literature of film is international in its scope, it is also important to organize access to that literature in more than one country. For an ongoing if limited list of specialized film-book dealers all over the world, see the annual issues of the *International Film Guide*, edited by Peter Cowie. The *Guide*, begun in 1964, each year surveys world movie production and in addition provides detailed listings of interest to collectors such as the names of dealers and information about film magazines currently being published.

There is a need to be at least aware of dealers in several countries, especially as a particular edition of a book may be distributed in only one country. Take, for example, what has happened to Lotte Eisner's pioneering study of expressionism in the German cinema of the 1920s. This study was first published as *L'Ecran Demoniaque* in Paris in 1952. Three years later an enlarged and revised edition, *Dämonische Leinwand*, was published in West Germany. In 1965 another edition with further revisions was published in France. This one served as the basis for the English-language edition, *The Haunted Screen*, which was published in England and the United States in 1969 with some appendices added. In 1975, 20 years after the first German edition, another and again somewhat different German edition was published. It would have been impossible to assemble all of these variants under my roof had I not been able to get in touch with dealers in several countries.

To the best of my knowledge, collecting film books and movie material is a field in which happily there is a paucity of what John Carter termed "issue mongers." But the multiplicity of Eisner editions and issues, while unusual, is not unique and does indicate the need for the serious collector to have some bibliographical help, to have what Carter refers to as "a systematic description of books according to subject, class, period, author, country or district. . . ."[12] Among the works I have found most useful are the bibliographical notes to G. P. Straschek, *Handbuch wider das Kino* (1975); the catalogue of the British

Film Institute book library, printed in three oversize volumes; and the two volumes of the *Internationale Film Bibliographie*, edited by Hans Peter Manz and covering the years 1952–1964. (Complete bibliographic information for these and other books is given in the Further Reading list at the end of the chapter.)

The increasing interest in all aspects of the movies, to which I referred at the beginning of this chapter, has meant not only a proliferation of new film books but also the reprinting of many older titles and of runs of periodicals. There has also been extensive microform publishing of such material. We should all be grateful to the Arno Press for reprinting the five-issue run of *Experimental Cinema* and the ten volumes of *Close Up*. But the reprints suffer by comparison with the original. The bold layout of the former and the striking and unique illustrations of the latter in the original become somewhat murky and ill-defined in the reprints, in much the same fashion that the wonderfully photographed, marvelously composed films of the 1930s suffer from the reception available on most TV sets. We are fortunate to have a trade journal such as the *Motion Picture Herald* available in microform, but think of the multihued ballyhoo advertising new movies in these trade journals reduced to black and white on a microform viewer—something is lost. It seems to me that for the collector only the original will do.

To this point I have discussed well-marked sections of a new path in collecting. Let me now turn to areas where it seems to me relatively few have taken steps along the path. American film is a subject that would hardly seem to qualify under that rubric. Yet during the past 15 years or so there has been an enormous proliferation in the literature on the nature and history of American film. As one historian has pointed out, "major new books now appear once a month, rather than . . . once a decade as in the twenties and thirties."[13] For the collector this situation is both exciting and dangerous—exciting because the choice is invitingly broad; dangerous because of the need to choose between the potentially worthwhile and the useless. One writer turns out (admittedly with the help of an acknowledged research team) more than a book a year. The value of such a book to the collector or the scholar is minimal. A generation ago a beginning collector could try to amass as much of the published material as he or she could lay hands on, and this was not an unrealistic goal. Given the rapid growth in the volume of published material in recent times, as well as the ever-increasing cost of this material, today's collector must of necessity make careful choices.

The following list of titles on the history of American film includes only books published during the last 15 years; a number of items are already out of print in hardback. This listing, which easily could be expanded, is arranged according to a roughly chronological history of American films: R. Sklar, *Movie-Made America* (1975); G. Jowett, *Film: The Democratic Art* (1976); G. Hendricks, *Origins of American Film* (a 1971 reprint in one volume of three difficult to find out-of-print books); K. Niver, *The First Twenty Years: A Segment of Film History* (1968); A. Slide, *The Big V: A History of the Vitagraph Company* (1976); G. Pratt, *Spellbound in Darkness: A History of the Silent Film* (1966); W. Kerr, *The Silent Clowns* (1975); J. Spears, *Hollywood: The Golden Era* (1971); K. Brownlow, *The Parades Gone By* (1968); R. W. Henderson, *D. W. Griffith* (1972); K. Brown, *Adventures with D. W. Griffith* (1973); A. Sarris, *The American Cinema: 1929–1968* (1968, paperback); S. M. Kaminsky, *American Film Genres* (1974); S. Solomon, *Beyond Formula* (1976); J. Tuska, *The Filming of the West* (1976); C. McArthur, *Underworld USA* (1972); F. Capra, *The Name above the Title* (1971); P. French, *The Movie Moguls* (1971); B. Deming, *Running away from Myself* (1969); J. G. Dunne, *The Studio* (1969); L. Alloway, *Violent America: The Movies 1946–64* (1972). Not to be overlooked are the two volumes of the *American Film Institute Catalog of Motion Pictures: Feature Films, 1921–30* and *Feature Films, 1961–70* (published in 1971 and 1976 respectively).

A more difficult new path to follow, but one with the same destination, is to assemble a collection of books that view Hollywood through foreign eyes. The movies do come from America, and over the years the American film industry has been the subject of much foreign comment, as is indicated by the following list, which is drawn just from the literature published between the two world wars and which is but a sample of that literature: A. Ferro, *Hollywood, Capital des Imagens* (Lisbon, 1922); R. Florey, *Filmland: Los Angeles et Hollywood, les capitales du cinéma* (Paris, 1923); K. Organesov, *Amerikanskie Kino-atel's* (Moscow, 1926); A. Fraccaroli, *Hollywood paese l'aventura* (Milan, 1928); E. Debries, *Hollywood wie es wirklich ist* (Zurich, 1930); A. Hubert, *Hollywood: Legende und Wirklichkeit* (Leipzig, 1931); J. F. Otten, *Amerikaansche filmkunst* (Stockholm, 1935); E. H. Rideout, *The American Film* (London, c. 1937). There are many more such books not only for these years but for the period before World War I and the years since World War II.

Yet another new path is one that would be more theoretically oriented. The aesthetics of the cinema has preoccupied filmmakers and film viewers ever since motion pictures were seen only in peep shows. A fascinating if expensive collection could be built on the works (or even the English-language translations thereof) of the theorists and of their critics. Again I am listing relatively few works in an area where many books and articles are to be found. Good general overviews that can serve as guides are A. Tudor, *Theories of Film* (1974) and J. D. Andrew, *Major Film Theories* (1976). Hugo Munsterberg, a German–American professor at Harvard University, was among the first serious film theorists in the United States. The collector should have *The Photoplay: A Psychological Study* (1916) by Munsterberg, which was reprinted in 1970 as *The Film: A Psychological Study*. Gestalt psychology played a role in the theories set forth by Rudolph Arnheim, a German art critic who thanks to the Nazis became a faculty member at Sarah Lawrence College. Arnheim's seminal work *Film* appeared in English translation in 1933. The Soviet film director Sergei Eisenstein had strong ideas about the validity and utility of film, and his ideas are spelled out in books such as *Film Form: Essays in Film Theory* (1949). Andre Bazin, the vigorous French critic, was a progenitor of the auteur theory, which has pervaded much of the director-oriented American film criticism; his ideas (somewhat poorly translated) are summed up in two volumes entitled *What Is Cinema?* (1967, 1971). Another Frenchman, Christian Metz, is the prime exponent of applying the techniques of structural linguistics to movies, and in books like *Film Language: A Semiotics for the Cinema* (1974) he argues that the movies have a language all their own. There are, of course, any number of other theorists who easily could be added to the above sample.

The cinema of the Third World is yet another byway that may prove an exciting one for collectors. The dramatic cultural and social changes taking place in the world today highlight the effectiveness of making such a collection. The following again is but an introductory selection: F. Amado and A. Echeverria, *El cine en Mexico* (1960); E. Garcia Riera, *Historia documental del cine mexicano* (1969–); R. Andrade et al., *Il Cinema Brasiliano* (1961); A. Campos Periera, Jr., *Cinema Brasiliero: 25 anos* (1971); M. Hairabedian, *Les Films egyptiens et ceux de Hollywood* (1950); M. R. Bataille and C. Veillot, *Cameras sous le soleil: le cinéma en Afique du Nord* (1956); J. M. Landau, *Studies in the Arab Theater and Cinema* (1958); W. Holmes, *Orient: A Survey of Films Produced in Countries of Arab and Asian Culture* (1959); G. Sadoul, *The Cinema in the Arab Countries* (1966); *Film in Aufbruch: Eine Dokumentation ueber Filmentwicklungen in Afrika und Südamerika* (1966); E. Barnouw and S. Krishnaswamy, *Indian Film* (1963); R. D. Jain, *Economic Aspects of the Film Industry in India* (1960); P. Shah, *The Indian Film* (1950); J. I. Anderson and D. Richie, *The Japanese Film* (1959); J. Mellen, *Voices from the Japanese Cinema* (1975); J. Leyda, *Dianying: Electronic Shadows* (1972); R. Daudelin, *Vingt ans de cinéma au Canada François* (1967).

Some readers may well find the preceding paragraphs too detailed or too constricting, wishing instead to find only the vaguest signposts placed on the new path. For them, and for those readers who are not interested in the subjects I have suggested above, perhaps one of the following would be rewarding: pre-cinema; published and unpublished screenplays as well as the literary properties on which the screenplays draw; novels in English and other languages that deal with American movies; the treatment of sex; political and moral censorship. Each has potential because of past, present, and prospective writings. There is a growing body of literature in each of these areas, as there is now on almost every aspect of film. In the final analysis, whatever part of the path the collector chooses to follow, the important thing is a firm and comfortable footing and a safe arrival at the final destination.

A few general comments about my collection and collecting habits are in order here. I began to buy film books and other movie material during my college days in the mid-1950s. I bought then and later (indeed until relatively recently) with no thought of building a systematic collection and I had no overall scheme of organization. My purchases were undertaken for purely pragmatic reasons. First, while still an undergraduate, I bought books and periodicals in order to produce program notes for film series I had organized. Later as I began writing about various aspects of cinema, my primary concern became the putting together of a working library that would assist my research.

Until about six years ago, I ignored the traditional conventions that marked collecting. I ignored what a late-nineteenth-century English writer has dubbed "the craze for first editions."[14] Instead I opted to obtain the latest corrected editions that would incorporate an author's latest thoughts and research. I must note here that my scholarly work did not deal with theory, where, of course, the first edition is important, even vital, for comparison with later editions and for an understanding of the writer's intellectual development. Association and signed copies held no particular interest for me. I did not spurn such books but neither did I seek them out. Whether a book had its original dust jacket, whether that dust jacket was frayed, torn, or taped mattered not a whit. In general, condition only mattered to me insofar as determining that a book was usable.

In the 1970s I did begin to make some concessions to the more traditional techniques of collecting. As I became known in the film-study field through my writings and lectures, I came into contact with people hitherto known to me only through *their* writings and lectures, and I asked these men and women to inscribe copies of their books and articles in my possession. Scholars who used my collection also provided inscribed first printings of the resulting books. And I began to seek out first printings of certain of the older classics such as Frederick A. Talbot, *Moving Pictures: How They Are Made and Worked* (1912), and Henry V. Hopwood, *Living Pictures* (1899), even if I had a copy of a later edition or a reprint.

Over the years I bought material from individuals, dealers, and institutions; and, except for an occasional trade for something more desirable, I neither sold nor gave away any item that came into my possession. *In fine,* over a quarter of a century of collecting I put together a working research library for myself and in the process of so doing built what proved to be a valuable and unique collection—one that other scholars have used because it contained books, periodicals, and other material that were not readily available elsewhere.

Recently, however, I sold the collection to the Australian National Library. The thought of any kind of financial return on my expenditures for film books and other movie material never occurred to me over the years. But the burgeoning of my collection, to the point where it was even larger than most American institutional holdings in this area, brought with it serious problems, mostly centering around costs of maintaining and adding to it. Just before I sold the collection I was subscribing to or buying regularly more than 20 periodicals, all of which I was having bound in cloth at the end of each year—and the price of subscriptions and binding had risen to dizzying heights. Furthermore, many film books and related material have been printed on low-quality paper —this is especially true of the French books published in the 1940s and 1950s. It was not in my power to provide optimum storage conditions such as proper humidification. Access for others was difficult—a home cannot readily serve as a public library. Although the collection was shelved roughly according to the Dewey system and I thus knew where everything was, I just did not have the time or the funds to catalogue the collection properly. Insurance, moreover, was becoming prohibitively expensive.

The solution to these problems came from an unexpected quarter as a direct but oblique result of being invited in 1977 while a Fulbright senior lecturer in West Germany to participate as a speaker at the scholarly conference that accompanies the annual business meeting of the Federation of International Film Archives. The site that year was Varna, Bulgaria, and while there I met an Australian whose duties included scouting for collections that might be of interest to the Australian National Library. Mine proved to be such a collection.

Why did I sell? Essentially because the National Library of Australia offered me a solution to my problems and because it was the perfect home for my collection. The National Library has the resources and facilities to take splendid care of the material. Moreover, while the film-study field was growing in Australia and elsewhere, there my material could be of more use than in any other English-speaking country. For the National Library much of my collection would be unique, despite the undoubted strength of the holdings they already had in film books and movie-related material. Finally, and a most important point, the National Library could make my material accessible to a degree that I never could.

Sometimes now I am asked if I have any regrets about selling my collection and if I intend to continue collecting film books. The answer in both instances is a resounding and unqualified "yes." My collection simply had grown too large for one individual to handle at will; it was better off in a library. However, the sale does not mean that I intend to stop collecting film books and movie-related material. The part of the new path that I have staked out now is the use of film as an evidentiary tool in the writing of history, a subject that I have written about before and intend to tackle again.[15]

I am especially interested in the various manipulative uses to which newsreels, documentaries, and other so-called nonfiction films have been put—as well as the public reaction to them. An excellent bibliography is to be found in Paul Smith, ed., *The Historian and Film* (1976). Among the books dealing with this subject are splendid histories by Raymond Fielding of the American newsreel and of the *March of Time*. Other important works are Jay Leyda, *Film Begets Film* (1964), a gem of a book about compilation film; E. Bradford Burns, *Latin American Cinema: Film and History* (1975), an intelligent approach utilizing a varied and until recently unknown cinema; Anthony Aldgate, *Cinema & History: British Newsreels and the Spanish Civil War* (1979), a good case study; and W. K. L. Dickson, *The Biograph in Battle* (1901), an early and somewhat naive view of the uses of "actuality film." The subject has engaged the interest of a variety of authors in various countries for some time; important non-English studies include Marc Ferro, *Analyse de film/Analyse de societes* (1975), a fascinating analysis that also touches on feature film; Wolfgang Klaue et al., eds., *Film contra Faschismus* (1965), an uneven East German view; and Günter Moltmann and K. F. Reimers, *Zeitgeschichte in Film-und Tondokument* (1970), a pioneering collection of diverse articles. To me the potential of the subject as an area of collecting seems limitless and extremely topical given contemporary interest in media manipulation.

The attitude toward film has changed a great deal since I began collecting. No longer is the medium disparaged. No longer do we find statements such as we did a generation ago that "the cinema's reputation with the intelligent public is . . . relatively low."[16] Film has become a respectable subject that is studied intensively by scholars and collected extensively by institutions. Indeed, film books and periodicals have now achieved the cachet of being sold at auction. Among the movie items recorded as sold by the 1978 *American Book Prices Current* are a complete run of *Close Up* (which sold for £95, much less than the cost of the authorized reprint) and Charlie Chaplin's *My Life in Pictures* (which inexplicably sold for $35 or considerably more than it was fetching on the remainder tables of book shops, let alone its $19.95 publication price three years earlier).

Nearly half a century ago the anonymous author of the foreword to a catalogue of an exhibition arranged to illustrate the new paths in book collecting circa 1934 unabashedly asserted that "the fun of book hunting is in the chase, and the pursuit of items not universally known and valued gives a maximum chase, with, at the end, a minimum of investment."[17] I wholeheartedly endorse these sentiments, which for film material were never truer than now. The collector of film books and movie-related material still has the opportunity to blaze a trail, to know the exhilaration of the pioneer. Some of the underbrush has been cut away, parts of the path are no longer untrodden, but much of the way is still rough and barely explored—making for an exciting and jaunty adventure.

Notes

1. Gore Vidal, *Matters of Fact and Fiction: Essays 1973–1976* (New York: Random House, 1977), pp. 5, 26.
2. Ivan Butler, "The Film Books of the Year," in *Film Review 1978–79*, ed. by F. Maurice Speed (London: Allen, 1978), p. 175.
3. William Everson, *American Silent Film* (New York: Oxford, 1978), p. 351.
4. John Carter, *Taste and Technique in Book Collecting: A Study of Recent Development in Great Britain and the United States* (Cambridge: Cambridge Univ. Press, 1948), p. 136.
5. John Carter, ed., *New Paths in Book Collecting: Essays by Various Hands* (London: Constable, 1934), p. 3.
6. J. Douglas Gomery, "The Coming of Sound to the American Cinema" (Ph.D. diss., Department of Communication Arts, Univ. of Wisconsin, Madison, 1975), p. 1.
7. Daniel J. Leab, *From Sambo to Superspade: The Black Experience in Motion Pictures* (Boston: Houghton, 1975).
8. Daniel J. Leab, "The Black in Films: An Annotated Bibliography," *Journal of Popular Film* 4 (1975): 345.

9. Everson, *American Silent Film*, p. 351.
10. For an annotated bibliography that deals thoroughly with the literature to 1975, see Leab, "The Black in Films," pp. 345–356.
11. David Robinson, *The History of World Cinema* (New York: Stein & Day, 1973), p. 124.
12. John Carter, *ABC for Book Collectors*, 5th ed. (London: Granada Publishing, 1978), p. 34.
13. Charles F. Altman, "Towards a Historiography of American Film," *Cinema Journal* 16 (Spring 1977): 1.
14. William Roberts, quoted in Robin Duthy, *Alternative Investment* (London: Michael Joseph, 1978), p. 22.
15. Daniel J. Leab, "Some Problems in the Use of Film in Historical Research," *University Vision*, no. 10 (June 1973): 41–47.
16. Roger Manvell, *Film, A Reader's Guide* (Cambridge: published for the National Book League by the Cambridge Univ. Press, 1947), p. 5.
17. *Catalogue of an Exhibition Arranged to Illustrate New Paths in Book Collecting Held at the Old Court House . . .* (London: J. & E. Bumpas, November 1934), p. 1.

Further Reading

Catalogue of the Book Library of the British Film Institute. 3 vols. Boston: G. K. Hall, 1975.

Dyment, Alan R. *The Literature of the Cinema: A Bibliographical Guide to the Film as Art Entertainment, 1936-1970*. London: White Lion Publishers, 1975. This is a copy of the thesis originally submitted for the fellowship of the Library Association in April 1972.

The Film Index, vol. 1: *The Film as Art*. Compiled by workers of the Writers' Program of the Works Project Administration in the City of New York. New York: The Museum of Modern Art Film Library and the H. W. Wilson Co.; reprint edition, New York: Arno Press, 1966.

Gottesman, Ronald, and Geduld, Harry, eds. *Guide Book to Film*. New York: Holt, 1972. Useful mainly for its chapter "Theses and Dissertations about Film," which will be superseded by the publication in late 1979 or early 1980 of Raymond Fielding's massive compilation *A Bibliography of Theses and Dissertations in Film, 1916-1977* to be published as Monograph no. 3 in a series sponsored by the *Journal of the University Film Association*.

Jackson-Wrigley, M., and Leyland, Eric. *The Cinema: Historical, Technical, Bibliographical—A Survey for Librarians and Students*. London: Grafton, 1939.

Manz, Hans P. *International Film-Bibliographie, 1952-1962, 1963-1964*. Zurich: Verlag Hans Rohr, 1963, 1964. Since 1964 a variety of supplements have been issued at various times during the year to update these volumes.

Rehrauer, George. *Cinema Booklist*. Metuchen, N.J.: Scarecrow Press, 1972.

————. *Cinema Booklist: Supplement One*. Metuchen, N.J.: Scarecrow Press, 1974.

————. *Cinema Booklist: Supplement Two*. Metuchen, N.J.: Scarecrow Press, 1977.

Repertoire Mondial des Periodiques Cinematographiques/World List of Film Periodicals and Serials, 2nd ed. Brussels: La Cinematheque De Belgique, 1960.

Straschek, Günter Peter. *Handbuch wider das Kino*. Frankfurt am Main: Suhrkamp Verlag, 1975. An examination of world cinema with splendid and detailed bibliographies.

Traub, Hans, and Lavies, Hans Wilhelm. *Das deutsche Filmschrifttum: Eine Bibliographie Der Bücher Und Zeitschriften Über Das Filmwesen*. Leipzig: Verlag Karl W. Hiersemann, 1940.

Vincent, Carl; Redi, Riccardo; and Venturini, Franco. *Bibliografia generale del cinema/Bibliographie generale du cinema/General Bibliography of Motion Pictures*. Rome: Edizioni dell'ateno, 1953; reprint edition, New York: Arno Press, 1972.

5

American Mass-Market Paperbacks

Thomas L. Bonn

For 40 years contemporary paperback books have been the disposable container of the printed word. Those that have survived in basements and barns are surfacing in secondhand shops and other out-of-the-way places. Through their cover designs, early examples of these publications often reveal a freshness or outrageous innocence, which is understood by older generations and fascinates or puzzles the young. It is not surprising that these early pocket-size packages of print are being pursued with enthusiasm today. Magazines for collectors of paperback books, often outgrowths of "fanzines," offer descriptions of the history and nature of early softcover series, provide "checklists" of series, authors, and imprints, and offer collectors of particular writers or genres the opportunity to exchange observations, reviews, anecdotes, and checklists.

Beginning with the early almanacs in the seventeenth century and continuing through dime novels, yellowbacks, Tauchnitz, Little Blue Books, and Penguin, small softcover books—originals and reprints— have been fancied by collectors the world over. Today, the American paperback-book industry is a thriving and dynamic part of American culture. Publications first produced in softcover 30 or 40 years ago continue to be reprinted or reissued today. A wealth of fresh insights and interpretations reward the collector who compares today's softcover editions with those of the past.

But because of the ephemeral nature of paperback books, they tend to be disregarded by collectors. They are not valued and preserved as hardcover editions are. However, they are a part of the historical record of a book's publication and, as such, have their place in the recording of bibliography. More than one bibliographer has been heard to lament the difficulty in locating paperback editions for examination. A comprehensive collection of paperback editions of an author or of a publisher's output constitutes a valuable bibliographic record.

Although authorship, content, and imprint are important considerations in collecting, cover art, too, may determine a collector's selection. Familiar books, for instance, are acquired because of the accuracy with which a particular scene or mood is portrayed, frequently because of the way it is distorted, exaggerated, or otherwise misrepresented.

Paperbacks are rarely printed in editions of less than 50,000 copies; first printings often exceed 100,000 and have been known to surpass 1 million. "Rarity," therefore, is a term not usually applied to softcover editions. Whereas a handful have achieved some modest degree of value, perhaps exceeding $75 or more, the vast majority will seldom be priced over a few dollars and most at much less. Those that are more costly often represent first paperback editions either of collected authors or of science fiction and mystery titles, genres with large and dedicated numbers of collectors. The most collectible titles are often most entertaining to read. Condition, of course, also influences price. Early softcover editions of popular works in fine condition are more difficult to obtain and usually priced above the average.

Although this chapter touches on precursors, it focuses mainly on publications issued in the early years of American mass-market publishing, 1939–1952. It briefly summarizes the early history of modern softcover publishing, presents a few definitions when they seem needed, and, most importantly, suggests to the potential collector some areas of approach. Most of these approaches are based on my personal tastes and interests and are not to be considered exhaustive.

Characteristics

What are American *mass-market* paperbacks? Today, a strict definition may not be possible, but the term "mass market" generally does have relevance and meaning to those in the book trade, both inside and outside paperback-book publishing. Mass-market paperbacks are "rack size," roughly 4¼ by 7⅛ inches, though many early paperback publishers issued books that were shorter, approximately 4¼ by 6½ inches.

Wrapped in eye-catching paper covers, their leaves are trimmed on all four sides and are bound together by an adhesive process called perfect binding. The books are predominately reprints of successful hardcover titles, but a growing percentage are original publications.

Publishers of mass-market paperbacks issue their titles somewhat like magazine publishers. Each month approximately the same number of titles are produced to ensure display in a basic number of pocket (or rack) spaces at retail outlets across the United States. Promotion and advertising are wide-ranging though not as intensive as for other mass-market products. Emphasis is given to "lead" titles, those books for which the publisher often pays large royalty advances for reprint rights.

Over 50 percent of domestic mass-market sales are accomplished through a system of "national distributors," marketing organizations that also handle mass-circulation magazines, tabloids, and comics. Eleven major national distributors sell to approximately 450 regional independent distributors (IDs). The IDs in turn supply 100,000 local retail outlets throughout the United States.

Because mass-market paperbacks are distributed to trade bookstores and bought by schools and libraries, they also compete with trade (or "quality") paperbacks. Trade paperbacks, often larger in physical size, are published for smaller, more specialized audiences. They are marketed and distributed by the same methods used for hardcover general (trade) books.

The chief characteristic that separates mass-market paperbacks from other categories of book publishing is the conduit linking publisher to national distributor to independent distributor to local retail outlet. Historically, this supply system contributed most to the establishment, growth, and dominance of mass-market paperbacks in American book publishing. Today, all of the dozen or so major producers of mass-market books engage in other forms of publishing, including hardcover, trade paperbacks, and premium books. At least one is now marketing greeting cards, a natural outgrowth of recent trends in paperback cover design and artwork.

History and Imprints

Although true mass distribution of paperbacks did not begin until almost 1941, it is universally recognized that Pocket Books successfully published the first mass-market paperback books in 1939. Drawing on his years of experience in the hardcover reprint business, Robert de Graff, the principal founder of Pocket Books, printed in late 1938 a 2,000-copy test edition of Pearl Buck's *The Good Earth* (Plate 13). This unnumbered reprint is probably the rarest of mass-market paperback editions. (The title appeared in 1939 as number 11 on Pocket Books' list.)

Following favorable reaction to the sample volume, de Graff published a carefully chosen list of ten titles that had been successful in hardcover.[1] A full-page advertisement in the *New York Times* offered the first ten titles with a "money-back guarantee without any strings" and proclaimed Pocket Books' intention to "revolutionize New York's reading habits" by offering "famous bestsellers—complete, not digests. Unabridged and unexpurgated, in brand-new pocket-size editions; beautifully printed in large, clear type on easy-to-read opaque cream paper. Sturdily bound with soil-proof, Dura-gloss cover."[2]

The basic design first used on the sample edition of *The Good Earth* has remained the same, but almost every format feature described in that advertisement has undergone some evolution. The original size was a stubby 4¼ by 6⅜ inches. Early pages were surrounded by a Smyth-sewn binding reinforced with crash to which endpapers and a stiff but flexible cardboard wrapper were glued. But the war years and postwar inflation dictated changes in the physical appearance and makeup. Generous page margins disappeared so that more text could be crammed on a single page. Paper with high ground-wood content replaced more durable book-quality paper; perfect binding became a universal substitute for sewn bindings; and thinner, more flexible cover stock appeared. Readers of this period delighted in the feel of the plastic lamination that, with use and temperature extremes, often separated from the paper cover and provided nervous fingers with the job of stripping off the clear laminate as a book was read. Following their disappearance during World War II, the laminations reappeared only to be permanently replaced by coated cover stocks and varnished cover finishes.

As a reprinter of a new kind of book series, de Graff depended on the cooperation of his hardcover-publishing colleagues. This, together with his sensitivity to charges of cheap and shoddy publishing practice, resulted in early Pocket Books cover designs that reflected hardcover dust jackets: dignified, if somewhat poorly illustrated. Similar in size and design to Pocket Books were the first 12 Avon Pocket-Size Books, which Joseph Meyers started publishing in 1941. (The Avon books were ¼ inch wider.) Like de Graff, Meyers's experience rested

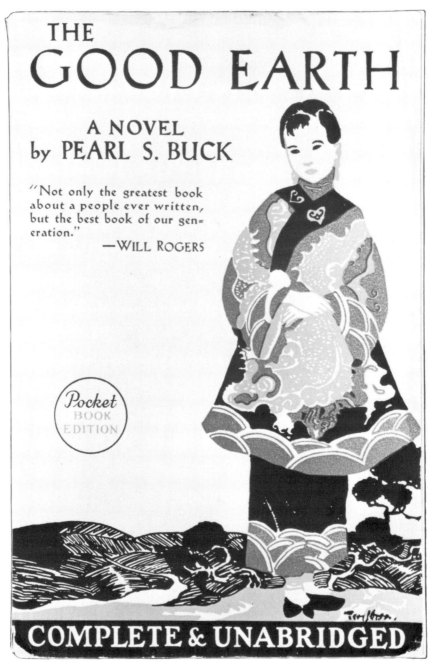

THE

GOOD EARTH

A NOVEL
by PEARL S. BUCK

"Not only the greatest book about a people ever written, but the best book of our generation."

—WILL ROGERS

Pocket
BOOK
EDITION

COMPLETE & UNABRIDGED

PLATE 13   Cover to the rarest of all contemporary paperbacks, Robert de Graff's sample edition of *The Good Earth*.

on hardcover reprint publishing, and like Pocket Books, Avon Pocket-Size Books appealed to hardcover readers (as proclaimed in this self-evaluation, which appeared in Avon's first title, *Elmer Gantry*).

> AVON Pocket-Size Books come to you after many months of careful planning (and shall we say not a few headaches) in an endeavor to give you not only the best authors and their writing, fiction and otherwise, but also to offer what we think is the best achievement to date in tasteful and dignified design, yet well printed and strongly bound books in a handy format.
>
> Note particularly the large readable type, the decorative end-paper, title page design, frontispiece and pictorial cover. Everything has been done to make this Avon Pocket-Size Edition something pleasing to handle, yet still at no more than a modest price.
>
> We say, and not without full appreciation of the breadth of the statement, that it is, we feel, the best value yet offered in every respect.

But with the appearance of Avon Pocket-Size Books, Pocket Books' designs became the subject of legal scrutiny. Following a precedent set 80 years earlier when Erastus Beadle tried to stop his brother Irwin from publishing dime novels similar in appearance and name to his own, de Graff went to court to enjoin Meyers. Litigation lasted more than two years, resulted in three separate decisions, and ended with a New York State Court of Appeals decision on January 20, 1944, favoring Avon. All of the decisions recognized that there were similarities in format between Pocket Books and Avon (see Plate 14). The final decision in Avon's favor was based on their prominent display of the distinguishing legend, "*AVON* pocket-size *BOOKS*" and their Bard's Head trademark. Avon's success on the newsstands, as well as in the courts, encouraged other magazine and pulp publishers to start softcover lines. Even prior to the final court decision other softcover imprints already had begun.

Red Arrow, launched on the heels of Pocket Books in October 1939, like so many softcover publishing ventures before and since, died within a few months. Published by Columbia Art Works, a Milwaukee printer, they were printed by offset and trimmed to a taller 4⅜ by 7⅛ inches, thus matching in size the English Penguin Books Series. Like imported Penguins of the time, they contained no cover illustrations but were color-coded by subject.

The Dell paperback imprint appeared in 1943 with a keyhole trademark that reflected its pulp-magazine parentage. Most early Dells were mystery reprints. A small red heart was superimposed on the keyhole for romances, while an ominous long-horn skull was used for western

PLATE 14   The first titles published by Pocket Books and Avon. The Avon format generated a series of court cases initiated by Pocket Books.

titles. Today, collectors prize these early Dell "mapbacks" for their back covers, which contain labeled illustrations of one or more settings described in the text.

Beginning in 1935 England watched the growth of Penguin Books, founded by Allan Lane. In 1939, one month after the start of Pocket Books, Lane set up a branch in New York City under the direction of Ian Ballantine. Initially the American Penguin branch distributed only English-produced titles, but it soon began to issue American-made publications as well. In the summer of 1945, Ballantine, with two other key staff members, left Penguin and founded Bantam Books to begin another chapter in his colorful and productive career in American softcover publishing.

Following Ballantine's departure, Kurt Enoch and Victor Weybright shared the direction of the American Penguin branch. Like Ballantine, they had difficulty working with the mercurial Lane. Part of the American branch's differences with the Englishman centered on his expressed distaste for cover illustration. Lane believed illustration cheapened and often misrepresented content.

Enoch and Weybright worked out a separation from Lane in 1948 and founded the New American Library. On their backlist were many titles that had been issued by the American Penguin branch over the preceding nine years. Within a short time, the Signet and Mentor imprints of Enoch and Weybright established NAL as one of the largest and most successful reprint houses in the United States. The Mentor line confirmed that there was a solid market for serious nonfiction and paved the way for the trade paperback imprints of the 1950s.

In January 1950, Fawcett Publications entered the paperback field. They rejected what was then considered the raison d'etre of softcover publishing—reprinting—and issued Gold Medal Books, an imprint devoted solely to original publications. Such a commitment today might be viewed as venturesome, but when announced in 1949, Fawcett's intentions bordered on the heretical. Fawcett was accused, among other things, of undermining the mutually beneficial relationship that existed among author, hardcover publisher, and paperback reprinter. Gold Medal Books succeeded in large measure because of the attractive royalty scales it offered to writers; the resulting list encompassed a varied range of talent.

With the launching of Gold Medal Books, all major factors essential to the present-day success of mass-market paperback books were established in the industry: intelligent selection of reprint and original material; fast and inexpensive manufacture; a nationwide system of local distribution; and arresting "packaging." It only remained for sophisticated and extensive advertising and promotion to expand dramatically the readership.

One of the more interesting early imprints is Ace Books, which merged original and reprint functions. The concept at Ace Books was to wrap a paperback original with a reprint, and in 1952 Ace Double Novels were launched. The volumes had two front covers, each with a pulp-inspired illustration usually painted by the same illustrator. The same "double" idea with different formats continues to be used occasionally by other paperback houses. As recently as 1977, a series of titles, which New American Library had earlier published singly, were issued two to a volume in a "double" series.

Price changes brought about a different kind of "double" volume. For almost 12 years, 25 cents was the standard price for rack-size paperback books. The amount was so well known and accepted that some publishers did not print the figure on the cover. As costs increased and larger books were published, however, publishers believed they had to convince the public that they were still getting a bargain at 35 cents or 50 cents. Some publishers chose to start a new series of "giants" or "extras" and increased book size by ½ inch. In the summer of 1950, New American Library inaugurated "double volumes" for its 50-cent Signet titles. Willard Motley's *Knock on Any Door* (Signet number 802 AB) was the first in this series. The title appeared twice on the spine, each with a different color background to simulate two books side by side. Even the serial numbers were broken apart: half of the spine read 802A, and the other 802B.

Since 1939, hundreds of publishing imprints have found their way to wire paperback racks. Some of these imprints are difficult to locate now, because the companies that published them went bankrupt or discontinued the series. Such imprints are a challenge to collectors who want to have a copy of each title issued under those particular imprints. The "Publisher Specifications" section of Robert Reginald's *Cumulative Paperback Index, 1939–1959* lists most discontinued imprints, including Eton Books, Bonded Mysteries, Bart House, Bantam (of Los Angeles), Checkerbooks, Graphic, Hillman, Black Knight, Novel Library, Hangman's House, Permabooks, Pony, and Royce. Early Permabooks imprints, published by Doubleday, had hard covers that resembled paperback books rebound with hard covers for libraries and schools. This line of pocket-size books was a successor of sorts to Doubleday's popular hardcover reprint series, Triangle Books, a training ground for Robert de Graff and his successor at Pocket Books, Freeman Lewis. In 1954, with both de Graff and Lewis at Pocket Books, the firm acquired the Permabooks imprint from Doubleday.

Certain other imprints of publishers are noteworthy because of content or design. Handi-Books issued pamphletlike, stapled editions at 15 cents in the early 1940s. Beginning in 1951, Dell used a similar format to publish three dozen 10-cent editions. In 1948, Pocket Books was the first mass-market publisher to issue a juvenile series, Comet Books. Trimmed to a digest size, 5⅛ by 7⅛ inches, they contained comic-book inspired plot summaries on the back cover. In 1950, Comet Books was succeeded by Pocket Book Jrs., designed in the smaller rack-size format.

Special mention must be made of the Armed Services editions. Sponsored by the nonprofit Council on Books in Wartime, these books were given away overseas to World War II servicemen. Most of the softcover volumes were reprints of successful hardcover titles. Staplebound on the short side and printed on magazine presses, they measured either 5½ by 3⅞ inches or 6½ by 4½ inches, half the size of *Reader's Digest* and half the standard pulp magazine size, respectively (see Plate 15).

In the spring of 1944 Pocket Books designed Ellery Queen's *Halfway House* (PB number 259) to resemble an Armed Services edition. It was bound on the short side and had two columns of type per page. The design exchange took one more step after the war when Armed Services Series II editions appeared in a size and shape similar to Pocket Books. The Infantry Journal and Superior Reprint editions of the mid-1940s were also aimed at servicemen. Ian Ballantine handled the distribution of these titles, first at American Penguin and later at Bantam. This probably accounts for the fact that their design was similar to early American Penguin and Bantam.

Prior to 1939 there were a number of twentieth-century American attempts to publish books in inexpensive, softcover formats. From a design standpoint the most interesting example is the Boni Paper Books, published between 1929 and 1931. Two series were issued, the first of which was sold as a book-club subscription. Founder Charles Boni envisioned bringing fine literature to a national audience at an inexpensive price of $5 for twelve issues, or 42 cents per copy. For $1 a copy Boni even offered to put a hardcover binding on returned editions. Later, a second series, almost identical to the first, was issued and sold through the book trade, but the experiment ended in 1931. The books are interesting because of their cover and page designs. Rockwell Kent created the covers and endpapers for many of the quarto-size (roughly 5-by-7½-inch) books (see Plate 16).

In the fall of 1937 another publisher of quarto-size books, Modern Age, issued its first books under three separate, color-coded imprints: Red Seals (not to be confused with a later Fawcett imprint) were reprints priced at 25 cents; Blue Seals and Gold Seals were originals priced at 25 cents and 35 cents, respectively, and were also available in hardcover. In one way or another, Modern Age Books employed almost all of the methods that later assured the success of mass-market paperbacks, including representation by a national magazine and newspaper distributor and manufacture using high-speed, rotary presses. Within two years of its first list, however, Modern Age gave up trying to publish for a mass audience and produced hardcover books for the regular book trade almost exclusively.

Other pre-1939 imprints of interest to collectors and students of American paperback history are the reprints of classic literature by the National Home Library, the digest-size imprints of American Mer-

PLATE 15   Examples of the Armed Services editions sponsored by the Council on Books in Wartime.

1302

ERLE STANLEY GARDNER

THE CASE OF THE
FAN-DANCER'S
HORSE

A PERRY MASON
STORY

ARMED
SERVICES
EDITION

Overseas edition for the Armed Forces. Distributed by the Special Services Division, W.D.,
for the Army, and by the Bureau of Naval
Personnel for the Navy. U. S. Government property. Not for sale. Published by Editions for the
Armed Services, Inc., a non-profit organization
established by the Council on Books in Wartime.

THIS IS THE COMPLETE BOOK -- NOT A DIGEST

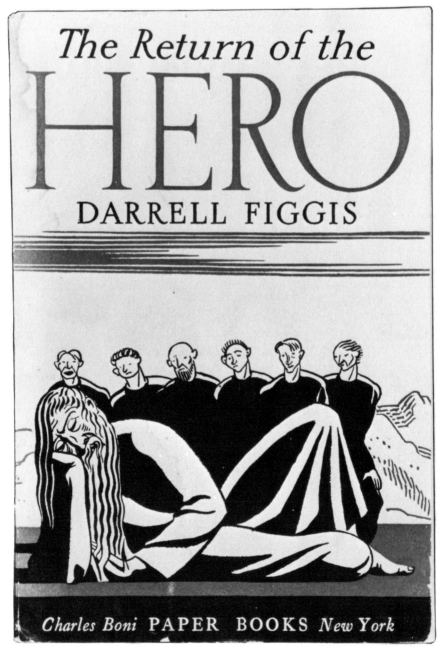

PLATE 16   A hardcover pre-1939 design and illustration by Rockwell Kent for the Boni Books.

cury Publications, and the well-loved and widely collected Little Blue Book editions of Emanuel Haldeman-Julius.

Although this chapter centers on American mass-market imprints of the twentieth century, I would be remiss if I did not refer to the European roots from which Robert de Graff and others drew inspiration and example. Beginning in 1841, the English-language, paperback Tauchnitz Collection of British (and, later, American) Authors series set high design and typographical standards. Sold only on the Continent, appearance in this series meant recognition and prestige for an author. Robert Louis Stevenson wrote to Baron Tauchnitz, the Leipzig-based founder, "I am pleased indeed to appear in your splendid collection, and thus to rise a grade in the hierarchy of my art."[3] (For an account of the Tauchnitz Series, see Chapter 3, "Books in Series," by William B. Todd.)

Tauchnitz was acquired in 1934 by the Albatross Modern Continental Library of English and American Fiction, a series started in 1931 and patterned after Tauchnitz. The Albatross format was designed by Giovanni Mardersteig,[4] considered by many to be the finest book designer and printer of the twentieth century. Manufactured in various European countries, Albatross established for the twentieth century the "elongated" duodecimo (roughly 4¼-by-7⅛-inch) paperback size that today is standard for mass-market books.

Penguin Books, referred to earlier, began publication in England in 1935 and through the years has sponsored the finest list in all paperback publishing. Although not issuing what might be described as massmarket titles since 1939, Penguin has employed a variety of different distribution channels in the United States, which have put their publications in direct competition with American mass-market publications.

Collectors of Penguin imprints exist throughout the world, and many belong to the Penguin Collectors' Society (see the second section of Further Reading at the end of this chapter). Among the various series prized by collectors are the American productions with cover illustrations, published prior to the 1948 independence of New American Library.

Authors, Titles, and Series

Today, the press seems to delight in the paperback numbers game by quoting not only the size of initial printings but also the advance given to popular authors for first paperback publication rights and by estimating publishers' break-even points. This fascination with numbers is nothing new to twentieth-century mass-market publishing.

It began in 1940 when Pocket Books, impressed by its own sales figures for Dale Carnegie's *How to Win Friends and Influence People*, printed individual copy numbers on the cover headband of later printings. For a short time after World War II, Pocket Books combined all of its printing figures so that each cover out of the bindery showed an even more impressive figure: each was numbered consecutively, based on the total number of Pocket Books copies printed since 1939.

The large numbers of copies printed—even early mass-market paperback editions rarely had printings of less than 50,000 copies, and frequently they ran to 100,000 copies or more—can be a distinct advantage to the collector whose aim it is to acquire the earliest edition of each title by a given author. But although prospects of success are greatly increased by the large print runs, this approach is not without challenges.

Pen names can create a problem for collectors. Some fiction writers, particularly those who wrote in a number of genres, employed a dozen or more pseudonyms. Harry Whittington, who wrote over two dozen books under his own name in the 1950s, has at least nine *noms de plume*, including "Hondo Wells" for westerns, "Hallam Whitney" for southern regional writing, and "Ashley Carter" for slave-plantation fiction in the Falconhurst series.[5] Mike Avallone uses fifteen different pen names for juveniles, science fiction publications, movie and television novelizations, and for suspense and mystery subgenres such as spy, hardboiled detective, occult, police procedural, and gothic fiction. E. Howard Hunt used several pseudonyms. These are traced in Gore Vidal's essay in *Matters of Fact and Fiction*.[6] Under the name of "Edgar Box," Vidal himself wrote mysteries reprinted by Signet in the 1950s.

Few paperback series gave more than passing recognition to authors. Notable exceptions were the American Penguin and early Signet imprints of New American Library whose back covers contained information readers were accustomed to find on the back flap of hardcover dust jackets—a brief biography and a photograph of the author. A search for a writer's true identity might begin with the National Union Catalog or the book catalogue of the Library of Congress. (Other specialized aids are included in the Further Reading section at the end of this chapter.)

Certainly one of the minor joys in collecting paperbacks is comparing an original title with its revision. By reading the book's content and examining the cover art and editorial copy, one can speculate on the rationale and appropriateness of the title change. But title changes create another difficulty in tracing paperback works. Reprinters of the 1940s and early 1950s excelled at title substitution, which was used to make a book more appealing or suggestive. The absence of conspicuous notice of title changes or abridgments on paperback reprints became a concern of the Federal Trade Commission in the late 1940s. In the finest of regulatory language, the commission summarized its concern when it stated that such practices "have the tendency and capacity to mislead and deceive a substantial portion of the purchasing public with respect to respondents' books, and the tendency and capacity to cause such portion of the public to purchase such books as a result of the erroneous and mistaken belief so engendered."[7] Most paperback publishers eventually signed agreements with the FTC, stipulating that "the substitute title must be 'immediately accompanied' by the original title in clear conspicuous type."[8]

Sometimes a mass-market softcover edition receives attention from rare-book dealers. Such a book is William Burroughs's first published book, *Junkie: Confessions of an Unredeemed Drug Addict* (Ace Double D-15), which appeared under the pseudonym William Lee. The edition subsequently achieved full recognition when two pages were devoted to it in a bibliography published by the Bibliographical Society of the University of Virginia.[9] Today, this volume fetches several hundred times its original 35-cent price. Gold Medal, Dell First Edition, and others published original material for writers who have since achieved fame or notoriety. These authors display a wide range of talent and include Kurt Vonnegut, John D. McDonald, McKinley Kantor, William Goldman, Arthur C. Clarke, John Jakes, Kathleen E. Woodiwiss, and E. Howard Hunt. (For a discussion of first editions issued in paperback, see Chapter 9, "American Fiction since 1960," by Peter B. Howard.)

Many early paperbacks cited the date of their first reissuing of another publisher's original hardcover work. Some, like the early Pocket Books, listed a history of the various editions of the work, including hardcover reprints that preceded the Pocket Books edition. Although usually correct, the information should not be the sole source used for establishing bibliographic accuracy. Some reprints, like early Dell titles, gave no information about the publication history and failed to show on the title page or its verso the year the softcover edition was published. With the exception of anthologies, few original works were published in paperback between 1939 and 1950.

To the delight of cover-art collectors, publishers periodically redesign paperback wrappers, substituting new cover art and editorial-promotion copy (blurbs) to reissue a previously published paperback. Reissues usually occur several years after first softcover publication. When there is a movie, television, or current-event tie-in, reissues may appear sooner, perhaps four to six months after the first softcover publication. As with title changes, comparison of cover changes leads to speculation on the reasons behind the change.

No discussion of paperback publishing can ignore the literary reviews sponsored by American mass-market houses and their predecessors. Several interesting literary series appeared in paperback form prior to 1939. In August 1891, *The Tauchnitz Magazine; An English Monthly Miscellany for Continental Readers* began. It lasted only two years, but it started a tradition of short-lived (usually) softcover literary collections in series. *The Albatross Almanac*, published in the 1930s, was a successor of sorts. The 1933 edition contained selections from James Joyce, D. H. Lawrence, Aldous Huxley, Sinclair Lewis, Katherine Mansfield, and George Bernard Shaw.

Nationally distributed softcover literary series, like today's little magazines, are also vehicles through which new writers gain recognition. Frankly acknowledging its inspiration from the English *Penguin New Writing* series, which had ceased publication two years earlier, New American Library issued the first volume in the *New World Writing* series in April 1952. New American Library's co-founder and then-president, Kurt Enoch, also took inspiration from *The Albatross Almanac*. Twenty years earlier Enoch took part in the founding of Albatross Books and was responsible for their distribution in prewar Europe. Fifteen issues of the *New World Writing* series were published by NAL under the skilled and loving editorship of Arabel Porter. In 1959 the series was taken over by Lippincott, which published seven additional numbers, concluding with number 22 in 1964.

In 1967 New American Library revived the paperback literary-magazine idea with *The New American Review*. The introduction by editor Theodore Solotaroff acknowledged its *New World Writing* roots. After ten issues, the softcover periodical was picked up by Simon & Schuster; issues 11–15 appeared with a Simon & Schuster imprint. Bantam continued the series as the *American Review* or *AR*. The final volume, still under the guidance of Solotaroff, was issued in 1977 as number 26.

Between 1953 and 1955, Pocket Books published six numbers in *Discovery*, edited by Vance Bourjaily. In 1955, Bantam sponsored an even shorter-lived series, *New Campus Writing*, which issued only two numbers.

Subjects, Categories, and Formulas

With the exception of Harlequin Books, today's dozen or so major mass-market paperback publishers distribute on a monthly basis a full range of fiction representing all popular categories, including westerns, mysteries, romances, and science fiction. All of the major areas have much finer breakdowns. In some fields, such as science fiction, there is no agreement among editors on what the subcategories are. To a list made up of various fiction categories, a publisher adds a "lead" title or two. Most often it is a hardcover best seller, but it may also be a book with only modest hardcover sales in which a publisher sees the potential for large paperback sales.

Nonfiction is published on every possible subject, but most titles stress topics that are currently popular. Nonfiction titles receive greater or lesser prominence, depending on the importance of the author and the currency of the topic. Somewhere toward the bottom of a publisher's list are game, puzzle, and cartoon books, along with reprints of one or more classics now in the public domain.

This mix and balance of publication types and categories was not always a mass-market publication pattern. With the exception of New American Library's Mentor series, early mass-market publishers issued few nonfiction titles. Self-help books with obvious mass-audience appeal were the only regular exceptions. Aside from NAL and Bantam, no other early publisher of mass-market books approached the balance of Pocket Books' early lists as demonstrated by the first ten Pocket Books titles. De Graff "experimented" with a list containing two fiction best sellers, a light comic-fiction title, an Agatha Christie mystery, a children's book, a book of verse, a self-help title, and three reprints of English literary classics. Four of the ten titles had recently been released or were soon to be motion pictures. The early "best seller" from the list was *Wuthering Heights* (PB number 7), produced that same year as a successful film.[10]

Various fiction genres were added in succeeding months. The first western was *Oh, You Tex* (PB number 78) by William MacLeod Raine. Pocket Books' edition of Daphne du Maurier's *Rebecca* (PB number 205) introduced millions of readers to a genre now known as "gothic romance," but it was not until the 1960 edition of Phyllis A. Whitney's *Thunder Heights* (Ace Star number K 158) appeared that the popular-fiction type was recognized (see Plate 17). It is a gold mine of speculation to compare Gene Marchetti's cover art for the Whitney title, which contains almost all of the acknowledged clichés of contemporary gothic cover design, to covers of earlier suspense novels, including Larry Hoffman's illustration for *Rebecca.*

The first attention given to science fiction by paperback publishers was the Donald A. Wollheim-edited anthology, *The Pocket Book of Science*

PLATE 17   Covers of two early gothic romance editions.

Fiction (PB number 214), published in 1943. However, it was not until the early 1950s, with Ballantine, Ace editions, and occasional titles from NAL and Bantam, that the audience was deemed large enough to support systematic publication in this category.

Murder mysteries and detective fiction dominated the lists of early publishers of paperbacks. Though Robert de Graff was disappointed with the initial sales of Christie's classic mystery, *The Murder of Roger Ackroyd* (PB number 5), he discovered that several mysteries grouped together on a rack attracted attention and sales from readers of this genre. (Approximately 40 percent of his first 180 titles were mysteries.)

From its first publication in 1943, Popular Library sponsored 76 mystery titles before it offered the public a western, *Buckaroo!* (Popular Library number 77). Between 1942 and 1947, Avon published almost 50 titles in its digest-size series, Avon Murder Mystery Monthly. Similar in format to the American Mercury editions, they included some of the best hard-boiled writers of the time. Pyramid's Green Door series,

Gold Medal's Classic Murder Trials, and Avon's Classic Crime series are other collections prized by mystery and detective fans.

Among the most widely collected imprints are the Dell "mapbacks." As mentioned earlier, these were mostly mysteries with a keyhole logo and an illustration of an important setting on the back cover. To the delight of crime-solving readers, the illustration frequently showed a detailed and labeled floor plan of the scene of the crime. The quality of the front-cover illustrations in this series varied greatly. Detail in the back-cover map declined by the time the illustrations were dropped in the early 1950s.

The growing and expanding literature of fan and amateur press alliance publications in the mystery, western, science fiction, and fantasy categories give the prospective paperback-book collector numerous paths to follow through plot summaries and reviews, as well as author and publisher checklists. (See Further Reading section at the end of this chapter for follow-up suggestions.)

Two types of publications closely identified with mass-market publication are media-tie-in books and "instant books." The former began when publishers timed new editions or releases of film-related titles to Hollywood distribution schedules. Today, it is not uncommon for complex, cooperative planning among paperback, hardcover, and film people to take place even prior to hardcover publication.

Pocket Books takes credit for the first movie-tie-in title, *Wuthering Heights* (PB number 7) (see Plate 18). It is not clear, however, how actively the fledgling softcover house associated its 1939 reprint with the newly released film. The following year, however, a Connecticut bookseller observed, "The movie tie-up, of course, is excellent and accounts for many sales. We are still selling what they prefer to call 'Withering Heights' to Laurence Olivier fans."[11]

Some very interesting but not necessarily attractive early paperback covers combined a black-and-white photograph of a film's stars with color background art provided by an illustrator. The faces usually had a ghostlike cast. Early covers were printed by letterpress, a method that generally did a poorer job of reproducing cover art than offset presswork. It also underscored the questionable wisdom of combining halftones in a layout with painted illustration. Cover artists' attempts at four-color sketches of principal stars generally created better, if less interesting, cover designs.

"Instant books," "instant edition," "quick books," and "extras" are all terms used by paperback houses for titles of immediate currency, written, edited, manufactured, and distributed at high speed to take

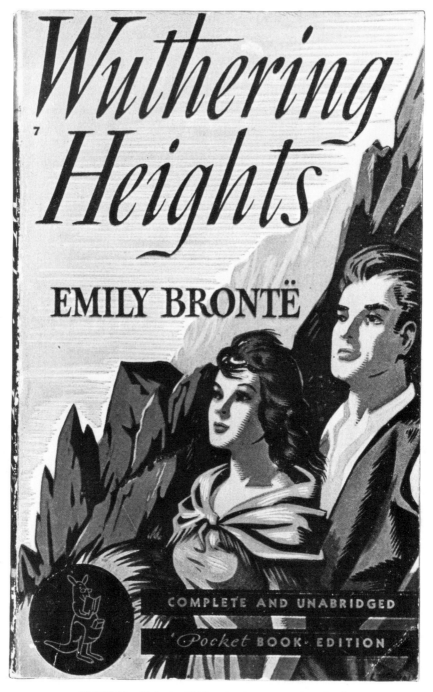

PLATE 18 *Wuthering Heights*, the first movie-tie-in book.

advantage of widespread but temporary public interest in an event, topic, or personality. "Instant books" were popularized by Bantam in 1964 when it prepared and published within 80 hours of its release by the government an 800-page, 1-million-copy edition of the *Report of the Warren Commission* (Bantam number PZ 2935). Subsequently, other mass-market publishers experimented with this rapid publication process. To celebrate its twentieth anniversary in 1965, Bantam issued a 48-page report entitled *The Making of a Book*, which outlined the steps through which the commission report was published.

At one time Bantam claimed a place in the *Guinness Book of World Records* under the heading "Fastest Publishing" for a volume it produced a year after the *Report of the Warren Commission*. Bantam's second "instant book," *The Pope's Journey to the United States* (Bantam number SZ 322), was put together with the cooperation of 51 strike-bound writers and editors of the *New York Times*. A mere 66½ hours elapsed between the arrival of the first manuscript page and the production of bound copies.

Ironically, the visit of Pope Paul VI to the United States also produced one of the rarest editions sponsored by a mass-market publisher. In a cooperative effort with American Book-Stratford Press, Pocket Books distributed 15 presentation copies of a morocco-leather-bound, slipcased edition of *Pacem in Terris*, proceedings of the International Convocation on the Requirements of Peace held in New York in February 1965.

Bantam may have coined the term "instant books," but we again turn to Pocket Books for the first twentieth-century paperback example of the fast-book-publishing phenomenon. Six days after the death of President Franklin D. Roosevelt, Pocket Books published *Franklin Delano Roosevelt: A Memorial* (PB number 300). The 300,000-copy first edition was printed over a weekend on the rotary-perfecting presses of Colonial Press (Clinton, Massachusetts), the manufacturer of most Pocket Books editions until the end of World War II.

Special events, personalities, and, especially, fads and fashions have long tempted book publishers, both hardcover and softcover, to put out a "quickie." CB radios, trucks and vans, disco music, and running are only a few of the popular fads exploited by paperback books. Larger, more significant trends, such as black American culture, the women's movement, the environment, and gay rights, find paperback publishers saturating the marketplace with speedy but often poorly conceived softcover responses. An individual interested in comparing the editorial treatment and packaging of both the serious and ephemeral concerns of our society can do worse than gather and compare these softcover publisher responses.

Cover Design and Art

The cover design (both front and back covers) for a paperback book
is usually made up of three elements: (1) an illustration (a photograph
or painted artwork); (2) required bibliographic information (author and
title); and (3) editorial-promotion copy (front and back matter: claims,
quotes from reviewers, and hints about the plot). The overriding objective is to attract potential buyers—to get them to pick up and feel the
book and examine its contents. The first requirement is for the design
to stand out and give strong hints about the contents or project a strong
image of the writer. In paperback publishing today, ideas for cover
design are often initiated by editorial, marketing, production, and design personnel at cover conferences. If cover art is required, a free-
lance artist is often hired. Because the artist is usually not a participant
in cover conferences, his or her assignment and guidance come from
the publisher's art director, who is a participant.

Most often a cover artist deals with the problem of projecting
the book's contents by creating an image or series of images that attract
and flash content signals to the potential reader. The artist tries to
capture the essence by painting one scene, drawing a composite of
scenes, or by creating certain symbols—people, places, and things—to
represent the book as a whole.

Cover art is often the primary or the most important secondary
reason for owning a particular mass-market edition. Because it is designed to appeal to all ages, tastes, and educational backgrounds, early
mass-market paperback art ranges from the most imaginative and art-
ful to the most laughable and tasteless. It reflects the time in which it
was created, the market it was created for, and the status of the writer
whose work it illustrates.

Early paperback covers were generally inspired by hardcover dust-
jacket design and illustration. Pocket Books, Avon, and American Penguin often issued covers framed with neat borders reminiscent of the
dust jackets of some hardcover books. But after World War II designs
and illustrations began to change. Cover art became less symbolic or
juvenile and more realistic, as in the case of the Signet covers of New
American Library, or more like pulp-magazine covers, as in the case of
Bantam, Popular Library, Avon, and most others. Then in the early
1950s the realistic and pulp styles merged to create a style that was
bold, exaggerated, and often sadistic and sexist. Mass-market publishers were faced with a hail of protest.

In December 1952 the House Select Committee on Current Pornographic Materials,[12] popularly known as the Gathings Committee,

heard testimony from several mass-market publishers, including Ralph Daigh of Fawcett, whose Gold Medal number 132, *Women's Barracks* by Tereska Torres, repeatedly raised the committee's ire. This period, described as one of "sex, sadism and the smoking gun," led to a variety of experiments in cover design in the mid-1950s and eventually to the poster-art layouts and the white-cover backgrounds that dominated the paperback racks of the late 1950s and the 1960s.

Today greater attention is given to graphic and illustrative symbols for mass-market paperbacks than was the case in the past. Frequently content is reflected through the selection of particular type styles for author-title cover graphics. In the case of the Signet cover for *Coma* (number E 7881, 1977) a graphic is integrated with the cover illustration by having it serve a practical function and at the same time strengthen the symbolism. The large block letters serve as a ceiling support for wires suspending a human body.

While the cover design of paperback books always has had a selling function and has reflected the book's contents, it also has mirrored the time in which it was created and the status of the author whose work it portrays. One can trace the growth in stature of writers such as Hemingway, Faulkner, Lewis, or Wilder through the covers of their various reissued paperback titles (see Plate 19). Early covers tend to concentrate on the story; later designs tend to be less illustrative, use more typography, and stress author identity and importance.

The collection and identification of the cover illustrations of particular artists offer almost unlimited challenges, especially those artists who span a number of years. Sheer quantity alone can make attempts at acquiring complete lists almost impossible. Techniques and styles of successful artists such as James Avati, James Bama, Robert McGuinnis, and the Hildebrandt brothers have been widely imitated through the years and reduce the certainty of identification.

Some artists of early paperbacks did not sign their work; some signed only those paintings that they liked; and signatures of those that did sign often were cropped in the final design. Few artists or publishers have complete records of early paperback-cover assignments. (Until fairly recently, original artwork remained the property of the publisher, and older cover paintings were given away or disposed of by publishers.) To further complicate identification, some artists used pseudonyms at different points in their careers or for different styles of art. Expressionist and "knothole" artist Robert Jonas's last name appears clearly in lowercase Ultra Bodoni Italic type on most of his American Penguin and New American Library covers. On a series of

PLATE 19   Early covers of two reissued paperback titles.

rather poorly illustrated Signet western covers, however, a hand-printed "Robjon" signifies cover illustrations he was less anxious to acknowledge.

Although artists generally did not get credit for their illustrations on early paperback titles, an exception to this was Bantam editions published in the late 1940s. For example, on the ad card page (opposite the title page) for *Relentless* (Bantam number 251, 1948), a short promotional paragraph about the cover described the scene depicted on the front cover, naming the artist who painted it. (See Plate 20.)

When illustrator Cliff Young finished reading *Relentless* he tried to summon up enough breath for a whistle. The part that really got Cliff was Nick Buckley's gun battle for his life *with his hands manacled*. From his artist friend Harvey Dunn (who owns an eye-popping display of small-arms) he borrowed a gun, and from the famous magazine and book illustrator Dean Cornwell, Cliff got the holster and other equipment. Add to this a dash of memory—Cliff rode quite a bit when he was a farm kid in Ohio—and that smashing climax becomes the real thing, in full, unbridled color that smacks of the roaring West.

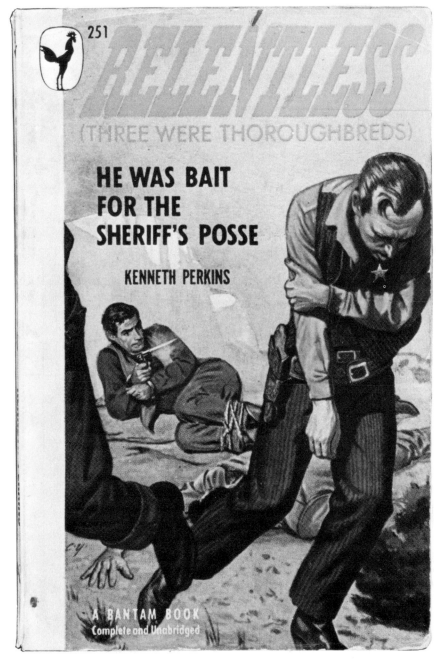

PLATE 20   Even the illustrator got into the action in this typical "shoot 'em up" cover of the late 1940s (Bantam number 251).

Among the art directors who often have illustrated covers, perhaps one of the best known is Leonard Leone. His 25 years at Bantam Books have made him the acknowledged master of creative paperback design. Leone's signature as illustrator can be found on Lion and Bantam western titles from the early 1950s. Milton Charles of Pocket Books also received much recognition for his cover art and designs. Charles created some very interesting, decorated, stark-white sculptures that appeared on Pocket Books covers in the late 1960s.

Compared to the number of artists involved in other commercial art media, the list of artists who have illustrated paperback-book covers is probably very small. Many have belonged to the Society of Illustrators in New York City, but there is no one association or club with which all have affiliated. Also, no comprehensive study of mass-market paperback art and design is known to exist. The annual reviews of the Society of Illustrators and Art Directors Club (also in New York City) are limited research sources, though some of them do contain artists' addresses. Between 1960 and 1964, the American Institute of Graphic Arts did publish a catalogue for its annual exhibition of the best mass-market and trade paperback covers. Although many commercial artists have agents, it is probably easier to find and reach those active today through publishers for whom they have worked.

It is not necessary to have industry information to collect examples of certain themes that have appeared on paperback covers through the years. Sexism abounded in early paperback cover art and continues even today. The chief difference between the sexist art from the first 15 or so years of paperback publishing and today is the better execution of the illustration and the disappearance of the heavy-handed, pulp-magazine styles of presentation. Ironically, however, it is this bold and exploitive pulp style that makes the early covers of Popular Library, Avon, Lion, and others attractive to many collectors.

Combined with objects splashed with bright yellows and reds, women appear on paperback covers in just about every imaginable position of disarray or compromise. Artists of the early period seemed enchanted with women's undergarments, particularly the brassiere. And when a half-dressed bosom could not be incorporated into an illustration of a female, a bra strap often appeared from under a dress, draped suggestively over a shoulder.

Women's breasts, backs, or legs (and any combination thereof) may have sold more books, but other parts of the human anatomy were not ignored. The covers of some very early Avon titles carried suspended heads (no necks or shoulders) like so many balloons. Hands were another interesting artistic device used generally to represent dread or intrigue. Grasping objects or empty, fleshy, or boney, they appeared in every shape, color, and size—delights to have and hold!

On early covers, blacks were usually portrayed with more dignity than were women. For the sake of southern book sales, however, racial origin was often disguised when one of the characters in a multiracial love match was black. An example is James Avati's first cover for Signet's *Last of the Conquerors* (number 706, 1949). Here, the face of one of the two main characters, a black American soldier, was shadowed. Blacks positively portrayed in a novel's text were illustrated with lighter skins and strong Anglo-Saxon features; unsympathetic blacks had darker skins.

Archaeological studies could be made from various hand-held, dress, and background objects that appeared on early covers. Along with all manner of weaponry, furniture, telephones, handbags, and hats abound. Tenements, skyscrapers, and automobiles, dominant symbols of postwar American society, were backdrops for stories of adventure and longing.

Probably the most overworked artistic device for presenting a scene on a softcover was the "peephole." Besides lending an air of prohibition and intrigue to the cover mood, the peephole device serves as a gunsight—which it occasionally is—and focuses viewer attention on the principal object in the cover illustration. It also allows designers to lay out necessary typographic elements around the outside borders of the viewfinder without diverting attention from the central object. Some early publisher formats literally framed an artist's illustration with headbands and borders. In other cases, the knotholes, keyholes, and window frames of the 1940s and 1950s were illustrative devices ideally suited to the limited dimensions of a paperback cover. Use of these devices began with the Robert Jonas's knothole cover for *God's Little Acre* (Penguin [American] number 581, 1946), and continues to this day.

Present-day gimmick covers, especially die-cut front covers, can mechanically accomplish similar objectives. Taking inspiration from the greeting-card industry, gimmick paperback covers feature foil stamping and embossing, fold-out front covers, and front covers trimmed back to expose endpaper illustrations (step-backs). A variety of foil covers are used to highlight cover features; on Donald Westlake's *Too Much* (Fawcett Crest number K2750, 1976), twin bikinis were cov-

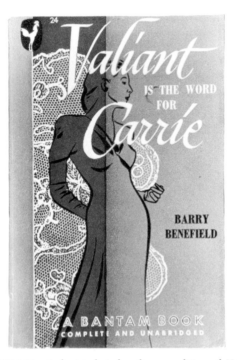

PLATE 21A   A dust-jacketed, softcover edition of *Valiant*
Is the Word for Carrie (Bantam number 24). (Cf. Plate 21B)

ered in pink flock! This was the first and perhaps the only cover to use
this particular tactile device.

Dust jackets occasionally appeared on paperback editions of some
American publishers. Unlike Penguin and Albatross volumes on which
dust jackets were identical to the bound, softcover wrapper, American
mass-market dust jackets were usually wrapped around older warehouse stock to hide an undesirable cover. (See Plates 21A and 21B.)
Among the more interesting is the first Bantam number 8 edition of
The Great Gatsby, reprinted in 1945. When the film appeared in 1949, a
dust jacket featuring an illustration of Alan Ladd as Gatsby was placed
over the original cover art.[13]

Few are the species in the animal kingdom that at one time or another have not been captured for a softcover spine logo (the distinctive
trademark device that symbolizes a particular publishing house or
imprint). Through the years these animals evolved along with the lists
they symbolize (see Plate 22). Bantam's cocky rooster was redesigned

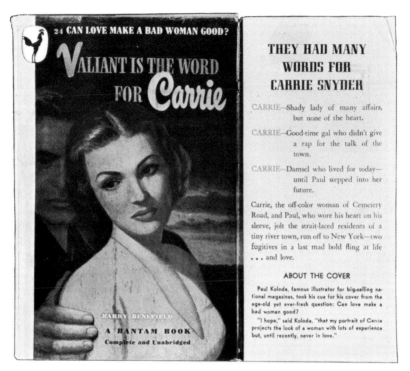

PLATE 21B   Another dust-jacketed, softcover edition of *Valiant Is the Word for Carrie* (Bantam number 24). (Cf. Plate 21A)

after criticism that he looked emaciated. The second Penguin logo had a relatively short life. One wag described the dancing bird as in the throes of an attack of appendicitis. The best known, Pocket Books' "Gertrude," was named after the mother-in-law of her designer. At first she wore glasses, but these were removed by a Walt Disney design in 1945. It was feared that a bespectacled kangaroo might give the impression that reading promoted nearsightedness!

In Conclusion

Because paperback books are relatively easy to obtain, collectors may be tempted to accumulate rather than select. The most interesting collections, however, are those that are built with knowledge and purpose. Through history, example, and anecdote, this chapter has highlighted some aspects of paperback books in order to show a range of

Plate 22   The Bantam, Penguin, and Pocket Books logos.

collecting possibilities. One can easily succumb to the temptation to collect "everything" merely because of low price and easy availability. However, whether one is attracted to Agatha Christie softcover whodunits, first paperback editions of Lion Books, animal logos, Bantam endpaper maps of Rafael Palocios, the cover art of Harry Bennett, or any of the other endless possibilities in the paperback field, the collection one forms should have an organizing principle. Lasting satisfaction comes from choosing examples that, when put together as a whole, shed new light on previously unexplored areas of knowledge. Knowing what to look for is the foundation of intelligent collecting; it is what distinguishes a book warehouse from a collection.

Notes

1. The titles were: James Hilton, *Lost Horizon;* Dorothea Brande, *Wake Up and Live;* William Shakespeare, *Five Great Tragedies;* Thorne Smith, *Topper;* Agatha Christie, *The Murder of Roger Ackroyd;* Dorothy Parker, *Enough Rope;* Emily Bronte, *Wuthering Heights;* Samuel Butler, *The Way of All Flesh;* Thornton Wilder, *The Bridge of San Luis Rey;* and Felix Salten, *Bambi.*
2. *New York Times,* June 14, 1939, p. 34.
3. "The Story of the Tauchnitz Edition," *Publishers Weekly* 80, no. 2 (July 8, 1911): 82.
4. Author's tape-recorded interview with Kurt Enoch, November 20, 1971.
5. Bill Crider, "Paperback Writers," *Paperback Quarterly* 1, no. 1 (Spring 1978): 9, 15.
6. Gore Vidal, "The Art and Arts of E. Howard Hunt," in Vidal, *Matters of Fact and Fiction* (New York: Random House, 1977), p. 19.
7. "Trial Examiner's Initial Decision (5811)," *U.S. Federal Trade Commission Press Release,* April 27, 1951, p. 5.
8. "Two Reprint Houses Sign FTC Stipulations," *Publishers Weekly* 164, no. 12 (September 19, 1953): 1203.
9. Joe Maynard and Barry Miles, comps., *William S. Burroughs, A Bibliography, 1953–73* (Charlottesville, Va.: Univ. Press of Virginia, 1977), p. 18.
10. For other titles on the list, see Note 1.
11. "A Report from Pocket Books," *Publishers Weekly* 137, no. 9 (March 2, 1940): 29.
12. U.S., Congress, House, Select Committee on Current Pornographic Materials, *An Investigation of Literature Allegedly Containing Objectionable Material.* Hearings. December 1–5, 1952 (Washington, D.C.: U.S. Government Printing Office, 1953), p. 34.
13. For a fuller description of this cover and dust jacket, see James L. West III, "The Bantam 'Gatsby,'" *Book Collector's Market* 3, no. 6 (November–December 1978): 15–18.

Further Reading

The following is a highly selective list of books and periodicals basic to knowledgeable paperback-book collecting. For those who wish to read more deeply into the history and practice of paperback publishing in America, I recommend: Thomas L. Bonn, "Mass Market Paperback Publishing, 1939–Present: An Annotated Bibliography," *Paperback Quarterly* 1 (Winter 1978).

HISTORY AND REFERENCE

Paperbound Books in Print. New York: Bowker, 1955–. A trade bibliography, listing by author, title, and subject, the paperback books currently available from United States publishers.

Peterson, Clarence. *The Bantam Story: Thirty Years of Paperback Publishing.* New York: Bantam, 1975. Although this history focuses on Bantam Books, it also credits the contributions of other publishers. Bantam's publishing practices, not unlike those of other large mass-market publishers, are also described.

Reginald, R., and Burgess, M. R. *Cumulative Paperback Index, 1939–1959: A Comprehensive Bibliographic Guide to 14,000 Mass-Market Paperback Books of 33 Publishers Issues under 69 Imprints.* Detroit: Gale, 1973. The single, most useful volume to the paperback collector. Basic for reference and research, it lists by author and title 20 years of mass-market paperback output.

Schick, Frank L. *The Paperbound Book in America.* New York: Bowker, 1958. Out of print for a number of years, this remains the only comprehensive history of paperback publishing in the United States. Schick's doctoral dissertation (same title) is available in hard copy or microfilm from Xerox University Microfilms, 300 North Zeeb Road, Ann Arbor, Michigan 48106.

COLLECTOR AND FAN PERIODICALS

Collecting Paperbacks? ed. by Lance Casebeer, 934 S.E. 15, Portland, Oregon 97214, 1979–. A new paperback collectors' newsletter and successor to Louis Black's *The Paperback Collector's Newsletter*, 1977–1979, nos. 1–12.

Guide to Current Fantasy Fanzines and Semi-Prozines. Published by Rosemary Pardoe, Flat 2, 38 Sandown Lane, Liverpool 15, England. 1978.

Guide to Current Fanzines. Published by Peter Roberts, 38 Oakland Drive, Dawlish, Devon, England.

Mystery Fancier. Published by Guy Townsend, 1120 Bluebird Lane, Memphis, Tennessee 38116. An annual feature is "The Line Up," a list of other mystery and detective fan magazines. 1977–.

Paperback Quarterly: A Journal for Paperback Collectors. Pecan Valley Press, 1710 Vincent, Brownwood, Texas 76801. 1978–. A periodical by collectors for collectors, it contains informative articles, checklists, and information queries and answers. In *Paperback Quarterly* one will find the names and addresses of book-sellers and collectors who buy, sell, or trade paperbacks.

Penguin Collectors' Society Newsletter. Cambridge, England: Penguin Collectors' Society, 1975–. A subscription is included with society membership. Address inquires to: A. K. Dalby, Editor, Penguin Collectors' Society Newsletter, 5 Primrose Way, Linton, Cambridge CB1 6UD, England.

BIOGRAPHY, BIBLIOGRAPHY, AND PSEUDONYMS

Atkinson, Frank. *Dictionary of Literary Pseudonyms: A Selection of Popular Modern Writers in English.* London: C. Bingley, 1977.

Ball, John. *The Mystery Story.* San Diego: Univ. Extension of the Univ. of California, San Diego, in cooperation with Publisher's Inc., 1976. Contains articles on book collecting and pseudonyms.

Bauer, Andre. *The Hawthorn Dictionary of Pseudonyms.* New York: Hawthorn, 1971.

Bruccoli, Matthew, and Clark, C. E. Frazer, Jr. *First Printings of American Authors.* 4 vols. Detroit: Gale, 1977–1979.

Contemporary Authors: The International Bio-bibliographical Guide to Current Authors and Their Works. Detroit: Gale, 1962–.

Gribbin, Leonore S. *Who's Whodunit: A List of 3218 Detective Story Writers and Their 1100 Pseudonyms.* Chapel Hill: Univ. of North Carolina Library, 1968.

McGhan, Barry. *Science Fiction and Fantasy Pseudonyms with 1973 Supplements.* Dearborn, Mich.: Misfit Press, 1973.

Sharp, Harold S. *Handbook of Pseudonyms and Personal Nicknames.* 2 vols. Metuchen, N.J.: Scarecrow Press, 1972.

Writers Dictionary, 1976–1978. New York: St. Martin's Press, 1976.

ARTIST INFORMATION

Annual of Advertising, Editorial, TV Art and Design. New York: 1921–. Published for the Art Directors Club of New York.

Illustrators; The Annual of American Illustration. New York: Hastings, 1959–. Published for the Society of Illustrators, New York City.

Paperbacks U.S.A. New York: American Institute of Graphic Arts, 1960–1964. Four annual catalogues of AIGA-sponsored paperback exhibitions.

Pitz, Henry. *200 Years of American Illustration.* New York: Random House, 1977. Sponsored by the Society of Illustrators, New York City.

Reed, Walt, ed. *The Illustrator in America, 1900–1960s.* New York: Reinhold, 1966.

6

Photography as Book Illustration, 1839–1900

Stuart Bennett

IN EVERY collecting field there seem to have been halcyon days when one could have had virtually anything, or everything, one wished. The early Victorian book collector Thomas Phillipps stated his intention of owning a copy of every book that had ever been printed, an approach shared until the early or even mid-1970s by practically everyone in the photography field. Nobody would have suggested that one should, or might necessarily be constrained to, collect anything less than the entire realm of historic photography, from daguerreotypes onward.

There is an additional relevance in comparing Sir Thomas to photography collectors of today: Phillipps, who was a friend of the photographic pioneer W. H. F. Talbot and some of whose early photographic possessions survive in an American private collection, lived during the great era of Victorian inventive achievement. Although he was not an inventor himself, his eclecticism and supreme confidence as a collector clearly derive from the same progressive impulse. The mercurial rise of photography collecting at the end of the 1960s and at the beginning of the 1970s derived from a similar confidence in the art market: in a politically and financially uncertain climate, art was something that could be both a considerable economic asset and an aesthetic pleasure. Traditional collecting fields were witnessing a strong and developing interest in Victoriana. In photography one had a specimen of Victoriana with a distinct advantage—it could be collected comprehensively from its origins to its essentially modern state by covering a period of about 50 years, all of them during Victoria's reign. The collector could be a latter-day Phillipps in microcosm.

History

The prehistory of photography embraces any number of technological innovations, from Aristotle's description of the camera obscura and Renaissance developments of the concept, through various chemical experiments—most particularly those of Thomas Wedgwood at the turn of the nineteenth century. Nicephore Niepce finally gave birth to the medium by successfully fixing, via a day-long exposure, a photographic image on a metal plate in 1826. Niepce's nephew (and heir to his photographic researches) went into partnership in the 1830s with L. J. M. Daguerre, a successful marketer of a trompe-l'oeil concept known as the diorama.

However one interprets the conflicting evidence as to how much technical work on the processes actually was performed by Daguerre as opposed to Niepce,[1] the end product was immortalized as the daguerreotype. Daguerre himself was able to secure a French government pension in exchange for making the process known "free to the world," which at the very least suggests a high degree of acumen in the world outside the laboratory, and in England there were patent restrictions financially beneficial to Daguerre. Another possible indication of Daguerre's antipathy to the chemical side of the process is that very few of his daguerreotypes are known to survive—fewer than a dozen, including studies of French architecture and at least one fine still life.

The process itself was a messy one, involving quantities of iodine vapor and mercury vapor heated over a spirit lamp. The exposure of the whole business to light by means of the then very primitive camera required additional skill, and the result was a single highly polished image. The plate inserted into the camera was developed into the final positive, which was then protected by glass and encased. Exposure times at first were enormously long, up to 20 minutes in full sunshine, but successive sophistications by other inventors finally enabled the development of the first successful portrait, generally attributed to the American John W. Draper, who sent it to J. F. W. Herschel on July 28, 1840.

From this time on, use of the daguerreotype process rapidly proliferated. The artist Paul Delaroche, seeing a daguerreotype after the announcement of the process at the Académie des Sciences on January

7, 1839, exclaimed, "From today painting is dead!" and his prognostication was to some extent confirmed, although not in the way he anticipated. The growth of the daguerreotype industry so undercut the rates painters of miniature portraits could charge that many of them were forced into the commercial daguerreotype studios as mere colorists. However, in some instances, notably in the London studios of Claudet and Kilburn in the early 1850s, the quality of the work was of an almost breathtaking delicacy of execution.

In the 1840s daguerreotype portraiture expanded rapidly, with Americans in particular displaying an awareness of its immense potential for recording history. Prior to 1845 the American daguerreotypist Dan Adams traveled to photograph ex-President Andrew Jackson shortly before his death, and portraits of Presidents John Quincy Adams, Zachary Taylor, and John Tyler survive from the same period. We owe to an Englishman, the inventor and surgeon Jabez Hogg, our first record, dating prior to August 1843, of the photographer in action in a daguerreotype studio. There also survives a study, probably taken a couple of years later, of photographers at work outdoors in W. H. F. Talbot's calotype studio in Reading, England.

This same W. H. F. Talbot, an experimenter in the best Victorian tradition, had been tinkering with photographic chemistry throughout the 1830s; his papers concerned with the effects of light on certain chemical compounds were published in various learned journals. At quite an early date he was able to produce "photogenic drawings" by placing objects, such as ferns and feathers, against sensitized paper, which was then exposed to light. His first photographic negative, of a window at Lacock Abbey, was produced in 1835. Daguerre's announcement took him entirely by surprise. He rushed into print with explanations of his own process, the success of which he believed, with some justification, to antedate Daguerre's announcement. He also attempted to impose severe patent restrictions, which he rigorously defended in court, with the result that he impeded the acceptance of his process and ultimately drove himself into poverty.

Talbot's calotype (from the Greek *kalos*—"beautiful") had one enormous advantage over daguerreotype in that the camera produced a paper negative, which could produce innumerable (in theory at any rate) positive images—also on paper. The primary difficulty of the calotype was that it often remained sensitive to light and progressively faded, sometimes quite literally leaving only a blank sheet of paper. Thus Talbot and the daguerreotype practitioners were reduced to concerning themselves with the same problem—how to produce multiple images that were permanent. One of their primary concerns was the production of multiple images suitable for book illustration.

As early as 1827 Nicephore Niepce had concerned himself with this problem, producing a copy of a copperplate engraving of a cardinal by applying light-sensitive bitumen of Judaea to a polished metal plate and exposing it to light directed through the engraving. The areas protected by the ink of the engraving and so unexposed were cleaned, then etched, inked, and printed. In 1840 the French publisher N. P. Lerebours capitalized on the publicity surrounding the new art by publishing *Excursions Daguerriennes*, a series of engravings copied (with embellishments) from daguerreotypes, a number of which were taken as far afield as Moscow, Stockholm, Egypt, and Niagara Falls. Some of the daguerreotypes themselves were later sold by Claudet, and several of the best were selected by Queen Victoria and Prince Albert for their own collection in advance of public sale.

In the meantime the Frenchman Hippolyte Fizeau had developed and was attempting to perfect a process whereby daguerreotype images could themselves be etched to produce a plate suitable for printing. The daguerreotype was slightly recessed by electrolytic etching, so that the dark portions of the image were left above the lighter portions. Stiff ink was then applied and printing carried out, but it was found that the plates went "soft" and the images deteriorated after only a few impressions. Far more successful was a process known as photoxylography, whereby a photograph is produced on a chemically sensitized woodblock, which is then carved by the engraver. This process was first used on April 27, 1839, in the *Magazine of Science*. For some time, however, the process could be used only with inanimate objects due to the long exposure times required.

To the calotype, however, belongs the distinction of being the first purely photographic process applied to book illustration. In 1843 Talbot already was planning the treatise on the uses and potential of photography that was to become *The Pencil of Nature* (Plate 23). Before Part I was published Talbot supplied calotypes photographed from a portrait bust for the privately printed *Record of the Death Bed of C. M. W.* This work, dating from 1844, holds the record of being the world's first photographically illustrated book, although collectors without it asten to point out that *The Pencil of Nature* is still the world's first *published* photographically illustrated book. Collectors with neither of these, but in possession of a copy of Talbot's *Sun Pictures in Scotland* (1845), however, can point out that theirs is the world's first published photographically illustrated book to be issued in its entirety. After it had

PLATE 23   An upper wrapper from one of the parts of *The Pencil of Nature*, the first published photographically illustrated book (London: Longman, Brown, Green & Longmans, 1844–1846).

been completely produced and published, a progressively less enthusiastic public still was awaiting Parts V and VI of *The Pencil of Nature.*

One might say that Gutenberg's 42-line Bible established a standard of printing that successive generations of printers have failed to maintain by an increasingly wide margin. One hardly could impute to Gutenberg, pioneer though he was, the purpose of establishing such a standard, but Talbot's *Pencil of Nature* is precisely such a statement of purpose. Each of the 24 plates is intended to illustrate a particular aspect of photography—from city views, rural scenes, architectural details, and monuments, to sculptures, botanical tracings, facsimiles of books and etchings, and still lifes—whereas *Sun Pictures in Scotland* depicts photography at work in what was and is its most popular sphere—topographical illustration. Throughout the remainder of the 1840s, calotypes were produced for book illustration. (In 1846 Talbot's Reading, England, studio produced approximately 5,000 prints for a single number of *The Art Union.*) But by the early 1850s, disenchanted with the progressive fading to which his calotypes remained subject, Talbot attempted to develop other techniques.

Talbot's photoglyphic experiments performed during the period 1852–1860, although never commercially successful, anticipated many of the techniques of modern photogravure and halftone printing. His experiments with engraving techniques, attempts to compensate for the defects of his calotype process, were not to come to fruition until the 1880s, when first photogravure, and then type-compatible screen halftone processes, effectively supplanted the mounted photograph as book illustration. Until this time the history of photography and its history as book illustration had run parallel courses, with successive sophistications of photographic printing techniques providing increasingly permanent and decreasingly expensive prints for all kinds of artistic and illustrative purposes.

The first significant improvement on Talbot's calotype was the introduction of the waxed-paper negative, by Gustave Le Gray in 1851. This new development enabled more prints of a higher quality to be taken from an individual negative. While Talbot was fighting his court battles in England for control over this and other sophistications of the positive-negative photographic process, several books illustrated with salt prints from waxed-paper negatives were produced on the Continent, the most striking of which, and now excessively rare, were Maxime du Camp's *Egypte, Nubie, Palestine et Syrie* (1852)—the first French photographically illustrated book—Auguste Salzmann's *Jerusalem* (1856), and Felix Teynard's *Egypte et Nubie: Sites et Monuments* (published between

1853 and 1858). The last was published at the intimidatingly high price of 1,000 gold francs, doubtless explaining its rarity.

Although the waxed-paper negative, with its attractively soft tonalities and almost "pointilliste" graininess, continued to be used by photographers into the 1860s, Frederick Scott Archer's invention of the albumen-on-glass technique in 1852 soon supplanted the paper negatives for his 1854–1855 reporting of the Crimean War, and by the end of the decade a number of Englishmen were at work producing books illustrated with mounted photographs taken by means of the albumen process. Albumen printing remained widely used through the 1880s, and even beyond the turn of the century such an important practitioner as Eugene Atget was producing his magnificent studies of Paris and its environs by means of a sophisticated version of albumen printing.

But fading, imperfections in print, and variations in color and tone remained problems with albumen prints—to say nothing of the chemical complexities and forbidding stains and smells attendant on their use, as, among others, guests of Julia Margaret Cameron testify—and the quest for simplicity and permanence in photographic printing continued. As early as 1856 Paul Pretsch developed a successful photo-gravure printing technique, which was, however, unsatisfactory in its rendering of detail. He called the technique photogalvanography, because the production of the final copper printing block involved electrolytic deposition. A number of individual photographs, most significantly those by Roger Fenton, were reproduced this way and marketed, but the project was not a financial success and apparently was abandoned in 1859. By the mid-1860s carbon printing, first begun experimentally by the Frenchman A. L. Poitevin and perfected by the Englishman J. W. Swan, provided one alternative. It involved the application of different reliefs of pigmented gelatin, with the visible darkness and light in the image varying according to the depth of the carbon layer. Variations on this technique produced the autotype and, most beautiful of all carbon techniques, the Woodburytype, in which a gelatin relief was transferred to a lead mold and printed.

All of these techniques were used, along with the albumen print, and, of course, the entire range of metal, stone, and wood engraving available for book illustration, throughout the remainder of the 1860s and 1870s. The 1870s saw the introduction of bromide and platinotype printing, the first (at least in its early guise) visually almost indistinguishable from albumen, the second displaying a delicacy of detail and tonal splendor entirely befitting the precious metal used. The same decade, however, saw the onset of cost cutting, most particularly with the introduction of collotype printing. Its basic technique, which had a variety of trade names, utilized a gelatin-coated plate exposed to a negative so that the gelatin hardened according to the lights and darks of the image. The plate could be coated with a greasy ink, which was retained according to the hardness of the gelatin, and printed. The result reflected the quality of the ink used, and although special printing paper was required, the end product anticipated the type-compatible screen halftone process introduced a decade later—the death knell of pure photographic printing except in infrequently produced and expensive limited editions.

The development of a true photogravure process was not to come until the late 1870s, and although Karl Klic published his results in Vienna in 1879, the details remained secret for several years afterward. By the early 1880s, however, the British were publishing books illustrated with photogravures, mostly engraved by Annan and Swan. G. Christopher Davies's *Studies of the Broads of Norfolk and Suffolk* began a trend that was continued by P. H. Emerson and communicated by him to the British "Linked Ring," Albert Stieglitz, and the Photo Secession. Throughout this chronological and transatlantic progression, extending over two decades, several thousand miles, and a number of different countries, the photographers involved remained, almost without exception, true to two techniques: platinotype printing for individual photographs and, after Emerson's financially disastrous *Life and Landscape on the Norfolk Broads* (Plate 24), published in 1886, photogravure printing for publication. World War I in effect brought the movement to an end, with its inflationary effect on the cost of the expert labor required for photogravure printing and with the military's monopoly over available platinum supplies effectively pricing it out of the photographer's reach. The 1920s brought bromide printing and halftone publishing into almost universal use, the latter excepting, as indicated earlier, certain limited edition books and portfolios, and thus it has remained to the present day. The early 1970s, however, saw the advent of the experimental photographer bent on using platinotype regardless of cost and, rather more frighteningly, the forger, with the materials and expertise to produce salted paper and albumen prints often virtually indistinguishable from those of the photographic pioneers.

Collecting Photography: A Phenomenon of the 1970s

Isolated attempts to offer photographs to collectors were carried out by the London booksellers E. P. Goldschmidt and Maggs Brothers

PLATE 24   "Marsh Man Going to Cut Schoof-Stuff," plate XXII from *Life and Landscape on the Norfolk Broads*, by P. H. Emerson and T. F. Goodall (London: Sampson, Low, 1886). One of the 40 platinotype plates comprising what is arguably the most beautiful photographically illustrated books ever produced.

(through their Paris office) in 1939, celebrating the centenary of Daguerre, but few were sold. The two catalogues themselves are rarities, not to mention their contents; the prices are nothing short of tantalizing to the modern collector. Probably the first serious marketing attempt in the United States was a 1952 auction held by Swann Galleries, later followed by Parke Bernet with their 1967 sale of the Will Weissberg collection, in which a portrait of Tennyson by Julia Margaret Cameron (see Plate 25) made an astonishing $350, more than a complete copy of *The Pencil of Nature* in 1952. The 1970 Sidney Strober sale, again held by Parke Bernet in New York, was truly the birth of the goose that laid the golden egg. A copy of George Barnard's *Photographic Views of Sherman's Campaign* (1866) fetched the then staggering price of $5,400, and other books and individual photographs realized comparatively high prices.

These prices reflected an emerging interest on the part of Americans in a field that was richly illustrative of the formative years of the country, and by the late 1960s several museums and private collectors had begun eclectic collections of photographic "greats." Even a few

PLATE 25   Portrait of Alfred, Lord Tennyson as "The Dirty Monk." Frontispiece to
Volume I of *Illustrations to Tennyson's Idylls of the King*, by Julia Margaret Cameron (London:
Henry S. King, 1874–1875).

years previously, however, collectors such as Rolf Schultze could write: "There are probably not more than a dozen serious collectors of photographically illustrated books, private or institutional. This, fortunately, has kept the prices low, except for some 'firsts' and certain books known to be rare. . . . Prices should remain modest as long as . . . the fashion for Victoriana does not spread, and too many new collectors are not attracted."[2]

Needless to say, Schultze's provisos, published in 1962, were soon to be fulfilled as prophecies, as Victoriana became increasingly fashionable and the number of photographic collectors grew. London auctioneers entered the photography market in 1971, and soon both Christie's and Sotheby's were holding regular sales of photographic material. Several of the major American private collections were in the formative stages in these early years. Arnold Crane of Chicago, who had been active in the 1960s as well, bought the magnificent Edgar Allan Poe daguerreotype sold in Chicago in 1973 and owns a representative cross section of nineteenth- and twentieth-century work. By the mid-1970s both Samuel Wagstaff and Paul Walter, New York private collectors, had developed collections with a liberal sprinkling of work by the major nineteenth- and twentieth-century photographers. Both have demonstrated an awareness of specialized collection possibilities in the field and almost certainly have influenced institutional curators.

At the autumn 1978 symposium of photography collecting at Eastman House in Rochester, New York, Wagstaff presented a paper on collecting potentialities in the realm of nineteenth-century American stereo cards, a previously neglected field. Walter's interest in the photography of India has quickened interest not only in that field but in collecting by geographic area generally. There also have been a number of splendid exhibitions that, together with their attendant catalogues, have given indications of trends in contemporary photography collecting. Among them are the exhibitions of Photo-Secession work and photographs of the American West at the Metropolitan Museum and of selections from the Andre Jammes collection, first at the Philadelphia Museum of Art in 1969, and at the Art Institute of Chicago in 1977. In addition there have been several fine gallery shows, concentrated mostly on the American seaboards but spreading to Europe and Japan in the later 1970s.

For the most part the price structure of the photographic market has altered so substantially over the last decade that the formation of a comprehensive, or at any rate representative, photographic collection is now out of the question on a budget of less than several hundred thousand dollars. Admittedly one could point out that it is still possible to form a representative photographic collection for less than the cost of a single major impressionist painting, but the fact remains that either alternative is beyond the means of most acquisition librarians and private collectors. Specialization is the answer, and in a thoroughly unprogrammatic way the remainder of this chapter attempts to suggest collecting paths that are still open in the photographic world.

Collecting Paths in Nineteenth-Century Photography
COMPARISON OF PHOTOGRAPHIC STYLES

It is difficult now to estimate the impact that photography had at the time of its introduction in 1839. To many, the representation of an image as it actually was, coming into existence on a piece of paper or a metal plate, seemed nothing less than the result of divine agency. To engravers and painters, particularly portrait painters, concerned, as so rarely is the case in the twentieth century, with a lifelike representation of a subject, Paul Delaroche's prediction of the death of painting must have seemed all too real a prospect. And this concept was one with which much of the evolution of photography was concerned, this depiction of "things as they actually are."

As documentary sources, the value of nineteenth-century photographs is generally recognized, even if only to the extent that many universities in the eastern United States rely on ancient files of old Alinari and Sommer photographs to show art history students the relics of Italy. There is, however, enormous potential for research and documentation of the evolution of illustrative styles after the introduction of photography in the mid-nineteenth century, not only, for example, in the comparison of photographically illustrated books with their steel-engraved brethren of the period, but in the broader sense of how photographic realism necessarily modified the imaginative excesses of earlier illustrators.

The many topographical works devoted to the Near East and Egypt provide a good case in point when compared to Francis Frith's 1858 photographic studies of the area, but even Frith ran afoul of public opinion when it was felt that the crocodile depicted in one of his photographs simply could not exist. Comparison of works by the artist William Simpson and the photographer Roger Fenton, both chroniclers of the Crimean War, reveals enormous differences of style and choice of subject, even given that Fenton was prohibited by long exposure times from portraying action and by a directive from no less august a personage than Prince Albert from photographing corpses on the battle-field. The potential for comparative study is vast, and the photographic works absent from libraries whose specialized area collections are illustrated by other techniques can probably be obtained at less than prohibitive cost.

INDIVIDUAL PHOTOGRAPHS

Even from the earliest days of successful calotype production it has been impossible to categorize photographically illustrated books separately from individual image production. This fact could enable the discriminating collector of photographic incunabula, now generally accepted as works published before 1860, to amass a representative group of separately published images by many of the major photographers to complement what complete books are available within his/her budget. There will, nevertheless, necessarily be gaps.

Fox Talbot published many of the calotypes from *The Pencil of Nature* and *Sun Pictures in Scotland* separately, as did the Bisson Frères with the photographs in *Monographie de Notre Dame de Paris* and Francis Frith in his Egyptian books. However, as with illustrated books of other periods and techniques, the market for individual plates often has been more readily accessible to, and more lucrative for, the dealer than complete works have been. The considerable number of individual photographs available from, for example, Maxime du Camp's 1852 *Egypte, Nubie, Palestine et Syrie* and Auguste Salzmann's 1856 *Jerusalem* are almost certainly all from breakers—and so unacceptable to the purist. If one's concern is with the historical representation of the early progress of photography, then these individual plates are still useful—and many of them are of extraordinary beauty.

Some consolation can be taken from the fact that a complete copy of du Camp's work reportedly changed hands in Paris in 1977 at a figure between $30,000 and $40,000, and *Jerusalem* generally is considered to be in the same price category. There is no doubt, therefore, that collecting photographic incunabula per se is both difficult and expensive and, like the collecting of printed incunabula, is perhaps best left to those institutions already with substantial holdings and to the nearly extinct breed of private collector endowed both with unlimited funds and inexhaustible patience.

THE PUBLISHING HISTORY OF PHOTOGRAPHY

Particularly in the early days, the publishing history of photography reads as a virtual catalogue of disasters, with technical problems, long production delays, and undersubscription by the public most common. Most of the early photographically illustrated works were published privately, although for a time in the early to mid-1850s there seemed to be a sound economic base in France for the production of major photographically illustrated works—those of du Camp, Bisson, Salzmann, and others—by having negatives processed by a commercial developer, usually Blanquart-Evrard, and then published under the imprint of Gide and Baudry, or Baudry alone, in Paris.

In Great Britain and the United States several commercial publishers tried their hands at photography. The two first photographically illustrated works published in the United States were published in 1854 by the substantial houses of G. P. Putnam of New York and Ticknor & Fields of Boston. By 1856 the British publishers Agnew & Sons, Chapman & Hall, and Joseph Cundall had tried their hands, as had Low, Son & Co., a precursor of the firm that was to be so active in photographic publishing in the 1870s and 1880s. But these were isolated efforts for the most part, and in 1857 or 1858 Lovell Reeve was one of the first commercial publishers to undertake photographic printing on a regular basis. He is particularly well known for his publication of C. Piazzi Smyth's *Teneriffe*, published with stereoscopic albumen photographs in 1858 (and still surprisingly common), for his much rarer *Stereoscopic Magazine*, published erratically between 1858 and 1865, and other works of the same period.

The year 1862 saw the first appearance of the great publisher of photographically illustrated travel books, Alfred William Bennett, with the first series of William and Mary Howitt's *Ruined Abbeys and Castles of Great Britain*. Bennett continued to produce works illustrated by photographers as significant as Francis Frith, George Washington Wilson, and Ernest Edwards until the end of the decade. Sampson, Low, Son & Marston, a successor to Low, Son & Co., published Elihu Burritt's *A Walk from London to John O'Groats* in 1864 but remained relatively, if not completely, inactive in photographic production until the early 1870s, when they produced one of their greatest works, indeed one of the great photographically illustrated books of the nineteenth century, William Bradford's *The Arctic Regions* (Plate 26), published in folio with 129 mounted albumen prints. Sampson, Low continued to innovate in the field for the next two decades, publishing works in Woodburytype, P. H. Emerson's monumental *Life and Landscape on the Norfolk Broads* in platinotype, and in the late 1880s and 1890s producing some of the finest photogravure works of the period. Many of these nineteenth-century publications, particularly those of A. W. Bennett,

PLATE 26   Study of William Bradford's ship "The Panther," from *The Arctic Regions*, with 129 mounted albumen prints (London: Sampson, Low, 1873).

were surprisingly undervalued in the mid-1870s, and although they have become increasingly scarce, they provide an approach to photography collecting that both constitutes a challenge for the diligent collector and repays scholarly investigation.

PHOTOGRAPHS OF WORKS OF ART

Another realm of scholarly investigation in which photographically illustrated books could play a useful part is that of art history. Vast numbers of books were produced from the late 1840s to about 1890, when it was more economical to mount photographs individually in small editions than to produce a lithographic or steel-engraved plate, and many of these reproduced such works of art as antiquities, porcelain, and paintings. The books themselves, displaying practically every photographic printing technique used during the period, provide an ideal cross section of these techniques as utilized in book production, and many of them, with such features as morocco bindings, gilt and gauffered edges, and color printing are splendid examples of the Victorian bookmaker's craft. Surely someone someday will rise to the challenge of determining how many of the works of art illustrated in these books are now lost to posterity.

PORTRAIT PHOTOGRAPHY AND ALBUMS

As is still the case with specialized art reference books, the market for Victorian examples was limited, but concurrently with these scholarly productions ran one of the most popular of Victorian collecting fashions, the carte-de-visite portrait, usually mounted on a 2½-by-4-inch card and earning its name by the use to which it most often was put. To the modern eye there is an almost irresistible magic in seeing Victorian celebrities as they actually were, and this spirit seems to have been shared by the Victorian middle classes, who collected these portraits, along with those of friends and relatives, in such quantity.

The commercial distribution of portraits of celebrities was made possible only by the use of a positive-negative process allowing multiple prints, and it would seem that the first successful marketing of such portraits prior to the introduction of cartes de visite in the late 1850s, was by the Edinburgh printseller Alexander Hill, distributor of the photographs taken by his brother David Octavius and the calotypist Robert Adamson. D. O. Hill and Adamson had begun collaborating on calotype portraits in 1843 when Hill won a commission to paint a group portrait of the 155 churchmen involved in the formation of the Free Church of Scotland. The photographs produced were of fairly limited and local appeal, but they are among the finest photographic portraits ever taken, all the more remarkable for their appearance in the very earliest era of photography, and their success prompted the photographers to undertake more ambitious portrait studies and even a few landscapes.

By the early 1850s there was a certain potential for the marketing of copy daguerreotypes, rephotographed in limited numbers from a master original, and Negretti and Zambra, opticians, sold among other views of the Crystal Palace a number of stereoscopic daguerreotypes taken on April 20, 1855, showing Napoleon III and Empress Eugénie in the company of Queen Victoria and Prince Albert posed on a platform in the Great Hall at the time of their state visit to the palace. The London photographers Maull and Polyblank in 1856 introduced a series called *Men of Mark*, which was to anticipate the later Lock and Whitfield and Alvin Langdon Coburn publications of the same name. The 1856 series was particularly rich in scientists, Darwin and Faraday among them, and at least two copies are recorded of the compilation *The Literary and Scientific Portrait Club* with fine portraits of the most eminent Victorian men of science, several of whom were dead before 1860, posed with their apparatus and specimens.

The late 1850s saw the introduction both of the photographic portrait frontispiece and, as previously mentioned, the carte-de-visite photograph. It is to the popularity of the latter that we owe so many of the fine portraits of celebrities in all fields and most nations dating from the 1860s onward, and collecting portraits, whether by period, nation, or subject, is still a possibility with rich potential. Some English Victorian albums are full of literary figures; one album from the 1860s is recorded as containing 18 different poses, mounted one to a page, of Charles Dickens. Less commonly, portraits of artists and composers turn up, or studies of such subjects as European costume, circus acts, inventions, humorous tableaux, usually with an appropriate caption, and sententiae photographed from embroidery. Most common in European albums, apart from the ubiquitous compilations of family photographs, are portraits of royalty and nobility, particularly of the English royal family. Many of these portraits are by the most distinguished photography studios of the period, taken, one can be reasonably assured, by the proprietors themselves, such as Mayall, Disderi, Claudet, and Hughes. Some of the finest of all are by Camille Silvy, a Frenchman who practiced his art in London, and these display a sensitivity for composition and pose that make them distinguishable even without reference to the photographer's credits usually so helpfully printed on the versos.

In the United States carte-de-visite portraiture was gaining popularity at about the time of the outbreak of the Civil War, and a number of albums survive with portraits of Abraham Lincoln, his cabinet, and the various generals and officers of the Union armies, and sometimes including copy prints of prewar portraits of Confederate officers or, more rarely, portraits produced in Southern studios. Many of the best were taken in Mathew Brady's Washington, D.C., studio, and some records survive of the studies of Lincoln taken at various times during the war. In 1866 the negatives of the by-then bankrupt Brady were taken over by the New York firm of E. & H. T. Anthony and republished with a suitably revised credit "from photographic negative by Brady" on the reverse. The albums compiled during the Civil War do not have the Anthony credit on Brady's photographs and can often be quite precisely dated by reference to the successive generals of the Union Army of the Potomac. Confederate albums are extremely rare, and American albums of any period devoted to literary and artistic celebrities are by no means common, although both in the United States and Europe albums were compiled of portraits of favorite theatrical and operatic performers.

Until recently albums were likely to be offered on the market as found, but the growth of interest in cartes de visite—one exceptional album, consisting almost entirely of circus acts, costume studies, nudes, and other esoterica including self-portraits of photographers, sold in a London auction for £2,000—has made it necessary to keep in mind that albums can easily be made up, and unless there is physical evidence of provenance it is wise for the collector to regard the total as no more than the sum of its parts, that is, of the individual portraits.

Carte-de-visite photography persisted in one form or another virtually until World War I. Over the decades the format grew larger, with the cabinet portrait and "imperial-size" cabinet portrait introduced as attempts to retain public interest. There were also successive publications of portraits of eminent personalities in book form, with varying degrees of commercial success. In the United States and England engravings taken from photographic portraits were published in the 1850s and early 1860s, Brady's *Gallery of Illustrious Americans* (1850) being perhaps the most notable and apparently least commercially successful. Although for the most part portraiture in the 1860s and early 1870s was dominated by the carte de visite, there were some fascinating oddities produced in book form, such as E. B. Hilliard's *The Last Men of the Revolution*, published in Connecticut in 1864, with mounted portraits of six survivors of the American revolutionary war.

The mid-1870s saw major undertakings in portrait publishing begun on both sides of the English Channel. Arguably the finest series of portraits ever produced was the French *Galerie Contemporaine*. Begun in 1876 and printed in Woodburytype from negatives by the best of the French photographers—such as Nadar, Carjat, and Adam-Soloman—it contained portraits of George Sand, Baudelaire, Rossini, Dumas, and virtually every other artistic notable in France at the time. Less impressive, although still a substantial undertaking, was the earlier *Paris-théâtre* published between 1873 and 1875, with each issue containing a portrait of a French performer. The firm of Lock and Whitfield began their massive *Men of Mark* series the same year as the *Galerie Contemporaine*. Published by Sampson, Low, it does not approach the artistic heights of the French publication, but it contains 252 portraits published between 1876 and 1883 of most of the eminent personalities of the period. Judging from the number of copies that have survived, it seems to have been a successful venture and was followed by such publications as W. & D. Downey's *Cabinet Portrait Gallery,* Bassano's *Our Conservative and Unionist Statesmen,* and other works of the 1880s and 1890s.

Portrait publishing in book form in the United States was limited largely to frontispieces and the occasional esoteric and privately printed compilation, such as the 1876 *Biographical Sketches of the Leading Men of Chicago,* a copy of which is in the New York Public Library. In the twentieth century even the great American photographer Alvin Langdon Coburn produced and published his fine *Men of Mark* and *More Men of Mark* in London, and it is not beyond the realm of possibility that his titles were chosen as recognition of the English portrait tradition in which he was working.

If portraiture itself provides the most fertile ground for the prospective collector, there are areas in which portraiture can overlap and complement nonphotographic collections. The most obvious is the Victorian obsession with the interaction of psychology and physiognomy. Darwin's 1872 *The Expression of the Emotions in Man and Animals,* illustrated with heliotypes by Oscar Rejlander, is the photographically illustrated classic on this subject. There also are distinct possibilities for collecting photographically illustrated books on scientific subjects, Piazzi Smyth's 1858 *Teneriffe* being perhaps the first, but for the most part these works are few and far between. When they began to be produced in some quantity in the 1890s and later, they were almost invariably printed with screen halftones.

ALLEGORICAL PHOTOGRAPHS

Another intriguing, and largely unexplored, area of nineteenth-century study, embracing literature and art, is the use of allegory in photography. Literature, academic painting, and indeed musical compositions were rife with allegorical subjects during the period in which photography was born, and the new art was quick to climb on the bandwagon, as can be seen in the remarkable calotypes of the 1840s by the Frenchman Hippolyte Bayard and in the use of allegory in early still-life daguerreotypes.

The English painter Lake Price was the first to introduce "picture-making" into photography, with his 1856 studio composites "The Baron's Feast" and "Don Quixote in His Study." One of Lake Price's compositions, "A Scene at the Tower," depicting the young princes murdered by Richard III, caught the imagination of Lewis Carroll— "a capital idea for making up pictures."[3] Exhibitions of these studies caught the interest, and ultimately won the patronage, of Prince Albert.

Oscar Rejlander introduced a technically more complicated form of allegory in his 1858 study "The Two Ways of Life," displaying the virtuous and the dissolute in a series of biblical tableaux, printed from 30 different negatives. Prince Albert bought a print of this study as well, and the photographers Lake Price and later H. P. Robinson followed Rejlander's lead by producing ever more complicated compositions, as Roger Fenton did more subtly in his Eastern tableaux vivants and *odalisques* and as David Wilkie Wynfield did in his studies of artists in period costume.

Julia Margaret Cameron produced one allegorical study after another, killing the swans in Freshwater Bay in order that their wings might transform children into angels, and many of these compositions are, to say the least, appallingly unsuccessful. Some of the groups, however, notably those without wings, have an undeniable power, and Cameron's *Illustrations to Tennyson's Idylls of the King* (1874–1875), which utilized servants and artisans in many of the principal roles, captures in photographs, such as "The Parting of Lancelot and Guinevere," some of the finest allegorical work of the nineteenth century.

Denounced in its own time, neglected since, and only recently sought by collectors dismayed at what has turned out to be the extreme rarity of examples of the genre, it may even now be too late for a comprehensive collection of allegorical photographs of the nineteenth century ever to be assembled.

PHOTOGRAPHY AS SOCIAL HISTORY

Any attempt to indicate paths in photography collecting would be incomplete without some reference to the mine of photographic material available for social documentation. Some of the photographically illustrated books are classics: Mayhew's *London Labour and London Poor* (1860), illustrated with woodcuts taken from Beard daguerreotypes (the daguerreotypes themselves are lost); John Thomson's *Illustrations of China and Its People* and *Street Life in London* (Plate 27); and Jack London's *People of the Abyss*. There is, however, an even greater wealth of material outside the photographically illustrated book, much of it only beginning to be collated.

One area of social history ripe for more thorough study is the progress of the photographic war reporter. The few surviving daguerreotypes of the Mexican War are now well documented, as for the most part is the work of Fenton and Robertson in the Crimea. The Brady studio's work during the American Civil War, and monumental books on the subject by Barnard and Gardner, are generally known, although

PLATE 27   A sign painter from *Street Life in London*, by John Thomson and Adolphe Smith, with 36 Woodburytype plates (London: Sampson, Low, 1877–1878).

there is much work to be done in tracing the steps of the various photographers working for Brady in order to document their individual work. Although these are well-known areas, at present no satisfactory catalogue exists for the 1858 Indian Mutiny, which was photographed in depth by Felix Beato, as was the 1860 China Opium War and subsequent movements of British troops. Little has been done by way of documentation of the Franco-Prussian War and its aftermath, partly no doubt due to the anonymous character of most of this work and its suppression by the French authorities, but a considerable quantity has survived nevertheless. Even less is known about John Burke's movements during the Afghan campaigns from 1878 to 1880, even though he produced prints in some quantity, and a collection and comparison of the work of other traveling photographers would doubtless reveal more reporting of local insurrections so far undocumented.

Another collecting area still very much open is that of photographic documentation of cities. Many of the photographically illustrated books produced on the subject document ancient relics, as does Dixon and Boole's project for the Society for Photographing Relics of Old London in the 1880s. At least as fruitful an endeavor would be the documentation through photography of the rise of many of the world's great cities. This is particularly possible in the case of the United States and the Far East, where, particularly in the American West, itinerant and later local photographers produced views of cities for tourists; for example, Thomas Houseworth and later Taber published views of San Francisco, including many from early negatives by photographers such as Muybridge and Watkins. Savage documented Salt Lake City, while Jackson documented the Denver area, as well as the progress of railroads in the West generally. In the Far East there are early views by Beato and Thomson of Hong Kong and Canton, and Beato and others later produced views of unwesternized Japanese cities, particularly Nagasaki, Tokyo, and Yokohama. Later photographers covered many of the South Sea islands; Notman, in particular, published fine Canadian studies beginning in the 1860s; and Marc Ferrar in Brazil, Samuel Boote in Argentina and elsewhere, and other traveling camera artists documented the rise of the city in South America.

Financial Pitfalls

Potential collections in photography cover virtually the entire nineteenth-century subject catalogue. Although there is still a vast amount of collectible material available, it is well to point out that there are pitfalls, particularly financial ones, for the unwary collector. Beginning with the Parke Bernet auctions of the late 1960s, photography began to elevate itself from the realm of ephemera to that of fine-art collecting, with all the revisions in prices such a shift entails. To a certain extent modern taste has reverted to that of the Victorians, and once again it has become fashionable to hang photographs on walls, whether they be in private homes or galleries. Generally speaking this has meant that photographs of interesting subjects large enough to be satisfactorily hung, whether Jackson landscapes or Cameron portraits, have escalated in price most substantially, and sometimes the price escalation occurred before the relative scarcities of various photographers' work were established satisfactorily. Certainly it has proved to be the case that Jacksons and Camerons are less rare than was thought in the early 1970s, although examples with fine tonal ranges are still seldom seen and command an appropriate premium. A number of the illustrated books of the 1860s that brought high prices on first appearance in the auction rooms fell considerably on repeated subsequent appearances. Many of these works, however, are now turning up less frequently, as are really fine compilations of cartes de visite, and it seems likely that one day the 1970s will be seen as the halcyon days of photography collecting. Many public and institutional collections of photographs remain uncatalogued or unchecked against other holdings, and very little in the nature of a census of copies of photographs or of illustrated books has appeared. The few that have appeared suggest a terrifying rarity of major works; a recent Harvard article, for example, suggested that as few as a dozen copies of Cameron's *Illustrations to Tennyson's Idylls of the King* may survive.

Nevertheless, it is as well to beware of the collector or dealer who refers to a carte de visite or stereo card, or even a book, as "rare"; it may mean simply that the collector has not seen it before, and it is entirely legitimate to ask how diligent a search was done. Those fortunate enough to travel would do well to investigate photographic archives whenever possible to gain their own ideas of comparative rarity. One generalization that appears safe from the commercial market of the 1970s is that very often what is common is exceedingly common and what is rare, exceedingly rare. Many of the finest individual paper photographs of the nineteenth century are known only in one example. It is probably also safe, in conclusion, to generalize that the collector of photographs enters a field in which there is an enormous wealth of material available, and the collector who is also a scholar may rest secure in the knowledge that any serious research he/she may undertake is virtually certain to be original.

Notes

1. The one certain chemical development in the art of photography we can attribute to Daguerre was the result of an accident; mercury from a broken thermometer spilled onto a discarded photographic plate and produced an image. It seems likely, however, that Daguerre also discovered the fixing properties of common salt. See Gernsheim, *The History of Photography . . . up to 1914* (New York: Oxford, 1955), p. 50.
2. Rolf Schultze, *Victorian Book Illustration with Original Photographs and by Early Photomechanical Processes* (London: National Book League, 1962), p. 1.
3. Helmut Gernsheim, *Creative Photography: Aesthetic Trends, 1839-1960* (Boston: Boston Book & Art Shop, 1962), p. 76.

Further Reading

The still-standard work for any approach to photographic history is Helmut and Alison Gernsheim's *The History of Photography . . . up to 1914* (New York: Oxford, 1955), which was later published under the title *The History of Photography from Camera Obscura to the Beginning of the Modern Era* (New York: McGraw-Hill, 1969). A valuable abridgment of this work, and a good introduction to the subject, is *A Concise History of Photography* (New York: Grosset & Dunlap, 1965). Beaumont Newhall's *The History of Photography*, first published in 1939, has also recently been reissued (New York: Museum of Modern Art, 1972).

So far there has been no satisfactory, or even unsatisfactory, attempt to document photographically illustrated books comprehensively. Two useful articles are Rolf Schultze's *Victorian Book Illustration with Original Photographs and by Early Photomechanical Processes*, the catalogue of a National Book League exhibition held October 8–13, 1962, and Julia van Haaften's "Original Sun Pictures: A Check List of the New York Public Library's Holdings of Early Works Illustrated with Photographs" (*New York Public Library Bulletin* 80, no. 3, Spring 1977).

A large proportion of the books on photographic subjects currently available are of the coffee-table variety. Some of the best on individual subjects are listed here.

Borcoman, James. *Charles Negre, 1820–1880*. Ottawa: National Gallery, 1976.

Ford, Colin. *The Cameron Collection*. Washington, D.C.: The National Portrait Gallery, 1975.

Ford, Colin, and Strong, Roy. *An Early Victorian Album.* New York: Knopf, 1977.

Gernsheim, Helmut. *Creative Photography: Aesthetic Trends, 1839–1960.* Boston: Book & Art Shop, 1962.

———. *Lewis Carroll: Photographer.* New York: Dover, 1970.

———. *Julia Margaret Cameron, 1875.* Millerton, N.Y.: Aperture, 1974. (Some of the attributions in this and the preceding work have required revision.)

Gernsheim, Helmut, and Gernsheim, Alison. *L. J. M. Daguerre.* New York: Dover, 1969.

———. *Roger Fenton.* London: Secker & Warburg, 1954.

Newhall, Beaumont. *The Daguerreotype in America.* New York: Dover, 1976.

Taft, Robert. *Photography and the American Scene.* New York: Dover, 1964 (c. 1938).

Thornton, Ann, trans. *Rome in Early Photographs: The Age of Pius IX.* Copenhagen: The Thorvaldsen Museum, 1977.

Since the early 1970s several excellent exhibition catalogues with information unobtainable elsewhere also have been published.

Naef, Weston J., and Wood, James N. *Era of Exploration: The Rise of Landscape Photography in the American West, 1860–1885.* New York: Metropolitan Museum of Art, 1975.

Pfister, Harold Francis. *Facing the Light: Historic American Portrait Daguerreotypes.* Washington, D.C.: The National Portrait Gallery, 1978.

Une Invention du XIXe Siècle: Expression et Technique—La Photographie. Paris: Bibliothèque Nationale, 1976.

Anyone intending to collect will find all auctioneers' catalogues indispensable. Many of these are out of print, but some back copies, with price lists, are usually available from Sotheby Parke-Bernet, Swann Galleries, Phillips, Christie's (New York), Christie's, South Kensington, and Sotheby's Belgravia (London). A number of the art galleries on both sides of the Atlantic, particularly those in New York and Washington, issue catalogues of photographs. Many of these are well documented and well illustrated and provide good indications of available subject matter and prices. Charles B. Wood of South Woodstock, Connecticut, has issued two catalogues under the title *The Photograph and the Book*, which provide bibliographical information and useful price guides for some of the photographically illustrated books.

7

Book Catalogues

Wm. P. Barlow, Jr.

"THE TRUE book-lover is usually loath to destroy an old book-catalogue. It would not be easy to give a reason for this, unless it is that no sooner has he done so than he has occasion to refer to it."[1] So wrote A. Edward Newton, and so, one might think, began a collection. But it would be more accurate to say: so began an accumulation; for Newton's closet of old book catalogues was not a collection, nor was it regarded as one. When the closet was full, some had to be destroyed, however regretfully, to make room for the continuing stream of dealer and auction catalogues that every serious collector receives.

Newton's remark also makes it clear that he did not regard book catalogues as *worthy* of collection. His excuse for keeping them is the same one we all use for cluttering our lives with useless objects: "I never know when I might need that again." It is the same excuse that allows us to retain obsolete timetables, out-of-fashion bric-a-brac, and political campaign buttons. For those who collect these objects decades later, it is this accumulative habit that makes collecting possible.

Newton was not the only one not to collect book catalogues. Few of the major public and university libraries have reasonably adequate runs of the ephemeral pieces that surely once passed through their hands. Those that have respectable collections have generally acquired them much later from collectors, bibliographers, or the dealers and auction houses themselves.

One institution that can hardly be faulted in this respect is the Grolier Club of New York. As a club of book collectors it is fitting, though not necessarily inevitable, that it would concentrate on the history of book collecting. Its collection of seventeenth-century English auction catalogues is rivaled only by that of the British Library, and its private library catalogues are unmatched. But if Newton's dismissal of a sizable fraction of today's book collections as "obsolete medical and scientific books"[2] now seems particularly shortsighted, his judgment on book catalogues would seem perfectly rational to most modern collectors and librarians.

That is not to say that *all* catalogues have been uncollected, even by Newton. I have A. Edward Newton's copy of *The R. B. Adam Library Relating to Dr. Samuel Johnson and His Era* (Buffalo, 1929–1930). It is a presentation copy inscribed "To my best friend and Brother Johnsonian A. Edward Newton." Newton wrote an introduction for this catalogue, but even without this personal association, the four volumes would surely have occupied an important position in Newton's library for their Johnson interest alone. And the auction catalogues of Newton's own library (New York: Parke Bernet Galleries, 1941) must be one of the most common sets known to bookselling, even complete with the introductory brochure and with the three sales volumes priced, as they should be.

Most serious collectors have a few auction or dealer catalogues on their shelves listing books within their collecting specialties, to be used as a bibliography or a want list or for organized wishful thinking. The collecting of catalogues, as catalogues, however, is a rather recent phenomenon that seems to have first arisen among the scholar-collectors who most needed to use the materials the catalogues contained. Seymour de Ricci was a pioneer, and his Sandars Lectures published as *English Collectors of Books & Manuscripts* (Cambridge Univ. Press, 1930) is one product of that collection. A. N. L. Munby and William A. Jackson, both librarians and bibliographers, also put together impressive collections and used them effectively in their published works.

In very much the same way, my own collection of catalogues originally had only a reference purpose. My principal book-collecting passion has always been John Baskerville, the eighteenth-century printer and type designer. It was my intention to develop an index to all catalogue appearances of Baskerville Press books. The index would give an impression of comparative scarcity, serve as a guide to value in the collectors' market over the years, help in tracing provenance of specific copies, and indicate contemporary bibliographical thinking about the books. Shortly, however, the reference material became a collection in itself, and the lack of Baskerville Press books in a catalogue no longer discourages me from purchasing the catalogue. Nonetheless, the original purpose is still there (as evidenced by the frequent appearance of Baskerville in this chapter).

It seems doubtful that the collecting of catalogues will ever achieve great popularity among private collectors. Perhaps this is fortunate for the few who are now collecting, although there is much room for specialization. But if the field does not need a host of eager new collectors, it does need a more widespread appreciation of the value of book catalogues and the importance of their preservation.

If A. Edward Newton, as a great friend and promoter of the love of books, is reluctant to destroy old catalogues (but does so anyway), those who clean up after a book collector or dealer is gone have no such inhibitions. And let us hope that libraries, at least, will find a way to keep what comes their way and make it available to future generations. There are those—and I am not one—who cry that all good books are disappearing into institutions, but almost anyone can find frustration in libraries buying from the marketplace what they threw away a decade before.

There are several types of book catalogues that can be collected; each presents different collecting problems and has its own allure. In terms of sheer volume, book dealer catalogues must head the list. Many collectors receive several hundred of these each year, and major libraries are deluged with well over a thousand.

Auction catalogues are only slightly less numerous, and the auctions had a head start on the dealers. For the past five years *American Book Prices Current* (which, despite its name, includes most English and some Continental sales along with the American) has listed an average of over 190 sales a year. Auctions by Continental and other foreign houses, dozens of obscure and short-lived American houses, and the widespread, if occasional, charitable fund-raisers would multiply this annual output several times.

Exhibition catalogues can range from mimeographed handouts to such elaborate treatises as that produced after the "Printing and the Mind of Man" exhibit (London: Cassell, 1967). Almost every library, famous or humble, has produced these over the years, and it seems doubtful that most have complete runs of their own catalogues, let alone selections of those produced by others.

Published institutional catalogues are fewer in number but bulk large. A collector could devote a fair sized room to the *National Union Catalog* alone, but this would not be advisable.

The elite of the book catalogue world is the private library catalogue. Often lavishly produced, almost always printed in small quantities, and frequently distributed in a perverse fashion, these volumes represent a tiny fraction of the book catalogue output but have always attracted the greatest collector interest.

There are several other groups of books that could be, or have been, described as book catalogues but that will not be considered here. Bibliographies are certainly catalogues of books. So are such volumes as *American Book Prices Current* and *Bookman's Price Index*. There are also catalogues of new-book dealers and publishers, and trade bibliographies, from the Term catalogues of the seventeenth century to our present-day *Books in Print*. Each of these has its place and its value, but all lack the common elements of the five categories we have included, all of which describe books brought together from various sources for some purpose and, at least theoretically, existed together at a single point in time. I think it is this sense of existence at a time and place that gives these books their essential character and appeal.

In all, it is a collecting field with well over a million different items from which to choose, with values ranging from $1,500 or so for a Pforzheimer Library catalogue to items many librarians, collectors, and even dealers would be pleased to have you haul away, and with availability running from very common indeed to altogether unobtainable. Clearly, specialization or, at least, restraint is essential.

Book Dealers' Catalogues

Most readers of this book, I would expect, are familiar with catalogues of antiquarian book dealers. The book dealer's catalogue is such a common and obvious method of retailing rare books that it seems it must always have been with us. In fact the antiquarian dealer's catalogue is one of the more recent of those we shall consider, and the number of them produced annually probably did not exceed the production of auction catalogues until the present century.

The origin of antiquarian book dealers' catalogues is somewhat obscure, not only because they have been so poorly preserved, but also because the earliest examples tended to imitate auction catalogues. In a necessarily cautious statement Graham Pollard says, "General antiquarian catalogues seem to have started with Robert Scott's catalogue of the library of Humphrey Henchman, bishop of London, in 1677."[3]

This catalogue, in common with those that followed for the next 50 years, appeared without printed prices. The catalogues indicated that the prices were marked in the books themselves, but in every other respect these early dealer catalogues could be taken for auction sales. Prices began to appear in the 1720s, and within another decade book-sellers' catalogues had taken on the style that they have to this day. Nevertheless through the end of the eighteenth century book dealers' catalogues are commonly included in lists of auction sales because of their similarity.[4] The use of wording reminiscent of auctions is illus-trated by a dealer's catalogue in my collection. "They are now selling, this Day, 1790, for Ready Money only, at the low Prices marked in the Catalogue, and on the first leaf of each Book."[5] This catalogue also has a section of "Books Omitted" and concludes with an advertisement of the same dealer operating as an auctioneer.

Whether a collector would regard these eighteenth-century cata-logues as integral to, or distinct from, a collection of auction catalogues is perhaps moot, because all of these are fairly scarce. In the nineteenth century, however, some major dealer catalogues appear that are clearly things apart from auctions and are much more readily available for collecting as well.

An interesting collection of the great "general catalogues" of the mid-nineteenth century would not be impossible to assemble today. The title pages recall the important dealers of the period: Thomas Thorpe, Henry G. Bohn, Bernard Quaritch, and Willis and Sotheran. The most famous of these is the final in a series from Bernard Quaritch: *General Catalogue of Books*, 17 vols. (London: 1887–1897). This multi-volume catalogue was preceded by some of the thickest books ever bound. The 1880 catalogue is an octavo of 2,395 pages some 6½ inches thick.

Books of this size are not likely to be thrown away, and this ac-counts for their reasonable availability. Whether all of the books listed in the catalogues were available when the catalogue was issued, how-ever, is questionable. The general catalogues were mostly compila-tions of monthly lists issued over the preceding two to three years, and many of the books listed in the final volume must have been sold. Whatever else they represent, the great general catalogues recall an era of book collecting and bookselling that is gone.

With the catalogues of the late nineteenth and the twentieth cen-turies the greatest problems of the collector are selection and organiza-tion. How much can a collector keep of what is sent by dealers or given to him or her by relieved collectors reluctant to retain but unwilling to destroy? How much and what should one buy, knowing that a house full of dealers' catalogues will yet be uncomprehensive? What does one do with masses of catalogues when they are acquired? How can one refer to an entry at a later date when nothing exists comparable to the auction records that index the sales catalogues?

I wish I could offer sound advice in this area, but I have yet to solve the problem myself. Meanwhile I keep everything that comes my way and buy whatever I think must ultimately belong to the collection. I can, however, offer a few suggestions. The most obvious is to select a dealer or group of dealers and try to complete runs. Another approach would be to collect catalogues of dealers in your own city. The catalogues are likely to be around—somewhere—and a history of bookselling in the area may well be the result of such a collection.

First catalogues are intriguing, but the collector should be aware that not all "catalogue number one's" are numbered; there may be both "lists" and "catalogues"; and at least one dealer started a series with a two-digit number to avoid appearing wet behind the ears. The whole problem of the numbering and dating of catalogues is a fascinating and maddening one. In the preface to the recently reprinted Rosenbach catalogues (New York: McGraw-Hill, 1967) the editors frankly state that they have ignored the catalogue numbers assigned by Rosenbach and used their own.

Anniversary catalogues are often interesting and may contain historical information about firms. Specialized subject catalogues are the most useful of every dealer's output—unless no one is interested in the subject. Even then, dealers' catalogues have been known to establish collecting trends or have proved to be just a few years premature.

I find it difficult to pass up long runs of almost any dealer, no matter how seemingly unimportant. A complete run of any dealer in business for more than a decade is really quite rare, and chances are that the dealer personally lacks a complete run. Completely irresistible are dealers' own copies of their catalogues. My set of the J. Halle catalogues (Munich: 1890–1935) is a mine of information that cannot otherwise be available: date of issue, buyers' names, indications of books sold before the catalogue was issued, books receiving multiple orders, and books remaining unsold. I wish I had a dozen more sets like it, but most such material does not survive the dealer.

If the selection problem is difficult to solve, the problem of organization is impossible. Any system that allows you to find a given catalogue knowing the dealer's name and a date or catalogue number is better than anything I have, and a system that allows you to find a given book in a given catalogue is utopian. One small practice that I regret not following consistently is stamping all catalogues with receipt dates and indicating the source of those acquired in lots.

Auction Catalogues

READER,

It hath not been usual here in *England* to make Sales of BOOKS by way of *Auction*, or *who will give most for them:* But it having been practised in other Countreys to the Advantage both of Buyers and Sellers; It was therefore conceived (for the Encouragement of Learning) to publish the Sale of these Books this manner of way; and it is hoped that this will not be unacceptable to Schollers; and therefore we thought it convenient to give an Advertisement concerning the manner of proceeding therein.

With this address, book auctions were introduced to England to dispose of the library of Dr. Lazarus Seaman on October 31, 1676. As the introduction indicates there were several countries that had preceded England in adopting auctions as a method of selling books. Holland was first in 1593 and was the exporter of the idea to England, although, according to Pollard,[6] Belgium (1635), Denmark (1639), and Sweden (1664) had adopted the technique in the intervening years. Once started the practice quickly took hold, and nearly 400 English catalogues prior to 1700 are known to exist.

It would be a mistake to assume, based on their number, that the seventeenth-century auction catalogue represents a fruitful collecting field. A collector can be considered lucky to run across one or two of these in a lifetime, and the same can be said for catalogues of eighteenth-century auctions in America, where the practice of selling books by auction started in 1713. If the earliest auction catalogues are essentially uncollectible, English sales from the middle of the eighteenth century and American sales from the middle of the nineteenth century are available enough to make a collection and elusive enough to make it fun.

I must admit a strong prejudice for auction over book dealers' catalogues—a prejudice in which I wish I were alone. Although I dislike continually disparaging the remarks of the man who introduced me to collecting, I cannot concur in A. Edward Newton's condescending view of auction catalogues: "Auction catalogues come, too. These must also be scanned, but they lack the element which makes the dealers' catalogues so interesting—the prices. With prices omitted, book-auction catalogues are too stimulating. The mind at once begins to range. Doubt takes the place of certainty."[7]

Perhaps it reflects change in the book world, but in current catalogues I prefer the certainty that a book is there to be bought over the certainty that the price is fixed, which means little when ten orders precede mine. In old catalogues, price lists or priced auction catalogues answer Newton's complaint and provide somewhat greater assurance that the price has some meaning (only somewhat, since books are still bought in, of course).

There are other attractions to auction catalogues. There are lists of what there is to collect. English catalogues to 1900 are noted in the British Museum *List of Catalogues of English Book Sales, 1676–1900;* American catalogues to 1934 are in George L. McKay's *American Book Auction Catalogues, 1713–1934; Book Auction Records* and *American Book Prices Current* carry on from 1934.

There are dates. For every auction labeled only "Monday, May 2nd" there are a hundred book dealers' catalogues without so much as a year of issue. And "Monday, May 2nd" can probably be pinned down with a perpetual calendar and a little intelligent guesswork.

And there are names. Even though more and more books turn up as "Other Properties," auctions do disclose some owners' names. Dealers rarely do. For those collectors, like me, to whom provenance means something, auctions have the edge.

One of the recurring nightmares of collectors in any field is running across more items at one time than they can afford to buy. Those on a limited budget are well advised to acquire a sound basic collection before advertising to all dealers who may be interested that they want everything in a given area. The results of such an advertisement could be embarrassing.

For some time I have freely advised dealers that I am interested in auction catalogues from 1750 onward, and I have yet to be embarrassed. In part this is due to the fact that dealers are collectors of auction catalogues as well. (One of the great mysteries of life—disarmingly similar to the question of where elephants go to die—is what happens to these catalogue collections on the death or retirement of a dealer.) In part this is due to the fact that dealers do not generally sell catalogues. They are always "around here somewhere" but rarely in a condition to be seen or sold. Another factor inhibiting dealers is that they are really not sure how to price catalogues beyond those famous sales that appear with some regularity. And in part this is due to the fact that auction catalogues have become somewhat scarcer than one would have thought.

The appearance of plenty—small piles of catalogues in every dealer's shop—is deceiving because of the number of auction catalogues to be collected. Except for the major sales and the sales of the major houses, which are more likely to be kept, there is a considerable attrition in auction catalogues. In my own run of Parke Bernet book sales, for example, I do not lack copies of the Streeter sales, but I do lack catalogues of a couple of "residence" sales with a few pages of books. And while my run of American Art Association-Anderson Galleries (1929–1939) is virtually complete, my runs of Plaza and Ritter-Hopson, from the same period, are far from it.

The most practical way to collect auction catalogues of the present century is to acquire large accumulations. Finding an accumulation is not easy, but they do exist, and often their owners would rather be rid of the entire lot than to take the trouble of sorting and pricing them individually and the risk of ending up with the unimportant sales unsold. This will result in duplicates, to be sure, but the overall cost is likely to be less, in spite of the duplication, and the duplicates may be valuable for sale or trade, if you can find anyone else who collects.

In the same spirit I have often volunteered to sort out a cache of auction catalogues myself for the opportunity of buying those I lacked. If you wait for a dealer to go through these accumulations you may wait forever, and once it is finally done, you should certainly expect to pay for the labor.

Occasionally a cache of nineteenth-century catalogues turns up, but these cannot now be counted on. Most of these are being sold individually these days, and they turn up ever more frequently in dealers' catalogues. They are apparently selling now, too. Two early pioneers in cataloguing auction catalogues were Irving Lew of Battery Park Books and James Carr. Both have told me that their initial attempts at catalogues of catalogues in the early 1960s were financially disasterous.

When buying in quantity, discrimination must be forgotten, but when buying individual catalogues it becomes a necessity. Fine condition, of course, is desirable but not a practical goal on the whole. Whether a catalogue is better rebound or in the original wrappers is a matter of taste, although I prefer the latter and detest the former when the volume contains several auctions from different houses or years.

The first level of quality in an auction catalogue is pricing. Printed price lists will do, but hand pricing by the auction house is preferable (they do not do it any longer), and pricing by someone at the sale with notes on condition or correction of descriptions is Elysian. Copies with names of buyers added are another step up the scale. English houses have long printed buyers' names in their price lists (although they are often aliases), but the American houses have not. At the top of the line are auctioneers' copies with order prices or names of consignors or buyers, and consignors' copies with such delicious information as original acquisition prices.

Before embarking on a full-scale collection of catalogues, either auction or dealer, consider the space requirements. Adequate shelf space is the first requirement for organization. While it might be possible to house an important collection of eighteenth- and nineteenth-century catalogues on a half dozen shelves, a collection of modern catalogues will not begin to become impressive before consuming 100 feet of shelf space.

It is probably easiest to arrange catalogues by auction house, because this places similar sizes together, but arrangement by date works well enough, and for earlier catalogues is probably best. A card file, again by auction house or by date, is a second step along with a portable list of some sort, because no one can be expected to remember which of several thousand catalogues one has and which one lacks. I use a marked copy of McKay up to 1934 and lists of either "haves" or "lacks" thereafter depending on which approach produces the shorter list.

Further refinements should depend on your own uses of the collection. A consignor index is useful; the major sales are easily located, of course, but thousands of small consignments are not indexed anywhere. A general subject index is also possible or an index to specific books or manuscripts in which you are interested.

It is hardly conceivable that anyone could be so well organized, but it is useful to decide what indexing is to be done before starting on any. The prospect of going back through several thousand catalogues a second or third time to develop a new index is usually enough to defer the project indefinitely.

Exhibition Catalogues

Each time some of my books have been placed on exhibit I learn something new about them. Similarities and contrasts in design become more apparent when books are spread out rather than removed from the shelves one or two at a time, and historical and literary relationships can be highlighted. Through borrowing, books, manuscripts, and related materials that could not otherwise be brought together can be seen at one time. A well-planned and well-illustrated exhibit catalogue can enhance and later recall the exhibit experience for those who saw it and reproduce the experience for those who could not. Not many exhibit catalogues are this successful, but those that are make an important contribution to the book world.

The exhibit catalogue, like the book exhibit itself, is a late comer to institutional library practice. I am unaware of any catalogues printed prior to the mid-nineteenth century. This, and the fact that there has been very little research into exhibit catalogues as a class, makes an intriguing opportunity for the development of a significant collection.

Certainly there are hundreds of exhibit catalogues that are little more than mimeographed checklists and can safely be ignored, but there are still hundreds more that are worth collecting. Many such catalogues have been distributed only in conjunction with the related exhibit, offering a real challenge to the collector in tracking them down or even learning of their existence. Others have been widely distributed, almost, it would seem, independently of the exhibit.

Printing and the Mind of Man (London and New York, 1967), coming four years after the exhibit in London, falls in this latter category, but it should be no less welcome to the collector's shelves on this account. With Joseph Blumenthal's two books, *Art of the Printed Book, 1455–1955* (New York: Morgan Library, 1973) and *The Printed Book in America* (Boston: Godine, 1977), one can well wonder whether the catalogue was the excuse for the exhibit or the exhibit the excuse for the catalogue. The answer is that neither needs any excuse at all, the book and the exhibit creating a sum more useful than its parts.

These three books represent a new tradition in exhibit catalogues, but the old tradition continues to serve well. A run of the exhibit catalogues issued by the Grolier Club would be a valuable collection, bearing in mind that many of these catalogues are tucked away in the pages of the Club's *Transactions* (1884–1919) and *Gazette* (1921–1976).

Major exhibits are regularly noted in the pages of *The Book Collector* and other periodicals, as is the existence or prospect of a catalogue. A review of back copies of such periodicals would develop an excellent collecting checklist. A great many catalogues are available from the exhibiting libraries years later, and this source should not be overlooked.

If the field of exhibit catalogues seems too large there are opportunities for specialization. With the attractiveness of the individual items for display, exhibits of finely printed books have been frequent as have exhibits illustrating the history of printing. A very interesting collection could be made of exhibit catalogues honoring the five-hundredth anniversary of the invention of printing. Because this date is rather indefinite, these exhibits began about 1940 and continued for over ten years. The Morgan Library exhibit catalogue mentioned above could be considered a part of such a collection and provides a terminal date of 1973.

A sense of changes in taste could be drawn from a collection of "high spot" exhibit catalogues. Start with the various Grolier Club

"100 Bests," include the *Fifty Books of the Year* exhibits (New York: American Institute of Graphic Arts), and add the many "Treasures of the Library" catalogues.

Institutional Library Catalogues

A collection of institutional library catalogues is likely to contain a more substantial percentage of early books than would a collection of dealer, auction, or private library catalogues. This is not only because the institutional catalogue appeared on the scene earlier and in less ephemeral form, but also because collectors will be forced to establish a terminal date for their acquisitions—at least for general catalogues —if sanity is to prevail.

As useful as the general catalogue of the British Library may be, it is of a very low order of interest for the collector. Nowadays a general catalogue, running into hundreds of volumes, is the product of one institutional library and the acquisition of another. Beyond the nineteenth century the general catalogue of the major institutional library ceases to have much appeal for the private collector, but in the earlier periods, the general catalogues have both charm and utility and can still be found to collect.

That is not to say that there are no catalogues beyond 1900 of collecting interest. It is only the general catalogues that have mushroomed out of proportion. Catalogues of special collections within a major university or public library or catalogues of specialized institutions remain collectible and, indeed, are frequently the bibliographies of the specialized subjects that they cover. A nice example of this is one of William A. Jackson's most frustrating books, *An Annotated List of the Publications of the Reverend Thomas Frognall Dibdin, D.D.* (Cambridge, Mass.: Houghton Library, 1965). It is difficult to be sure whether this was intended to be a bibliography of Dibdin, a catalogue of the Dibdin collection at Harvard, or—and this is what makes it frustrating—a subtle parody of Dibdin's bibliographical style.

This is not the only border dispute in the institutional catalogue field. There is an equally fuzzy line between institutional and private library catalogues. There are catalogues of private libraries that are clearly destined for institutions; there are catalogues of private libraries issued by institutions after their acquisition of a private library; and there are catalogues of private libraries that have been begun by the collector and completed by the acquiring institution. In addition there are the private libraries that have themselves become institutions. Occasionally dealers' and auction catalogues have been bought *in toto* by institutions; David Magee's three-volume *Victoria R. I.* (San Francisco, 1969–1970) was completed after the collection had been acquired by Brigham Young University and at the insistence of that institution. Collectors will have to draw their own lines in this area or take the easy way out by collecting institutional catalogues, private library catalogues, and subject bibliographies, not being too concerned over the proper shelf for any given volume.

Printed institutional catalogues go back to the late sixteenth century, although the practice of publishing such materials did not become common until later. From the middle of the seventeenth century, when Leyden University published its second catalogue (1640, the first was 1595) until the middle of the eighteenth century, when Leyden University published the supplement to its third catalogue (1741, the catalogue itself is dated 1716), it seems that every Dutch university felt obliged to publish a catalogue. The vogue was not universal, however, and it was not until the next century that the largest libraries began to publish general catalogues.

The first British Museum catalogue of printed books, for example, is dated 1787 and is contained in two folio volumes. A second required 8 volumes (1813–1819), a third, 58 volumes (1881–1900) and a 10-volume supplement (1900–1905). Although such undertakings have demonstrated that the largest libraries can be catalogued, they have also demonstrated how unlikely an acquisition these massive works are for the private collector.

Specialized catalogues of institutions are another matter, and British Museum publications like *Books Printed in the Fifteenth Century* (1908–1962, now reprinted), *Manuscripts in the Cottonian Library* (1802), and *Punjabi Printed Books* (1893, supplement 1961) show the wide diversity and usefulness of such publications. Every other major library has issued its share of important special collections, and a listing in a short chapter such as this would omit more of importance than it could include. There is ample material for collection, however, and the collector is aided by the fact that these publications are often heavily subsidized and represent unusual bargains—at least until they go out of print.

The large institution is not the only source of fascinating catalogues by any means. Lacking though it is in bibliographical detail, comprehensiveness, or even a scholarly introduction, my copy of the *Catalogue of Books in the South Gardner Social Library, February 15, 1867* (Fitchberg, Massachusetts) is a delightful possession that is a valuable indication of contemporary popular reading habits and education. There are probably hundreds of similar examples.

Private Library Catalogues

There could hardly be a book-collecting field with a wider range of rarity and a wider range of quality than that of private library catalogues. All of this has been brought about by the wide range of objectives that have produced these books.

The first private library catalogues were probably intended as inventories to aid in the sale or transfer of books from a deceased collector's library. The famous *Bibliothecae Cordesianae Catalogues* (Paris, 1643) compiled by the great librarian and early bibliographer Gabriel Naudé, began with a view toward sale of the books but was used in the latter part of the seventeenth century as one of the most important "universal" bibliographies.

Other early catalogues may have been intended as checklists or shelf lists for the private collector, with outside distribution limited or nonexistent. Still others were planned to make private libraries available to scholars in a period when public libraries were few.

The most frequently mentioned motive, that of self-aggrandizement, was perhaps a later phenomenon, but it was nonetheless important. After the well-known Barberini catalogue (*Index Bibliothecae qua Franciscus Barberinus*, Rome, 1681), an Italian cardinal was not regarded as fully successful until he had published his library catalogue in a lavish folio or two. Other wealthy individuals felt obliged to follow suit.

Regardless of the purposes that spawned them, these catalogues—most of them Continental—were the bibliographical literature of the seventeenth and eighteenth centuries prior to the arrival of Brunet, Lowndes, and others in the early part of the nineteenth century.

If the need for private library catalogues as bibliographies declined, the need for prestige or a display of erudition did not, and private library catalogues multiplied throughout the nineteenth and early twentieth centuries. Some of them have considerable value. A. N. L. Munby required an entire volume of the five-volume *Phillipps Studies* (Cambridge Univ. Press, 1951–1960), a very important and extremely scarce reference work, to describe the catalogue of the manuscripts of Sir Thomas Phillipps. At the other end of the scale, when *A Choice of Books from the Library of Isabella Stewart Gardner, Fenway Court* (Boston, 1906) was given to Daniel Berkeley Updike to print, he was so dissatisfied with its lack of scholarship—indeed, outright errors—that he refused to attach the Merrymount Press imprint to it.

In recent years the quantity of private library catalogues has decreased as a result of the escalating cost of printing them, and the bibliographical value has improved as collectors concentrated their activities on specialized subjects and had their catalogues prepared by eminent bibliographers. A valuable example is *The Rothschild Library* (Cambridge, Eng.: Privately printed at Cambridge Univ. Press, 1954). Few private library catalogues today are intended exclusively for presentation to friends by opulent collectors and instead have at least a limited commercial distribution. Under the circumstances it is easy to see why scholarly excellence is so important.

In collecting private library catalogues a serendipitous approach is useful. A large number of catalogues have an extremely small press run. An edition of 500 copies is large, and 100 is not uncommon. Some catalogues have been issued in editions of 25 or less, and there are often five or ten copies of a somewhat larger edition for presentation or other purposes.

As a result you may not always find just what you are looking for, but you will find others, equally limited in edition size. I take what comes, and sooner or later everything does. Private library catalogues turn up far more frequently than their limited edition size would suggest. They were, after all, always collectible or at least easily shelved and surely too nice to throw away. That explains why *The Ashley Library* (11 vols., London, 1922–1936) published by Thomas J. Wise in an edition of 200 copies turns up for sale a couple of times a year, whereas a minor Sotheby's auction sale of the same period, published in an edition of several thousand, may not turn up at all. It might also be explained by the rather casual attitude of Thomas Wise toward limitation notices, but that is a different story.

It would be inexcusable to leave this subject without mentioning an even more limited form of private library catalogues. These are the manuscript catalogues or shelf lists that are occasionally to be found. Even if a catalogue is not identifiable as to the collector or specific date, it is still a library catalogue and a fascinating document as well.

Just for Fun

The principal merit that catalogues have for the bibliographer is that they are lists of books that existed. Although there are some instances where this assumption has proved invalid, the principle is sound. However, a small group of catalogues is entirely fictitious. These are the catalogues of imaginary books written either for the purpose of hoax or satire. Although the humor of these pieces is transitory—after all, a hoax exposed is no longer a hoax, and a topical satire whose topic is forgotten is impenetrable—they form a fascinating addition to any catalogue collection.

By far the most noted of the genre is the Fortsas hoax. The preface to this catalogue, which selected bibliophiles and librarians received in the mail in the summer of 1840, declared that the late owner of the books to be offered by auction, one Comte de Fortsas,

> admitted upon his shelves only works unknown to all bibliographers and cataloguists. It was his invariable rule, a rule from which he never departed. With such a system, it is easy to conceive that the collection formed by him—although during forty years he devoted considerable sums to it—could not be very numerous. But what will be difficult to believe is, that he pitilessly expelled from his shelves books for which he had paid their weight in gold—volumes which would have been the pride of the most fastidious amateurs—as soon as he learned that a work, up to that time unknown, had been noticed in any catalogue. This sad discovery was indicated upon his manuscript list in a column devoted to this purpose, by these words: "Mentioned in such or such a work," etc.; and then—"sold," "given away," or (incredible if we did not know to what extent the passion of exclusive collectors could go) "destroyed"!![8]

In response to this tempting tale, many of Europe's leading book collectors and librarians or representatives bearing commissions gathered in the small town of Binche in Belgium for the August 10 sale of these priceless books only to discover, as some had already suspected, that the sale and the library and the count were part of an elaborate hoax.

The number of copies printed of this catalogue has been variously reported, but the most frequent citation is 132 of which 10 were on various colored papers and 2 on vellum. There is also a close facsimile reprint, apparently produced when the original catalogue became a collector's item itself, and several later editions and reprints.

Most of the examples of satire I have seen are all but impenetrable now. One that is not is the sale of "The Classical Contents of Gooseberry Hall," a parody of the puffery employed by George Robins in placing the library of Horace Walpole at Strawberry Hill "to sell by Public Competition." The original is so nearly ludicrous that it required very little alteration to make the parody. On one title page, for example, we find "and it may fearlessly be proclaimed as the most distinguished gem that has ever adorned the annals of auctions," and on the other "and it may unhesitatingly be proclaimed as the most brilliant feather that has ever adorned the cap of an auctioneer." The latter is the parody, but it is not immediately apparent.

There are only a few imaginary books here, but no matter. The parody works today because the original catalogue of the Strawberry Hill sale (1842) is relatively easy to acquire for comparison.

The catalogues of most of these imaginary libraries are rather scarce, but a few of the modern ones, such as the *Catalog of Rare Books & Manuscripts* offered by The Caveat Book Shop in 1946 and printed at the Grabhorn Press, do occasionally turn up. The best list available is a Houghton Library exhibit catalogue prepared by William A. Jackson for a 1962 meeting of the Bibliographical Society of America, *Bibliotheca Chimaerica.*

But Have You Read Them All?

In this era of issues and endangered expectations, nothing seems so relevant as "relevance." Perhaps the modern visitor, on seeing a room full of catalogues, is too sophisticated to ask the time-honored question that heads this section, but he might well ask what purpose there is to all of this. It is no longer adequate—even though it is perfectly proper— to evade the question as Harry B. Smith evaded a similarly time-honored question in the "Apology" to *A Sentimental Library* (1914): "If a man's mind can be so uncouthly practical that he can think of asking, 'Why first editions?' he is beyond the reach of sentimental argument." And perhaps sentiment is a weak argument for a shelf of book dealers' catalogues.

It is equally inadequate—though, again, perfectly proper—to defend a collection of catalogues for the joy provided by filling the gaps in the series. This is pure hedonism and, besides, is so dangerously close to the commonly perceived pleasures of stamp collecting as to risk isolation from fellow book collectors. Whatever the real motive, a sensible purpose for collecting is a valuable refuge to have at hand. Fortunately it is not so difficult to construct.

As we have seen, in the seventeenth and eighteenth centuries, catalogues were the principal bibliographical tools. Evidence of this is plentiful. Here is a description from the first edition of Lowndes, *The Bibliographer's Manual of English Literature* (London: Pickering, 1834). "_____ The Bible. Cambridge, 1763. folio. From Baskerville's press. One of the most beautiful books ever printed. Constable, 278, morocco,

7£. 7s. Williams, 371, morocco, 8£. 10s. Heath, 443, morocco, 9£. Roxburghe, 26, 10£. 15s."

The references are to sale catalogues: David Constable, 1827; The Rev. Theodore Williams, 1827; Dr. Benjamin Heath, 1810; and John Duke of Roxburghe, 1812. The references were, no doubt, familiar enough to readers of the day, even though the Constable and Heath sales did not name their consignors on the title page. In later editions edited by Henry G. Bohn (London: Bell & Daldy, 1869) the entry is almost identical, but the following has been added. "Gardner, 9£. A few copies in LARGE PAPER. Duke of Sussex."

The additional references are to later sales: John Dunn Gardner, 1854, and Augustus Frederick, Duke of Sussex, five parts, 1844–1846. The existence of large paper copies (which probably do not, in fact, exist) has been announced, probably on the basis of a cataloguer's description in one of the Sussex sales, although the Williams copy was also described as large paper in 1827.

Further evidence of the position of book catalogues is their frequent appearance in major auction sales. In the Askew sale (Baker & Leigh, 1775) 38 of the 3,570 lots are of auction catalogues. In the Roxburghe sale (Evans, 1812) there are 18 lots of catalogues, and a priced copy of the Askew catalogue brought £2, a price greater than most of the seventeenth-century Shapespeare quartos brought in the same sale.

Now that we have newer and more accurate bibliographical tools available, catalogues have lost much of their day-to-day utility. But they still record books that may no longer exist or that are hopelessly scattered; they still give a view of contemporary scholarship and popular thought; and they still tell us something about the book trade. Moreover they are being used increasingly in bibliographical research.

Extensive use of catalogues was made by Allen T. Hazen in preparing *A Catalogue of Horace Walpole's Library* (New Haven, Conn.: Yale Univ. Press, 1969). A portion of the description of item 2208, *Select Fables of Esop and Other Fabulists* (Birmingham: Baskerville for Dodsley, 1761) shows the extensive material that was gathered.

SH SALE, iv.100 (with Catullus and Terentius), to Thorpe, £2; offered in Payne & Foss Catalogue for 1845, lot 4, for £3.3.0; Sotheby's, 21 June 1851 (Granville Penn Sale), lot 1338, to Lilly, £1.10.0; Sotheby's, 23 March 1868 (Windus Sale), lot 4, to Lilly, £1.13.0; offered in Lilly Catalogue for 1868, for £2.12.6; Christie's, 2 July 1945 (Sir Hugh Walpole Sale), lot 412, to Maggs for WSL, £19.

An incredible accumulation clearly based on an extensive collection of auction and dealer catalogues, but what happened to the volume between 1868 and 1945? Even more catalogues are required to complete the provenance.

In amassing this material Allen Hazen recognized the existence of a bookseller's "ring" in operation at the 1842 Strawberry Hill sale of the property of Horace Walpole. For lot after lot, priced copies of the auction sale showed one book dealer as the buyer, yet shortly after the sale a different book dealer offered the volume in his catalogue. The evidence is strong that the sale was followed by a "knock-out" where dealers, who refrained from bidding against each other during the sale, split up the spoils. Strong as the evidence is, Hazen laments that it could have been stronger: "There seems no doubt that other types [lots listed as purchased by one member of the ring but subsequently resold by another] could be added if Kerslake, Pickering, or Rodd Catalogues of 1842 could be traced, or a Payne and Foss Catalogue earlier than 1845."[9]

One of the most important uses of catalogues today has been in preparing editions of the letters of authors. Letters of the famous are often widely scattered in the autograph market, and the task of reassembling the material for a scholarly edition becomes almost impossible. The habit booksellers and auctioneers have of quoting all or parts of such letters in their catalogues has provided at least partial texts of reasonable accuracy for letters that cannot otherwise be traced.

My own collection of catalogues has produced the texts of several letters for the Mark Twain Papers at the University of California in Berkeley and has identified a good many otherwise uncitable references. The Mark Twain Papers has quantities of catalogue descriptions nicely transcribed but with vague references and of uncertain accuracy. In many cases I have been able to turn up the original catalogue for them. A catalogue description of a letter may not be as desirable as the letter itself, but it is far better than nothing.

For my own part, book catalogues are an illustration of the history of book collecting—an imperfect history perhaps, when it is considered how hastily auction catalogues must be put together, usually without the benefit of the accumulated knowledge of the collector—and an incomplete history as well. Because only a fraction of the exhibits assembled are preserved in catalogue form, only a fraction of collectors produce private library catalogues, and only a fraction of the libraries sold pass through auctions or are listed in dealers' catalogues, the thousands of catalogues to be collected can represent only a fraction of the history of book collecting. But, as display windows illustrate the contents of a shop, the catalogues give us some idea of the whole.

Most catalogue collectors begin with a book-collecting specialty and slip into the collecting of catalogues. Eventually the "real collection" is confined to a few dusty shelves while the "reference material" expands uncontrollably through the house. This, however, seems a not improper course of events. As the eminent bibliographer Falconer Madan said in reference to bibliography, "It is better to choose a limited subject, one within your capacity, and let it expand, rather than too wide a subject which you have subsequently to contract."[10] Book collectors often apologize for their collections. I can offer no apology for what seems a reasonable collecting progression. The question one should ask on viewing another's collection is not "Have you read them all?" or "Of what use is it?" but rather "How did it happen?" *That* question always gets an answer, and sometimes an essay.

Notes

1. A. Edward Newton, *The Amenities of Book-Collecting and Kindred Affections* (Boston: Atlantic Monthly Press, 1918), p. 65.
2. Newton, *The Amenities of Book-Collecting*, p. 65.
3. Graham Pollard and Albert Ehrman, *The Distribution of Books by Catalogue* (Cambridge: Printed for presentation to members of the Roxburghe Club, 1965), p. 155.
4. For references to these lists, see *List of Catalogues of English Book Sales, 1676–1900, Now in the British Museum* (London: British Museum, 1915); George L. McKay, *American Book Auction Catalogues, 1713–1934: A Union List* (New York: New York Public Library, 1937); and A. N. L. Munby and Lenore Coral, *British Book Sale Catalogues, 1676–1800: A Union List* (London: Mansell, 1977).
5. T. King, Bookseller, *A Catalogue of Books; Containing a General Assortment of the Best Authors in Every Branch of Literature* (London: 1790), title page.
6. Pollard and Ehrman, *The Distribution of Books by Catalogue*, p. 218.
7. Newton, *The Amenities of Book-Collecting*, p. 30.
8. Quoted from the translation attributed to William Blades reprinted in *The Fortsas Hoax* (London: Arborfield, 1961). There is considerable doubt about the attribution, however, because the translation was first printed in volume 2 of the Philobiblon (New York, 1863) and the manuscript, which is in the St. Bride Typographical Library, is not in Blades's hand.
9. A. T. Hazen, "The Booksellers' 'Ring' at Strawberry Hill in 1842," *Studies in Bibliography* 7 (1955): 197.
10. Falconer Madan, "Some Experiences of a Bibliographer," *The Library*, 4th series, 1, no. 3 (1920): 132.

Further Reading

British Museum. *List of Catalogues of English Book Sales, 1676–1900, Now in the British Museum*. London: The British Museum, 1915. 523 pp.

Collison, Robert. *Published Library Catalogues: An Introduction to Their Contents and Use.* London: Mansell, 1973. 184 pp.

de Ricci, Seymour. *English Collectors of Books & Manuscripts (1530–1930) and Their Marks of Ownership.* Cambridge: Cambridge Univ. Press, 1930. 203 pp.

Lawler, John. *Book Auctions in England in the Seventeenth Century (1676–1700): With a Chronological List of the Book Auctions of the Period.* London: Elliot Stock, 1898. 241 pp.

McKay, George L. *American Book Auction Catalogues, 1713–1934: A Union List.* With an introduction by Clarence S. Brigham. New York: New York Public Library, 1937. 540 pp. Reprinted with supplements of 1946 and 1948. Detroit: Gale, 1967. 560 pp.

Munby, A. N. L. *The Cult of the Autograph Letter in England.* London: Athlone Press, 1962. 117 pp.

Munby, A. N. L., general ed. *Sale Catalogues of Libraries of Eminent Persons.* London: Mansell, 1971–1975. 12 vols.

Munby, A. N. L., and Coral, Lenore. *British Book Sale Catalogues, 1676–1800: A Union List.* London: Mansell, 1977. 146 pp.

Pollard, Graham, and Ehrman, Albert. *The Distribution of Books by Catalogue.* Cambridge: Printed for presentation to members of the Roxburghe Club, 1965.

Taylor, Archer. *Book Catalogues: Their Varieties and Uses.* Chicago: The Newberry Library, 1957. 284 pp.

Towner, Wesley. *The Elegant Auctioneers.* New York: Hill & Wang, 1970. 632 pp.

8

Publishers' Imprints

Jean Peters

I T HAS BEEN nearly 20 years since I bought my first book published by the Hogarth Press in a small bookshop on West Fourth Street in New York City. On the surface, the book, *King's Daughter*, by Vita Sackville-West, Volume 11 in the Hogarth Living Poets series, hardly seemed a significant purchase. It was not an early book of the Press, nor an important one, and its physical condition made it an undistinguished copy of an unimportant book. Obviously, the shop owner had considered it of no importance, for the price penciled lightly in the corner of the free endpaper was 25 cents. Yet, I was as captivated by this book as I had been by the story of the Press, which had started me on my search a few months earlier. I had been looking in the secondhand bookshops of New York City throughout one whole summer for a book, any book, published by the Hogarth Press. *King's Daughter* was only the first of many Hogarth Press purchases, and it marked the beginning of my long preoccupation with that remarkable press.

In recent years the story of Leonard and Virginia Woolf's Hogarth Press has become so well known that it hardly bears repeating: the story of how the Woolfs' mutual interest in printing and Leonard Woolf's search for a manual occupation for his wife that would take her mind completely off her writing for some time each day led them to inquire about printing lessons at the St. Brides School of Printing in London; of how they were turned down by St. Brides, which was in the business

198

of teaching union apprentices, not amateurs; of how the Woolfs then bought a small hand press, type, and instruction book, installed the press in the dining room of their home, Hogarth House, in Richmond, and taught themselves to print; of how, in 1917, after a month of studying, they printed their first publication, *Two Stories*, a pamphlet of 32 pages containing one story by each of them; and of how, finally, the success of this first publication led to their printing and publishing other works in which commercial publishers had no interest, and ultimately to the development of their own full-fledged commercial imprint.

To present-day collectors, the building of a collection of books issued under the Hogarth Press imprint might well be considered a well-traveled course. Certainly, it is an already accepted "new path," with books of the press now listed by imprint in many book dealers' catalogues, with a published checklist of press publications issued through 1938, and with prices of the books raised to new highs by the interest of both private and institutional collectors. Hogarth Press books are no longer difficult to locate, although they are sometimes difficult to afford. All of this seems to indicate a "fashion" in book collecting. However, collecting Hogarth Press imprints was not always so fashionable, not even as recently as the early 1960s when I first became interested in the Press. Even today, the collecting of publishers' imprints in general has not become a fashion in collecting. Yet the importance of this kind of collecting to the history of publishing seems clear: the history of the publishing industry can be most accurately recorded through a study of its imprints.

By definition, an imprint is the statement that identifies the printer or publisher of a piece of printed material. The imprint usually contains the name of the printer or publisher, place and date of publication, and often includes a device or logo (Plate 28).[1] By extension, imprint can refer to the printed or published item itself, and it is in this context that the term will be used in this chapter.

As book collectors and dealers know, it is not uncommon to collect *printers'* imprints. In this kind of imprint collecting, the interest is in the printer, or in the history of books, or in their production. Books printed by Aldus, Elzevir, Caxton, Baskerville, and other early printers have always held collectors' interests. Fine printing by modern private presses has also attracted large numbers of collectors. Collecting the imprints of such modern private presses of the late nineteenth and early twentieth centuries as the Kelmscott, Ashendene, Doves, or Vale presses continues a tradition of imprint collecting that now extends to the

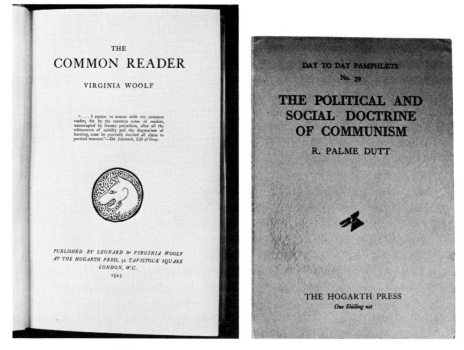

PLATE 28   Devices of the Hogarth Press. (*Left*) The wolf head in a medallion, designed by Vanessa Bell, in its first appearance on the title page of Virginia Woolf's *The Common Reader* (1925), where it appeared in a larger size than elsewhere. (*Right*) The stylized wolf head designed by E. McKnight Kauffer for the Day to Day Pamphlet series in 1930.

imprints of scores of contemporary private presses.[2] Collectors' book clubs such as The Limited Editions Club, The Heritage Press, or The Folio Society offer another possibility in imprint collecting, especially for those attracted to handsomely designed and illustrated books. Today no one would consider collection of printers' imprints an unusual form of collecting.

Oddly enough, this interest in the history and production of books does not ordinarily extend to the collecting of *publishers'* imprints, even though the publishing of books is as much a part of the history of books as is their printing and production. Perhaps as a result of this lack of interest by collectors, the antiquarian and used-book trade is not organized for this kind of collecting. Except for certain isolated instances —as in the cases of such publishing firms as Stone & Kimball or Copeland & Day and now of the Hogarth Press—where publishers' checklists or bibliographies are available, it is not possible to locate a book by publisher either in a book dealer's catalogue or by the shelf arrangement of a bookstore. In a book dealer's catalogue it is not customary even to find a publisher's name included anywhere in an entry, to say nothing of an arrangement or cross-reference by publisher's name.

During the early years of my search for Hogarth Press imprints, I had a difficult time locating any of the books. I was soon to learn that arrangement by publisher's name was not one of the ways booksellers organized their stock. There was not even a card file that could provide a cross-reference by publisher. The usual response from a bookseller to my request for books published by the Press was to ask for authors and titles of particular books. Here I was at a disadvantage during the first few years of my collecting because, until I learned of John Lehmann's autobiography, which included an account of his years at the Hogarth Press, I had no source to go to for titles issued by the Press.[3] I was aware, of course, that the Press had published T. S. Eliot's *Poems* and *The Wasteland* and Katherine Mansfield's *Prelude*, and most of the books by Virginia Woolf, but not until much later did I know titles or authors of lesser-known books of the Press, books that stores I visited might have had on their shelves under the names of Prewett, Limebeer, Gates, Palmer, Ainslie, or Plomer, to name but a few. Occasionally, I would speak with someone who recalled having seen books of the Press in London bookstores, but only rarely in those days did I find a Hogarth Press book in a New York bookstore. When I did, it was because a bookseller knew he had one in stock and where it was sitting on the shelf, or because of my own methodical searching of the shelves of every bookstore I entered.

In those days I busied myself with making my own abbreviated checklists of Press publications from information I found in the few books I was able to locate, either from lists printed in the books themselves, or from lists on publicity brochures that were occasionally laid in the books. Titles issued in series were usually certain to include a list of all previously issued books in the series. A joyful examination of my first purchase revealed that *King's Daughter* contained a list of 11 other titles in the Hogarth Living Poets series, ten earlier titles and one to come. I was delighted to see on the list collections of poems by Robinson Jeffers, F. L. Lucas, and C. Day Lewis, as well as other poets with whose work I was unfamiliar, but nevertheless now I knew *of* them. For some time afterward on visiting bookstores I felt unusually well informed, armed for the first time with the names of so many authors and titles of books published by the Press. Even so, the new information proved to be of little help; I simply could not find the books on any bookstore shelf. It was many years before I located the companions to *King's Daughter*.

Today collectors of the Hogarth Press are not faced with this problem. Since 1972 an extraordinary number of books have been published on the lives and work of the Woolfs, some of which include information about the Press and its publications.[4] More importantly, however, was the publication, in 1976, of J. Howard Woolmer's *A Checklist of the Hogarth Press, 1917-1938*.[5] Although incomplete lists of press publications had previously appeared in three of the five volumes of Leonard Woolf's autobiography,[6] and a list with additional early publications of the Press had appeared in the *American Book Collector*,[7] Woolmer's *Checklist* was the first comprehensive treatment of Press publications during its early years. It provided the roadmap collectors and dealers had needed for so long. As a result of all this interest in the Woolfs and in their press, books never before considered important were unearthed and began to appear in book dealers' catalogues. Some dealers even began to group books of the Press together on a shelf in their stores. However, a combination of factors—the small press runs of many of the early books (fewer than 500 copies), the frequent pulping of later unsold books with larger press runs, the fragile bindings and delicate paper wrappers of many of the books, and a number of authors who never became well known—has made the general survival rate low and available copies scarce. The usual response from a bookseller today when I ask if the store has any books published by the Hogarth Press is: "I wish we had."

For those who attempt to assemble collections of the imprints of most publishers, however, the way is not so clearly charted, and conditions still resemble those of my Hogarth Press collecting experience in the early 1960s. Books are difficult to locate by imprint, but this is not to say they do not exist. They are on the shelves and in the catalogues, arranged by author or subject, or sometimes not arranged at all. Patience and ingenuity are required to track down the imprints of a publisher before authors or titles are known. However, collectors who persevere are rewarded with books that are generally low in price and often in fine condition, and with collections that are both interesting and of scholarly value.

The importance of such collections to the study of publishing history is enormous. Those of us who are involved with publishing history in our work and in our studies are constantly aware of the incomplete and often superficial record that exists. In the past, the writing of publishing history has often taken the form of broad general histories of the industry as a whole rather than the detailed studies of individual publishing firms, and a trend for this kind of publishing history still prevails. Although general histories are important and useful, the kind of information that is often sought can be found only in carefully researched, in-depth studies of individual publishers and their imprints. Few of these exist. There are, of course, commemorative or anniversary volumes issued by the firms themselves, as well as reminiscences of publishers, but few independent, carefully documented individual company histories or catalogues of publications (let alone full-dress descriptive bibliographies) have been issued. Among those that come readily to mind are: Sidney Kramer's *History of Stone and Kimball and Herbert S. Stone and Company, with a Bibliography of Their Publications, 1895– 1905* (Chicago: Norman W. Forgue, 1940); Joe W. Kraus's *A History of Copeland and Day, 1839–1899, with a Bibliographical Checklist of Their Publications*, issued in 1941 as a thesis by the University of Illinois Library School, and recently published in book form as *Messrs. Copeland and Day, 69 Cornhill, Boston, 1893–1899* (Philadelphia: MacManus, 1979); Raymond L. Kilgour's *Messrs. Roberts Brothers Publishers* (Ann Arbor: Univ. of Michigan Press, 1952); his *Estes and Lauriat: A History, 1872–1898* (Ann Arbor: Univ. of Michigan Press, 1957); and his *Lee and Shepard, Publishers for the People* (Hamden, Conn.: Shoe String Press, 1965); Carl J. Weber's *The Rise and Fall of James Ripley Osgood* (Waterville, Maine: Colby College Press, 1959); Eugene Exman's *The Brothers Harper: A Unique Publishing Partnership and Its Impact upon the Cultural Life of America from 1817 to 1853* (New York: Harper, 1965); and his *The House of Harper: One Hundred and Fifty Years of Publishing* (New York: Harper, 1967); James Penn Pilkington's *The Methodist Publishing House: A History* (Nashville, Tenn.: Abingdon Press, 1968); and Ellen B. Ballou's *The Building of the House: Houghton Mifflin's Formative Years* (Boston: Houghton, 1970). More individual publisher histories on the order of these need to be written, and the foundation of any such history is a study of the imprints themselves. By seeking out the books of particular publishers, even books that are of little importance in themselves, and by organizing and preserving them as a record of a publisher's output, collectors can lay the groundwork for the writing of this kind of history.[8]

The initial response to this kind of collecting by those who have never considered publishers' imprints as the likely theme of a collection might be to balk at the sheer size such a collection would eventually reach. For would-be collectors who might be discouraged by this aspect of imprint collecting, however, there are ways to narrow the scope of a collection. For example: by collecting books only up to a particular date, or only books on a particular subject (or subjects), or only books issued in a particular series. To use my own collection as a specific example, Woolmer's Hogarth Press *Checklist* includes publications only up to 1938, the year Virginia Woolf sold her partnership in the Press to John Lehmann. For a long time my own collection was limited to publications issued prior to 1941, the year of Virginia Woolf's death. However, if I had wanted a different scope, though still narrowed in some way, I might have limited the collection to only those books that were handprinted by the Woolfs, or to one of the many subject areas of the Press, regardless of date. In my own case this would have been works of literature. (The reissuing by the Press in 1978 and 1979 of the novels of Henry Green is, after all, no less interesting or important in understanding the nature of the Press and its literary policy than was the firm's original publication of these books in the 1940s.) Or, if I had limited my collection to a series, I might have collected one or more of the many pamphlet series of the Press, a format that had considerable influence on its development (Plate 29). In discussing the first series that was issued by the Press, the Hogarth Essays, which were begun in 1924, Leonard Woolf wrote: "This series consisted of pamphlets, a form of publication which nearly all publishers fought (still fight) shy of because they always involve a good deal of work and a loss of money. I was eager to have a series of pamphlets in which one could have essays on contemporary political and social problems as well as on art and criticism."[9] Some of the later pamphlet series are the Day to Day Pamphlets (1930–1939), the Hogarth Letters (1931–1932), and the Hogarth Sixpenny Pamphlets (1939). Two other series were issued in boards: the Hogarth Lectures on Literature, First Series (1927–1931), Second Series (1934), and the Hogarth Living Poets, First Series (1928–1932), Second Series (1933–1937).

However, regardless of an initial desire on the part of an imprint collector to limit the scope of the collection to some well-defined collecting plan, it often becomes difficult to stay with such a plan. As one learns more about a publisher and sees more of the imprints, new possibilities for the collection continue to unfold. It is often true that eventually nothing less than a complete collection of all the imprints becomes the collector's goal.

My own curiosity about the Hogarth Press began as the result of my interest in the work of several authors published by the Press. It would seem impossible that one interested in twentieth-century litera-

PLATE 29   The four cover designs by Vanessa Bell for the Hogarth Essays.

ture would not also be interested in this publisher that issued the early work of Katherine Mansfield, T. S. Eliot, John Middleton Murray, E. M. Forster, Robert Graves, Conrad Aiken, Edwin Muir, Edith Sitwell, Gertrude Stein, and C. Day Lewis, as well as nearly the entire output of Virginia Woolf, and English translations of Gorky, Dostoevsky, Tolstoi, Rilke, and Freud—especially when one learns that the very reason for this publisher's existence was that many of these authors could not find publishers elsewhere. However, the history of literary publishing is filled with such stories—though possibly not so dramatic or long-lived as the Hogarth Press—and a would-be collector has only to read casually in the history of publishing to find them.

For example, a small booklet in my own library containing a brief history and checklist of imprints of Frederick Leypoldt, whom I find among the most interesting (though least recognized) of all publishers in U.S. book-trade history, serves as a constant temptation to begin another imprint collection.[10] Prior to the compilation and publication of the monumental bibliographical work for which he is chiefly remembered, *The American Catalogue*,[11] Leypoldt had his own publishing firm in Philadelphia and later in New York, from which he issued during the years 1863 through 1869 a variety of trade books in the fields of literature, history, and music, as well as translations of many European classics. Leypoldt's career as a trade publisher has been little explored, and a collection and study of these imprints would add another dimension to our knowledge of this important figure in book-trade history.

For a brief time I considered collecting Egoist Press imprints, enticed by reading Jane Lidderdale and Mary Nicholson's *Dear Miss Weaver* (New York: Viking, 1970), the biography of Harriet Shaw Weaver, whose short-lived Egoist Press published James Joyce, Marianne Moore, Ezra Pound, Wyndham Lewis, H. D. (Hilda Doolittle), and T. S. Eliot at a time when these authors had difficulty finding a publisher for their work. However, I soon learned that prices of Egoist Press imprints were beyond my means because of the interest of author collectors in almost every work of the Press. However, I did acquire later editions of two books of the Press, Joyce's *Chamber Music* (first published by Elkin Mathews) and *A Portrait of the Artist as a Young Man* (first published by B. W. Huebsch), so that at least there are representations of this important literary imprint in my library. Although I have seen a number of individual Egoist Press imprints, I have never viewed an entire collection assembled for the imprint alone. From a literary standpoint such a collection would be as fascinating as a Hogarth Press collection, and its smaller size would make it easier to assemble and more likely to be completed.

Of course, one need not consider only imprints available from the antiquarian market as the focus of a collection. By using these earlier imprints as examples, I do not mean to imply that they are the only ones suitable for collection. Imprints of contemporary publishers also offer collecting possibilities: two examples that come immediately to mind are the publications of David Godine (Boston) and of the Northland Press (Flagstaff, Arizona). Both of these firms issue books that are worthy, both in content and design, of imprint collections of significance.

Yet, in spite of many possibilities awaiting the imprint collector, a search of periodical literature reveals relatively little interest in this area of collecting. One of the few imprints that has received any attention at all is Penguin Books, which was distinguished by three brief essays in the very first volume of *The Book Collector*.[12] Quotations from two of them will serve as a further example of the nature of this kind of imprint collecting. In "The Penguin Collector," by John Willesley, serious Penguin collectors are identified as those "who either buy all Penguins as they appear, or who specialize in some series, such as King Penguins or the Classics." The author foresaw future Penguin collecting as being of two kinds: first, those books that are collected as first editions in author collections because of the new material they contain; and secondly—characteristic of true imprint collecting—Penguins that are collected for themselves in categories such as the first 100 Penguins, or the first 50 Pelicans, or foreign issues, or first editions of Penguins that have sold over 200,000 copies. Willesley concludes with an observation that might be applied to this kind of imprint collecting as a whole: "Such a collection might not suit everyone, but let no one think that it would be easy to assemble."

However, in "The Penguin Achievement," Brooke Crutchley gets to the heart of imprint collecting and gives a reason for the appeal of this kind of collecting: "There can be little doubt that the Penguin Books group of publications is the most important and influential British publishing venture of this century, for it has penetrated the various economic and sociological barriers to bring new reading to thousands of people. . . ." And therein, he might have added, lies the appeal of Penguins to so many collectors. The distinguished achievement of Penguin has given the imprint a special place in publishing history, and in so doing, has captured the attention of an extraordinary number of collectors.[13]

Another collector of publishers' imprints, G. Thomas Tanselle, writing in *The Book Collector* about the imprints he collects—Boni & Liveright, Huebsch, Kennerley, Knopf (pre-1930), and Seltzer, as well as several lesser imprints that "served a similar function"— explains the rationale behind his collection in this way:

> In the belief that there was a clearly defined group of American publishers, in the first three decades of this century, who were willing to take risks on new and experimental young writers and who thus bore the same relation to the large established houses as the "little magazines" and "little theatres" did to the popular commercial magazines and the Broadway theatre, I have been attempting to assemble the total output of these "little publishers" as one way of illuminating the literary milieu of a major period in American literary history.[14]

For whatever other reasons a collector may be attracted to a particular imprint, at the heart of the collecting usually lies the belief that the imprint has made a significant contribution to some aspect of literary or publishing or social history. Other reasons exist, but this one seems paramount.

Price often plays a role in determining what one will collect. Where price is a consideration, publishers' imprints offer a decided advantage over most other kinds of collections. The high-priced books in a collection of publishers' imprints will be those that are sought competitively by collectors in other areas. Most of the time the competition comes from author collectors. The problem with collecting Egoist Press imprints, as I mentioned earlier, is that every author published by the Press is today a collected author! In my own collection, the highest priced books are predictably the widely collected authors; for example, Virginia Woolf, T. S. Eliot, and Christopher Isherwood. Occasionally, though, there are surprises. I was recently disappointed to learn from a book dealer that a copy of Rilke's *Duineser Elegien*, which I was hoping to buy, had been sold. I expected to hear that it had gone to a Rilke collector, but was surprised to learn that it had been sold instead to a collector of Eric Gill, designer of the book. Similarly, books of interest to subject collectors will also be among the higher-priced books in the collection. Julia Margaret Cameron's *Victorian Photographs of Famous Men & Fair Women* is costly, not especially because it was published by the Hogarth Press, but because it is sought after by collectors of photography as well. And, as if it were not enough to have *these* collectors vying for copies, the book has an introduction about Mrs. Cameron by Virginia Woolf (who was her niece) and a second introduction about Mrs.

Cameron's photographs by Roger Fry, giving the book a place in both Virginia Woolf and Roger Fry collections as well. Obviously, such competition creates a wider market and a greater scarcity of available copies and thus higher prices.

However, in a collection of publishers' imprints, there will be many low-to-moderately priced books, for many of the books of most publishers are of little interest in themselves to present-day collectors. Yet, collectively, they all tell something about their publisher. It is doubtful that there is much interest today in B. Bowker's *Lancashire under the Hammer*, a study of the Lancashire cotton trade, published by the Hogarth Press in 1928; or in R. Fitzure's *It Was Not Jones* (Number 2 in the Hogarth Living Poets, First Series) issued the same year. Yet they are both examples of the kinds of books the Press was interested in publishing from its inception: the former, a reflection of Leonard Woolf's interest in economics, and the latter, of the Woolfs' interest in new poetry. They have just as much of a place in a collection of imprints of the Press as do the remembered books in these areas: the economic studies of John Maynard Keynes, H. G. Wells, and Leonard Woolf, and the poetry of T. S. Eliot, Robert Graves, and John Crowe Ransome. They all have a place in the history of the Press. It was the Press's purpose to take chances on new writers. The work of many of them has survived; the work of many others has not. But this does not make the latter any less desirable in assembling a collection of the full output of the Press. It sometimes makes them even more desirable because, not having been saved for themselves, they are more challenging to locate, completely new in content, and always less expensive to purchase.

For those who collect the work of contemporary publishers, there is the opportunity to acquire books at publication price; occasionally small publishers even offer a discount to those who subscribe to all the works of the press. If readers do not realize what an advantage this is, they have only to turn to the last chapter of this book, "American Fiction since 1960," to learn how quickly books can become "collectible" and what prices one must pay for the more desirable ones once the publisher's supply has become exhausted and the books find their way into the antiquarian market.

Another attraction of collecting publishers' imprints is their constant and often surprising variety. A collector need not settle for one author or one subject, but has the opportunity to collect many. Frequently, comprehensive author collections can be built under the imprint of just one publisher. Within my Hogarth Press collection, for example, a near-complete Virginia Woolf collection is possible, as well as sizable collections of books by Sigmund Freud, C. Day Lewis, Edwin Muir, and Vita Sackville-West. One can only thrill at the thought of a collection of Scribner's imprints of the 1920s, 1930s, and 1940s, which would contain all the novels of Hemingway, Fitzgerald, and Thomas Wolfe.

Similarly, most publishers' lists contain an extraordinary variety of subjects. The Hogarth Press published widely in the areas of art, biography, drama, fiction, history, literature and criticism, music, poetry, politics and economics, psychoanalysis, and travel. Even so, as fully aware as I am of the varied subject interests of the Press, it was still startling recently to come across a book on what I find to be quite an unlikely subject for the Press: *Diet and High Blood Pressure*, by Dr. I. Harris (1937).

In short, imprint collectors have little chance of ever becoming bored with their collections. Aside from the organizing principle, the imprint itself, there are endless interests within the collection to attract every kind of collector. Even if a collector wearies of a particular author or loses interest in a once-favored subject, there is an astonishing array of other authors and other subjects to take their place.

Because book collectors are interested in books as physical objects, it is not surprising that many collectors are interested in the design and appearance of the books they collect. In this respect some collectors find themselves especially drawn to the "look" of the books of some publishers, and this attracts them to imprint collecting. Unlike the private press, for which fine design and production are usually the chief concern, the small publisher recognizes the importance of good book-making, but places it secondary to the concern for content. The small publisher's concern with bookmaking shows itself more in the production of "interesting-looking" or "unusual-looking" books than it does in the production of "fine books." On this point Leonard Woolf wrote:

> We did not want the Press to become one of those (admirable in their way) "private" or semi-private Presses the object of which is finely produced books, books which are meant not to be read, but to be looked at. We were interested primarily in the immaterial inside of a book, what the author had to say and how he said it; . . . We wanted our books to "look nice" and we had our own views of what nice looks in a book would be, but neither of us was interested in fine printing and fine binding.[15]

Although anyone who has seen a collection of Hogarth Press imprints would agree that in practice the Woolfs followed this design philosophy, they would also have to agree that the design of Hogarth

Press books is one of the features that sets them apart from the books of all other publishers. The design is totally original. Especially striking is the design of the books that were handprinted by the Woolfs (see Plate 30).[16] They carefully and beautifully designed, printed, and bound these books themselves, in a style that was completely unlike the books of other publishers of the period. Some were in wrappers and others were bound in paper over boards. All of the papers used were striking and unusual, and the Woolfs took great pains to find them. Some were colorful wallpaper, others were brilliantly patterned papers from Czechoslovakia, and still others were marbled papers made in Paris for the Woolfs by Roger Fry's daughter.[17] The Press soon became known for these unusual covers and, according to Leonard Woolf, within 10 or 12 years the use of such paper for binding all kinds of books, particularly for volumes of poetry, was widely adopted by publishers.[18]

By 1920, only three years after the first pamphlet had been issued from the Press, the Woolfs were forced by the number of manuscripts coming in and by the flood of orders for books already published to turn to a commercial printer for help. It was at this point that Leonard Woolf began to think of the Press as a commercial operation and that output began to increase dramatically. In spite of the move to mechanized operations, the books never lost their handmade appearance, nor the Press its original purpose of publishing books that were unlikely to be published elsewhere. And even the success of the Press as a business venture did not gain acceptance for it in the book industry. Writing about this time, Leonard Woolf said:

> The Hogarth Press, in these early years, met with a rather chilly welcome, or rather cold shoulder, from the booksellers. If you compare the thirteen books which we published in that year [1923] with any thirteen similar books from other publishers, you will find that all of ours have something more or less unorthodox in their appearance. They are either not the orthodox size or not the orthodox shape, or their binding is not orthodox; and even worse, what was inside the book, what the author said, was in many cases unfamiliar and therefore ridiculous and reprehensible, for it must be remembered that, if you published 42 years ago poetry by T. S. Eliot, Robert Graves, and Herbert Read, and a novel by Virginia Woolf, you were publishing four books which the vast majority of people, including booksellers and the literary "establishment," condemned as unintelligible and absurd. . . .[19]

With the publication in 1922 of Virginia Woolf's *Jacob's Room*, the Press produced its first full-length novel. This was also one of the first books of the Press to be issued in dust jacket, and like the jackets of

PLATE 30　Some of the early handprinted books of the Hogarth Press.

all the Virginia Woolf titles that were to follow, it was designed by Virginia's sister, Vanessa Bell. One might expect that once the Press began to issue full-length novels, printed and bound by commercial printers and binders, the look of the books would become more orthodox. But this was not so. Even the dust jackets of Hogarth Press books had an unusual appearance that caused the Woolfs continued difficulty in persuading booksellers to handle books of the Press (see Plate 31). In recounting the reaction of booksellers to *Jacob's Room*, Leonard Woolf wrote:

> The reception of *Jacob's Room* was characteristic. It was the first book for which we had a jacket designed by Vanessa. It is, I think, a very good jacket and today no bookseller would feel his hackles or his temperature rise at the sight of it. But it did not represent a desirable female or even Jacob or his room, and it was what in 1923 many people would have called reproachfully post-impressionist. It was almost universally condemned by the booksellers, and several of the buyers laughed at it.[20]

There is no evidence from the books in my collection, ranging in date from 1918 into the late 1940s, that during those years the design of the books ever changed to make them more orthodox in appearance. Each book in its own way has the distinct look of a book that could only have been published by the Hogarth Press.

I have dwelt at some length on the design of Hogarth Press books because they are a perfect example of how a publisher—not a private press or fine printer—can issue books of distinctive design. For collectors to whom design is important, collecting publishers' imprints can often be an ideal kind of collecting.

To conclude this discussion of the attractions of collecting publishers' imprints I have only to underscore the underlying principles of purpose and organization that form the basis of any good collection. Collecting publishers' imprints offers an exceptional opportunity to preserve material that might otherwise be lost or destroyed, to look at forgotten books in a new light, and to find new uses for these books in building a collection that may not have been previously assembled and that may be put to scholarly use.

It is in the nature of a book collector to look for ways to expand his or her collection. Because the search for the imprints of a specific publisher is often long and frustrating and because frequently there are considerable time lapses between purchases, relevant ways of expanding this kind of collection are particularly desirable.

One method of expanding and strengthening an imprint collection

PLATE 31   Dust jackets by Vanessa Bell for *Jacob's Room* (1922) and *Mrs. Dalloway* (1925).

is by acquiring later printings and editions. As this is discussed in detail by G. Thomas Tanselle in "Non-Firsts," the first chapter in this book, I will only describe how the addition of this kind of material has enriched my own collection.

As already noted, the early publications of the Hogarth Press were printed and bound by hand at the Woolfs' dining room table. This method of hand production had considerable effect on later editions. The original press runs were understandably small: the first issue of the Press was in an edition of only 150 copies and none of the handprinted books produced during the following three years exceeded 250 copies. However, in 1919, upon publication of Virginia Woolf's *Kew Gardens*, the Woolfs sent a review copy to the *Times Literary Supplement*. An extremely favorable review appeared after which the Woolfs were overwhelmed with orders for *Kew Gardens*. Until then, they had sold fewer than 50 copies, but after the appearance of the review they found they hadn't enough copies to fill all the orders. Unable themselves to produce enough handprinted books to meet their need, they went to a commercial printer for a second edition of 500 copies, and later, in 1927, they issued a third edition of 500 copies from still another printer.

This was the first instance of a policy they were to follow from time to time with later editions of their handprinted books. As might be expected, the commercially printed books usually have quite a different appearance from the handprinted ones. Although the second edition of *Kew Gardens* resembles the first, differing only in the use of less striking paper wrappers (I have seen it only once, and it may be even rarer than the first edition), the third edition has a decidedly different look. It is bound in printed boards rather than in marbled paper wrappers, was issued in large paper format rather than small octavo, contains a printed limitation notice, and, in some copies, is signed by the author and the illustrator (Vanessa Bell). Following the accepted traditions of book collecting, I was not interested in later editions at the time I had (and missed) the opportunity to purchase the second edition. But by the time I came across the third edition I was well aware of what I had lost, and without hesitation added the third edition to my collection. In these three books, standing side by side, one would see the transformation from handprinting to commercial representation of a handmade book, to a commercially produced limited edition.

Even more striking are the differences in the handprinted and commercially printed editions of E. M. Forster's *Pharos and Pharillon* (1923). Both editions were issued the same year, but the second edition is clearly identified on the title page. In size, binding, and quality of paper, the commercially produced edition is distinctly inferior to the hand-produced book. In fact, the former looks like an ordinary paperback book (Plates 32 and 33).

The addition of variant bindings is another way to expand an imprint collection. Bindings can change not only from edition to edition, but also within the same edition. The Hogarth Press, however, must be exceptional for the astonishing numbers of variant bindings that were used. So many variants turn up that it often seems the Woolfs never had enough of one kind of paper on hand to complete the binding of any one edition of a book. Binding variants of this sort can certainly lead to duplicate purchases for collectors not interested in this kind of expansion, particularly if they do not carry want lists with them but rely on their memories of a book's appearance to determine whether they already own a copy. Hogarth Press bindings are generally distinctive enough from one another—with the exception of the common binding designs of the series publications—to warrant such dependence on memory alone, but the variant bindings are deceptive.

The dust jackets in any collection of publishers' imprints contribute an additional important source of information about the publisher and about each particular book. Books should be sought in dust jacket and the jackets always preserved. In addition to telling a great deal about a publisher's style of design, the jacket can also illustrate a publisher's advertising style as can perhaps nothing else that has survived. Jackets sometimes also contain other information that is available nowhere else: numbers of copies printed, endorsements by well-known persons, quotations from elusive reviews, and occasionally other curious information.

Variant dust jackets sometimes turn up on Hogarth Press books, but with far less frequency than do variant bindings. However, they are always interesting. I recently purchased an edition of Christopher Isherwood's *Lions and Shadows* (1938) that seems to have absolutely no differences from an edition of the same date that I purchased some time ago (and that I assume to be the first edition) except that the second copy has an entirely different dust jacket (Plate 34). It is typographic rather than pictorial, containing quotes from reviews (which definitely implies that it is a later jacket), and carrying the identification of the Hogarth Crown Library. This identification is not contained anywhere within the book itself, and there is no mention of it in Woolmer's *Checklist*. Nor have I yet turned up any information about such a series in my reading. The same plates and quality of paper have been used for both editions. The same frontispiece, a portrait of the young Isherwood, appears in both. Only the dust jackets are different, and only from this variant dust jacket do I now know that the Press must have issued a Hogarth Crown Library series.

Advertising and promotional brochures, catalogues of publications, broadsides, and the like, all can be useful in expanding and strengthening the collection. I have already mentioned my own uses of this kind of material to learn about publications of the Hogarth Press before Woolmer's *Checklist* was available. Such material, usually regarded as ephemeral and quickly discarded, can tell much about the character of a publishing firm, its methods of announcing and promoting its publications, and its mode of operation in general. It should always be sought out and preserved.

In the foregoing pages, the value, the attractions, and the pleasures of collecting publishers' imprints have been discussed. The difficulties have been touched upon realistically, but only briefly, and then, in a way that I hope has turned these difficulties to challenges. Few collections that I know of offer such variety and such pleasure, or such an opportunity to make a scholarly contribution to a field of study that

PLATE 32   Binding and title page of the handprinted edition of *Pharos and Pharillon* (1923).
The imprint of the handprinted books always reads: Printed and Published by Leonard
and Virginia Woolf at the Hogarth Press. . . , whereas the imprint of the commercially
printed books reads: Published by Leonard and Virginia Woolf at the Hogarth Press. . . .
(Cf. Plate 33.)

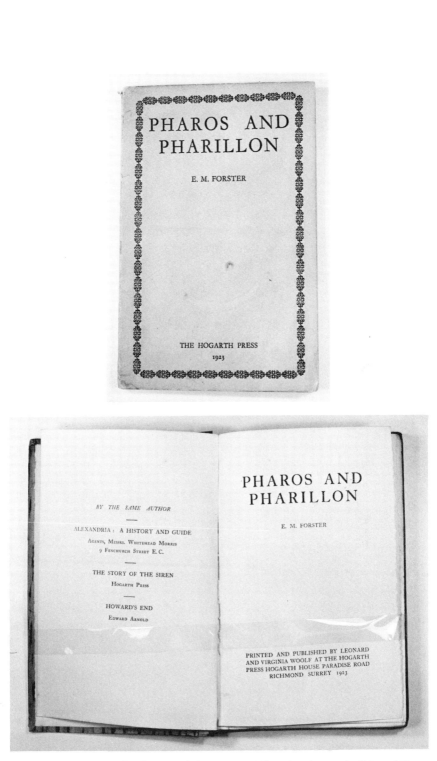

PLATE 33   Binding and title page of the commercially printed second edition of *Pharos and Pharillon* (1923). (Cf. Plate 32.)

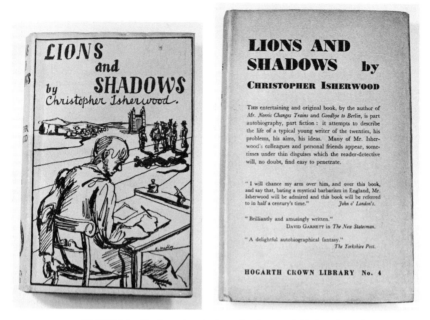

PLATE 34   Variant dust jackets for *Lions and Shadows* (1938).

Mr. Tanselle described more than ten years ago as a field "where the labors of many men for many years to come will make only a beginning."[21]

Of the many thousands of publishers that exist or have existed, only a fraction have been studied historically or bibliographically, and even fewer have had systematic collections of their imprints assembled. The possibilities for new collections are endless, innumerable stories wait to be told, and ideas turn up everywhere. Anyone who reads is constantly exposed to them. I cannot forget that a few lines I read almost 20 years ago were the catalyst that started me on the search for Hogarth Press books and led me to the collecting of the imprints of this publisher who "drifted into the business with the idea of publishing things the commercial publisher could not or would not publish,"[22] and in so doing, produced over the next 40 years one of the most extraordinary lists in modern publishing.

Notes

1. The term *device* or *logo* is the correct designation for a publisher's mark of identification, and it appears with the publisher's imprint on the title page.

In modern book publishing such marks as the Knopf borzoi or the Holt owl are examples of publishers' devices so recognizable to most readers as to be almost interchangeable with the firm name. Although the term *colophon* is sometimes used to indicate a publisher's device or the publisher's imprint as a whole, this is incorrect usage. The colophon is the note usually appearing at the end of a book, containing the *printer's* imprint. The colophon gives the details of the production of the book (the name of the printer, the number of copies printed, the paper and type used) and is often accompanied by the printer's device or mark. In present-day publishing the printer's imprint has disappeared entirely from the publications of many U.S. commercial publishers. These books bear only the notation, appearing usually on the verso of the title page, "Manufactured in the United States of America."

2. The work of the earlier private presses has been well documented, but, although some magnificent work is presently being turned out by contemporary private presses, it is often difficult to learn of the existence of the presses or to locate examples of their presswork. And sometimes there is only a fine line of difference in what today constitutes a private press or a small publisher. An exhibition of the work of approximately 40 contemporary private presses in operation from 1968 to 1978 was held at the Grolier Club in New York City in early 1979. The imprints of these presses offer collecting possibilities for those interested in fine printing and bookmaking, and who wish to take advantage of the lower prices usually offered to buyers of books upon publication. However, the traditional nature of this kind of imprint collecting—a primary interest in the printer or the designer of the book rather than in the publisher—necessarily keeps it outside the range of this chapter. Those interested in this kind of imprint collecting will find a list of the presses included in the exhibition and a commentary in *Bibliography Newsletter 7*, nos. 1–3 (March–April 1979): 6–7, and in *Book Collector's Market* 4 (March–April 1979): 36–37. For an ongoing account of the work of contemporary private presses, see issues of the periodical, *Fine Print*.

3. Volume 1 of the autobiography, *The Whispering Gallery* (London: Longman), was published in 1955, and Volume 2, *I Am My Brother* (London: Longman), in 1960. The subject of the Hogarth Press had not been brought out in the library cataloguing of these books, and it was only through the knowledge of my former teacher and friend, the late John Neal Waddell of the Columbia University Libraries, that I came to know of them at all. They provided my most valuable source of information about the Press for several years. The third and final volume of the autobiography, *The Ample Proposition* (London: Eyre & Spottiswoode), was published in 1966. But by then Leonard Woolf's own autobiography was being issued in parts, and I was learning about the Press from another—and quite different—point of view.

4. For authors and titles of books that discuss the Press, see Further Reading at the end of this chapter.

5. J. Howard Woolmer, *A Checklist of the Hogarth Press, 1917-1938; With a Short History of the Press by Mary E. Gaither* (Andes, N.Y.: Woolmer-Brotherson, 1976).

6. The Hogarth Press is covered extensively in the last three volumes of the autobiography: *Beginning Again: An Autobiography of the Years 1911 to 1918* (New York: Harcourt, 1964); *Downhill All the Way: An Autobiography of the Years 1919-1930* (New York: Harcourt, 1967); and *The Journey Not the Arrival Matters: An Autobiography of the Years 1939-1969* (New York: Harcourt, 1969).

7. George A. Spater, "The Paradise Road Publications of The Hogarth Press," *American Book Collector*, May 1971, p. 18.

8. For a survey of research and publication in the field of American literary publishing, as well as a suggested research procedure for further historical and bibliographical studies in the field, see G. Thomas Tanselle, "The Historiography of American Literary Publishing," in *Studies in Bibliography*, 18 (1965): 3–39. For a more complete list of historical studies of publishers, see G. Thomas Tanselle, "Studies of Individual Printers and Publishers," in *Guide to the Studies of United States Imprints* (Cambridge, Mass.: Harvard Univ. Press, 1971), pp. 405–762.

9. Leonard Woolf, *Downhill All the Way* (New York: Harcourt, 1967) p. 161.

10. Jay W. Beswick, *The Work of Frederick Leypoldt, Bibliographer and Publisher* (New York: Bowker, 1942).

11. *The American Catalogue* (New York: Office of Publishers Weekly, 1880–1911), the standard American national bibliography for the period 1876–1910, was Frederick Leypoldt's bibliographical dream, although the finished work fell somewhat short of his ideal.

12. "Penguin Books: Three Short Essays," *The Book Collector* 1, no. 4 (1952): 210–214.

13. For other articles on collecting Penguins see David J. Hall, "The King Penguin Series," in *The Private Library*, 2nd series, 10, no. 4 (1977): 143–148; and David J. Hall, "The Penguin Collectors' Story," in *Antiquarian Book Monthly Review* 5, no. 9 (1978): 361–367. The latter is concerned with the Penguin Collector's Society, the only association, to the author's knowledge, "at present devoted to the output of a single publisher."

14. G. Thomas Tanselle, "Collecting Modern Imprints," *The Book Collector* 19, no. 2 (1970): 203–213.

15. Woolf, *Downhill All the Way*, pp. 79–80.

16. A list of the 35 books handprinted by the Woolfs is included in Woolmer, *A Checklist of the Hogarth Press*, p. 155.

17. Leonard Woolf, *Beginning Again* (New York: Harcourt, 1963) p. 236.

18. Woolf, *Downhill All the Way*, p. 77.

19. Ibid., pp. 75–76.

20. Ibid., p. 76.

21. Tanselle, "The Historiography of American Literary Publishing," p. 3.

22. Woolf, *Downhill All the Way*, p. 80.

Further Reading

HOGARTH PRESS

The Hogarth Press has been studied bibliographically in two checklists: J. Howard Woolmer, *A Checklist of the Hogarth Press, 1917–1938* (Andes, N.Y.: Woolmer-Brotherson, 1976) and Suzanne Henig, "Bibliography of Hogarth Press Publications, 1917–1946" (*Virginia Woolf Quarterly* 2, nos. 1–2 [1975]: 106–152). The latter extends the recording of Press titles eight years beyond Woolmer's *Checklist*, but gives no bibliographical information other than author and title within a chronological framework that is further subdivided by subject. Woolmer, on the other hand, includes such additional information as printer, description of binding and dust jacket, size, number of pages, number of copies printed when known, and includes notes about variant bindings, designers and illustrators, author pseudonyms, and the like. It is indispensable for the study of the Press.

The most valuable study of the operations and history of the Press is contained in the last three volumes of Leonard Woolf's autobiography: *Beginning Again* (New York: Harcourt, 1964); *Downhill All the Way* (New York: Harcourt, 1967); and *The Journey Not the Arrival Matters* (New York: Harcourt, 1969). An account of Press operations in the 1930s and 1940s is given by John Lehmann in his three-volume autobiography: *The Whispering Gallery* (London: Longman, 1955); *I Am My Brother* (London: Longman, 1960); and *The Ample Proposition* (London: Eyre & Spottiswoode, 1966); and again recently in a volume devoted entirely to his relationship with the Woolfs and the Hogarth Press: *Thrown to the Woolfs* (London: Weidenfeld & Nicolson, 1978). A concise history of the Press by Mary E. Gaither appears as an introductory essay to Woolmer's *Checklist*, and a light-hearted illustrated memoir by Richard Kennedy, *A Boy at the Hogarth Press* (London: Heinemann, 1972) offers glimpses of the Woolfs and the workings of the Press in the late 1920s from the viewpoint of a 16-year-old office boy. Included is a fold-out map drawn by Kennedy of the pressroom about 1928. Information about the Press can also be found in Quentin Bell's *Virginia Woolf: A Biography* (New York: Harcourt, 1972) and in volumes two, three, and four of *The Letters of Virginia Woolf*, edited by Nigel Nicolson and Joanne Trautmann (New York: Harcourt, 1975–1979).

OTHER PUBLISHERS

Comprehensive histories that provide an overview of the U.S. book industry and serve as a useful general introduction to the field include

Hellmut Lehmann-Haupt, with Lawrence C. Wroth and Rollo G. Silver, *The Book in America* (New York: Bowker, 1951) and John Tebbel, *A History of Book Publishing in the United States*, 3 vols. (New York: Bowker, 1972–1978). A listing of additional general histories as well as studies of individual publishers can be found in G. Thomas Tanselle, *Guide to the Study of United States Imprints*, 2 vols. (Cambridge, Mass.: Harvard Univ. Press, 1971). This bibliographical guide as well as Mr. Tanselle's "The Historiography of American Literary Publishing" (*Studies in Bibliography* 18 [1965]: 3–39) are indispensable to anyone who needs to know what research has been done in book-trade history. They are the starting point for any serious study of the field. Annual catalogues of publishers are collected in the multivolume set, *Publishers' Trade List Annual*, which began publication in 1871 (New York: Bowker) and continues to be issued annually. Because it is difficult, if not impossible, to locate retrospective publication lists of individual publishers, the *Publishers' Trade List Annual* is a basic research tool for studying the output of U.S. publishers. The book industry journal, *Publishers Weekly* (New York: Bowker, 1872–) serves as an invaluable history of the industry and continues to provide in its current issues an ongoing account of industry developments and information about new and forthcoming books.

For a historical overview of the British book trade, see Frank Arthur Mumby and Ian Norrie, *Publishing and Bookselling* (London: Cape; New York: Bowker, 1974) and Marjorie Plant, *The English Book Trade* (London: Allen & Unwin, 1965). References to other general histories as well as to studies of individual publishers are included in Robin Myers, *The British Book Trade . . . A Bibliographical Guide* (London: Andre Deutsch, 1973). A new journal, *Publishing History* (Cambridge: Chadwyck-Healey; Teaneck, N.J.: Somerset House, 1977), thus far emphasizing British publishing history but promising broader area coverage in the future, should not be overlooked as an important source of historical information on the book trade. For an ongoing account of contemporary British publishing and information on new and forthcoming books, see issues of the weekly journal of the British book trade, *The Bookseller* (London: Whitaker, 1858–).

For bibliographical references to book-trade literature of European countries, see the "Europe and International" section in *The Book Trade of the World*, vol. 1 (Hamburg, Germany: Buchmarkt-Forschung; New York: Bowker, 1972).

9

American Fiction since 1960

Peter B. Howard*

ALL OF US were a part, however much we remained in the background, of the landscape of the 1960s. That landscape, in turn, has become a significant part of many of *us*. It made an impression. To put it in the most general terms: we found the 1960s, in the United States at least, to be simply more *interesting* than the decades just before and after. More was openly and excitedly going on, more seemd to be changing: all sorts of new drugs and varieties of religious experience (many of which, of course, are very old in other parts of the world); a "sexual revolution" that resulted in an expanding popular notion of what is permissible in sexual relations and in living arrangements generally; a drawn-out losing war, the first in our history, waged against both a tenacious "enemy" far away and a more and more powerful—and unprecedented —resistance to war at home. Unprecedented, too—or at least unknown since the founding—was the extent and depth of people's loss of faith in conventional politicians and politics, particularly toward the end of the decade.

All these, if they did not determine, at least contributed to, an unusual freedom in writing, with respect to both subject matter and

*Writing about bookselling, like bookselling itself, is often a cooperative effort. I wish to thank my friend Burton Weiss for his careful reading of the second draft of this essay and for his many perceptive suggestions for improvement, most of which I have followed. All responsibility for error remains, of course, my own.

form. Some critics have observed that freedom of written expression in the United States, more than being merely unusual in the 1960s, grew to be greater than ever before. Most of these critics take pleasure in that observation. I understate—they're exhilarated by it! The fact that I, as a bookseller, share their opinion, their pleasure, and their exhilaration has had more than a little to do with the account that follows.

Two antiquarian booksellers have recently issued catalogues limited to American fiction since 1960: Christopher P. Stephens in New York (Catalogue 35, 1974) and myself in Berkeley (Catalogue 38, 1979). Both catalogues are dedicated to Frank Scioscia, a Harper & Row executive and book enthusiast whose practical knowledge in this area of modern fiction combined with personal goodwill has encouraged and informed many an inexperienced book buyer. The intent of each dealer is put succinctly by Stephens in the foreword to his catalogue: it is to offer "a comprehensive catalogue of serious writers who had not had a novel published before 1960." There was cordial cooperation between us in our separate projects—each of us selling these authors constantly in the interim between the two catalogues, often to each other—and certain common assumptions underlay our efforts. Chief of these was the acceptance of critical opinion that a new generation of prose writers had risen, roughly speaking, during the decade 1960–1970 and the Vietnam War, and the conviction that though accessible to us as book scouts, their works were not widely available for long to buyers and readers—having, in some instances, been poorly merchandised by their publishers—and would consequently sell in the antiquarian market if presented in a logical, organized fashion. We were informed by our reading of the fiction, by critical reviews, by the literary studies that had appeared, by the suggestions of knowledgeable friends and prescient customers, and not least by the tempting vision of book after book being hustled to the remainder tables to allow room for ever more titles in the hardback publishers' warehouses. Finally, no other dealers seemed to have taken comprehensive interest in the period. Every year through the 1960s, 2,000 to 3,000 new fiction titles appeared from standard publishers, of which an average of just under 1,000 per year were hardcover. Of these, an average of 110 were *first* novels.[1] Our self-appointed task was to identify, secure, and offer the best 20 percent of this diffuse lot, and our checklists of authors and their works grew rapidly. If an author flourished after 1960 but began just before, our arbitrary time frame was nudged backward. We hoped to frame a period of literature in a bookseller's manner. Because the books themselves seemed to us plentifully available on each coast as long as the remainder lasted and were as inexpensive as any sort of book in any market (those were the days of the $1 remainder), and because we could count on almost every promising novel by a beginning writer being somewhere remaindered, we hoped to sell the books over and over again.

In 1974 Stephens offered 429 books by 157 authors. The average price was close to $13, and the catalogue was mailed almost exclusively to university libraries. Individual titles were offered in first printings, together with later printings if available, in dust jacket or without, with appropriate distinctions in price. The range in format and genre was intentionally limited; only an occasional proof, essay, juvenile, critical work, anthology, or association copy was included. By any measure the catalogue was a considerable success. Hardly a title was left unsold, as many as ten copies of certain books were placed, and as many as ten back orders were accumulated for titles Stephens could reasonably expect to acquire in the trade within a year.

In 1979, with the advantage of another five years during which I madly expanded my list of authors and recorded the newly published titles and new editions of works by writers already included, and with the experience of having supplied numerous duplicates for Stephens to relay to his customers, I ventured forth with the second 1960s fiction catalogue. The trick was to have held on during these intervening years to all the books I wanted to offer. In this I was fortunate because I had been commissioned to build similar collections at two universities. Building them helped me delineate and pay for my own.[2]

In Serendipity Books Catalogue 38, 2,752 books of 429 authors are priced, in one format or another. I note with rue, but no apology, that the average price is beyond $20 and that "high spots" have increased in price an average of fivefold, or occasionally even more.[3] Three thousand copies of this catalogue were mailed to institutional libraries, new and old private customers, and every dealer who evinced even minimal curiosity. The consequences of all this business and busyness are some opinions (and facts) that may interest all parties: publishers, sellers of new books, scouts, antiquarian dealers, critics, librarians, and, especially, private collectors and readers. With some attempt at objectivity, I should like to consider what one might expect to find in catalogues such as Stephens's or mine, to consider which authors' books might be wanted today, or ought to be wanted, in what formats, and why. Other questions arise as well. What is the role of price, and from whose point of view? What trade practices prevail of which the buyer should be aware? What have a few exemplary collectors already accomplished in this field?

Authors and Genres

One certification of the lasting value of a particular author, though by no means the only one, is the degree of scholarly attention paid either to the author or to his or her place in a larger context. In fact, academic study is well advanced upon the authors of the 1960s. Even though only 5 of the 429 Serendipity authors are known to have died (William Brammer, Richard Farina, Sylvia Plath, Edward Wallant, and Herbert Wilner), and the others may be presumed to be still alive and in mid-career, there are nonetheless a good number of critical and historical essays, as well as working bibliographies and checklists already in print. In compiling our catalogue we surveyed this research and occasionally added to it. Brief consideration now of available resources may suggest to the reader the range and quality of contemporary criticism and bibliography.

Criticism has addressed contemporary fiction in a variety of ways, which we can separate into several broad categories. The most obvious, and to the average collector apparently the most congenial, is the author study. Already, almost every one of the major novelists of the 1960s has had several books devoted entirely to him or her, although no full biographies have been published. First to appear is usually the brief monograph in a series of similar author studies, like the Minnesota or Twayne series on American writers or "Contemporary Writers in Christian Perspective." For a writer as prominent as Updike, there are, besides the formulaic treatment of a series, no fewer than five additional full-length critical works and more than 150 articles and essays.[4] Similarly, for Roth, there are more than 60 scholarly articles (through 1976), for Pynchon, more than 50, for Kesey, more than 30. Introductions to the period, like that of Ihab Hassan, insistently focus on "major" and "prominent" novelists and broad genres, and the latest novels by the dozen or so writers thus singled out are almost as quickly assimilated by the critics as they are reviewed or "collected."[5] In short, the most heavily collected authors are the best studied. But only a few writers in each generation receive such immediate and extensive scrutiny.*

Some collectors have traditionally collected, and may be in fact limited (or ennobled) by their devotion to, a particular genre, such as

---

*The labor of graduate students corroborates our general conclusions. The unpublished dissertation, that lumbering, devouring beast, has already sniffed out (between 1970 and 1979) 12 authors from our 1960s list for individual consumption. As might be expected, John Updike leads the list, having been digested 13 separate times, more than twice as often as the next closest victims, Joyce Carol Oates, Walker Percy, and Thomas Pynchon (6 dissertations each). Robert Coover, Ken Kesey, and Philip Roth have all en-

science or detective fiction. And as the books from earlier decades begin to run thin, they look for these forms among modern books. A good deal of contemporary literature remains conventionally recognizable; for instance, houses like Doubleday and Ace have exclusive lines of science and detective fiction. The Gothic novel, the historical novel, the Jewish novel, the southern novel, the war novel (the Civil War and World Wars I and II) all flourish, are published in generous quantities, and find their traditional readers. But it is safe to say that some new genres and techniques in fiction have recently been introduced. These are often named and labeled on covers and in reviews, sometimes receive precise definition and explication by critics, and might well compel the attention of collectors seeking to understand better what they already have on their shelves or might find in the stores. Who are the "surfictionists," "transfictionists," "black humorists," and "absurdists"?[7] Updike and Pynchon are customarily found in the same book collection, but do they really have any points of view, beliefs, or techniques in common?

While it is impossible here even to begin to separate out all the possible distinctions of technique, it may be useful to point to a single genre, *the nonfiction novel*, as an example of how one can consider as a group several works of literature that otherwise might too readily be dismissed or overlooked by the collector. The one book about this genre is Maś ud Zavarzadeh's *The Mythopoeic Reality, The Postwar American Nonfiction Novel*, which deals theoretically with a few of the best-known works of our generation: Capote's *In Cold Blood;* Mailer's *The Armies of the Night;* Styron's *The Confessions of Nat Turner;* and Wolfe's *The Electric Kool-Aid Acid Test*. But we find in the same discussion all of Carlos Castaneda's books; Hersey's *The Algiers Motel Incident;* three works by Oscar Lewis; Theodore Rosengarten's *All God's Dangers;* John Sack's *M.;* Andy Warhol's *a.;* Joseph Wambaugh's *The Onion Field;* and books by Studs Terkel and Hunter S. Thompson. Zavarzadeh finds that the new sensibility and method that these books reveal were foreshadowed by isolated novels of the past, although he concludes that there have been *absolute* changes in the way some contemporary writers see and relate to the actual world.[8]

---

joyed more than a single study, the fate to date of Donald Barthelme, William Gass, Joseph Heller, and Edward Wallant.[6] These dissertation counts do not include the many other dissertations devoted to more than one of our authors, or those that consider one of the 1960s writers at the end of a historical study that progresses to the present. For the last decade there are more than 30 directly relevant dissertations; some of the most pertinent are cited in the Further Reading section at the end of this chapter.

Before World War 2, the imagination of the fictionist was ahead of the actualities, thus enabling him to formulate a private metaphysics of life in his culture and weave his vision—his view of man and his experience in relation to a larger order—into the fabric of his novels to provide his reader with a pattern of the underlying order of external reality. The advent of technetronic culture in the postwar years, however, has changed the nature of the relationship between the fictionist and the world around him: the actualities, in their freakish behavior, now move far ahead of the imagination of the writer. Contemporary reality is invested with fictive power and unfolds with a shape so fictional that not even Kafka, Joyce, or Beckett could have fully anticipated it. The forces unleashed by postwar scientific and technological innovations have created such historical disruption and discontinuity that the permutations of events have now reached a degree of bizarreness beyond the wildest imaginings.[9]

The point for the collector is that disparate novelists and journalists, in their similar approach to "historical facts," write books that it makes sense to read together, because they may reinforce and substantiate each other.

On a different level, but with the same purpose, one may collect fiction not by author or technique, but by *subject*. Not many collectors have interests so refined that they are moved by categories like the "family" novel or the "academic" novel, but this cannot be said of the "beat" novel, the "Chicano" novel, the novel about the Vietnam War experience, or about being black in America.[10] There is a growing literature of the aesthetics of sport.[11] The critic may precede the collector in exploring these fields, but he certainly does not preempt him. The careful reader and the watchful hunter of books will jointly add to the rapidly accumulating evidence that these persist as enduring subjects of modern fiction, whatever the technique or style of the author.

Nowhere is this assertion so relevant as in the area of homoerotic (gay male and lesbian) literature. Dozens of contemporary novelists have written books which espouse and/or reflect homoerotic ("homosexual" is an inappropriate and hybrid word) feelings and attitudes.[12] Many are obvious—C. D. B. Bryan, Robert Gover, William Herrick, Sanford Friedman, Rosa Guy, Margaret Laurence, Marge Piercy, John Rechy, and Jane Rule are but a few. Some are less well known, even though their books all appeared from major trade publishers: Ann Bernays, Roy Doliner, Edwin P. Murray, Peter Rand, George Selcamm, Shane Stevens, and Philip Van Rensselaer, for instance. To evergrowing lists like these must be added the obscure or rare book or small-press author whose readership is severely restricted by the problem of accessibility of text. Included in this group are Doris Grumbach's *The Spoil of the Flowers* (Doubleday, 1962); all the books by Alma Rout-song[13]; fiction by Leo Skir[14]; William Carney's *The Real Thing* (Putnam, 1968); Hunce Voelcker's *Logan* (Cowstone, 1969); and the early, pseudo-nymous, erotic paperback originals by the mystery writer Joseph Hansen.[15]

Another perspective on modern fiction is that of region. The modern southern tradition from Faulkner and Welty and before is certain to be sensed and its continuation measured in the works of Wendell Berry, John William Corrington, James Dickey, Jesse Hill Ford, George Garrett, Josephine Haxton (using the pseudonym "Ellen Douglas"), Madison Jones, Harper Lee, Romulus Linney, Reynolds Price, and many others who have emerged as talented writers since World War II.[16] Collecting writers by geographical origin is often the preoccupation of those who live within that region, if the traditions are long and strong enough. Particularly true of southern collectors and Cape Codders for a long time now, it is becoming true for another region, the Southwest, and east Texas especially, in which a host of young fiction writers of note have recently appeared, where it may fairly be said none at all existed before. It is likely to be the collecting reader who adds to the once short shelf that now preserves together books by Max Crawford, John Graves, Sherry Kafka, Larry L. King, Vassar Miller, Hughes Rudd, Edwin Shrake, Mach Thomas, R. G. Vliet, and Dorothy Yates. More narrowly still, one can put together a collection of desert literature, Los Angeles fiction (there are several anthologies of Los Angeles already), or even Bolinas, California, fiction (greatest number of authors per capita in the world!). Not only *can* small collections of these writers be built, they *should* be. These authors should be gathered, read, and understood to the extent that they choose to live in proximity to each other, write about each other, and the common horizon.

Of the 429 authors represented in Serendipity's Catalogue 38, which is a carefully assembled and (I hope) comprehensive list, only 61, or 14 percent, are women. Rather than an expression of partiality or insensitivity, this figure is, I feel, an accurate reflection of the fact that disproportionately few novels by women were published between 1960 and 1970. But the percentage is increasing, and figures for the 1970s may show that twice as many novels by women were accepted for publication in this decade as in the previous one. I think readers will find that the woman's point of view is better represented now by authors of both sexes. Women's writing deserves the same serious attention from collectors in general that it has continuously enjoyed only from the liberal women's college library. Lamentable in this regard is the paucity of female book collectors, whatever their interests, a fact doubtless to be attributed in part to the rare-book trade's traditional capacity for alienating women in general. However, more and more women are effectively engaged as antiquarian booksellers, and about 20 percent of the full members of the Antiquarian Booksellers' Association of America are women. Perhaps modern women's literature as a whole will affect these imbalances for the better.

Beginning with Tony Tanner's *City of Words* (London: Cape, 1971), which takes Ken Kesey as a point of departure, there has appeared about once a year a sympathetic work of criticism of the fiction since 1960. The best of these seem to be Charles Harris on the "absurdists," Glicksberg on sexual revolution, the overviews by Hassan and Kazin, Schulz's study of "black humor" fiction, Kenner on American modernists, and Boyer's essays. In several articles and books Jerome Klinkowitz has examined and promoted the "surfictionists": Donald Barthelme, Richard Brautigan, Raymond Federman, and Ronald Sukenick. Anthologies of stories abound, as editors gather between covers examples of new short fiction for pedagogical purposes.

The best single treatment of the fiction of the 1960s that is not simply a summary or a guide to the period is Raymond M. Olderman's *Beyond the Wasteland*, which assays novels by 50 writers strictly belonging to the 1960s, as well as 8 others who began a few years before 1960. Olderman finds that the work of these authors reflects certain trends, tendencies, and characteristics: the blurring of fact and fiction (ending for some, as we have seen above, in the "nonfiction" novel), the mystery of fact, the helplessness of protagonists, the movement away from the realistic novel, two-dimensional characterization, dominance of plot and action over character, abandonment of the possibility of reconciliations, movement toward romance, barest affirmations of life, and the "controlling metaphor in the image of the wasteland."[17] Olderman is able to synthesize these particular abstractions by analyzing a specific group of writers. But in fact ten times as many writers have flourished contemporaneously with those discussed by Olderman, many of whom have as yet hardly anyone as advocate. Few, if any, collectors or scholars have turned yet to the fiction of Thomas Baird (nine novels), Richard Bankowsky (four novels), Gina Berriault (three novels, one volume of stories), Don Berry (three novels), William Butler (eleven novels, five published only in England), Stanley Crawford (three novels), Thomas Curley (three novels), John Hopkins (two novels)—to name but eight writers who are not even mentioned in the revised edition of *Contemporary Novelists*.

Bibliography

Bibliographers seek to identify what scholarship and criticism hope to understand; in a modest, uneven way, a number of bibliographies and checklists have appeared that can aid the librarian and collector in sorting out a pleasing variety of authors of varying talents and diverse origins. Separately published bibliographies already exist for Donald Barthelme, LeRoi Jones, and John Updike, and for Updike two, plus a bibliography of secondary studies.[18] Checklists of primary works have been compiled in considerable detail (if not final exactitude) by Gary M. Lepper and collected in one volume for Thomas Berger, Wendell Berry, Richard Brautigan, Robert Coover, James Dickey, Diane DiPrima, George P. Elliott, Bruce Jay Friedman, John Gardner, William Gass, Joseph Heller, Larry McMurtry, David Meltzer, Joyce Carol Oates, Reynolds Price, Philip Roth, Paul Theroux, and Edward Wallant.[19] Gale Research Company has an ongoing series, *First Printings of American Authors* (general editor, Matthew Bruccoli, four volumes to date), which adds 42 lists of books by 1960s novelists.[20] The conjunction of particular authors in these volumes is highly arbitrary, undoubtedly because candidates for checklisting were nominated on the basis of availability of collections for study, rather than on a sounder principle such as geographical origin or style or merit. Though of widely varying quality, depending upon the aptitude of the investigator assigned to a particular author and the quality of the base collection examined, these checklists with their "points" and "issues" invariably spur the dealer, collector, and librarian to acquisition. With much greater sweep, but less precision, the St. Martin's Press series on *Contemporary Novelists, Dramatists*, and *Poets* provides short lists of major titles only and publishers, along with biographical information, for some 600 living English-language novelists, including at least 45 novel writers of the 1960s not yet covered by Bruccoli or Lepper.[21] And there is hardly an American writer so obscure that some mention of him cannot be found in the *Contemporary Authors* sequence published by Gale, now numbering 80 volumes, cumulatively indexed.[22]

The black authors of the United States have been fairly well served by bibliographers. The handiest, amazingly useful work in this regard, simple checklist though it may be, is the supplement to Whiteman's pioneer work compiled by Deodene and French, which identifies every prose work by almost every black author born or living in the United States published between 1952 and mid-1969.[23] Translations, juveniles, and anthologies are excluded. From this reference tool one may derive the irritating and challenging information that one American black writer wrote only a single novel, in 1958, and it was published only in England. Richard Gibson's *Mirror for Magistrates* (London: Anthony Blond) is an instructive example of a recent, intriguing, historically significant, and hopelessly unobtainable book. The assumption behind a list like Deodene and French's, or any catalogue or collection that attempts to survey a period comprehensively, is that a fictional work by an American black writer is important per se to someone and that preservation of the book and the securing of a wider readership for it are of more immediate moment than imposition of critical judgment on the part of the compiler. Mass-market paperbacks, wherein much original literature by many black writers has appeared since the early 1950s, are desperately difficult to identify and, correspondingly, badly in need of additional lifeguarding *after* they are found (Plate 35). The Serendipity catalogue lists 38 black writers (about 9 percent of the whole), including one claimed by Canadian literature, Austin C. Clarke (a Barbadian educated in Canada, now teaching in the United States).

Interest in Canadian writers is not widespread in the United States, though a handful are fairly popular and enjoy an informed audience, notably Leonard Cohen and five women: Margaret Atwood, Marian Engel, Mavis Gallant, Margaret Laurence, and Jane Rule, the last an outspoken feminist in nonfiction as well as in the novel. Of all the other Canadian novelists of the 1960s, only Daryl Hine, Hugh Hood, Robert Kroetsch, and Jack Ludwig have been distributed in the United States. The best survey of achievement in contemporary Canadian fiction is Frank Davey's *From Here to There, A Guide to English–Canadian Literature since 1960* (Ontario: Porcepic Press Erin, 1974), but very little descriptive bibliography of these Canadian books has been written. Informative and occasionally sparkling comment on the Canadian scene is usually included in the catalogues of the two Canadian antiquarian dealers who concentrate on the contemporary literature of their country, William Hoffer in Vancouver and Nelson Ball (William Nelson Books) in Toronto.

Until recently the small-press movement in America was devoted to poetry, but its capacity and inclination to publish prose have vastly increased, due in large measure to National Endowment support not only of writers but also of presses, a printing plant, and distributors.

PLATE 35 Two paperback originals, *Weed* and *Black*, by the black author Clarence L. Cooper, Jr. (Regency, 1961 and 1963).

Checklists of small presses, together with files of reviews like *Fine Print* and *The San Francisco Review of Books*, which are devoted exclusively to the small press, are becoming more and more important as sources of information about fiction writers. The first 100 publications of the Black Sparrow Press were noted in 1971 in a separate book, and descriptive lists of the productions of the Cummington, Stone Wall, and Perishable presses (to name but three of the finest that have persevered through the last decade or two) have been carefully constructed. The Dust Books *International Directory* keeps annual tabs on most little magazines and small presses, but it requires many of the facilities of a university reference library and lots of spare time to chart a desired course through this kaleidoscopic world. The fourteenth edition (1978–1979) of the Dust *Directory* records more than 290 little magazines and as many small publishers receptive to new *prose*. Important writers have been published by some very obscure houses. The curious are invited to track down information on, or books from, Apocalypse, Assembling, Aurora,

Baker, Bay, Carp, El Corno Emplumado, Frommer-Pasmantier, Identity, Illuminations, Jihad, Kiepenheuer & Witsch, Links, or Thing Press, each of whom published at least one work of fiction by a 1960s writer. It is difficult enough to garner bibliographical facts about books from a publisher as established as Alan Swallow.

Similarly, it is nearly impossible for the small bookdealer to order for five customers five copies of the first printing of a paperback original from Ace, Bantam, Belmont, Fawcett, Lancer, Award, Berkley, or Avon, should he or she be so studious as to learn of the existence of the book within seven weeks of publication. After that time it is likely to have gone away forever. Some mass-market publishers themselves, as well as certain small-press publishers, have disappeared entirely, within the 1960s period, together with, it would appear, all copies of the hundreds of books they published. Try to find a Regency or Lion or Brandon House or Essex House paperback original!

The original price of the earliest mass-market paperbacks, like Pocket Books, was so low that now no used-book store can afford to process and shelve them at the customary 50 to 60 percent of original price, and hardly any of those same stores are inclined to treat the early paperback original as a valuable, out-of-print item. Bibliographical guides to this endlessly difficult world of popular culture, the paperback original, the pseudonymous publications, are just now beginning to appear, particularly from the detective and science fiction sector. One study, with checklists of the publications of Olympia-New York, Essex House, and similar publishers, has already examined modern erotic literature, while a companion magazine article reexamines the speculative erotica of Essex House alone.[24] Most of the books mentioned in these two particular studies are paperback fiction originals.

So the bibliographers, with whatever skills, pursue information *about* the books, even as the dealer and collector chase the physical object itself. Let me turn now to a survey of the sorts of books all parties will find.

The Texts

Institutional libraries almost necessarily and individuals almost invariably (alas!) collect by author. In doing so for the period 1960–1979 they will be confronted with possibilities for getting an individual text in a variety of formats. An orderly and hierarchical approach to the questions of format, with illustrative examples, may facilitate an understanding of contemporary bookmaking, advertising, and antiquarian pricing.

PREPUBLICATION

Manuscripts and Corrected Typescripts

Rough and working drafts of accomplished recent fiction are seldom made available on the open market for several reasons. On the one hand, many authors entertain the logic in an age of inflation and mercenary attitudes that if someone thinks their manuscripts have some value, then they ought to have considerable value, whereas collectors, on the other hand, are customarily unwilling to acquire (*invest* in, they might think) a manuscript for which there is no precedent in terms of public sale price. Occasionally what occurs is the placement in a university library by a given author (in response to solicitation or otherwise) of a whole archive, on terms known only to the parties involved, with a dealer functioning perhaps as appraiser or agent on commission; or an author's archive or estate may be deposited without being sold; or it may be willed to a particular institution. So we find that James Dickey's archive is at Washington University in St. Louis; Ed Dorn's at the University of Connecticut; Joseph Heller's at Brandeis University; Larry McMurtry's chiefly at the University of Houston; Sylvia Plath's chiefly at Indiana University; and John Updike's at Harvard University.[25]

But in canvassing 600 libraries and their holdings of 2,750 authors, J. A. Robbins located astonishingly few collections of manuscripts by the writers included in our 1960s catalogue, other than those mentioned. The University of North Carolina has some manuscripts of Kristin Hunter; two holdings are recorded for Ken Kesey; three letters from Jerzy Kosinski are spread among three institutions; four small holdings of N. Scott Momaday are located. There are eight holdings for Walker Percy, three for Reynolds Price, five for Susan Sontag, eighteen for John Updike, and that is all. However incomplete these records (they seem incredibly spotty), the implication is inescapable that a vast quantity of contemporary manuscripts remains available, depending upon the attitudes of the authors themselves toward "being collected" and their sense of their own dollar value.

The average individual collector never gets the chance to buy manuscripts, except at the very occasional benefit auction, unless he or she is willing to approach an author directly. Both parties in such circumstances are unlikely to be able to appraise manuscripts to mutual satisfaction. It is possible that 90 percent of the collectors of modern authors do not want to collect manuscripts, except perhaps a token specimen, for aesthetic and financial reasons combined. The number of dealers likely to handle contemporary manuscripts is very small indeed, but at least they are well or easily known. This is a world of commission and propriety, usually, rather than speculation, where the responsibility of the dealer and the library is to serve the author's needs and best interest. Or so one would hope. But largely, it is a world as yet unexplored.

Setting Typescripts

These days the publisher usually receives a relatively clean typescript from the author, often signed, but rarely evidencing much composition or correction. Occasionally, setting typescripts pop up in the market, or they are lost by the publisher, to the author's distress (or delight, when he receives negotiated recompense). The very existence of setting typescripts implies earlier and more complex drafts of the text, and the former should not sell for much, though one meets them in dealers' catalogues misrepresented as "the author's manuscript." Xerographic copy and carbon paper invite confusion and mystery. One is reminded of the nearly final draft of a recent novel by Jerzy Kosinski, which now circulates in an edition of four copies, properly numbered and signed by the author, one of them offered at $100. It appears to be a photocopy but is legitimately signed. It is of interest because Kosinski is known as a late reviser, and the final, published text differs from this so-called proof. Is it really a proof? How did four sets get back from the author, to be placed so quickly on the market? Who set the price? How are these "authenticated" proofs different from the publisher's uncorrected proof, which circulates in cream wrappers, or the galley sheets in folio form that were sent about to reviewers with a cover letter?

A more disgusting creature is the totally clean typescript prepared by a collector or speculator transcribing a poem or story, which has along the way acquired the author's signature, *so that it appears that it is the author's typescript.* However proud an author may be to autograph a transcription of his work, the item itself appears to us barely worth the price of the signature. Almost every author makes a public appearance and becomes available to the autograph seeker. One ought to view such productions, and dealers who misrepresent them, with outright hostility.

Letters

Holograph and typed letters from one or another (but not from every one) of our authors make frequent appearances in the market either singly or in lots. Many collectors are content with a single example; others generate their own correspondence in the most obvious way (by writing the author directly). This is done particularly by collectors who become bibliographers or checklist compilers. No author should be surprised to find that someone collects him or her, though many authors are surprised. An unfortunate few are astonished at how quickly their letters to a dear friend or fellow writer are converted to cash. Some, of course, are hurt by such a commercialization of friendship. When a son offers his famous writer-father's letters (written the day before), what should the dealer do? The range in quality of contemporary letters is wide, as at other times in history. A great letter may have been written yesterday. The finest letters will be between equals—fellow writers, lovers, family. Occasionally we find available the letter that begins "Dear collector, I am returning to you under separate cover my first book, which you have sent for my signature, and for a explanation of its genesis, to be inscribed on the flyleaf. This was rather a presumptuous request it seems to me, and I demur, but here is the photograph you wanted. . . . Sincerely, your favorite author."

Letters and manuscripts turn up in publishers' archives all the time; these packages are sometimes attractive to the research library, particularly when some degree of intactness can be guaranteed, and a secure option on future materials at fair prices is included in the bargain. Rumors of three different archives of the same small press being sold to three different institutions are unsettling. Sometimes what looks to be an important archive has in fact been stripped of significant literary materials over the years, though a mass of less important financial and other business records may remain. It is very difficult for an archivist always to know what might have been present before his or her school commits itself to a purchase. It is difficult to remain calm when one espies carbon copies and photocopies of archival materials floating in different directions.

Rare is the contemporary archive that finds a willing private buyer. But many publisher's and author's archives must be available. The prime, collectible single holograph letter (or item) will always find a buyer. It is much too early, however, for us to know what *cannot* be obtained of 1960s authors. To date, no one has been able to buy publicly, and no collector of our acquaintance has, a signed Pynchon book or a letter from Pynchon or a photograph of Pynchon. There is without question a growing mystique about Pynchon, which will serve to justify an incredible price for the first good item that will, inevitably, appear, despite at least one published article that does identify him as a live and palpable human being and attempts to dispel the nonsense. Collectors should be reminded that Pynchon letters are already at the Ford Foundation Library in New York City, that proofs are at the University of Texas, and that a manuscript is held by the Ford Foundation Library. One of the loveliest stories ever to come south to California insists that the reference books used by Pynchon when he composed *V.*—each volume annotated—are safely stowed in bank vaults in Seattle, but not by the author.

AFTER PUBLICATION—PRINTED TEXTS

Galleys—Corrected and Uncorrected

Corrected galley proofs are maintained either by publisher or author; they seldom appear for sale, but should prove very attractive to the private collector loyal to his or her author. Modern first-edition collecting concentrates on uncorrected galley proofs, for this is the earliest form of the printed book that the collector can reasonably expect to acquire. Proofs like these are used by publishers to promote reviews or to alert book clubs and film agents of a forthcoming work of merit (Plate 36). The proof may assume any of a number of specific forms, noted here in order of desirability and rarity.

1. *Folio sheets, folded or unfolded, uncut, printed on the rectos only.* Jerzy Kosinski's *Blind Date* (Houghton, 1977) appeared thus, with a cover letter; this proof is of interest because of later revisions to the text. Almost every trade novel takes this form in its printing history, but folio sheets are so unwieldy and heavy that they are seldom mailed out to reviewers.

2. *Sheets cut to page size, banded (usually with butcher paper).* Harper & Row preserved William Gass's *In the Heart of the Heart of the Country* (1968) in this manner, as well as N. Scott Momaday's *House Made of Dawn* (1968). Again, not many books are distributed in this format: the sheets are printed on one side only, and if one removes the band, one finds 250 sheets in the lap, askew.

3. *Sheets, folio or quarto size, secured by a ring or rings (as opposed to spiral bound, again printed on one side only, with printed cover(s).* This too is an awkward format, but at least the sheets are kept in numerical order. These crude objects, unbound galleys, bespeak hastiness of assembly and urgent desire on the part of the publisher to get a book before the public eye as soon as possible. Frederick Exley's first novel, *A Fan's Notes* (Harper, 1968) was first gotten up like this, with a rich blue printed upper cover, the sheets tied with a white ribbon; the whole was only a bit taller than the published book, but twice as thick. We know of two copies; perhaps as many as two dozen were made.

Dutton took out the scissors, cut the galleys of Robert Coover's *A Theological Position* (1972) into dozens of scraps, photocopied the rearranged scraps onto legal-sized sheets, added a plain blue cover with a typed label stuck on and a handwritten title, and whisked it out to a reviewer. Not many could thus have been assembled. Five?

4. *Perfect bound, narrow quarto, infrequently octavo.* Probably the most irritating format for a book ever devised. The cost-conscious promotion department is in a rush again. There is no spine, only glue. As the covers are opened, they fall off; as the pages are turned, they loosen and fall out. The corners are soon dog-eared. Nevertheless, this is a popular and widely used vehicle to convey the publisher's intent. Books such as Richard Brautigan's *The Abortion* and *Revenge of the Lawn* (both 1971), Thomas McGuane's *The Sporting Club* (1968), and Geoffrey Wolff's *Bad Debts* (1969), all four from Simon & Schuster, all first entered the world in this guise.

5. *Spiral bound, printed card covers.* This is also a popular method of promotion, and one finds a number of very significant novels in this form, notably Robert Coover's *The Universal Baseball Association, Inc., J. Henry Waugh, Prop.* (Random House, 1968) (Plate 37), Leonard Gardner's *Fat City* (Farrar, 1969), Larry McMurtry's *The Last Picture Show* (Dial, 1966), Jay Neugeboren's *Listen Reuben Fontanez* (Houghton, 1968), Cynthia Ozick's *Trust* (New American Library, 1966), two Walker Percy novels, *The Last Gentleman* (Farrar, 1966) and *Love in the Ruins* (Farrar, 1971), Marge Piercy's *Small Changes* (Doubleday, 1971), and Tom Robbins's *Another Roadside Attraction* (Doubleday, 1971). Experience suggests that as many as 25 copies of a proof are gotten up in this way, though it would be a happier situation for both customer and dealer if more exact figures were available.

6. *Sheets glued or sewn into printed, full wrap-around covers, octavo or narrow quarto, with or without printed label.* This is by far the commonest means by which uncorrected proofs are circulated for review, particularly in the 1970s. A multitude of titles appeared this way, in a limited range of solid colors: red, green, gray, yellow, salmon, mustard, orange (the British tend to mute these colors). In the smaller size have appeared William Butler's *The Ring in Meiji* (Putnam, 1965), Gass's *Fiction and the Figures of Life* (from Harper in 1970, though Knopf and *not* Harper in fact published the first edition in 1970!), Percy's *The Message in the Bottle* (Farrar, 1975) and *Lancelot* (Farrar, 1977), and Robert Stone's *Dog Soldiers* (Houghton, 1974). In the large, narrow format we find copies of Thomas Berger's *Who Killed Teddy Villanova?* (Delacorte, 1977), Carlene Polite's *Sister X and the*

PLATE 36   Uncorrected proofs, specially designed, of a first book, Stephen Schneck's *The Nightclerk* (Grove Press, 1965).

PLATE 37   Uncorrected proofs of a major novel, Robert Coover's *The Universal Baseball Association, Inc.* (Random House, 1968).

Victims of Foul Play (Farrar, 1975), and several of the more recent titles of John Gardner, Philip Roth, and John Updike. In the case of Roth, *The Great American Novel* (Holt, 1973) was first sent around in green covers, subsequently in red. E. L. Doctorow's best seller *Ragtime* (Random House, 1971) circulated in red covers, but in two different cover settings, with the Random "house" logo present on one but not the other.

Galleys may differ significantly from the published text, as we have mentioned; it is likely that the collector will make the discovery, unless it is obvious, for most dealers rarely take the time to collate proofs with first printings. In fact, the private buyer will often chance upon the proof in the shop of a dealer before the book is even published or available for collation. Furthermore, the dealer learns that many institutions have no interest whatsoever in proofs, save for those schools that collect particular authors in depth. One cannot but muse over what revelations about contemporary book-making and advertising practices a massive collection of galleys might yield to the imaginative scholar. We know of no such collection abuilding. Proofs in this last form are probably manufactured in quantities of 75. The major reviewers number perhaps a dozen, two dozen at the outside if one includes newspapers like *The Rolling Stone* and journals like *Time*. The prepublication reviewing services like *Library Journal, Publishers Weekly*, and the Kirkus Service raise this figure only a fraction. There remain the several book clubs, specialized agents, sales representatives, and individuals like college professors. Galley proofs are expensive to assemble; the sheets must be hand pulled. If an editor wants four sets instead of the usual two, his or her department may well be billed for them. Such is corporate cost accounting. The uncorrected galley proof has a propensity for taking on the appearance of a great rarity only a few years after the publication of the first edition. It is a far different story for our next category.

The Advance Reading (or Promotional) Copy

In 1978 an advance issue in white coated wrappers of *The World According to Garp* by John Irving was distributed by Dutton to promote what was the most heralded and coincidentally the most praised novel of the season. This issue now changes hands rapidly in the trade at $75. Such salability attests either to fear on the part of the buyer that if one does not obtain the advance issue when it is first offered, one will never see it again, or ignorance on the part of the seller of the actual number of copies printed, for $75 is about the price for a limited edition (350 copies) of a recent novel like Joseph Heller's *Something Happened* (1974). Yet 1,500 copies of the advance issue of *Garp* were made, a generous number, to say the least. To put it in practical rather than moral terms, $75 seems too much, so we may expect that this book will not rise above that price plateau swiftly, as the facts become better known. Moreover, uncorrected galley proofs in either mustard or blue-green wrappers (narrow quarto format) preceded the white promotional copy. The customer can expect that if the advance issue is $75, the galleys will approach $400.

Incidentally, it is within the period of time under discussion that the specially designed advance reading copy comes into its own. There were scattered examples in the 1950s and before (even as far back as the 1920s), but in the 1960s it seems to have been the practice of *most* trade publishers to introduce the first books of their most promising authors with an attractively designed or hard-hitting advance copy. Many of the most desired and best written met their reviewers and a portion of the public in these forms: *A Fine Madness* by Elliott Baker (Putnam, 1964); *Red Sky at Morning* by Richard Bradford (Lippincott, 1968); *Hard Rain Falling* by Don Carpenter (Harcourt, 1966); *The Carpenter Years* by Arthur A. Cohen (New American Library, 1967); *The Origin of the Brunists* by Robert Coover (Putnam, 1966); *Gascoyne* by Stanley Crawford (Putnam, 1966); *Boswell* by Stanley Elkin (Random House, 1964); *A Fan's Notes* by Frederick Exley (Harper, 1968—in printed red wrappers, quite distinct from, and subsequent to, the blue-wrappered galleys mentioned above); *Totempole* by Sanford Friedman (Dutton, 1965); *Catching Saradove* by Bertha Harris (Harcourt, 1969); *Catch-22* by Joseph Heller (Simon & Schuster, 1961); *The Martyred* by Richard Kim (Braziller, 1964); *The Orchard Keeper* by Cormac McCarthy (Random House, 1965); *A Smuggler's Bible* by Joseph McElroy (Harcourt, 1960); *To an Early Grave* by Wallace Markfield (Simon & Schuster, 1964); *The Ballad of Dingus Magee* by David Markson (his first *hardbound* novel, Bobbs, 1965); *True Grit* by Charles Portis (Simon & Schuster, 1968); *A Long and Happy Life* by Reynolds Price (Atheneum, 1962); *V.* by Thomas Pynchon (Lippincott, 1963); *Looking for Baby Paradise* by John Speicher (Harcourt, 1967); *Orpheus on Top* by Edward Stewart (Putnam, 1966); *Up* by Ronald Sukenick (Dial, 1968); *Hurray for Me* by S. J. Wilson (Crown, 1964). Though used at this time primarily for promoting first books, this format has been used for other books by the same or similar authors to advertise potential best sellers in the chase for the consequent benefits of paperback sale and movie rights on which many publishers depend. Included in this group are books such as *Killing Time* by Thomas Berger (Dial, 1967); *We Can't Breathe* by Ronald Fair (Harper, 1972); *Lightning Bug* by Donald Harington (Delacorte, 1970); *The Charisma Campaigns* by Jack Matthews (nonfiction from Harcourt, 1972); *Them* by Joyce Carol Oates (Vanguard, 1969); and *Sissie* by John A. Williams (Farrar, 1963).

Uniquely conceived formats that introduce (either by design or historical accident) a new writer are always appealing to the collector. Donald Barthelme's first book, *Come Back, Dr. Caligari* (Little, Brown, 1964), was preceded by two stories from that collection separately printed and laid into a labeled box that circulated to a few. The bibliographers report that 100 sets were made, but the item is far scarcer than that large number would seem to warrant. N. Scott Momaday's first separately printed fiction was a design project at the Santa Barbara campus of the University of California and was illustrated with an

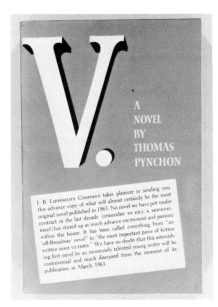

PLATE 38   Advance reading copy of Thomas Pynchon's *V.* (Lippincott, 1963).*

PLATE 39   *Philip*, a juvenile by the mystery writer Donald Westlake (Crowell, 1967).

original print. An entire font of type was especially designed and cast, but then that typeface was abandoned. This book, *The Journey of Tai-Me*, may well be the only original fiction issued during the 1960s that is issued in full leather; 100 copies were made in 1967 and divided among illustrator, author, and printer, none for sale.

    In fine condition, these advance and special issues are much sought. The best are not necessarily the scarcest, though the best promise never to be inexpensive. The advance *V.* by Pynchon is decidedly common, even in impeccable condition; at least 100 must have been made (Plate 38). It will not now sell readily at $750, though one sees it offered for as much as $900, but neither will it last long in a dealer's catalogue below $500, because another dealer will order it. In contrast, the advance *Catch-22* by Heller is very scarce in any condition, and fine copies are rare, though the printing run must have been comparable to that of *V.* Prevailing prices would indicate that these two books are three times dearer than any other mass-produced, advance review copy of a 1960s novel, and the great majority are available for considerably less than $100 each.

Occasionally the "special advance edition" carries bibliographical information from which one can learn and even generalize about publishing practice. Dutton used a ring-bound uncorrected proof to promote *Other Men's Daughters* by Richard Stern. This was immediately followed by the "advance edition" in green wrappers, picturing the jacketed first printing soon to be available, together with information directed to the new-bookseller: "DUTTON'S FICTION LEADER FOR FALL, 1973/ OCTOBER, $6.95/20,000 FIRST PRINTING/$15,000-INITIAL AD BUDGET/LITERARY GUILD ALTERNATE/CO-OP ADVERTISING AVAILABLE/1-FREE-WITH-TEN OFFER" —all printed on the upper cover; on the lower cover is a 145-word blurb by Philip Roth.

Simple Review Copies

The common practice with ordinary review copies is for the publisher to lay a slip in the published book announcing the date of publication and price, with a request for two copies of any review and possibly also an admonition that no review be published before the specific date of publication. Or this information may be rubber-stamped on the flyleaf (an old New Directions custom). Sometimes a mimeographed or photocopied letter or press release is also inserted. A promotional photograph of the author may be loosely inserted as well, as was done in the case of review copies of Reynolds Price's *A Palpable God*. To the collector, slip, sheet, and photograph are properly welcome, one hopes at not too great a premium (for new books). Slips and photographs have a way of moving about, and their original purpose can be obscured. Publisher's photographs are themselves sometimes collected in their own right. A marvelous example of an abused photograph (relevant here only by correlation) is that of William Faulkner, arms folded, mustachioed, young; it bears the rubber-stamp facsimile of his signature and was placed by the publisher into some review copies of *Sanctuary*. The photograph is not even an original print, but it has been offered as such by the unknowing or the unscrupulous, with a huge price for the "signature."

Infrequently, but often enough to require notice, the publisher will lay gathered and sewn (or unsewn), unbound (or tied) signatures of his latest offering into the dust jacket, and mail the bundle to the reviewer (*Bijou* by David Madden from Crown in 1974) or will simply glue the gathered signatures into plain, unmarked covers (*Tattoo the Wicked Cross* by Floyd Salas from Grove in 1967) or into the dust jacket itself (*Soldier in the Rain* by William Goldman from Atheneum, 1960). These practices have a long, if spotty tradition. *The Sound and the Fury* was sent to reviewers in unbound signatures in 1929.

The charm for collectors of all of these advance states lies perhaps in their transitoriness. They wish to preserve what was designed to be discarded.

The First Edition

All the critics and bibliographers cited above and appended in the Further Reading at the end of the chapter guide the buyer to this sacred object. Its acquisition and preservation are the common goal, for whatever reason. Two thousand novels by North American writers published between 1960 and 1975—excluding other genres—give the least imaginative collector plenty of room to stumble onto an interesting book or two to accompany runs of John Gardner, Joyce Carol Oates, and John Updike and an incipient file of the Joyce Carol Oates *Newsletter*. Fashion will always have its place, its genuine function, its servants. So do author newsletters, though one expects their proliferation will result any day now in dealer advertisements on the final leaves quoting market prices today, yesterday, and tomorrow for each title, underscored with the straightforward broker's legend, "we make a market in this author's first editions." There are 2,000 serious novels available to the reader every 15 years or so, depending upon range of taste and breadth or quality of interest. It is a pity 80 percent of modern collectors collect 10 percent of the available authors, even if those 10 percent are the "best" 10 percent. For institutional libraries the situation is modestly better. The natural respiratory cycle will suck in at least 50 percent of all the fiction that deserves to be preserved. But the remaining 50 percent is not to be acquired by automatic reflex reactions to advertisements and reviews.

The first edition can be a serious challenge. It may exist in 20,000 copies or in fewer than 1,000 (or 500 or 100). Serendipity Books is currently nursing 2,000 copies each of Gilbert Sorrentino's *Steelwork* (1970) and *Imaginative Qualities of Actual Things*, each remaindered by Pantheon, but has never even seen Doris Grumbach's first two novels, *The Spoil of the Flowers* (Doubleday, 1962) and *The Short Throat, The Tender Mouth* (Doubleday, 1964) and in 16 years has owned (twice) only a single copy of John Knowles's first book, *A Separate Peace* (London: Macmillan, 1959).

As should be abundantly clear by now, first editions are often paperbacks. In two and one-half years Essex House in Los Angeles published 41 paperback originals by collectible authors like Charles Bukowski, Kirby Doyle, Philip Jose Farmer, and David Meltzer, and by some very obscure authors like Richard Geis. The editions ranged from 15,000 to 30,000 copies. The Meltzer and Bukowski titles were saved by poetry dealers and collectors and friends of the authors; the remaining 32 titles have almost vanished. Many trade paperback originals from regular houses present comparable problems. In 1969 New American Library published at 60 cents a bit of fluff by W. H. Manville called *Am I Too Heavy, Dear?* It has taken ten years to find the first copy, which was sought because Manville wrote two conventional 1960s novels, *Breaking Up* (Simon & Schuster, 1962) and *The Palace of Money* (Delacorte, 1966). Now we find that he has a co-author for *Am I Too Heavy, Dear?*—James Wright. Could it be the poet?

Published screenplays and novelizations of films should be sought by author collectors. But they are usually consigned (or confined) to the rack jobbers and the paperback stores, where they possess an apparent half-life of seven weeks. *Pretty Baby* was novelized by William Harrison (Bantam, 1978), as was *Pat Garrett and Billy the Kid* by Rudolph Wurlitzer (New American Library, 1973), who had previously done an original screenplay, *Two-Lane Blacktop*, for Award Books in 1971. Rosalyn Drexler turned the successful film *Rocky* into a paperback original using the pseudonym "Julia Sorel." Her nonfiction paperback from Bantam, *Alex: Portrait of a Teenage Prostitute* (1977), is already very, very out of print. *Tides of Lust* by Samuel Delany was the last book published by Lancer in New York City before that firm discontinued in 1973. The book was not well distributed; its life was short-circuited. This first erotic novel by an acclaimed master of science fiction is unobtainable, except at great expense. These, and innumerable other paperback originals, were once available to the industrious and sharp-eyed, across the land, in drugstore and supermarket and airport, at 25 cents or 50 cents (not so long ago) or, more recently, $1.95. Once a dollar or so in the racks, soon ten to fifty times that at the antiquarian's.

We have concentrated on the cloth and paper novel by our authors, but many of them were active in other genres as well. Opportunity for author collectors is virtually limitless. An unexpected juvenile pops up now and again—Barthelme's *Slightly Irregular Fire Engine* (Farrar, 1971), which won a National Book Award in its field; *Tucky the Hunter* by James Dickey (Crown, 1978); *Gudgekin* (Knopf, 1975), *Dragon, Dragon* (Knopf, 1976), and *King of Hummingbirds* (Knopf, 1977) by John Gardner; *Jason's Quest* by Margaret Laurence (McClelland & Stewart or Knopf, 1970); *The Bed Book* by Sylvia Plath (posthumously from Harper & Row, 1976); and at least four titles by John Updike. Donald Westlake, the mystery writer, who also uses the pseudonyms "Richard Stark," "Curt Clark," "Timothy Culver," and "Tucker Coe" depending upon what sort of story he is creating, also wrote a juvenile, *Philip* (Crowell, 1967), for which he modestly abbreviated his name to D. E. Westlake (Plate 39). Such appearance of juvenile books is uncommon. In most cases, it seems, these juveniles reflect the publisher's willingness to capitalize on the popularity of a newly successful writer, but that fact does not impugn their quality; some, no doubt, had been buzzing in the heads of their creators for years.

These books are best bought when they are new, for when out of print they are invariably among the author's scarcest titles. They either go straight to the public libraries or, if they are good, are read to death by Easter. The collector should note that publishers bind juveniles in two different ways, generally: paper boards with dust jacket for the bookstore traffic; coated cloth, sidestapled, without dust jacket, for the library market. Because a book in the latter binding is never sold over the counter, though it can be ordered from the publisher, it is always troublesome for the recorder of binding variants to track down. A related genre is the fictional work for young adults. Chester Aaron followed his fine first novel *About Us* (McGraw-Hill, 1967) with four books for teenagers; *Giveadamn Brown* by Robert Dean Pharr (Doubleday, 1978) is directed to the same audience.

The Limited or Signed First Edition

As in the 1920s, publishers are hyperactively engaged in making books designed to appeal to the collector who values exclusivity. Although they always have the right (if not the ability) to say no, collectors nevertheless may have some grounds for the complaint that these days they are being manipulated by publishers and dealers. It may be wise to sort out different forms of "limited editions" and perhaps to probe a few motives. Commonly, especially with the major publishers, a limited edition will be very different from the trade issue. It is printed on better paper, is better bound, and is often designed with better taste. Examples are numerous, but I cite all of the limited editions of John Updike from Knopf as typical of this pleasing species. The publication price of $20 to $25 for such a book, limited to between 350 and 500 copies each, seems compatible with the quality of bookmaking and the reputation of the author. And apparently the burgeoning buying public agrees. Whereas an edition of this sort used to stay in print six months to a year, it is now frequently oversubscribed. Random House received more than 2,000 orders for the special edition of *The Coup* by John Updike, limited to 350 copies (publication day was December 7, 1978, but the limiteds were not delivered to booksellers until at least six weeks after the trade issue). The latest signed and otherwise special editions of writers such as Heller and Malamud have been accorded a similar reception. Even if the magnitude of this response is wholly attributable to sizable orders from dealers (most dealers did not get even 50 percent of their prepublication order for *The Coup* because so many dealers subscribed), still, *their* interest is only a measure of real or anticipated desire in their customers.

A variant of the specially printed and bound edition is the signed issue of a trade book created by the publisher at the request of a particular bookstore. Sometimes a new book bears an extra, inserted leaf, signed by the author. The annual convention of the American Booksellers' Association has occasionally been the venue for distribution of such books—that is, for distribution among booksellers and visitors. A good example of a book with an extra leaf is Updike's collection of pieces *Assorted Prose* (Knopf, 1965). Some few copies of the first printing have a blank leaf signed by Updike inserted *between* the blank flyleaf that follows the free front endpaper *and* the leaf bearing the Knopf logo. This issue was made for a Chicago bookstore, Kroch and Brentano's Inc., that at the time was promoting Updike to its "First Edition Circle" club, in part because he had won the National Book Award with his previous book. Other books with such signed issues are Bernard Malamud's *The Tenants* (Farrar, 1971), Norman Mailer's *Of a Fire on the Moon* (Little, Brown, 1970), and the American first printing of John Fowles's *The Ebony Tower* (Little, Brown, 1974). Some books that were similarly promoted—in these cases, by Pickwick in Hollywood—but that were signed on a regular, integral leaf, are *A Book of Common Prayer* by Joan Didion (Simon & Schuster, 1977), *The Devil Tree* by Jerzy Kosinski (Harcourt, 1973), and *The Breast* by Philip Roth (Random House, 1972). Buyers should be aware that signed copies of these books are plentiful.

The trade publishers infrequently have a sublimitation in their signed editions, a run usually of 26 copies lettered "A" to "Z." Such issues are often different with respect to paper and binding. The traditional and, I am certain, the original intention of such sublimitation was to designate gift or presentation copies for friends of the author and publisher; they were free to such friends and one would hope, treasured by them. Sometimes a lettered issue is not mentioned in the colophon; the fact that the limited, signed edition of *Finnegan's Wake* (Faber, 1939) exists in lettered copies is a most recent revelation.

The small, private publisher nowadays finds it advantageous to create lettered issues within an already small press run because it is highly profitable. The customary justification for this practice is that the publisher needs the money (always true); or the publisher will give a portion of the lettered run to the author in partial payment for royalties. But the practice is abused. Too frequently, the extra limited issue has been produced as cheaply as possible, and its price is hardly justified by the "enhanced" quality of the production. The lettered issue may become an instrument of extortion. The dealer is not permitted to buy a lettered copy unless he agrees to purchase a certain number of regular copies. Whereas the collector who must have every issue of every one of "his" or "her" author's books, and many collectors could be named who suffer from this peculiar psychology, is a sitting duck, and the publishers have been firing three to a blind.

Some publishers are so dedicated to simulated rarity that they seem to publish only limited editions. They solicit easily obtained short pieces, like a story or poem from a periodical, only from popular and already highly collected authors. In a recent first-edition catalogue we observe two new, small "fine" presses announcing books and broadsides by, among others, Bradbury, Fowles, Updike, Everson, Percy, Gass, and Oates, all of whom have already enjoyed this treatment. The regular editions are limited to 150–350 copies; the prices are not limited: $25 to $50. One of the books has four pages of printed text. There are at least three very strong and differing attitudes toward such books. Some dealers, librarians, and particularly collectors feel confronted with out-and-out exploitation, for which the publisher is chiefly to blame. Or they are wont to regard these items as if they were newly printed stock certificates, with a degree of enthusiasm proportional to the soundness of investment they perceive in their books. In such cases one could wish for a regulatory commission.

Yet many buyers of all temperaments never question the price of a book or the motive of its publisher. They simply enjoy their acquisitions, they want their authors complete, they collect open-mindedly. They may imagine the author is flattered to sign his or her name 100 times for faceless buyers (and how many thousand times for buyers of Franklin Mint publications?). They may even understand the usefulness of books like these to the *dealer*, for whom the books bear a certain, substantial profit, if he or she has standing orders or loyal customers. It is very possible that moralists hostile to artificial rarities severely underestimate the market potential for such first editions, but, then, they do not base their objections on practical grounds. When one discovers unnumbered overruns of limited editions and "issues" of "seven for review" or "seven for the publisher" and all these instantly in the antiquarian market but not in the colophon, one must be permitted to suspect chicanery.

The next step for the unprincipled publisher is to take advantage not only of the buyer, but also of the author, by manufacturing piracies of the much-collected authors. A few years ago J. D. Salinger's uncollected stories were pirated in two volumes and sold door-to-door for enormous profits.[26] A few days ago the uncollected stories of Larry McMurtry (first printed in *Avesta*, the literary magazine of North Texas State College) were pirated in an edition of 35 (with overrun sheets of title and colophon). The rationalization of the pirate was that no harm was intended, that the stories "deserved" being made available, that no profits were sought. The pirate overlooked the consideration that he was using McMurtry to obtain for himself about $10,000 worth of goodwill, not to mention the possibility that the author might object.

Another species of limited edition, the broadside, began to flourish again in the 1960s (chiefly as a vehicle for poetry), encouraged by a small-press movement centered in California, where the tradition of fine printing has not faltered in 70 years. The innumerable psychedelic posters printed in San Francisco in the mid-1960s reinforced and broadened awareness of visual material, and many poetry broadsides were lovingly produced and given away or sold at a nominal price. Large stocks of these broadsides await customers in the several stores on both coasts that have cared to conserve them. Altruism never kept a small press in paper, however, and such broadsides, both poetry and prose, are appearing at ever-increasing prices. They are frequently the means by which a new, optimistic publisher introduces itself to the world.

One often delightful alternative to the artificial rarity is the first separate edition of a favorite author's work that slips out into the world quietly, unknown to collectors. For instance, a story by an American writer is printed in Japan or Russia for students of English, with notes in Japanese or Russian. My favorite book of this type is *Eli the Fanatic*, a story extracted from Philip Roth's *Goodbye, Columbus* (first published by Houghton Mifflin in 1959) and printed in Israel in both English and Hebrew, with key words color coded. The series in which *Eli* appears is The Colour System for Teaching Languages, edited by Mordehai Hochberg. *Eli* comes in two states (differently colored covers) and first appeared in 1973. In 1939 a William Faulkner story was separately published in Canada by a Sherwin-Williams paint-seller to support national morale at the onset of war. It was bound in purple suede and went unnoticed by American collectors for 40 years!

Screenplays

Printed first editions, limited signed editions, and first separate editions are all old forms of collectible books. A new form for collectors that also represents a relatively new literary genre is the unpublished screenplay. I think it would be instructive, before discussing its collectibility, to outline the stages of evolution of a typical screenplay. Our point of view will be that of a collector of a particular author.

Typically, before World War II, an author on contract to a studio produced a treatment or prose story that his agent or supervisor transmitted to editors of the film company, who then handed it over to other, more malleable writers who in turn transformed the treatment into a workable screenplay. Sometimes the original writer would see the project through to the end. Treatments are rare; they are usually in the form of original and carbon typescripts, of which perhaps four copies were made. Nevertheless, studios gradually clear their files of unwanted material; an extended treatment, bearing manuscript corrections and extensive rewriting by one or more hands, will occasionally turn up in the market. The covers may be stamped "File Copy" or "Vault Copy." Documents like this bear the sense of complex, creative acts. When any one of the collaborators on a screenplay is a significant writer, research and commercial values are enhanced. For the bookdealer, the screenplay is a little explored and chaotic world of obscure sources, muddied rights, photocopying, and surprise. For instance, thousands of pages of original William Faulkner typescripts (uncatalogued and unread) were recently placed on the market by one studio. However, much material deemed of no interest after a film is completed must frequently be destroyed.

Improvements in the technology of duplication have resulted in the preservation of more screenplays by younger writers. Original typescript is much less common in the 1960s than it used to be. Nowadays the author's draft is quickly mimeographed or dittoed by a stenographer's service or by the studio's own printing department. But stages of development are revealed by the scripts themselves. After the treatment comes a first draft screenplay, a second draft, a third revised draft, and a final draft. Technicians correlate the dialogue with timing and footage sequences and produce a dialogue continuity (a much less desirable form than an early draft screenplay). After the film is made, a release script is prepared to enshrine in print what actually is heard in the theater. Four or five copies of the screenplay may have been submitted to the studio. The editors may create a dozen additional copies for internal study and decision making. There may be as many as 50 working drafts, for the cast and others. Up to 150 copies of a release script will eventually be printed; it may subsequently be published either by the studio (Warner Bros. has a publishing arm) or by a trade house. The largest institutional holdings of published and unpublished screenplays are at the University of California, Los Angeles, and a transcription of their Theater Arts Collection card catalogue has been printed by G. K. Hall.[27]

Sale of rights to the film industry is a major goal of the publishers of trade novels. Because a screenplay adaptation of a new novel may expedite, if it is not a necessary prerequisite to, such a sale, one ought not be surprised to find that a large number of young authors have written unproduced (or produced) screenplays. One does not easily learn of this activity, however, if the film is never made, unless a copy of the screenplay turns up. Larry McMurtry has written several screenplays (Plate 40), in addition to whatever assistance he may have rendered in the conversion of his own first three novels into films. Don Carpenter wrote a screenplay based on Charles Bukowski's novel *Post Office*. Evan S. Connell converted his own novel *The Diary of a Rapist* into the unsuccessful screenplay *Mr. Wasp* for Warner Bros. Agents for John Gardner circulated his screenplay conversion of his own novel *Grendel* among prospective producers, but they were rebuffed, despite plans to unite the talents of Gardner, Marjoe Gortner, Tom Smothers, and Orson Welles. Reynolds Price collaborated with Richard Neubert to adapt for the screen his first novel, *A Long and Happy Life*, with no luck to date. Stephen Schneck fashioned an original screenplay that he named *Something Soft and Evil Stirring Here*. John Seelye wrote a screen story, based on his novel *The Kid*, called *A Territory of the Mind*. Hubert Selby adapted *his* first book, *Last Exit to Brooklyn*, but two versions have failed to find a producer. The above are all examples of novelists who have unsuccessfully attempted to convert their own or comparable fiction into movies. Sometimes it is the professional or amateur *screenwriter* who approaches the novel (rather than the novelist, the screen), often with equal lack of success. Robert Schlitt drafted *Been Down So Long It Looks Like Up to Me* by Richard Farina for the movies; Morton Fine and David Friedkin took on *Blessed McGill* by Edwin Shrake, all to no avail.

Some original, produced screenplays by authors of the 1960s are *Viva Max* by Elliott Baker (Cine Rome, 1969); *The Panic in Needle Park* by Joan Didion and John Gregory Dunne (her husband), adapted from James Mills's novel; *Butch Cassidy and the Sundance Kid* (Bantam, 1969) and *The Great Waldo Pepper* (Dell, 1975), both by William Goldman; *The Missouri Breaks* (Ballantine, 1976) and *Rancho Deluxe* (FP Films, 1975), both by Thomas McGuane; *Pat Garrett and Billy the Kid* (MGM, 1970) and *Two-Lane Blacktop* (Award Books, 1971), both by Rudolph Wurlitzer. Joseph Heller wrote the entire script for a fine film, *Sex and the Single*

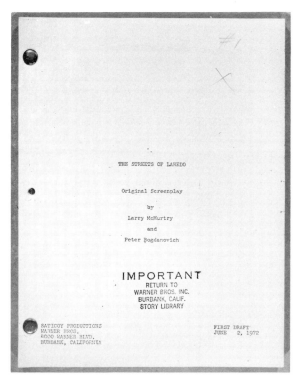

PLATE 40   "The Streets of Laredo," an unpublished screenplay by Larry McMurtry and Peter Bogdanovich.

Girl. James Dickey found appealing themes in Jack London and created
a television version of *The Call of the Wild.*

Or one finds the authors happily adapting their own novels into
realized films, as did Didion, again with her husband, with *Play It as It
Lays;* William Goldman with *Magic;* Dickey with *Deliverance;* and McGuane
with *92 in the Shade,* which he also directed. Hollywood professionals
may also be effective here: Laurence Haben and Bo Haube wrote the
screenplay of *One Flew Over the Cuckoo's Nest,* based on Kesey's novel;
only last year Marjorie Kellogg converted Sylvia Plath's *The Bell Jar;*
Kenneth Kantor wrote a screenplay of Joel Lieber's *Move!* for Twentieth
Century-Fox; Paul Sylbert tackled *The Steagle* by Irwin Faust, which was
made into a movie with Richard Benjamin.

Because screenplays are so infrequently published—they do not
sell well—the awkward, 8½-by-11-inch screenplay is often the only
physical record of a particular author's effort in this field. Each of the

examples given above is known by such a script. Obviously, every film has a screenplay or two behind it, but collecting them is a difficult matter. Scripts used to be offered in Hollywood by local dealers on the basis of the popularity of the film or the collectibility of its stars, rather than because of who wrote it, though after a Billy Wilder corrected script was catalogued in northern California by Alta California Bookshop in the mid-1960s, perspectives began to shift. The source for scripts remains principally the studios themselves and their agents or employees, most of whom are confined to the Los Angeles area. Although dealing in scripts is a recent phenomenon, it is hardly free from sharp practice. Photocopying of scripts from the pre-Xerox era occurs innocently enough within the studios, less innocently without. One major research library refuses to touch a photocopied script. A new problem here is that xerography has replaced other methods of reproduction, and the xerographic screenplay may be the only obtainable form of the text (other than the author's original typescript, which may not have survived). Misrepresentation is another problem. Both Aldous Huxley and Jane Murfin worked on the filmscript of *Pride and Prejudice*. Some dated versions bear only Murfin's name, but are offered as if they were of considerable Huxley interest and priced as such. In truth, Huxley worked on the script independent of Murfin, to the extent that the scripts that contain his contribution bear both his name and Murfin's, and his revisions are clearly attributed. None of Huxley's writing is reflected in the scripts that carried only Murfin's name. Similarly, we have in hand a very heavily corrected script for the film *Another Thin Man* (1938). Scholarship reveals that Dashiell Hammett was paid $40,000 for rights to his conception of characters involved. One would like to conclude that he must have written a treatment. He may have, but there is no evidence of it. He wrote other screenplays, but not necessarily this one. It should not be priced as if he did.

Other Texts, Other Formats

A physical object similar to the unpublished screenplay is the unpublished playscript, which always precedes official publication, if any. Found usually in stenciled form, with stenographer's or agent's covers, are such playscripts as "A Mother's Kisses . . ." by Bruce Jay Friedman and "We Bombed in New Haven" by Joseph Heller. Unlike the film industry, however, the legitimate theater has developed a reliable mechanism by which to preserve the texts of plays. In addition to normally published first editions of plays such as those brought out by Random House or New Directions, printed "acting editions" exist for almost every produced play. These are available at nominal prices from one of the few houses committed to theater alone, such as Samuel French, Inc., or Dramatists Play Service. The English acting edition may differ slightly from the American for the same play. It is sometimes difficult to determine which is the *first printing* of an acting edition. A later printing is to be inferred if the cover does not have a printed price; rises in price occur through various printings. A careful perusal of the current catalogues of these play-publishing firms is guaranteed to produce wonderment galore.

The enlightened—and/or wealthy, masochistic, or mad—collector collects in depth. Modern bibliographies systematically identify "A" items (primary works), "B" items (secondary works to which the author has made an original contribution), and "C" items (contributions to periodicals). Each of these categories has adherents in the modern collecting world. Usually an individual can take on only one or two authors in such absolute terms, and an institution collects thoroughly in this manner only when it possesses a certain author's archive. Dealers and collectors are frequently up to the minute when it comes to new objects or ways to collect. Formosan (Taiwanese) piracies, for instance, have drifted into the United States for several years now, via servicemen, tourists, immigrants, and possibly by direct commercial importation. Shoddily made, reduced in format from the original, the Formosan piracy could still conceivably be mistaken for the first edition by an inexperienced bookhand, particularly because the piracy may come into existence within ten days of the publication of the original in the United States. Shades of the mid-nineteenth-century, precopyright agreement, transatlantic pirates! Novels of the 1960s have been favorite game, including *A Fine Madness* by Elliott Baker, *Killing Time* by Thomas Berger, *The Hawkline Monster* by Richard Brautigan, *Play It as It Lays* by Joan Didion, and *Nickel Mountain* and *October Night* by John Gardner. Although we know of no collection of these piracies formed for their own sake, one fine scholarly study of the laws and pertinent diplomacy appeared in 1969.[28]

Large-type editions for the visually impaired are published by G. K. Hall. *Catch-22* and *Grendel*, along with such diverse fare as *I'm Glad You Didn't Take It Personally* by Jim Bouton and *Bear Island* by Alistair MacLean, have been printed in this format. Similarly, certain paperback printings of novels that originally appeared in cloth may prove attractive to collectors and students. Philip Roth's novel on Nixon's shenanigans, *Our Gang*, first published by Random House in 1971, was reprinted in paper by Bantam in 1973 in the "Watergate" edition, with a new preface by

Roth, and again reprinted in paper by Bantam in July 1974, in a "special Pre-Impeachment edition" with yet another "new introduction" by Roth. Boxed sets of paperback editions of novels by Oates, Gardner, and Updike will be hard to find in their first printings soon enough. John Irving's *The World According to Garp* has six differently colored covers in the first printing of the paperback issue.

Records and tapes of prose writers reading their own work are comparatively new on the market, though Joyce recorded "Anna Livia Plurabelle" in 1926, and Columbia Records issued a literary series in 1953, a multirecord set of poets and prose writers. A Contemporary Fiction series started in St. Louis in 1974, with Stanley Elkin on tape cassette. John Hawkes, James Baldwin, and John Barth are a few who appear on phonograph records. A complete kit involving Ernest Gaines was manufactured by Paul S. Amidon and Associates in Minneapolis, comprising a "Teacher's Guide" and six cassette recordings of Gaines reading from *Bloodline* and *A Long Day in November*, all enclosed in a black fabricoid springbound notebook, available in 1971 at $39.50.

Dust jacket art was at its nadir in America during the 1960s, at the same time when concern for the condition of dust jackets reached its zenith among collectors. Although one university in Texas has a large collection of jackets and undoubtedly there are a few quiet souls solemnly and secretly gathering up examples of a particular artist or style (the "vorticists," for example, or art deco or Edward Gorey), the 1960s have precious little to offer. The plain, typographical jacket, with possibly a modest abstract design, is the norm. For all its commitment to advertising, New York has not tapped much talent lately for dust jacket art—with the constant exception of Gorey, who is the beneficiary of the most extraordinary marketing efforts, efforts commensurate, I hasten to add, with his talents. Some isolated examples come to mind, but there were many books in between: Jackson Pollack's original design for the entire jacket of *Out of This Century* by Peggy Guggenheim (Dial, 1946); Grace Hartigan's cover for *But Not for Love* by May Natalie Tabak, with endpapers by Saul Steinberg (Horizon, 1960) (Plate 41). The late 1970s seem to have introduced a more adventuresome spirit—for example, the elaborately stylized pictorial jacket on *Falling Angel* (Harcourt, 1978) by William Hjortsberg. A study of this or a number of other aspects of the art of trade bookmaking in the 1960s and 1970s would have to be based upon some unusually perceptive book collecting. It would likewise require the talents of an extraordinary bookperson to find out what happened to the illustrated novel popular at the turn of the century or to find many examples of its rebirth since the death of the serializing weeklies like *Collier's* and the *Saturday Evening Post*.

PLATE 41 Dust jacket by Grace Hartigan for *But Not for Love*, by May Natalie Tabak (Horizon, 1960).

Total loyalty to an author or an idea drives the dedicated collector to incredible minutiae. The ultimate collector tracks down every Thomas Pynchon dust jacket or paperback cover blurb. Eight have been noted by one collector, so far.

Condition, Price, Fetishism

Every dealer in modern first editions is aware of the high standard for condition that is demanded in the marketplace. Every specialist in the Victorian novel can but shake his or her head sadly at the apparent madness of the modern collector. Many librarians cast aside the dust jacket of the newly arrived 1960s novel that is destined for the stacks. No matter what oddity or rarity the modern dealer scouts in the wastelands, he or she must answer for (or defend) its condition to his or her best (pickiest) customer. In days when not two of ten new books come unbumped from the publisher for lack of wrapping and gross lack of concern, the collector wants his first edition of *Catch-22* mint, in an unfaded, unnicked dust jacket. Because the buyer is willing to pay, no one complains. But it cannot always be the norm. The collector will not get all the books he or she *should* have, from the dealer's point of view. In this regard, the most miraculous event in recent years was the surfacing of the library of Norman Ungar, a collector who for 30 years or so bought multiple copies of all the books he liked, and wrapped them up carefully on the day of purchase. Here was perfection, and my how the news (soon followed by the books) moved about the country. Who, after all, had ever seen snow-white sheets in Norman Mailer's first book, *The Naked and the Dead* (utterly without the usual tanning)? A miracle of book madness; probably a unique library; and surely an important one, because the books have gone back into the marketplace for others to enjoy, one at a time.

Collectors who are otherwise quite articulate begin to mumble and paw the ground when asked either why they collect or just why they will not settle for "slightly worn dust jackets" on otherwise perfect first editions. So it is fortunate that we are in receipt of some self-examination, in the form of a letter, quite unexpected, from a friend who modestly collects modern and other books. He writes:

> When I look, nervously or with pleasure, at the books on my shelves, I know of course which of them could be better. Though I may have blocked this or that defect out of memory awhile, I am soon (sometimes painfully) aware of every one. My eye moves along from spine to spine, from desired object to desired object, and there is no way to prevent a twinge as it automatically locks in on each of the—shall we say?—most improvable ones.

Almost every book, of course, *could* be better. Condition is just a species of "quality" (which includes not only association value but also historical and/or literary value, comprehensiveness of the collection as a whole, etc.). Even a mint copy—i.e., one in "perfect" condition—is far from perfect, it is just the beginning. After all, it could have been—and, if one gets lucky, and the animal exists, one can upgrade it to—a mint signed copy, a mint copy with contemporary inscription, the mint dedication copy, the dedication copy with copious corrections in the author's hand, and so forth.

So, although I am aware of *each* defect, each lapse from perfection (a part of me no doubt believing that every issue of every book has its "Idea," its perfect archetype, in Paradise), what actually bothers me as I look at my books, and even gives me pain, are, *given the context* (i.e., age and kind of book, and standard I've set for that age and kind), only the most egregious defects. Thus I turn away, irresistibly look back, then turn away, feeling increasingly both nervous and impotent, having once again noticed the ever-so-slight chip in the dust jacket of *Myra Breckinridge*. I am not avid for an inscription here, have never thought of upgrading it *that* way, but it would make me feel better—indeed, for a moment, it would make everything all right—to acquire a perfect dust jacket.

On the other hand, when I happily examine my very fine *Bertram Cope's Year* (1919) by Henry Blake Fuller, inscribed at about the time of publication to Julia Cooley Altrocchi, I don't feel pain or even a twinge; I'm just (calmly) wistful, because I know someone who has a good-only copy, uninscribed, but accompanied by a dust jacket (worn and in three pieces) which is not for sale. When I look through my Paul Goodman collection, however, I want *all* (of the "A" items at least) to be both mint and importantly inscribed; I'd gladly upgrade every one to that quality, even by paying real bucks just for a perfect jacket. Finally, as I gently remove from its custom-made box my first of *Sexual Inversion* (1897), fragrant with both extreme rarity and vivid association (not to mention historical and literary value), the less-than-mint condition, so far from bothering me in any way, actually confirms its status in my eyes.

More on quality. I want my books to be the best of their kind, the best in the world—best condition, best associations, best literary and/or historical values, most comprehensive as a collection or series of collections. Insistence on condition is a species of insistence on, and striving toward, ἀρετή—the old Greek ideal very roughly translated "excellence."

A word on order. I like to see all of my books by one author together on one shelf, or successive shelves, every spine neatly flush with the edge, and arranged more or less chronologically. It's annoying that some books are too tall or too fragile for that and must be preserved in more or less disorderly ways—the former on "mixed" oversize shelves; the latter, in acid-free envelopes either lying flat on a shelf of their own, piled one on top of another, or standing upright in a file drawer. Broadsides are the most annoying of all; they are safe only in immense, clumsy boxes which are too much for *any* shelf, and it's usually too great a production to locate and take a look at just one particular title. Anyway, when I do look at my broadsides or, more often, at the books or spines of books on my shelves, I want to see uninterrupted perfection, which is a kind of order in itself. And I do mean "order," not mere "uniformity"—for since "perfection" in books (as I have understood and even sensed it) is scarcely possible and, no two examples of it, any more than of near perfection, are or look alike; each has been achieved, and can be described, only in the terms of its unique context.

Completeness. Naturally I desire my collections to be "complete." This is sometimes possible in the case of author collections, impossible in the case of collecting a subject—unless the collector cannot bear a long drawn-out losing battle, and has defined his or her subject in an achievably narrow way. That's just the opposite of how I have done it; I guess I've made almost a life out of long drawn-out losing battles.

A last word on completeness. It's not just collections: I also desire each *book* to be complete—i.e., in its original form; nothing missing, blemished, halt or lame. In short, whole. I've always been attracted to whole, individual beautiful books (or bodies). I desire them. Yet as I grow older I find (having begun perhaps to ascend that ladder the mysteries of which Socrates outlined to the drunken company), that I also desire beautiful books (or bodies) *as* a whole. Strange tastes? And, at least in the case of book collecting, even stranger practices? Perhaps. Yet the cause appears to be simple (and mysterious), though I have forborne to mention it until the end. It is just as Aristophanes remarked to that very same company long ago: the desire and pursuit of the whole is called Love.

Every collector might consider developing a rationale for himself or herself, which would cover an era or a generation of books. Here are two practical questions he or she might entertain. What sort of book is customarily fine? Where lie the *challenges?* So many good novels are remaindered that it is useful to consider what happens to them. If a lot of copies of one title stay together for a time, they tend to remain in good condition, unless, of course, their jackets are black. Black jackets betray the slightest rubbing more quickly than jackets of other colors, in particular when placed spine to spine and transported here and there. So Ken Kesey's *Sometimes a Great Notion* (Viking, 1964) is difficult to find looking unrubbed, as will be Paul Theroux's first novel *Waldo* (Houghton, 1967). Other jackets tend to fade, especially if printed in pale colors. Perfect copies of *V.* by Pynchon are notoriously scarce because the yellow on the spine fades; moreover, *V.*'s jacket is easily chipped at the crown. *Green: A Novella and Eight Stories* by Norma Stahl Rosen (Harcourt, 1967) comes in a green dust jacket. Appropriate packaging, but the spine is almost always badly faded. Many novels are now oversize; one thinks especially of the two books by Richard Marius or of *A Smuggler's Bible* (Harcourt, 1960) and *Lookout Cartridge* (Knopf, 1974) by Joseph McElroy or *The Sotweed Factor* by John Barth (Doubleday, 1960). Their weight strains their inadequate hinges. Paper boards are an insubstantial binding for large formats. Recognizing a format that is susceptible to wear will help the buyer to accept (at least temporarily) condition short of ideal, or allow him or her to decide promptly that a really sharp copy is worth extra.

One cannot conclude a discussion of condition without a footnote on techniques of preserving dust jackets and the dealer's common practice of switching jackets. The lending libraries and public libraries that keep dust jackets at all in general protect the jackets on their books by gluing or taping plastic covers to the books' covers. When such books reappear in used-book stores, often through Tartan Book Sales, the books are physically ruined, but the jackets are frequently perfect. Many dealers place a fine dust jacket on a fine copy of a book that came to them without a jacket, often without the courtesy of the appropriate notation "dust jacket supplied." All collectors should be advised that one brand of jacket protector, made by Bro-Dart but now discontinued, is characterized by a thin blue line of chemically unstable ink that will eventually offset and eat into the jacket proper. Damage of this sort has already been the basis for insurance claims and legal complaints. These protectors should be removed from books at once, if the owner has concern for either appearance or value.

Value itself is a troublesome subject, and we would rather avoid it. Price guides and auction records tell the reader what certain copies of specific books once brought or what their owners once *asked* for them. For modern books, they have a limited function. They provide a context for understanding what's going on. Dealers' catalogues are more useful. To our reading list are appended runs of catalogues from dealers who have represented 1960s and 1970s books consistently. The prospective buyer or researcher might well inspect these catalogues just for the mass of information presented, but he or she should never trust absolutely an otherwise unverified claim or description. Probably it is foolish for a bookdealer ever to question the motives of any bookbuyer. So if the collector chooses to "invest" in a particular book, he or she should be allowed to do so. Most dealers believe that the real investor in books is the dealer; he or she is the only one who can, *as a rule*, buy at a wholesale price and sell retail. The evidence that many collectors edge their way over into this position is scratched on scraps of paper in their wallets, where they have recorded newly obtained resale numbers or the numbers of friends who are in business. One must recognize "investment" as a *real* motive for bookbuyers; it certainly affects the market prices. But it is surely the basest motive of all.

How much the uncorrected proofs of Pynchon's *Gravity's Rainbow* should cost, or are likely to cost, is another matter entirely. The first dealer who owns it may well have obtained it from his friend the reviewer for $15, before publication day. He may buy lots of all sorts of review copies from his friend, and sometimes he may pay a little too much. He has had many review copies around, for three years now, and still has never heard of the author's amounting to much. So he prices the Pynchon proof at $400, and it sells to the first collector in the door, a week before the catalogue in which it is listed splashes down about the country. Six dealers order the proof by phone, and four do not want any other book in the catalogue. Had one dealer gotten the book, he would have paid $360 (with the courtesy discount) and reoffered it perhaps at $600. And it would have sold again, in all likelihood, to another dealer, who was first to phone and had some extra money. A normal pattern. No one erred. The dealer must make hundreds of snap decisions like these as a way of life, if he chooses to compete for the modern books that many modern book collectors *want*. The collector must make a like decision, when he is confronted with a book he desires. For most collectors, the money has far less meaning than does the book, or owning the book. The collector has the responsibility of learning which dealers *he* can trust with regard to consistency of pricing and integrity. When the dollar is really worth only 60 cents in Japan or Germany, the difference between $3,000 and $3,600 for a perfect copy of *Ulysses* sold in Los Angeles is less significant than one might have thought. After a while, the individual must develop a sense of what is preposterous, what is appropriate, what is sensible, and what is fair. Aided by this knowledge, he will soon be able even to sense what is a bargain. The availability of credit, often substantial, at first sight, even without substantiated references, is so common a phenomenon in the antiquarian book business that the relationship of dealer to customer is on an elevated plane almost from the beginning, and almost without parallel in other businesses. In consequence the trust between bookdealer and customer, once violated, is not easily repaired.

Four Collectors

I can think of no more vivid way to illustrate the opportunities for, and the principles of, book collecting that are described above than to sketch brief portraits of a few of the people who have made these opportunities *their* experience. They have different financial positions, live in different geographical areas, and put books to different uses. But their collective example and accomplishment have affected the lives of others, in addition to improving their own, more than they will probably care to measure.

A NAPA, CALIFORNIA, SCHOOLTEACHING COUPLE, in their early fifties. Once residents of Texas, with strong ties still, they had collected the traditional Texas folklorists, history of the American West, books about oil, and John Updike. Most of these interests persist. But chancing upon *In a Narrow Grave* by Larry McMurtry (in particular, the essay "Southwestern Literature?") they were guided toward other writers, the more than 30 cited by McMurtry, others slightly obscure like Georgia McKinley, and still younger authors of the 1970s with Texas origins. The later novels of McMurtry himself became central to their involved patterns of reading. They sifted *The Texas Observer* for political news and considered the degree of hostility toward McMurtry in the *Observer*'s reviews an index to the decline in perceptiveness back home.

These were not comforting practices, but they added dimension to Napa indoor life. It is a concerned reader who demands to know the thematic relationship of *Somebody's Darling* to McMurtry's preceding three novels, keeps track of Elroy Bode (he writes prose poems about Texas and was printed by Carl Herzog), tolerates Ronnie Dugger (editor and general manager of the *Observer*), and laments the imprisonment for drug trafficking of Texas's most promising Chicano politician, Ramsey Muniz. Within a narrowly delineated world they read and collect deeply. All of the southwestern prose writers are welcomed to the extent that they illuminate life originating in that region. Style or format are not cause for restriction or exclusion, though price may be. So William Brammer's *The Gay Place* will be sought inscribed, in dust jacket, and in its advance review format as well, but a clipping file of his periodical appearances are as important. A fair understanding of Brammer's brief career and unfortunate death is a necessary accompaniment to owning a copy of his novel.

Our friends were introduced to fine printing by Herzog. They are sensitive to the book as a physical object and are pleased to buy the special editions of their authors. A limited, signed Updike is nice, and never resented, but neither is it absolutely necessary, though the acquisition of the regular trade edition and the limited, signed Encino Press edition of McMurtry's essays is inevitable. Yet they can easily say no to the allegedly discarded "true" first printing of *In a Narrow*

Grave at $300, and two years later say no again when it surfaces once again at $500. For collectors so nice as these, and so wise, regionality is not a limitation but a window. Collecting is the self-indulgence of preserving for themselves in a modest way the literature that connects them to a larger world. Much involved with the content of their collections, they continue to educate themselves. Regularly, they check out a few stores selling new books, receive a few catalogues, and, once a month or so, visit an antiquarian. They still write letters by hand. Buying what they can afford, they return to the seller in appreciation and insight more than they take away.

A WALNUT CREEK, CALIFORNIA, LAWYER, age 36. He prosecuted murderers and robbers as a county district attorney; now he has a private law practice. Each side of this profession exacts its emotional toll. He finds book collecting an obligatory alternative to the daily stress, with these complications added: he pursues his avocation with the same compulsive diligence demanded by his profession and tops it off with amateur bibliography, one published compilation of checklists to his credit, and another scheduled to follow. He reads in history and modern fiction, and collects postwar prose writers, more than 30, all of them American except for J. P. Donleavy and John Fowles. His commitment to two standards for collecting overwhelms other considerations. Condition is paramount—no fading, no tears in dust jackets, no names on flyleaves. And he is driven by the aesthetic of completion. He wants every "A" item, every separately published book, pamphlet, broadside, and offprint for each of his authors. And he stops there. Association copies are of no interest; he will solicit an author's inscription, but not casually or for profit. He reads every book he collects, or tries to, but he will put one down if it is unsatisfying. The pursuit of books is very important to him, though his free time is severely circumscribed. Naturally efficient at correspondence, he accumulates bibliographical knowledge (willingly shared with others) as well as books by mail and supplements his needs for both by Saturday visits to his favorite first-edition shops, where he can scout and record, and simultaneously relish for their own sake the people he likes who also associate with books. Though our lawyer is unwilling to probe too deeply for an answer to the question of why he collects, one cannot help concluding that the answer lies not in the authors, but in the manner and style of collecting itself, the relentless push toward orderly perfection in condition and completeness in the bookroom, while these values erode more and more in the society outside that room. The books he collects are predictable, though he makes discoveries of literary value through his bibliographical work and often anticipates popularity by several years. He collects the best fiction of his own time. He is a genial man who likes all of his authors if not each and every one of their books. Although there is no modern book he cannot afford, the cost and current value of his books is never wholly irrelevant. When he feels exploited he will discard wholesale (but not at a loss) without a regret. When suddenly it cost $400 within six months simply to maintain already perfect Joyce Carol Oates and John Gardner collections, because new titles were offered in highly limited editions at high prices, out they all went. He would gladly invest all the time at his disposal in his authors and his bibliography, but he would as soon as not remain a bit ahead of the market, always.

A Los Angeles editor, often self-employed, age 38. Here is a *private* collector, oblique to every fashion and trend, who preserves in original form absolutely all the literature he can find, guided by intellect, curiosity, and a superb retentive memory, yet sustained only by a very modest purse, even in the best of times. He has a special talent for mining the seams of culture, where the novelist meets the movies, where conventional and science or detective fiction merge, where popular culture achieves integrity and art. The filmscript, the finest avant-garde fiction, the paperback original, European erotic fiction— all are specialties mastered without opportunity for traveling widely, without access to the stocks of out-of-town antiquarian dealers. He rarely buys from catalogues and never collects for investment, though what he does not wish to keep he sells. What he has found is proof of what *can* be found, what exists in the metropolis, threatened by neglect, oversight, abusive handling: screenplays (sometimes the original typescript) by major, minor, and unmeasured talents (Leigh Brackett, Albert Hackett, James M. Cain, William Goldman, John Steinbeck, Dashiell Hammett, Ray Bradbury, William Faulkner, Steve Fisher, Lucille Fletcher, Brian Garfield, Robert Bloch—the list would fill the page), and playscripts and television scripts as well; the "right" Star Trek scripts, some unproduced; paperback originals by Jim Thompson, Harlan Ellison, Ursula LeGuin, "Ross MacDonald"; paperbacks from Regency, New American Library, Lion, Olympia, Ophelia, Ophir. He will know ("knowing beforehand" is a rare aptitude) and have gathered some of the paperback soft-porn novels written by Robert Silverberg under the pseudonym "Don Elliott"; he knows most of the other pseudonyms used by contemporary authors as well. He himself edited and saw through publication more than 200 books in the fields of erotic and speculative fiction. He has bridged the vast expanse of ignorance that once lay between science fiction "fandom" and the research scholar and preserves in one eclectic library what he likes from hardback Double-day science and detective fiction, the beats, Updike, Mailer, Heller, the hard-boiled writers. Clear-mindedly, he will sniff at the artificial rarity but freely admit to coveting the Franklin Mint signed edition of *Catch-22*, no matter how many thousands of copies are pushed out into the market, because for him it is a cherished text. Because through the 1960s he fought as an editor both of newspapers and of experimental fiction to strike down all barriers to freedom of expression in literature, he still champions and promotes the books of that time, and beyond. The books that he has read and that he collects are his chief joy.

A MICHIGAN BUILDER, a man of means, age 51. At age 15 he began reading (and clipping) *Publishers Weekly* every week and never stopped. He has collected books since 1950, and over the years spent approximately $150,000. He is blessed with indefatigable energy and is happily mobile, for the home-construction business takes him everywhere in the United States and allows him to travel abroad with considerable freedom (Russia, England, Israel). Until recently his library was divisible into five distinct but related sections, part of one of which is relevant here. The divisions are American fiction before 1800, Russian literature in English (excluding expatriates like Nabokov), William Faulkner, Israeli literature since 1948, and American literature (chiefly prose and drama) since 1927, the year of his birth. In this last category he collects by author, intensively, and seeks every primary work in fine condition, including scripts, together with a published interview for every author, and all interviews for favorite authors: paperback first printings for every major and many minor titles; every bibliographical variant of "A" items, including proofs and galleys, revised editions, and all variant or trial dust jackets. For particular authors he will gather printed juvenilia, book appearances, periodical appearances, letters, a token manuscript, edited material, and original photographs. He preserves the work of every modern major dramatist (and many less well known ones), almost every modern serious novelist who was conventionally published, poets he has met or admired, and authors with Detroit origins. For the most part he chooses the authors themselves (rather than reacting to a dealer's suggestion), and has acquired 40 percent of his collection at publication price or less—by developing his own early warning system, clipping *PW*, reading critical reviews, patronizing new and all local bookstores, and buying carefully from the 40 or so antiquarian booksellers who have been aware of, and sympathetic to, his needs. He has bought from quotations in response to his want lists, from catalogues, and in person. No one has heard him bemoan a missed book or envy a fellow collector. Utter perfection in a dust jacket cannot tempt him beyond reasonableness, though he has never been ungenerous to his suppliers. The artificial rarity has been acquired uncomplainingly, always, but never under the illusion of accomplishment or with false pride in singularity. He allows himself one eccentricity. The books are separated in his library according to whether their authors are alive or dead. He moves the books of a deceased author on the day of death. He is partial to the living, to the future. Of the more than 350 author collections he has put together according to these principles, more than two-thirds are of writers who began in the 1960s and 1970s. It is the finest assembly of its kind in one private room in the country, I believe, *even if it is but a fraction of what is possible.* One of his controlling assumptions is that a national literature is continuous, and he feels responsible for the portion that was created in his lifetime; another is that the author is more important than any single book. "Not *Moby Dick*, but Melville. . . !" he will insist. Not one Gogol, one Tolstoy, one Dostoevsky on the shelf. Better three Tolstoys! He knows what being a collector means. One has to have time, money, and desire. One must spend all of these. This has been a strange achievement, to have gathered and preserved by oneself what others would have thought was the exclusive province of a (very) large university library.

What these very different collectors have in common, aside from interest in a few contemporary authors (all collect Updike, McMurtry, William Goyen) and one dealer, is a sense of commitment to what they are doing, what they have been doing for a good, long time. They take pride in that commitment and share an obligation to the present and to their own writers. Book collecting is *not* for them *a hobby*. One collector I know has put it rather negatively by allowing that "it's a disease, a serious disease. I don't know its cause. On the other hand, I guess I'm sufficiently confident in my psychological health in general, to support one serious mental illness without worrying about its aetiology."

None of our four examples is suffering from a lack of books to collect, or lack of a direction, which each has determined for himself or herself. Nor are they suffering from the frustration of competing with others at a disadvantage. It does not appear that any has the goal, or the slightest hope, of outdoing another (though that shallow motive obtains elsewhere in the collecting world). In fact, none of our friends is suffering at all. Their books have made them rather happy.

The Bookdealer

After the willing buyer has taken the trouble to look into *Books in Print* and a file of catalogues for the drama services and some small presses, after visiting Barnes & Noble and the Strand in New York, and B. Dalton's everywhere, after exhausting the search services, he or she may yet turn with broad needs and still strong desires to that sometimes maligned creature, the modern-first-edition dealer. The principal interests of this dealer are twentieth-century literature, of which he maintains a considerable stock: poetry, fiction, little magazines. He often, but not always, maintains a shop and has help in the form of an employee or two. He almost always has a car, a scout somewhere *out there*, at least one close friend in the book trade (usually at least 1,000 miles away). He has no extra money (there are now exceptions to this once hard and fast rule); he makes an average of one trip a day to the post office and one to the bank (because he is never paid by his customers within 30 days). With this primitive apparatus, in this situation, he tries to serve the needs of all the United States, a very thin slice of Canada, five people in England, three in Australia, and two in Japan. He is expected to have perfect copies of John Gardner's *Resurrection* and John Fowles's *The Collector* (first English edition, please!) at prices 10 percent below those of his competitor in Santa Barbara (from whom, in fact, he has just bought these very two books, on 90-day billing). He ought to be mobile and sweep both coasts semiannually; he represents his clients at New York auctions, usually to his dismay, and must ferry himself, staff, and 20 cartons of books to book fairs in New York City (twice a year, even), Boston, San Francisco, and Los Angeles. He must consider exhibiting at or scouting book fairs in Seattle, Washington, D.C., UCLA, London, and now, occasionally, even Charleston, Rochester, and Chicago. In between, he must publish one or more (usually many more) catalogues a year, educate his children, walk the dog.

There are not many modern-first-edition dealers. Not nearly enough. Santa Barbara has at least four; Knoxville, more than twice the size, has none. Almost all the modern-first-edition dealers established their businesses in the 1960s, or since, and have grown with inflation. They harvest books, whenever they can, from sources not usually open to the private buyer: the reviewer's review copies; the salesperson's advance copies; the small private collection; the stock of back rooms everywhere; the library duplicates. In addition, they are aware of new and forthcoming books; they have special knowledge, specialized bibliography. They sift book information and gossip equally well, even if they impart the latter with greater alacrity. They do not all get along well with each other. Most of them will allow to being subject to only two motive forces: to survive and to serve their customers as best they can.

The collective knowledge and experience of the fraternity of modern-first-edition dealers is very substantial. The old saw "there are no secrets in the book business" is nowhere more true than among these dealers. Whether it be the discovery of a hitherto unknown first book (for example, Adrienne Cecile Rich's *Ariadne, A Play . . . and Poems*, Baltimore, 1939) or the fact that *four* copies of Vladimir Nabokov's earliest surviving book, *Stikhi* (St. Petersburg, 1915) have been unearthed in two years—all book news will make the rounds with marvelous efficiency. The principal cause of inflation in modern books may well lie in the communications systems; what books sold from whose catalogue is common knowledge soon after the event. As dealers more often than ever before have access to their colleagues' books before most private customers even have a chance (there remain a few dealers who do not allow this to happen), it behooves both the private and institutional customer to develop understandings and working relationships with as many dealers as is comfortable. Soliciting a dealer's attention by means of an organized want list is the surest means by which one can test the dealer's skills and loyalty. Circulating the same list among numerous dealers is suicidal. Having interests beyond the commonplace always helps, whereas total commitment to an exciting cause will guarantee the collector the attentions of many dealers. We can illustrate this last principle with another reference to our friend the collector of Paul Goodman. He was inspired to collect Goodman after the death of Goodman's son, who had been his college classmate and friend, in a mountaineering accident. Goodman was neither expensive to collect nor widely collected. He wrote in a great number of genres, and was prolific. The collection was built in less than a decade, through the agency of many dealers, into the best of its kind in the world—every book, almost every book and periodical contribution, all in fine condition, with ephemera and correspondence. The collector's means were modest, his motives unmercenary. He wishes to give the collection to Cornell University as a memorial to both Paul Goodman and his son.

Enough. It is much too easy—indeed, it is inevitable—to digress when speaking about the world of modern books. A section devoted to the dealer has ended by referring to an author, a private collector, and a university library. Though unintended, this has surely not occurred by chance. It is, in fact, as it should be. Author, publisher, dealer, reader, private collector, and institutional librarian describe a full circle or, better yet, a complex pattern of intersecting circles. The individuals are interrelated, probably more today than at most other times in history. They depend on one another, for material advantage at least, if not always for fulfillment. Their interrelationships are mediated by their books, which also, I have no doubt, often mediate between them and the causes of their common human suffering. No, I can say more than that. As with our four exemplary collectors, their books have often made them—authors, publishers, dealers, readers, collectors, librarians, all of us—rather happy.

Notes

1. *A Survey of Trade Publishing, Poetry & Fiction, 1952–1977* (New York: Poets & Writers, 1978), pp. 1–3. Although the percentage of new fiction titles seems to be dropping (from 14 percent in 1950 to 8 percent in 1974), the absolute number of new titles seems to remain fairly constant. This problem is discussed by Maś ud Zavarzadeh, *The Mythopoeic Reality: The Postwar American Nonfiction Novel* (Urbana: Univ. of Illinois Press, 1976), pp. 33–34 n., where the reader is referred as well to Ronald Sukenick in the *New York Times Book Review*, September 15, 1974, p. 55; John Leonard in the *Village Voice*, June 27, 1974, p. 30; and Charles Newman in *TriQuarterly* no. 26 (1973): 7.

2. The library at the University of California, Santa Cruz, needed a fiction supplier after Richard Abel went bankrupt; the library at the University of Northern Iowa bought a base collection and new titles on approval.

3. Five examples should suffice: in Stephens's catalogue Donald Barthelme's *Come Back, Dr. Caligari* is $25; Wendell Berry's *Nathan Coulter* is $40; John Gardner's *The Resurrection* is $75 (uninscribed); Joseph Heller's *Catch-22* is $55; Ken Kesey's *One Flew Over the Cuckoo's Nest* is $35. The same books in the Serendipity catalogue are $110, $90, $750 (contemporary presentation from Gardner), $275, and $265, respectively. Each book was in fine condition in dust jacket and each book *sold*. Change in the prices of antiquarian books is not a much studied subject.

4. Mary Allen, *The Necessary Blankness, Women in Major American Fiction of the Sixties* (Urbana: Univ. of Illinois Press, 1976), pp. 208–216. Allen provides similar bibliographical references for studies of John Barth, Thomas Pynchon, James Purdy, Ken Kesey, Philip Roth, and Joyce Carol Oates.

5. Ihab Hassan, *Contemporary American Literature, 1945–1972* (New York: Ungar, 1973). Hassan nominates Bellow and Mailer as major; he calls Morris, Malamud, Salinger, Vonnegut, Purdy, Capote, Hawkes, Styron, Barth, and Updike "prominent." The "types and trends of fiction" he analyzes are

the short story, the war novel, the southern novel, the Jewish novel, the black novel, and science fiction.

6. Dissertations devoted solely to one author for this period, 1970–1979, are listed in the *MLA Bibliography*.

7. Zavarzadeh, *The Mythopoeic Reality*, pp. 38ff. Consistently, this critic makes precise distinctions among modern styles and techniques of fiction.

8. Some books cited as precursors of the nonfiction novel of the 1960s are Agee's *Let Us Now Praise Famous Men*, Clemens's *Life on the Mississippi*, Cummings's *The Enormous Room*, Defoe's *A Journal of the Plague Year*, Hemingway's *Green Hills of Africa*, Miller's *Tropic of Cancer*, and Orwell's *Homage to Catalonia*. See Zavarzadeh, *The Mythopoeic Reality*, pp. 251–252.

9. Zavarzadeh, *The Mythopoeic Reality*, p. 222.

10. Dissertations on the family novel, the academic novel, and the Vietnam War novel are specifically cited in the Further Reading section at the end of this chapter. There are numerous published works on black American fiction.

11. Those interested in the aesthetics of sport in fiction should consider Neil David Berman's dissertation on Leonard Gardner, Pete Gent, Don DeLillo, and Lawrence Shainberg or perhaps follow with Charles Reynolds an understanding of baseball in the continuum of American fiction that descends from Lardner and Broun through Malamud and Harris to Coover (also a dissertation). Among 1960s writers, Roger Angell and Marvin Cohen write about baseball, John McPhee about basketball and tennis, and James Houston about surfing and football. One of the very best books on sport in society is C. L. R. James's *Beyond a Boundary* (London: Hutchinson, 1963).

12. See *The Lesbian in Literature: A Bibliography*, 2nd ed. (Reno: The Ladder, 1975), compiled by Gene Damon et al., and Ian Young's *The Male Homosexual in Literature: A Bibliography* (Metuchen, N.J.: Scarecrow Press, 1965).

13. Particularly *A Place for Us* (New York: Bleecker Street Press, 1969), which was written under the pseudonym "Isabel Miller," and later reissued as *Patience and Sarah* (McGraw-Hill, 1972). Routsong wrote two novels under her real name before *A Place for Us* was published.

14. Skir wrote *Boychick* (New York: Winter House, 1971), which preceded by several paperback originals (erotic) under pseudonyms, including "Lon Albert," *Hours* (New York: Award Books, 1969).

15. Using the pseudonym "James Colton," Joseph Hansen wrote *Lost on Twilight Road* (Fresno, Calif.: National Library, 1964) and *Known Homosexual* (North Hollywood, Calif.: Brandon House, 1968). As "James Coulton" Hansen wrote *Gard* (New York: Award Books, 1969). As "Rose Brock" Hansen wrote at least two ordinary Gothic novels: *Tarn House* (1971) and *Longleaf* (New York: Harper, 1974). Under his real name, Hansen has written mysteries featuring a gay insurance investigator—*Fadeout* (1970), *Death Claims* (1973), and *Troublemaker* (1975), all from Harper & Row—and at least five other novels as well.

16. For the best checklist of the southern writers, see Richard Gray, *The Litera-*

ture of Memory, Modern Writers of the American South (Baltimore: The Johns Hopkins Univ. Press, 1977), pp. 347–363.

17. Raymond M. Olderman, *Beyond the Wasteland: A Study of the American Novel in the Nineteen-Sixties* (New Haven, Conn.: Yale Univ. Press, 1972), p. 8.

18. Jerome Klinkowitz, et al., *Donald Barthelme: A Comprehensive Bibliography and an Annotated Secondary Checklist* (Hamden, Conn.: Shoe String Press, 1977); Letitia Dace, *LeRoi Jones (Imamu Amiri Baraka): A Checklist of Works by and about Him* (London: The Nether Press, 1971); C. C. Taylor, *John Updike, A Bibliography* (Kent, Ohio: Kent State Univ. Press, 1968); B. A. Sokoloff and D. E. Arnason, *John Updike: A Comprehensive Bibliography* (Folcroft, Pa.: Folcroft Press, 1971); M. A. Olivas, *An Annotated Bibliography of John Updike Criticism 1967–1973, and a Checklist of His Works* (New York: Garland, 1975).

19. Gary M. Lepper, *A Bibliographical Checklist of Seventy-Five Modern American Authors* (Berkeley, Calif.: Serendipity Books, 1976).

20. Matthew J. Bruccoli, series ed., *First Printings of American Authors*, vols. 1–4 (Detroit: Gale, 1977–1979).

21. James Vinson, ed. *Contemporary Novelists*, 2nd ed. (New York: St. Martin's Press, 1976); James Vinson, ed., *Contemporary Dramatists* (New York: St. Martin's Press, 1973); Rosalie Murphy, ed., *Contemporary Poets* (New York: St. Martin's Press, 1975).

22. Frances Locher and Ann Evory, eds., *Contemporary Authors: A Bio-Bibliographical Guide to Current Writers in Fiction, General Nonfiction, Poetry, Journalism, Drama, Motion Pictures, Television, and Other Fields*, vols. 1–36 (revised), vols. 37–80 (Detroit: Gale, 1967–1979).

23. Frank Deodene and William P. French, *Black American Fiction since 1952: A Preliminary Checklist* (Chatham, N.J.: The Chatham Bookseller, 1970). The work covering earlier black fiction is Maxwell Whiteman, *A Century of Fiction by American Negroes 1853–1952, A Descriptive Bibliography* (Philadelphia: Maurice Jacobs, 1955).

24. Michael Perkins, *The Secret Record, Modern Erotic Literature* (New York: Morrow, 1976). Checklists begin on page 216. Essex House by itself and the editor Brian Kirby are examined in Maxim Jakubowski, "Essex House: The Rise and Fall of Speculative Erotica," *Foundation* 14 (1978): 50–64.

25. J. Albert Robbins et al., eds., *American Literary Manuscripts, A Checklist of Holdings in Academic, Historical, and Public Libraries, Museums, and Authors' Homes in the United States*, 2nd ed. (Athens: Univ. of Georgia Press, 1977).

26. In 1974 on the West Coast the pirates first printed the complete uncollected short stories of J. D. Salinger in two volumes that are dissimilar: the first volume is in yellow wrappers, saddlestitched; the second volume is perfect bound in white, coated paper covers. When the first printing was exhausted, the pirates made a second printing of two matching volumes, as pictured in *First Printings of American Authors*, vol. 1, p. 315, where it is *erroneously* entered as the first printing.

27. *Motion Pictures: A Catalogue of Books, Periodicals, Screenplays, Television Scripts and Production Stills*, Theater Arts Library, University of California, Los Angeles

(Boston: G. K. Hall, 1976). Approximately 2,300 unpublished screenplays are catalogued.

28. David Kaser, *Book Pirating in Taiwan* (Philadelphia: Univ. of Pennsylvania Press, 1969).

Further Reading

BLACK AMERICAN FICTION

Deodene, Frank, and French, William P. *Black American Fiction since 1952: A Preliminary Checklist.* Chatham, N.J.: The Chatham Bookseller, 1970.

Whiteman, Maxwell. *A Century of Fiction by American Negroes 1853–1952, A Descriptive Bibliography.* Philadelphia: Maurice Jacobs, 1955.

BOOK DEALERS' CATALOGUES

Ampersand Books, New York City. Catalogues 1–43.

Anacapa Books, Oakland, Calif. Catalogues 1–8.

Asphodel Book Shop, Burton, Ohio. Catalogues 1–62.

Colophon Bookshop, LaGrange, Ill. Catalogues 1–14.

Currey (Lloyd), Elizabethtown, N.Y. Science fiction. Catalogues 1–50.

Hoffer (William), Vancouver. Canadian literature. Catalogues 1–42.

House of Books, New York City. Catalogues 15–26 (since 1960).

In Our Time, Cambridge, Mass. Lists and catalogues, 1–108.

Joseph the Provider, Santa Barbara, Calif. Lists A–L; catalogues 1–16.

Morrow (Bradford), Santa Barbara, Calif. Catalogues 1–4.

Neville (Maurice F.), Santa Barbara, Calif. Catalogues 1–4.

Phoenix Book Shop, New York City. Catalogues 50–154 (since 1960).

Pieper (William), Whittier, Calif. (Deceased, shop closed.) Catalogues 1–45.

Rendell (Kenneth), Newton, Mass. Autographs. Catalogues 1–128; The Rendells 129–141.

Riley (William Michael), Kensington, Calif. Catalogues 1–7.

Serendipity Books, Berkeley, Calif. Catalogues 1–39.

Sylvester & Orphanos, Los Angeles. Catalogues 1–21.

Wenning (Henry W.), New Haven, Conn. (Retired, business closed.) Catalogues 1–10; Supplementary lists 1–2. With C. A. Stonehill: Catalogues 1–2; Supplementary lists 1–2; New acquisitions 1–3. These catalogues influenced a generation of dealers.

William Nelson Books, Toronto. Canadian literature. Catalogues 1–71.

Woolmer (J. Howard), Revere, Pennsylvania. Catalogues 1–56.

LITTLE MAGAZINES AND SMALL PRESSES

Cooney, Seamus. *A Checklist of the First One Hundred Publications of the Black Sparrow Press.* Los Angeles: Black Sparrow, 1971.

Fulton, Len, and Ferber, Ellen. *International Directory of Little Magazines and Small Presses,* 14th ed., 1978–1979. Paradise, Calif.: Dustbooks, 1978.

GAY AMERICAN FICTION SINCE 1960

Bibliography

Biblowitz, Iris, et al. *Women and Literature: An Annotated Bibliography of Women Writers,* 3rd ed. Cambridge, Mass.: Women and Literature Collective, 1976.

Damon, Gene, et al. *The Lesbian in Literature: A Bibliography,* 2nd ed. Weatherby Lake, Mo.: Naiad Press, 1975.

Young, Ian. *The Male Homosexual in Literature: A Bibliography.* Metuchen, N.J.: Scarecrow Press, 1975.

Criticism

Austen, Roger. *Playing the Game: The Homosexual Novel in America.* Indianapolis: Bobbs, 1977. Especially the chapter "Since 1960."

College English 36, no. 20 (November 1974). A special issue on "The Homosexual Imagination," edited by Louie Crew and Rictor Norton. Articles of particular interest: Roger Austen, "But for Fate and Ban: Homosexual Villains and Victims in the Military"; and James R. Giles, "Religious Alienation and 'Homosexual Consciousness' in *City of Night* and *Go Tell It on the Mountain.*"

Hall, Richard. "Gaybooks: From the Furtive World in the '50s to the Fad Style in the '70s." *The Advocate,* June 14, 1978.

Margins 20 (1975). A special issue on "Gay Male Writing and Publishing," edited by Louie Crew. Articles of particular interest: Louie Crew, "Editor Responses to Gay Material"; Daniel Curzon, "The Problem of Writing Gay Literature"; and Robert Gleissner, "Hunce Voelcker: A Beauty."

Perkins, Michael. *The Secret Record: Modern Erotic Literature.* New York: Morrow, 1976. Especially the chapter "Homosexual Erotic Fiction."

Rule, Jane. *Lesbian Images.* Garden City, N.Y.: Doubleday, 1975. Especially the chapter "Four Decades of Fiction."

Sarotte, Georges-Michel. *Like a Brother, Like a Lover: Male Homosexuality in the American Novel and Theater from Herman Melville to James Baldwin.* Garden City, N.Y.: Doubleday, 1978. Many discussions and brief references throughout.

MEXICAN-AMERICAN FICTION

The Mexican American, A Selected and Annotated Bibliography. Stanford, Calif.: The Center for Latin American Studies, 1969.

Schramko, Linda Fowler, comp. *Chicano Bibliography, Selected Materials on Americans of Mexican Descent*, rev. ed. Sacramento, Calif.: Sacramento State College Library, 1970.

MODERN FIRST EDITIONS

Bruccoli, Matthew J., series ed. *First Printings of American Authors*, vols. 1–4 (to date). Detroit: Gale, 1977–1979.

Kaser, David. *Book Pirating in Taiwan*. Philadelphia: Univ. of Pennsylvania Press, 1969.

Lepper, Gary M. *A Bibliographical Introduction to Seventy-Five Modern American Authors*. Berkeley, Calif.: Serendipity Books, 1976.

Locher, Frances, and Evory, Ann, eds. *Contemporary Authors: A Bio-Bibliographical Guide. . .* , vols. 1–36 (revised); vols. 37–80. Detroit: Gale, 1967–1979.

Murphy, Rosalie, ed. *Contemporary Poets*. New York: St. Martin's Press, 1975.

Robbins, J. Albert et al., eds. *American Literary Manuscripts, A Checklist of Holdings in Academic, Historical, and Public Libraries, Museums, and Authors' Homes in the United States*, 2nd ed. Athens: Univ. of Georgia Press, 1977.

Vinson, James, ed. *Contemporary Novelists*, 2nd ed. New York: St. Martin's Press, 1976.

———. *Contemporary Dramatists*. New York: St. Martin's Press, 1973.

SCREENPLAYS

Motion Pictures: A Catalogue of Books, Periodicals, Screenplays, Television Scripts and Production Stills. Theater Arts Library, University of California, Los Angeles. Boston: G. K. Hall, 1976.

STUDIES OF THE CONTEMPORARY NOVEL

Published

Allen, Mary. *The Necessary Blankness: Women in American Fiction of the Sixties*. Urbana: Univ. of Illinois Press, 1976.

Boyers, Robert. *Excursions: Selected Literary Essays*. Port Washington, N.Y.: Kennikat, 1977.

Bryant, Jerry H. *The Open Decision: The Contemporary American Novel and Its Intellectual Backgrounds*. New York: The Free Press, 1970.

Burchard, Rachel C. *John Updike: Yea Sayings*. Carbondale: Southern Illinois Univ. Press, 1971.

Coles, Robert. *Walker Percy: An American Search*. Boston: Little, Brown, 1978.

Dickstein, Morris. *Gates of Eden: American Culture in the Sixties*. New York: Basic Books, 1977.

Federman, Raymond. *Surfiction: Fiction Now . . . and Tomorrow*. Chicago: Swallow Press, 1975.

Galloway, David D. *The Absurd Hero in American Fiction*, rev. ed. Austin: Univ. of Texas Press, 1970.

Glicksberg, C. I. *The Sexual Revolution in Modern American Literature*. New York: Humanities Press, 1971.

Harper, Howard, comp. "General Studies of Recent American Fiction: Selected Checklist." *Modern Fiction Studies* 19 (1974): 127–133.

Harris, Charles B. *Contemporary American Novelists of the Absurd*. New Haven, Conn.: College & University Press, 1971.

Kazin, Alfred. *Bright Book of Life: American Novelists and Storytellers from Hemingway to Mailer*. Boston: Little, Brown, 1973.

Kennard, Jean E. *Number and Nightmare: Forms of Fantasy in Contemporary Fiction*. Hamden, Conn.: Archon Books, 1975.

Kenner, Hugh. *A Homemade World: American Modernist Writers*. New York: Morrow, 1975.

Klinkowitz, Jerome. *Literary Disruptions: The Making of a Post-Contemporary American Fiction*. Urbana: Univ. of Illinois Press, 1975.

Kort, Wesley A. *Shriven Selves: Religious Problems in Recent American Fiction*. Philadelphia: Fortress Press, 1972.

Luschei, Martin. *The Sovereign Wayfarer: Walker Percy's Diagnosis of the Malaise*. Baton Rouge: Louisiana State Univ. Press, 1972.

McMurtry, Larry. *In a Narrow Grave: Essays on Texas*. Austin, Tex.: The Encino Press, 1968.

Markle, Joyce B. *Fighters and Lovers: Theme in the Novels of John Updike*. New York: New York Univ. Press, 1973.

Olderman, Raymond M. *Beyond the Wasteland: A Study of the American Novel in the Nineteen-Sixties*. New Haven, Conn.: Yale Univ. Press, 1972.

Pinsker, Sanford. *The Comedy that "Hoits": An Essay on the Fiction of Philip Roth*. Columbia, Mo.: Univ. of Missouri Press, 1975.

Rupp, Richard H. *Celebration in Postwar American Fiction 1954–67*. Coral Gables: Univ. of Miami Press, 1970.

Scholes Robert. *The Fabulators*. New York: Oxford Univ. Press, 1967.

Schulz, Max F. *Black Humor Fiction of the Sixties: A Pluralistic Definition of Man and His World*. Athens: Ohio Univ. Press, 1973.

Tanner, Tony. *City of Words*. London: Cape, 1971.

Tri-Quarterly 26 (Winter 1973). A special issue on "Ongoing American Fiction I" with "Introduction" by Charles Newman and three critical essays by others, of which Philip Stevick's on the new fiction is particularly interesting.

Williams, Sherley A. *Give Birth to Brightness: A Thematic Study in Neo-Black Literature.* New York: Dial, 1972.

Zavarzadeh, Maś ud. *The Mythopoeic Reality: The Postwar American Nonfiction Novel.* Urbana: Univ. of Illinois Press, 1976.

Unpublished Dissertations

Dissertations are available from University Microfilms International, Ann Arbor, Michigan. *"DAI"* = *Dissertations Abstracts International.*

Ahearn, Kerry D. "Aspects of the Contemporary American Western Novel." *DAI* 35: 2975A. Berger, Clark, Davis, Fisher, Guthrie, Hawkes, McMurtry, Morris, Stegner, Straight, et al. 1975.

Berman, Neil David. "Play, Sport and Survival in Contemporary American Fiction." *DAI* 36: 5290A–91A. Coover's *Universal Baseball Association . . .* ; DeLillo's *End Zone;* Gardner's *Fat City;* Gent's *North Dallas 40;* Shainberg's *One on One.* 1976.

Bischoff, Joan. "With Manic Laughter: Secular Apocalypse in American Novels of the Sixties." *DAI* 36: 2818A. Hawkes, Heller, Mailer, Percy, Pynchon. 1975.

Freisinger, R. R. "To Move Wild Laughter in the Throat of Death: An Anatomy of Black Humor." *DAI* 36: 6655A. Barth, Elkin, Friedman, Heller, Kesey, Percy, Pynchon, Vonnegut. 1975.

Gregory, Thomas W. "Friendships between Adolescent Males in Selected American Novels 1945–70." *DAI* 33:6910A. Horgan, Knowles, Maxwell, Potok, Yaffe. 1972.

Hatley, Donald W. "The Contribution of Folklore to the Development of Plot, Theme and Character in Selected East Texas Novels." *DAI* 31: 2386A–87A. 1970.

Houston, Helen Ruth. "Afro-American Novels 1965–75: A Descriptive Bibliography of Primary and Secondary Materials." *DAI* 37: 1531A. 1976.

Jacobs, Rita Diane. "Individuals and Lusts: American Academic Novel 1960–70." *DAI* 35: 5409A. 1975.

Nelson, Robert M. "Some Instances of Double Vision in Post-War American Fiction: Essays on Knowles, Hawkes and Roth." *DAI* 36: 2826A. 1974.

Reynolds, Charles D. H. "Baseball as the Material of Fiction." *DAI* 35: 3005A. Asinof, Broun, Coover, Harris, Lardner, Malamud, Kennedy. 1974.

Steigman, Margaret Patton. "Evaluation and Record of Selected Novels and Authors Honored by the Texas Institute of Letters." *DAI* 37: 2881A–82A. 1976.

Stromberg, Peter Leonard. "A Long War's Writing: American Novels about the Fighting in Vietnam Written While Americans Fought." *DAI* 35: 4562A–63A. 1975.

Contributors

WM. P. BARLOW, JR. is a certified public accountant with his own practice in Oakland, California.

STUART BENNETT is head of the Book Department at Sotheby Parke Bernet in New York.

THOMAS L. BONN is Associate Librarian, State University of New York, College at Cortland.

JOHN ESPEY is Emeritus Professor of English at the University of California, Los Angeles.

CHARLES GULLANS is Professor of English and Director of Creative Writing at the University of California, Los Angeles.

PETER B. HOWARD is a bookseller in Berkeley, California.

DANIEL J. LEAB is Associate Professor of History at Seton Hall University and co-editor of *American Book Prices Current*.

WILLIAM MATHESON is Chief, Rare Book and Special Collections Division, Library of Congress.

PERCY MUIR is Managing Director, Elkin Mathews, Ltd., and a founder of *The Book Collector*. His publications, spanning a 50-year period, include *Printing and the Mind of Man* (1967), compiled and edited with John Carter, and most recently, *Victorian Illustrated Books* (1971).

JEAN PETERS is librarian of the Frederic G. Melcher Library, R. R. Bowker Company.

G. THOMAS TANSELLE is Vice President of the John Simon Guggenheim Memorial Foundation and author of *Guide to the Study of United States Imprints* (1971).

WILLIAM B. TODD is professor of English at the University of Texas at Austin, and editor of *The Papers of the Bibliographical Society of America*.

Index